OUTSOURCING

A Guide to . . . Selecting
the Correct Business Unit . . . Negotiating
the Contract . . . Maintaining Control
of the Process

Steven M. Bragg

JOHN WILEY & SONS, INC.
New York • Chichester • Weinheim • Brisbane • Singapore • Toronto

This publication is designed to provide accurate and authoritative information in regard to the subject matter covered. It is sold with the understanding that the publisher is not engaged in rendering legal, accounting, or other professional services. If legal advice or other expert assistance is required, the services of a competent professional person should be sought.

Library of Congress Cataloging-in-Publication Data:

Bragg, Steven M.
    Outsourcing : a guide to . . . selecting the correct business unit . . . negotiating the contract . . . maintaining control of the process / Steven M. Bragg.
        p.   cm.
    Includes bibliographical references and index.
    ISBN 0-471-24728-6 (cloth : alk. paper).—ISBN 0-471-25268-9 (pbk. : alk. paper)
    1. Contracting out.   I. Title.
HD2365.B73 1998   98-9842
658.7′2—dc21   CIP

Printed in the United States of America.

10 9 8 7 6 5 4 3 2 1

About the Author

Steven M. Bragg, CPA, CMA, CIA, CCP, CPM, CPIM, has been the COO of Isolation Technologies and consulting manager at Ernst & Young. He received a masters degree in finance from Bentley College and a masters in business administration from Babson College. He has also written *Just-in-Time Acounting* and *Advanced Accounting Systems,* and has co-authored *Controllership* and *The Controller's Function.* He is a past president of the 9,000-member Colorado Mountain Club.

SUBSCRIPTION NOTICE

This Wiley product is updated on a periodic basis with supplements to reflect important changes in the subject matter. If you purchased this product directly from John Wiley & Sons, Inc., we have already recorded your subscription for this update service.

If, however, you purchased this product from a bookstore and wish to receive (1) the current update at no additional charge, and (2) future updates and revised or related volumes billed separately with a 30-day examination review, please send your name, company name (if applicable), address, and the title of the product to:

Supplement Department
John Wiley & Sons, Inc.
One Wiley Drive
Somerset, NJ 08875
1-800-225-5945

For customers outside the United States, please contact the Wiley office nearest you:

Professional & Reference Division
John Wiley & Sons Canada, Ltd.
22 Worcester Road
Rexdale, Ontario M9W 1L1
CANADA
(416) 675-3580
1-800-567-4797
FAX (416) 675-6599

John Wiley & Sons, Ltd.
Baffins Lane
Chichester
West Sussex, PO19 1UD
UNITED KINGDOM
(44) (243) 779777

Jacaranda Wiley Ltd.
PRT Division
P.O. Box 174
North Ryde, NSW 2113
AUSTRALIA
(02) 805-1100
FAX (02) 805-1597

John Wiley & Sons (SEA) Pte. Ltd.
37 Jalan Pemimpin
Block B # 05-04
Union Industrial Building
SINGAPORE 2057
(65) 258-1157

Contents

Preface

Outsourcing is one of the most prevalent trends in today's business environment. Nearly every company outsources some part of its business, though it may not realize it. For example, the janitorial, payroll, and accounts receivable collections functions are outsourced so frequently that it has become, over the last few decades, an accepted method for running those functions. Other functions are being outsourced with more regularity, such as computer services, benefits administration, telephone customer support, and records management. Some functions are only being outsourced by a few companies, and may require a number of years before they are more widely outsourced. These functions include engineering, financial analysis, and management. The trend in outsourcing is to begin with the most clerical functions and to gradually move into more complex functions that may be more critical to the company, with a company's movement along this outsourcing path being driven by its ability to manage the outsourced functions, its comfort with the outsourcing process, and its previous experience with outsourcers. In short, there appears to be a gradual movement toward more outsourcing of more functions by a greater proportion of companies.

This book is designed to meet the needs of the company that wants to know the "nuts and bolts" of how to outsource any (or all) of its functions. It begins by discussing the strategic reasons for outsourcing a function, how to go about selecting a supplier who can take over a function, what should be included in the contract with the supplier, how to manage the supplier, and how to account for transactions with the supplier. The next section of the book discusses how to outsource all of the functions of a typical company, ranging from accounting to computer systems, manufacturing, and human resources, along with many other functions. A separate chapter is devoted to each clearly identifiable company function. Each of these function-specific chapters covers the advantages and disadvantages of outsourcing that function, as well as contractual and transition issues that are specific to that function, relevant ways to control the supplier, management issues, how to measure the supplier's performance of the function, potential customer service issues, and, finally, how to break off the outsourcing arrangement with the supplier. The final part of the book summarizes the previously noted outsourcing issues, discusses future trends in outsourcing, and lists selected readings for those who are interested in delving further into the field of out-sourcing. Finally, the book includes an appendix that contains measurements for tracking the performance of each company function if it is to be outsourced. In short, the book is designed to give the reader the complete range of information to use in making the decision to outsource, make the transition to a supplier, and manage the resulting relationship.

Chapters 1 through 3 cover various general aspects of outsourcing. Chapter 1 deals with the strategy of outsourcing. It covers why a company would want to out-source one or all of its functions, such as the acquisition of new skills, the reduction of costs, or to reduce the time spent by the management team in dealing with that function. It notes additional benefits from outsourcing, such as gaining access to the latest technology or application expertise, improving reliability, sharing risks, or having someone else handle an old application while the company's team works on new applications. It also points out the trend in outsourcing more strategic functions, whereby companies tend to outsource minor or low-cost functions—such as janitor-ial services—to gain comfort with the outsourcing concept, before they are willing to outsource very expensive functions or functions that involve high levels of exper-tise, such as computer services or engineering. In addition, it discusses the risk of outsourcing a function to a supplier that may become a competitor, and also the strategic reasoning from the supplier's perspective—why specializing in a particular function can earn a supplier an above-average profit. Finally, the reasons for stop-ping an outsourcing relationship are covered. In summary, Chapter 1 provides an overview of the decision-making process that underlies moving a function to a sup-plier, as well as taking the function away from that supplier.

Chapter 2 gives general information about outsourcing that should be used in con-junction with the detailed chapters related to specific functions that follow it. For ex-ample, if a company manager wanted to outsource the company's manufacturing ca-pability, the recommended reading would be Chapter 2 to gain an overview of the subject, and Chapter 10 to obtain detailed information related to outsourcing just the manufacturing function. Chapter 2 notes various methods for finding a supplier who is willing to take on a functional area and how to issue a request for proposals to prospective supplier finalists and evaluate supplier bids. The chapter also notes sev-eral issues regarding the cost of an outsourcing relationship, a large number of legal issues to be considered when negotiating a contract with the supplier, and how to change the company's organizational structure to accommodate the outsourced func-tion. Finally, the chapter deals with a variety of personnel issues related to moving employees to the supplier, various transition issues that are common to most func-tional areas, and the correct process for handling problems with the supplier on an ongoing basis. Chapter 2 covers topics that are common to outsourcing all functional areas: finding and evaluating suppliers, working out a contract with a supplier, tran-sitioning a function to it, and maintaining the relationship into the future.

Chapter 3 deals with how a company can handle its accounting function when other company functions have been outsourced. A traditional accounting department can rely on having other functions located nearby or at least under the direct control of company management, so that information can be exchanged quickly or processes modified rapidly on the command of top management. This is no longer the case in an outsourcing environment. The chapter deals with the difficulties of data collection and the impact on financial reporting when other functions are located at suppliers. In addition, it notes a variety of control issues and performance-measurement calculation problems that may arise, as well as how the transaction flow must be modified for most key transactions. This chapter is important for a company that wants to outsource some or all functions, but is concerned about the impact of outsourcing on its control over company assets, transactions, and reported financial results.

Chapters 4 through 13 are concerned with the details of outsourcing specific functional areas. These chapters have a common set of topics, which are as follows:

- *Advantages and disadvantages.* A detailed review of why the function should be outsourced, accompanied by a balancing set of reasons why it should stay as an in-house function. Various midway options are frequently noted, such as splitting up a function and outsourcing only a portion of it.

- *Contract-specific issues.* There are a variety of legal issues that should only be included in a contract for a specific functional area. This tends to be a long section for strategically important or complex functions, as well as those involving the transfer of assets or employees—such as computer services—and a much smaller section for less strategic functions, such as janitorial services.

- *Transition issues.* The bulk of the items involved in transitioning a function to a supplier are the same, irrespective of the function, but a few items will be added or deleted from the standard method, depending on the function. A graphical representation of the transition flow, integrated with a time line, is shown for each functional area.

- *Creating control points.* The controls needed by a company to have some oversight of an outsourced function will vary considerably by functional area. Controls may include company representation at supplier meetings, periodic internal audits, or the constant measurement of key activities. Examples of controls are included in each chapter covering a specific functional area.

- *Measuring the outsourced function.* The measurements needed to track a supplier's activities vary greatly from function to function. Accordingly, this topic is only lightly covered in the overview chapter, but is heavily discussed, along with numerous examples of measurements, in the chapters related to specific functions. Most measurements are not perfect—they can present misleading results depending on how they are used or how their usage modifies the behavior of the supplier. These issues are also discussed, along with recommendations to use certain measurements that are the most reliable and least subject to giving false results.

- *Managing the outsourced function.* The type of management needed will vary considerably by the functional area being outsourced. The less strategically important or inexpensive outsourcing suppliers, such as janitorial services, will require minimal management oversight, whereas strategically important or expensive functions, such as engineering, will require high degrees of company management to ensure that they do not stray from their assigned tasks for more than a few days at a time. Related issues regarding the best form of management for each functional area are covered. In addition, a graphical representation of the optimal management system for each function is included in each chapter.

- *Potential customer service issues.* Customer service issues vary considerably from function to function. If the customer is defined as not only external customers but also company employees, then any outsourced function will have an impact on a customer of some type. These issues may include cleaning problems within the company for a janitorial supplier, and how those issues may be promptly addressed, or problems with subcontracting engineering work from a customer to a supplier, whom the customers must then deal with through an intermediary at the company. Many other potential customer service issues are discussed under this heading.

- *Getting out of the outsourcing arrangement.* Some outsourcing arrangements do not involve a large investment of time or money by either party, and can easily be terminated with a notice letter. Other arrangements, however, may involve the transfer of large numbers of employees or the sale of large quantities of assets; these deals require considerable language in the original contract to ensure a smooth transition of the function back to either the company or a different supplier, and may involve the payment of termination fees or the transfer of assets back to the company.

In short, chapters 4 through 13 give the reader a detailed view of why a specific functional area should (or should not) be outsourced, and what specific issues should be kept in mind when doing so, including legal, transition, control, measurement, management, customer service, and termination issues.

These chapters cover those business functions that are used by the vast majority of corporations. Every function can be outsourced either completely or in part. Those functions are as follows:

Chapter   **Function Discussed**

4 *Accounting.* Covers the outsourcing of payroll, accounts payable, billings and collections, and cash management.

5 *Computer systems.* Covers the outsourcing of desktop services, voice and data networks, and data centers.

6 *Customer service.* Covers the outsourcing of field service, field service dispatch, and telephone customer support.

7 *Engineering.* Covers the outsourcing of engineering and drafting services.

8 *Human resources.* Covers the outsourcing of benefits and workers compensation administration, training, placement and outplacement, and employee relocations.

9 *Janitorial and maintenance.* Covers the outsourcing of the janitorial, in-house equipment maintenance, and fleet maintenance operations.

10 *Manufacturing.* Covers the outsourcing of all aspects of the manufacturing function.

11 *Materials management.* Covers the outsourcing of the warehousing, freight bill auditing, purchasing, and transportation functions.

12 *Sales and marketing.* Covers the outsourcing of the advertising, direct mail, field sales, outbound and inbound telemarketing, research, and foreign language telemarketing functions.

13 *Administration.* Covers the outsourcing of the copy center, desktop publishing, mailroom, records management, and clerical functions.

Thus, the reader will find that these chapters contain the information needed to outsource any function to a supplier, and then how to control, manage, and measure each function so that it contributes to the company's overall profitability.

Chapter 14 summarizes the findings from the previous chapters and points out those outsourcing issues that are common to all or most outsourced functions.

Finally, Chapter 15 covers the future of outsourcing. Like all industries, outsourcing within each of the functional areas will mature, and will go through several evolutionary steps that are common when any industry consolidates. These changes include an increase in supplier alliances, the emergence of a few very large suppliers, the appearance of smaller suppliers that focus on various market niches, a continuing search for higher profits through extra services as basic services become more competitive, and the increasing sophistication of companies in dealing with suppliers to whom services have been outsourced.

There are also two appendices. Appendix A contains a representative selection of outsourcing materials that have been published in the last decade. The preponderance of this information relates to outsourcing the computer services function, which is the functional area that has excited the most comment over the last few years (and is where the largest amount of the money in outsourcing contracts has gone). Most of these references are for articles. There have been very few books published, except for those related to computer services, that deal with outsourcing. Appendix B contains the performance measurements used to track the performance of outsourced functions. The measurements are sorted by functional area, and contain the name of the measurement and how to calculate the measurement. This appendix is intended to be a quick reference for those readers who do not have the time to hunt through the body of this book for the information. However, some measurements work better than others, and the measurement descriptions in the central part of the book contain the pros and cons for using each description, so the reader may want to read further about each measurement by referring back to the appropriate chapter for more information. In summary, Appendix A lists more sources of information about outsourcing, while Appendix B itemizes those measurements most appropriate for outsourced functions, and how they can be calculated.

Some of the terminology used in outsourcing is not clear, so some of the key terms are noted here. There is not common usage of names for the organization that outsources a function (the outsourcer?) or for the organization to whom the function is transferred (the outsourcee?). Consequently, as common terminology throughout this book, the organization that wishes to divest itself of a function is called the "company," while the name of the organization that takes on these services is called the "supplier." Finally, a company can assume that it is outsourcing an entire department, but in reality it may only be outsourcing a portion of the tasks provided by that department; thus, to be more accurate, anything being outsourced is referred to as a "function" rather than a "department," since there can be many functions within a department, only a few of which may be outsourced. For example, the payroll function is frequently outsourced, but the entire accounting department is rarely outsourced.

In summary, anyone who wants to outsource a function, or who wants to know more about how outsourcing works, can find within this book a discussion of why outsourcing fits the strategy of many companies, how to outsource every business function, how to select and manage suppliers who have taken over those functions, and the direction in which outsourcing appears to be headed.

CHAPTER ONE

The Strategy of Outsourcing

The "Trendsetter Barometer" survey conducted by Coopers & Lybrand L.L.P. shows that 83% of America's fastest-growing companies have turned to outsourcing for one or more functions. Why are so many companies diving into the pool of outsourcing? This chapter discusses many reasons, some strategic and others not so strategic, for this occurrence. In addition, since a decision to outsource should not be made without full consideration of the many risks that go along with moving a function over to a supplier, a list of risks is also itemized. Also, there is a discussion of who makes the outsourcing decision, and how this may vary by the function to be outsourced. In addition, since this chapter deals primarily with the major outsourcing decisions, there is a discussion of why a company should stop outsourcing—there are several key reasons for doing so, and other reasons why it may be a bad idea to stop outsourcing. Finally, there is a brief description of the suppliers who provide outsourcing services—how they operate and why they can provide services of higher quality than a company's in-house functions. This discussion is included in the strategy chapter because the executive who makes the decision to outsource must know the nature of the supplier to whom the executive is handing a large part of the company's functions. This chapter covers the most important decisions related to outsourcing—why to get into it, who makes the decision, and why to get back out.

1.1 AN OVERVIEW OF OUTSOURCING

There are a large number of reasons why a manager should consider outsourcing a function. These reasons, as enumerated in this section, include anticipated cost savings, the need for better skills and management, and handling overflow situations. A company will be more likely to outsource a function if there are several reasons for doing so, such as the need for reducing costs as well as selling off assets to the supplier (two reasons that go hand-in-hand for a financially troubled company). Each of the following reasons includes a short discussion, and, where possible, a related example:

1

- *Acquire new skills.* A company may find that its in-house skill set is inadequate for a given function. This may result in minimal improvements to the function in the future, if any. A company can overcome this problem by handing over the function to a supplier, who specializes in that function and who therefore is highly competent in its administration, using well-trained and experienced staff as well as the most current procedures and technological advances. This reason is most commonly used for outsourcing those functions that require high skill levels, such as engineering and computer services.

- *Acquire better management.* A company may find that an in-house function is not performing as expected, not because of any problems with the staff, but because of poor management. Symptoms of this are high turnover, absenteeism, poor work products, and missed deadlines. It can be very hard to obtain quality management, so outsourcing the function to a supplier just to gain access to the supplier's better management can be a viable option. It may also be possible to "rent" management from the supplier. This can be a good option in all functional areas, though it is more common in those areas requiring high levels of expertise, such as engineering.

- *Focus on strategy.* A company's managers typically spend the bulk of each day handling the detailed operations of their functional areas—the tactical aspects of the job. By outsourcing a function while retaining the core management team, a company can give the tactical part of each manager's job to a supplier, which allows the management team to spend far more time on such strategy-related issues as market positioning, new product development, acquisitions, and long-term financing issues.

- *Focus on core functions.* A company has a very small number of functions that are key to its survival. It may want to focus all of its energies on those functions and distribute all other functions among a group of suppliers who are capable of performing them well enough that company management will not have to be bothered with any of the details associated with running them. The company may even want to outsource those functions that are core functions at the moment, but which are expected to become less important in the near future due to changes in the nature of the business. In addition, a company could even outsource a function that is considered key to company survival if it can find a supplier that can perform the function better—in short, only keep those functions that are core functions *and which the company can do better than any supplier.* For example, a company may be the low-cost manufacturer in its industry, which allows it to maintain a large enough pricing advantage over its competitors that it is guaranteed a large share of the market. Management can focus on nothing but the manufacturing function, and outsource everything else.

- *Avoid major investments.* A company may find that it has a function that is not as efficient as it could be, due to a lack of investment in the function. If the company keeps the function in-house, it will eventually have to make a major investment in the function in order to modernize it. By outsourcing the function, the company can permanently avoid having to make this investment. For example, a company that owns an aging transportation fleet can sell the fleet to a supplier, who will provide an upgraded fleet to the company as part of its service.

- *Assist a fast-growth situation.* If a company is rapidly acquiring market share, the management team will be stretched to its limits building the company up so that it can handle the vastly increased volume of business. In such situations, the management team will desperately need additional help in running the company. A supplier can step in and take over a function so that the management team can focus its attention on a smaller number of core activities. For example, a company in a high-growth situation may outsource its customer support function to a supplier, who already has the phone line capacity and trained staff available to handle the deluge of incoming calls.

- *Handle overflow situations.* A company may find that there are times of the day or year when a function is overloaded for reasons that are beyond its control. In these situations, it may be cost-effective to retain a supplier to whom the excess work will be shunted when the in-house staff is unable to keep up with demand. This is a reasonable alternative to the less-palatable option of overstaffing the in-house function in order to deal with overflow situations that may only occur a small percentage of the time. This is a popular option for help desk services as well as customer support, where excess incoming calls are sent to the supplier rather than having customers wait on-line for an excessively long time.

- *Improve flexibility.* This is similar to using outsourcing to handle overflow situations, except that the supplier gets the entire function, not just the overflow business. When a function experiences extremely large swings in the volume of work it handles, it may be easier to eliminate the fixed cost of an internal staff and move the function to a supplier who will only be paid for the actual work done. This converts a fixed cost into a variable cost—the price of the supplier's services will fluctuate directly with the transaction volume it handles.

- *Improve ratios.* Some companies are so driven by their performance ratios that they will outsource functions solely to improve them. For example, outsourcing a function that involves transferring assets to the supplier will increase the company's return on assets (which is one of the most important measurements for many companies). The functions most likely to improve this ratio are those heavy in assets, such as maintenance, manufacturing, and computer services. Another ratio that can be improved is profitability per person. To enhance this, a company should outsource all functions involving large numbers of employees, such as manufacturing or sales.

- *Get rid of a rival manager.* A manager may promote outsourcing with the intent of eliminating the function of a rival within the company. Presumably, the outsourcing will also get rid of the rival. This is not an ethical reason to engage in outsourcing, but it happens nonetheless.

- *Jump on the bandwagon.* A company may decide to outsource a function simply because everyone else is doing it, too. If a major company suddenly dives into outsourcing, other companies will give the activity more credence and will be more likely to outsource, too. Also, a large amount of coverage of outsourcing in various national or industry-specific publications will give company management the impression that outsourcing is the coming trend, and they must use it or fail. For example, due to the large amount of publicity surrounding some of the very large computer services outsourcing deals, the bandwagon effect has probably led to additional outsourcing deals for the computer services function.

- *Enhance credibility.* A small company can use outsourcing as a marketing tool. It can tell potential customers the names of its suppliers, implying that since its functions are being maintained by such well-known suppliers, the company's customers can be assured of a high degree of quality service. In these instances, the company will want to hire the best-known suppliers, since it wants to draw off of their prestige. Also, for key functions, the company may even want to team up with a supplier to make joint presentations to company customers, since having the supplier's staff present gives the company additional credibility.

- *Maintain old functions.* A company may find that its in-house staff is unable to maintain its existing functions while also shifting to new technology or to a new location. Outsourcing is a good solution here, for it allows the company to focus its efforts on implementing new initiatives while the supplier maintains existing day-to-day functions. This reason is most common in computer services, where suppliers are hired to maintain old "legacy" systems while the in-house staff works on a transition to an entirely new computer system.

- *Reduce costs.* A company may emphasize cost savings for a variety of reasons, such as being in a poor financial position, or because of a goal to increase profits. Reducing costs by using a supplier is possible, but not in all situations. A supplier has clearly lower costs if it can centralize the work of several companies at one location, such as a central truck maintenance facility or a data-processing center. It can also lower costs if it can buy materials or supplies at lower costs by using volume purchasing. It can also purchase assets from a company and then lease the assets back as part of an outsourcing deal, thereby giving the company an up-front cash infusion. Otherwise, its costs will be higher than those of the company, for it must include a profit as well as sales and marketing costs in its budget—an internal department does not have to earn a profit, nor does it have a sales force. Thus, there are a few situations in which a company can reduce its costs by outsourcing, but there are many more cases where this is not a realistic reason for outsourcing.

- *Improve performance.* A company may find that it has a function that has bloated costs or inadequate performance. To "shake up" the function, company management can put the function out to bid, and include the internal function's staff in the bidding process. The internal staff can then submit a bid alongside outside suppliers that commits it to specific service levels and costs. If the bid proves to be competitive, management can keep the function in-house, but hold the function's staff to the specific costs and performance levels noted in its bid. As long as suppliers are told up front that the internal staff will be bidding, and that the selection will be a fair process, they should not have a problem with this type of competition. This approach can be used for any functional area.

- *Begin a strategic initiative.* A company's management may declare a complete company reorganization, and outsourcing can be used to put an exclamation point on its determination to really change the current situation. By making such a significant move at the start of the reorganization, employees will know that management is serious about the changes, and will be more likely to assist in making the transition to the new company structure.

Before deciding to outsource based on one or more of the previous reasons, a manager should consider the underlying reasons why outsourcing is being considered in the first place. It may be due to one of the previous reasons, but a deeper problem may be that the function in question is not doing a good job of presenting its benefits to management. In such cases, the function manager may not be doing a good job of trumpeting the function's accomplishments, or of showing management that the cost of keeping the function in-house is adequately offset by the resulting benefits. In these cases, it may do no good to outsource the function, because management may be replacing a perfectly adequate in-house staff that is not good at publicizing itself with a supplier who performs no better, but who is quick to point out how much it is doing for the company. If management suspects that this may be the reason why outsourcing is being considered, it is useful to bring in a consultant who can review the performance of the in-house employees and see if they are, in fact, doing a better job than they are saying. Sometimes, investigating the ability of in-house staffs prior to outsourcing functions will keep the outsourcing from occurring.

The manager who is making the outsourcing decision should also consider that it is not necessary to outsource an entire functional area—instead, the manager can cherry pick only those tasks within the function that are clearly worthy of being outsourced, and keep all other tasks in-house. This reduces the risk to the company of having the chosen supplier do a bad job of handling its assigned tasks, since fewer tasks are at risk, and it allows the company to hand over the remaining functional tasks to the supplier as it becomes more comfortable with the supplier's performance. For example, a company can outsource just the help desk part of its computer services function, or it may add network services, telephone services, application development, or data center operations tasks to one or more suppliers. These options are all available to the manager who is edging into a decision to outsource.

The typical outsourcing path that a company follows starts with a function that has minimal strategic value and will not present a problem even if the supplier does a poor job of providing the service. If the company's experience with these low-end functions proves successful, then company management will be more likely to advance to outsourcing those functions with more strategic value or with more company-threatening consequences if the provided service is inadequate. These functions include accounting, human resources, and materials management. Finally, if the company continues to perform well with all or part of these functions outsourced, it will consider moving to outsourcing the most important functions; typically, these are manufacturing, computer services, and engineering (though this may vary considerably by industry). This progression is shown in Figure 1.1. Thus, many companies experiment with outsourcing functions of low importance, and later include functions with more strategic importance, depending on their earlier experience with the other functions.

The list in Figure 1.1 appears to contain an overpowering number of reasons why a manager should outsource every corporate function. However, the following section contains a number of cautionary thoughts to consider before calling in a supplier to hand over a corporate function. Only by considering the reasons in favor of outsourcing alongside the associated risks can a manager arrive at a considered decision to outsource a function.

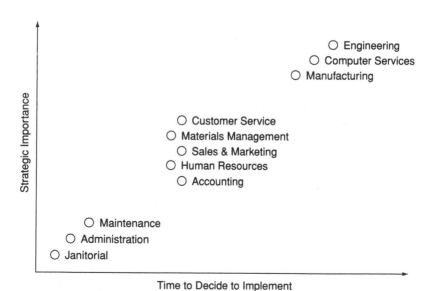

Figure 1.1   The Typical Outsourcing Path

1.2   OUTSOURCING RISKS

While there are many good reasons to outsource a function, there are also a number of risks associated with doing so. These can range from minor pricing issues to non-performance by a supplier of a key function. The person making the outsourcing decision must be aware of these risks before making the decision to hand over a function to a supplier. This section lists several of those risks, as well as how to mitigate them.

One risk is that the supplier's situation may change in the future, causing problems in the outsourcing relationship. For example, the supplier may have financial difficulties, be bought out by a company that does not want to be in the outsourcing business, or undergo a shift in strategy that forces it to provide different services. Also, the technology needed to service the company's needs may change over time, and the supplier may no longer be able to service that new technology. These risks can be lowered by ensuring that there is a termination clause in the outsourcing contract that allows the company to back out of the contract if any of the above circumstances occur. Also, these risks are less important if there are a large number of competing suppliers to whom the company's business can be shifted. Alternatively, the risk is greater if there are few competing suppliers. A major risk is that a supplier's ability to supply services may change over time.

Another risk is that available information about the success of outsourcing is usually skewed in favor of success stories. An excess of this type of information may lead company management to the conclusion that it must outsource a function (the "bandwagon effect") when in reality the number of outsourcing successes are fewer than reported. This skewing problem is caused by the timing of stories about outsourcing—they are almost always published for outsourcing deals that have just been signed, when no problems between companies and suppliers have yet surfaced. These stories find their way into various publications because they are being pushed by the public relations departments of the suppliers as a form of free advertising. These same suppliers are not going to go out of their way to advertise the failure of any outsourcing deals, nor will the companies for whom they are working, since neither party wants to acquire a reputation for not being able to manage an outsourcing deal. As a result, there is a skew in the press toward reporting more on successful outsourcing deals than failures, which may incline more companies to try outsourcing.

A very serious risk, especially for a large company that dominates a local economy, is that there can be significant fallout within the community if the company lays off a large number of workers as a result of an outsourcing arrangement. There are many outsourcing deals where employees are not rehired by the supplier, so this throws many employees out of work. If the local area is highly dependent on the company to maintain the local economy, this can generate a very large outpouring of bad feelings, quite possibly resulting in local boycotts, strikes, and bad publicity that may spill over into the national press. This is less of a risk for those companies located in large metropolitan areas, where laid-off workers can easily find new jobs within the region. One way to mitigate this risk is to only pick those suppliers who guarantee that they will hire a large proportion of the company's employees and retain them for a fairly long time, such as a minimum of one year. The person deciding to outsource should consider the impact on the local community before doing so.

Also, it is possible that a company can outsource a function that is critical to its existence, watch the supplier fail at providing the service, and have this bring about the failure of the entire company. This risk is heaviest for the major corporate functions, such as computer services, engineering, or manufacturing. Only by carefully selecting the appropriate supplier, tightly controlling the transition to the supplier, and then continually monitoring the supplier's subsequent activities can this risk be mitigated.

Finally, there is the risk that the person sponsoring the switch to outsourcing may lose his or her job if the outsourcing does not work. Outsourcing is a major change, in some cases involving a transfer of large parts of the company to a supplier and possibly having the supplier run a strategically major function for the company. If these changes do not work as planned, the outsourcing drive could backfire on the project sponsor and lead to a dismissal. In short, sponsoring such a major change and seeing it fail can lead to termination of one or more of a company's management staff.

Thus, there are a number of serious risks to be factored into the decision to outsource a function. These include changes in a supplier's business situation, trying outsourcing based on overly optimistic press reports, losing the support of the local community, having the supplier fail at providing a key service, and having the project sponsor fired if an outsourcing deal fails to perform as expected. These risks can, in some cases, bring down the company or significantly worsen its competitive or financial position, and so they must be carefully weighed alongside the many reasons why it is a good idea to outsource a function.

1.3 INITIATING OUTSOURCING

The person within a company who makes the decision to outsource will vary depending on the function. For example, a low-level manager can easily outsource the janitorial function, and may even be safe in not notifying senior management of the decision to do so. The same goes for most administrative functions and some aspects of maintenance. However, it is inappropriate for most other functions to be outsourced without the input of the most senior company executives. The reasons for this change in the level of decision-making is that most functions are not only more strategically important than janitorial services, but they also involve laying off large numbers of people or significantly changing the cost structure of the company. For all three reasons, it is most appropriate for someone at the chief executive officer or chief financial officer level to make the final decision to outsource. For major outsourcing decisions involving very large layoffs or cost savings, it is even possible that a company's board of directors will vote on the issue. If a lower-level manager tries to make the decision for any function but the few exceptions already noted, the decision should be moved up to the top of the company instead—the decision is just too important for a low-level manager to make. In short, the decision to outsource a function should be made by top management for all but the most insignificant functions.

1.4   WHEN TO STOP OUTSOURCING

A manager must be able to not only make an informed decision to begin outsourcing, but sometimes also to stop it. There are a variety of reasons why an outsourcing arrangement must be stopped.

One reason for stopping an outsourcing relationship is that a company only has a short-term need for the service being provided, and that need then goes away, as expected. One variation on this is called "transitional outsourcing," whereby a supplier is brought in to run an old system and sometimes the installation of a new system as well. Then the supplier, as arranged at the inception of the contract, moves the function back to the company's in-house staff and walks away. This is the most friendly of the situations where a company takes a service away from a supplier.

A reason that is subject to more dispute is when management does not feel that a supplier is providing the level of service that was promised at the start of the relationship. In these cases, if there is no clear set of performance measurements that both parties have agreed upon in advance, then the termination of the relationship may be rancorous in the extreme, and may involve litigation. Instead, this decision should be made based on performance measurements that have been verified and approved by the company and the supplier. If those measurements do not exist at the time when management is already questioning the ability of the supplier, it is still useful to begin calculating the measurements, since it gives senior management a better basis of information to use when deciding to terminate an outsourcing agreement.

If performance measurements are acceptable, then the remaining reason why an outsourcing contract may be canceled is the cost of the contract. Senior management may have to make a decision to cancel an outsourcing contract based on the allegation that the cost of the agreement is higher than expected. However, before doing so, management should establish a baseline cost for the outsourced service before it was given to a supplier, and compare this baseline cost to the current cost of using the supplier. In addition, the volume of transactions processed will probably have changed since the baseline period, so the comparison should include a before-and-after analysis of the cost per transaction. When armed with this information, senior management can realistically determine if the outsourcing cost has gone up, and then make a decision based on this information.

Once the decision has been made to cancel an outsourcing contract, the decision must then be made to either give the business to another supplier or to bring the function back in-house. One strong reason for bringing a function in-house is that the experience with the supplier was so bad—in terms of excessive costs, poor service, or a bad relationship—that company management refuses to even consider shifting the function to a different supplier. However, if management feels that there are other suppliers (or perhaps already knows of one) who can do a better job, then the function is more likely to be moved on to another supplier. If management thinks that the supplier possesses the talent to provide a high level of service but is not doing so, there may even be an option to buy the supplier outright and then impose new management on the supplier, so that the company is assured of the appropriate level of service. Thus, a key factor in deciding to bring a function back in-house or searching for a new supplier is the perceived presence of a viable alternative supplier who can match the service and cost expectations of company management.

Thus, backing out of an outsourcing agreement can be prearranged or due to the incompetence of the supplier, as well as due to friction between employees of the company and the supplier. Once the decision has been made to terminate a supplier, company management must then decide to either shift its business to a new supplier or take it back in-house. This decision is primarily driven by the perceived presence of another supplier who is considered able to adequately perform the work at a fair price.

1.5   COMPANIES THAT TAKE OVER OUTSOURCED FUNCTIONS

Moving a company function to a supplier is an important decision that may have a major negative impact on the company if the arrangement does not go well. The decision-maker should be aware of how suppliers operate and what their objectives are before making the decision to hand them a key company function, since this knowledge may impact the manager's decision. This section explores how suppliers make money in the outsourcing arena, how they compete against each other, the areas in which a supplier can truly provide a cost savings to the company, and how the company should treat a top-notch supplier. Only by understanding the supplier's operating paradigms can a company manager make an informed decision to outsource a function or not.

A supplier makes money by standardizing a portion of the work involved with a function. This means that the supplier has become so good at one activity that it can regularly beat the performance of any company with whom it does business. The supplier may achieve this cost advantage by paying particular attention to streamlining the function, by using only the most experienced and knowledgeable management, by using only the latest technology, or by having such a large-volume operation that it can obtain very low costs per transaction. For example, a computer services provider has lower processing costs because it can run all of the program processing for many companies through one large data-processing center, which combines the overhead for all of those companies into one facility—this is a permanent cost advantage that a company cannot match. Suppliers achieve lower function costs by standardizing portions of the activities within a function.

The key point to note in the preceding paragraph is that a supplier has a cost advantage in only a portion of a function. It usually does not have an advantage for any customized work that is, by definition, incapable of being standardized. For this part of the work related to a function, it is likely that the company and not the supplier is the low-cost provider. This is because the company does not have to earn a profit when it performs the function, nor does it incur any overhead costs to market the function. What this means for someone making the decision to outsource is that the supplier will focus on its ability to provide low-cost services during its presentation to company management, but there are many activities within a functional area that the supplier cannot provide at a lower cost—if anything, it will cost the company *more* money to outsource! Of course, a function may still be worth outsourcing for many reasons that are not related to cost, as were enumerated earlier in this chapter, but it is useful for the decision-maker to know that, despite all protestations to the contrary, suppliers only have a cost advantage over companies in a very small number of functional areas.

How do suppliers compete against each other? The decision-maker must know this in order to differentiate between the bids received from various suppliers. Nearly all suppliers try to lock in a company for as long a contract as possible. Not only does this give the supplier an assured flow of revenues, but it also locks out its competitors from dealing with the company. Second, suppliers try to keep the initial cost of a contract as low as possible in order to obtain a company's business, and then build various clauses into the contract that allow it to increase its prices later. This gives the supplier the lowest initial bid in order to obtain the company's business, but still allows it to earn a profit on a deferred basis. Third, suppliers like to offer free consulting services not only in advance but also during the term of its relationship with a company. These services are targeted toward recommending the services of the supplier to the company, and sometimes focus on the "FUD" principle: Fear, Uncertainty, and Doubt—e.g., if you do not outsource immediately with us—and not to the competition—all kinds of terrible things will happen. The decision-maker can counteract these supplier techniques by reducing the length of contract terms, examining the total cost of a supplier proposal over the full term of the contract, and taking the results of free supplier consulting work with a liberal degree of skepticism. Suppliers use a number of subtle techniques to compete against each other, which an informed decision-maker can counteract.

There are a small number of truly top-notch suppliers in every functional area. These suppliers usually have all of the business they can handle, for they have acquired a reputation for exceptional service that keeps companies coming to them for business. In these cases, the company must be extremely careful to treat the supplier as well as possible. If the company does not know how to treat a supplier, or abuses it as a matter of course (as some old-style purchasing managers are still prone to do), the top-quality supplier will shut down the relationship immediately, and nothing the company can do will bring it back. This can be a major problem for a functional area where the remaining suppliers are of a clearly lower quality, and may result in the company having to take a function back in-house because there are no other reliable suppliers left who can provide the service. The decision-maker should review the company's ability to handle suppliers prior to making the decision to outsource—if the company has a habit of "chewing up" suppliers, it may be best to forget about any outsourcing until the company's supplier relations problems are fixed.

When considering the services of a top-of-the-line supplier, the person making the outsourcing decision must realize that the supplier will want access to more information than the company has been used to revealing. This information may include the company's long-range plan, since the supplier may need to change its production capacity to meet the expanding needs of the company. In addition, and for the same reason, the supplier may need continuing access to the company's production schedules. Company management may even have to include key suppliers in the annual budgeting and long-range planning process—not as sources of information, but as active participants. If management is not comfortable with this prospect, it may not want to make the decision to outsource a function.

If a company is willing to engage in a tight relationship with a top supplier, it should envision further stages in the relationship with the supplier, which may include equity investments in each other, cross licensing, joint ventures, or even an acquisition by one party of the other. For example, Ernst & Young LLP has a business ventures subdivision that owns new businesses, wholly or with a partner who has related expertise, and that provides services to other companies. The relationship may become so close that the company and its supplier develop a "codestiny," meaning that the two entities do so much business with each other that each has a major stake in the survival of the other; this frequently leads to financial support by one entity if the other is in danger of failing. This type of close relationship is very uncommon with the more inexpensive functions or with those that have minimal strategic value, such as maintenance or office-administration functions, but is becoming more common with the suppliers of the more important functions, such as engineering, manufacturing, or computer services. Once again, if this level of commitment to a supplier is not something that a company is comfortable with, it may not want to outsource any functions, or restrict its outsourcing activities to the most low-level functional areas.

There is an important caveat to consider when envisioning a close relationship with a supplier: It may be more interested in earning a profit at the expense of the company than of forming a closer relationship with it. For many lower-quality suppliers or for those in the lesser functional areas (e.g., office administration or janitorial services), suppliers are not interested in a cozy relationship with a company unless it leads to more profits. They will not want access to company records or be involved in its budgeting or long-range planning activities. Instead, the supplier just wants to make a higher-than-average profit. In these cases, which are by far the most common of all outsourcing relationships, company management must realize that there is no point in inviting a supplier into company meetings, involving it in the company's budgeting or other planning processes, or creating strategic partnerships with it—the supplier will not have the company's best interests at heart, only its own. This will probably result in failed joint ventures, lowered expectations, and costs that are higher than anticipated. It is difficult for a company decision-maker to determine which kind of supplier—profit-oriented or relationship-oriented—is bidding to provide outsourcing services to the company, but it is important to find out, since this issue has an enormous impact on the long-term relations between the company and the supplier. For the decision-maker, the best source of information on this issue is the supplier's references, supplier's reputation in the industry, and face-to-face meetings with the supplier's management. It is critical that the manager who is deciding to outsource be able to determine if the supplier candidates are willing to enter into partnerships or not, because this has a major impact on how the relationship between the company and the supplier will proceed.

When a company manager makes the decision to give an important company function to a supplier, the situation is similar to a father giving his daughter away in marriage—he wants to know as much as possible about the person who is on the receiving end. This means that the manager must know the supplier's expectations for making money from the outsourcing deal, whether or not the supplier can really offer a cost savings, and how those savings are generated. Also, the manager must know how a supplier will behave when competing with fellow suppliers, and how this impacts its relations with the company. In addition, the manager must know how to treat the top-notch suppliers if they can be attracted in the first place, as well as the level of integration needed to retain this kind of supplier. Finally, the manager must be able to differentiate between the supplier who wants a long-term partnership and the supplier who is in it solely for the short-term profits.

1.6   SUMMARY

This chapter was concerned with the key decisions surrounding outsourcing: when to outsource a function, who makes the decision, and when to stop doing it. A large number of reasons were given that could form the basis for a decision to outsource a function, either individually or in combination. The deciding manager can then use the risks that were also itemized in this chapter to offset the reasons favoring outsourcing. Then, a short discussion of who should make the decision to outsource concluded that, for all but the most minor functions, this decision should be confined to senior management. The chapter also covered the underlying reasons why a manager might make the decision to pull back from an outsourcing relationship, either to take a function back in-house or to shift it to a different supplier. Finally, there was a brief discussion of the suppliers to whom functions would be given. This did not directly fit into the overall theme of the chapter, which was the decision-making process surrounding the key outsourcing decisions, but it is important for senior company management to understand the nature of the suppliers to whom they are giving control over large parts of their companies. In short, this chapter covered the reasons for getting into or out of an outsourcing arrangement, and who should make the decision to do so.

CHAPTER TWO

Outsourcing a Function

Most of the following chapters itemize, for particular functions, the advantages and disadvantages of outsourcing: control points, transition issues, legal concerns, management problems, possible measurements to use, how to back out of the outsourcing relationships, and the effect of outsourcing on customer service. To avoid repetition, those chapters only deal with the issues directly related to specific functions. This chapter, however, deals only with the general issues that are likely to arise when any function is outsourced. For example, the request-for-proposal process is about the same for all functions, so it is described in this chapter once, rather than in each of the succeeding chapters. There are many topics in this chapter that apply either totally or in part to most functions: the process of finding an outsourcing supplier, how to evaluate bids from a variety of potential suppliers, determining the cost of the outsourcing arrangement, different legal problems that may arise during the contract-negotiation phase, and how to change the organizational structure to accommodate the outsourcing arrangement. Also, there are personnel issues related to either moving staff to the supplier or laying them off, plus transition issues involved in moving each function to a supplier, how to conduct ongoing relations with the supplier, and how to measure each supplier's performance. By combining the general advice given in this chapter with more specific issues that are noted in the chapter devoted to more specific functional areas, the reader can gain a solid understanding of the issues involved in outsourcing a function.

2.1 HOW TO FIND AN OUTSOURCING SUPPLIER

When outsourcing is first being considered, company management will ask if an appropriate supplier exists who can take over the function from the company. If the person advocating switching to outsourcing cannot come up with a suitable list of suppliers, it is likely that the company's brush with outsourcing will end at that time. How, then, does one find a supplier that will take over a function?

One approach is to go to an outsourcing clearinghouse that advertises the services of a variety of suppliers. The principle outsourcing organization of this type is The Outsourcing Institute, located in Brooklyn, New York. This organization sponsors advertisements that include descriptions of a variety of outsourcing suppliers, publishes a directory of those suppliers, and also conducts various seminars on the subject.

Another source is industry trade journals. For example, some of the larger accounting firms advertise their auditing and accounting services in the magazines of the Institute of Internal Auditors and Institute of Management Accountants. Also, such computer outsourcing companies as Electronic Data Systems and Andersen Consulting advertise in *Information Week* and *Computer World*. Similarly, manufacturing suppliers tend to advertise in industry-specific trade journals.

For the more generic services that are common throughout the world, such as payroll processing, maintenance, and janitorial services, it is usually sufficient to look in the Yellow Pages or similar local advertising media to find an adequate list of suppliers. Also, suppliers will be present at industry trade shows, and are likely to send speakers to seminars and classes to give speeches. If the company is large enough to be a worthwhile target, it is very likely that company management will find itself on the receiving end of a series of sales calls by suppliers—there is no need to find the suppliers; they will find you.

In short, there are a variety of ways to obtain lists of suppliers who can potentially enter into an outsourcing relationship with the company. The only trouble a company should have in finding potential suppliers is when it is located in a geographically isolated area, or if the service it wants is so difficult to obtain—such as engineering skills in a highly specialized area—that there are no suppliers who can provide the service. However, for the bulk of a company's functions, there are usually a number of suppliers nearby who can provide the service.

2.2   EVALUATING POTENTIAL OUTSOURCING SUPPLIERS

The core of the selection process is creating a request for proposals and issuing it to suppliers, using a list of criteria to review the resulting supplier bids, and then checking the references of the top supplier candidates. This process, as described in this section, will result in the selection of a supplier.

Once a company has created a list of potential outsourcing suppliers, it should create a request for proposal (RFP) document to send to each one. The RFP gives the supplier background information about the company and its industry, describes the function it wishes to outsource, the specific tasks to be taken on by the supplier, current transaction volumes, the company's expectations for performance, and a deadline for when the RFP must be received at the company. The most important thing the company must get across in this document is exactly what the supplier is expected to do. This means itemizing all tasks that are to be outsourced in great detail, and their related transaction volumes. If a supplier bids on an RFP that contains incorrect task or transaction-volume information, the company will have to negotiate further with the supplier once the due diligence phase of the process is completed— this extra negotiation can be avoided if the company does adequate documentation of the function to be outsourced in the RFP. Also, there may be requests from suppliers for more information once they have received the RFPs. If the information requested is considered critical to all suppliers bidding on the contract, the company should send its response to all of the suppliers who received the RFP, not just the one who requested the information. This gives all of the suppliers a more equitable basis of information on which to submit their bids. The basic points to be covered by a standard RFP are as follows:

- *Company and industry information.* Briefly note the company's history, the range of products it sells, and the industry of which it is a part. This information gives the suppliers background information that may tell them if they want to submit a bid. Some suppliers prefer to specialize only in certain industries or avoid other industries, so this information may winnow out a few suppliers.

- *Scope.* Describe the boundaries of what the company wants to outsource. This is intended to be no more than an overview of the function, so do not include a large amount of detail. For example, the scope for a computer services RFP might say that the RFP's scope covers only the servicing of the company's local area networks and wide area networks, and does not include the outsourcing of all other computer services. By defining the scope, the number of potential suppliers willing to submit a bid may be reduced.

- *Current situation.* Note the key information related to the function to be outsourced. This can include transaction volumes, performance metrics, the number of personnel employed in this function, the geographical locations of the function, and how it is managed. This is a crucial part of the RFP, for suppliers will base a large part of their bids on the information provided in this section.

- *Key dates.* Note the dates in the selection process that will affect the suppliers. These should include the release date of the RFP, the date of an information session where prospective bidders can ask additional questions about the RFP, when (and where) bids are due at the company, and when a supplier will be selected.

- *Information the supplier should provide.* The company will want a standard set of facts to use for comparing submitted bids, so be sure to itemize all information that is mandatory on all submitted bids. This should include a baseline price, the services covered by the baseline price, all incremental pricing for other services, a list of all services the supplier intends to provide, resumes of the personnel to be assigned to the company in all skilled positions, financial information about the supplier, and a list of references.

- *Selection criteria.* Note the criteria to be used by the selection team in picking a supplier. This may include a weighting of a number of criteria, such as a supplier's price, experience, financial stability, and references. If a weighting system is being used, mention the details of the weighting system (e.g., 40% of the score comes from pricing and 60% from the supplier's perceived financial stability). This information will alter supplier bids, since they will present more information related to those criteria with the heaviest weighting.

- *Service responsibilities.* Itemize in some detail the services to be provided by the supplier. Also list those services *not* to be provided, if some parts of a function are being outsourced and other parts of it are being retained in-house. This information is critical for the construction of adequate supplier bids.

- *Use of subcontractors.* The supplier may seek to outsource its contract to subcontractors who have special expertise that the supplier does not have. The RFP should note that the use of subcontractors is to be approved in advance by the company. This is because the company will want to review the qualifications, experience, and stability of each subcontractor to ensure that required service levels will continue to be met.

- *Length of contract.* Suppliers will attempt to force the company into the longest possible contract term in order to lock in its business. By clearly stating the company's expectation in this area in advance, there will be a precedent set for later negotiations regarding the actual length of the contract.

- *Transfer of personnel.* Note the company's expectations regarding the disposition of those of its employees who will no longer be employed following the outsourcing of this function. For example, the company may expect that the supplier will hire at least 75% of the displaced workers, or that employment with the supplier will be guaranteed for all staff for one year. This information is needed so that suppliers can alter their pricing—taking on a large part of a company's employees rather than cherry picking only the ones it needs represents a staff-carrying cost that must be absorbed by the supplier, and which will probably be passed along to the company.

- *Performance standards.* List the exact performance standards expected of the winning supplier. For example, all discounts must be taken when an accounting supplier processes accounts payable. Alternatively, for an engineering supplier, all design changes for existing products must be completed within 10 days. If a bidding supplier realizes in advance that it cannot meet the requested performance levels, it will not submit a bid. This is also useful information for suppliers who are trying to determine the number of personnel who are needed to work on the function for the company—different performance standards require different numbers of staff, so making this information available results in more accurate bids.

- *Expectations for pricing.* Note that the winning supplier will, for example, be the one that includes the most services in the baseline pricing, allows credits if anticipated volumes are not met, and gives back some payments as a sharing of cost reductions. Also note that increases in payments will only be made if the supplier can improve performance in ways that will lead to either increased revenues or reduced costs for the company. This sets expectations for the suppliers who are submitting bids—they know that the winning bid must address some of these pricing expectations by the company.

- *Penalties.* List the penalties the company intends to impose if particular service levels are not met. Since suppliers will not want any penalties, this will serve as a basis for negotiating actual penalties later on, when the contract terms are being settled.

- *Termination.* List the conditions under which termination will be allowable. For generic functions such as maintenance and janitorial services, the termination may be upon written notice by either party, whereas other functions involving large numbers of employees or a large dollar volume of transferred assets may require mediation, a long notice period, or a substantial termination fee paid by the company before the termination will be legal.

Most of the above items should be included in an RFP for any substantial consulting project that a company is contemplating. The key items that are more frequently included in an outsourcing RFP are the length of the contract (since the outsourcing deal may last for many years), the transfer of personnel (since the entire function is to be eliminated), and the penalties and termination clauses (since the company must be able to hold the supplier to specific service levels, and get out of the arrangement if those levels cannot be met). The bulk of the RFP layout will be similar to that of a standard RFP.

One problem to avoid is sending the RFP to too many potential candidates. An inexperienced selection team will include all possible candidates, possibly to avoid any future complaints that all possible candidates were not included, to add any personal favorites to the search, and to mitigate the complaints of any suppliers who want to be included in the mailing. This can result in several dozen bids being received. With this many bids arriving, the selection team will be overwhelmed with the amount of work required to properly evaluate each bid and make a reasoned selection. Instead, because of the number of bids, the selection team will probably winnow down the pile of bids based on a small number of selection criteria—possibly just the price. This is dangerous, for a potential supplier finalist may not have the lowest bid price but could make up for this in many other ways, such as technical knowledge or the quality of services provided. In short, it is better to issue the RFP to just a half-dozen suppliers and avoid a larger mailing to additional suppliers who are not clear contenders for the work to be awarded.

One mistake made by many companies is to spend too little time evaluating the bids submitted by outsourcing suppliers before selecting one. The most common approach is to scan through the bids to look for the lowest price, and immediately award the contract to that supplier. However, this approach ignores a number of factors that should also be researched prior to awarding a contract.

- *Are bid prices comparable?* Carefully compare the bids to ensure that the quoted prices are all for the same baseline services. A common supplier ploy is to shrink the baseline services being quoted, which allows it to quote a reduced price while later charging higher fees for non-baseline services. If the baseline prices are not comparable, the company can either request new bids based on a common set of baseline services, or calculate estimated total costs based on the different pricing structures submitted by each supplier.

- *Is the supplier's operating style compatible?* The company's selection team should spend a large amount of time interviewing the management of each potential supplier, visiting supplier locations, and, if possible, talking to employees of the supplier. This gives the company a good idea of how the company operates. If the operating style of the supplier is similar to that of the company, this is a good reason for picking that supplier, since the supplier may potentially be working closely with the company for many years. Outsourcing companies may take over large portions of a company's operations, which means that they are, in effect, turned into large departments of the company, and if these large new departments do not operate in a manner similar to that of the other company departments, friction over a variety of issues is likely to develop. Also, if there is any question about a particular supplier's honesty, that supplier should be stricken immediately from the list of candidates—the company does not want to have to fight with the supplier to obtain adequate service and reasonable prices once the contract has been signed.

- *What is the supplier's reputation?* The reference lists of all supplier finalists should be used for lengthy phone interviews and possibly for on-site visits. Since the potential suppliers provided these reference lists, it is likely that the companies contacted will be effusive about the abilities of the suppliers. To look deeper for problems, the review team can ask these references for the names of other companies they are aware of that are using the supplier's services. These other companies that are *not* on the suppliers' reference lists may provide more typical information about dealing with the supplier. When conducting these interviews, the review team should use a standard set of interview questions so that the responses to all questions can be more easily compared between candidate suppliers.

- *What is the supplier's level of experience?* Another important issue is the experience level of each supplier. This issue should be explored on two levels. At a detailed level, the review team should request from each supplier a set of resumes for the group likely to be performing services for the company. These resumes should be summarized based on skill levels, industry experience, and years of functional experience to determine the quality of the group being provided by each supplier. A related issue is that outsourcing companies are well known for presenting a very experienced staff to the company during the bidding stage but then switching to a less experienced staff once the contract has been finalized. The best way to predict if this might happen with a specific supplier is to contact other companies that use that supplier's services and see if they have had this problem. On a higher level, the review team should find out the outsourcing experience of each supplier. If a potential supplier is new to the outsourcing arena, it may not know what it is getting into, resulting in a rocky relationship with the company if it is selected.

- *Does the supplier have special technical knowledge?* Some companies have developed an expertise in certain areas, protected by high levels of training or patents, that other suppliers cannot match. This knowledge is usually confined to very specific niches in the functional area to be served, so the company must be sure that the knowledge the supplier possesses is the same knowledge needed to service its needs. The presence of technical knowledge is not a factor in such areas as janitorial services, where the function requires no special skill, but can be very important in computer services, where the reverse is true.

- *Is the supplier located close to the company?* The company is not likely to receive a high level of service if the supplier is located a great distance from the company's headquarters. This is of particular concern if the outsourcing contract calls for emergency service on short notice. This is also a problem if the company has multiple geographical locations and the supplier does not, as the latter will probably have to subcontract work to other companies in areas where it has no presence, which can present logistical and management problems to the supplier that will be apparent to the company in the form of inadequate levels of service in some areas.

- *What is the supplier's financial condition?* Arranging most outsourcing agreements requires an extensive amount of work by the company, and the last thing a company needs after all of this review work is for the supplier to go out of business due to poor financial condition. Even if the supplier manages to save itself by selling out to another company, it is possible that the acquiring company will not have any interest in continuing in an outsourcing supplier role, and will back out of the agreement. This is a very difficult issue to guard against, since an outsourcing relationship may last for many years, and during that time the financial fortunes of the supplier may vary dramatically. The safest approach is to stay with a big supplier who has a history of longevity. However, smaller suppliers tend to be hungrier for the business and therefore provide better service, so there are reasons for not going with the biggest suppliers in the industry. At a minimum, any suppliers showing some financial strain on their financial statements should be avoided.

In addition, some employers will be very concerned about what happens to their staffs in the functions to be outsourced. Will they obtain jobs with the supplier, or will they be laid off and forced to fend for themselves in the marketplace? For the more socially responsible companies, this can be a major deciding factor in selecting a supplier—how many of the company's employees can they hire, and for how long will the supplier commit to retaining the staff? For most companies, this factor should at least be considered alongside the other previously noted selection criteria.

In short, it is more important to find a supplier that has the right mix of operating style, reputation, experience, geographical proximity, and price than to pick just based on the lowest bid price. This additional investigation work requires a significant amount of time, but will result in selecting a quality supplier with whom the company can work for a long time.

It is possible that, after having reviewed the supplier bids, the company finds that no supplier provides the correct mix of services that will adequately meet the company's needs. In this case, it may be possible to select a supplier to be a lead supplier, with several other suppliers subcontracting through it to provide services to the company. This approach has the advantage of allowing the company to create a tailor made package of services that exactly fit its needs. The downside of this approach is that there may be too many suppliers to effectively manage, and also that the suppliers may blame each other for service problems, resulting in some service problems being bandied about for too long before being solved. If the multiple-supplier approach is used, it is best to keep the total number of suppliers down to a manageable size—even if the resulting mix of services is not perfect—and assign total responsibility for the function to a single supplier, preferably the one with the best management expertise. This one supplier will take care of all billings to the company, and will handle all complaints. In exchange for providing this extra service, the lead supplier should be paid somewhat more than the market rate for its services. Using several suppliers to outsource a single function may work if no single supplier can provide the complete package of support that a company is looking for.

Once a potential supplier has been selected, the company should check its references. This should not be a cursory endeavor. On the contrary, the functional coordinator's team should devise a standard set of questions to be asked of each reference, and should obtain complete answers to all questions. The questions to be asked will vary by functional area. The following list covers only the most general topics that should apply to most functional areas, and are designed to yield lengthy responses— a "yes" or "no" answer is not desireable, since there may be details about the supplier that will not be revealed by such an answer. More detailed reference questions should be asked for those functional areas that are strategically important to the company, such as computer services and engineering, where it is most important to find out as much about the potential supplier as possible before a contract is signed. Possible questions to ask references are as follows:

- *How did the supplier handle the transition of the function to it?* The company should find out about the level of management expertise, the speed of the transition, if the transition occurred all at once or in stages, and any problems that occurred.

- *What level of resources were committed?* The company should find out about the experience level and quantity of the staff committed by the supplier, as well as the level of sophistication of the equipment used by the supplier to service the company.

- *How would you describe the supplier's level of service?* The company should find out if the expected service levels of other supplier customers were attained, and if not, how far off the actual service levels were from expectations.

- *How were employee transfers to the supplier handled?* The company should find out about the paperwork used to transfer staff, how humanely the staff were treated, and if they were moved to other clients—especially those requiring relocation.

- *Were there variations in pay and benefits for transferred employees?* The company should find out about changes in pay rates and benefit levels from what employees had prior to working for the supplier.

- *How did the levels of responsibility given to former employees compare to that of their previous jobs?* The company should find out about the job titles and responsibilities given to former employees.

- *What is the quality of the supplier's staff.* The company should find out about the experience levels, churn rate, and management expertise of the supplier's staff.

- *What is the supplier's level of responsiveness in regards to complaints about its staff?* The company should find out if the supplier has a regular review process or a person designated to receive complaints, and the ability of that process or person to correct the customer's complaints about its staff.

- *What level of technology does the supplier use?* The company should find out about how dated the supplier's technology may be, its willingness to use the most recent technology for the customer, and its willingness to train its staff in the use of the most advanced technology.

- *To what degree does the supplier use subcontractors?* The company should find out which functions the supplier typically gives to subcontractors. This is a good way to determine those functions in which the supplier has no expertise.

- *How does the supplier resolve disputes?* The company should find out if the supplier has a formal process for resolving disputes, how well that process works, the supplier's willingness to resolve disputes, and the customer's level of satisfaction with this item.

- *How agreeable is the supplier to renegotiating the contract?* The company should find out if the supplier has ever allowed its contract to be renegotiated to take out some of the more onerous terms, the level of negotiation required to make these changes, and the supplier's willingness to make these changes.

- *What is the level of supporting detail in the supplier's billings?* The company should find out if there is sufficient detail in the supplier's billings to support an audit review of line item costs.

- *Has the supplier shared cost savings with the company? If so, how did this work?* The company should find out the types of cost-sharing agreements, which cost reductions have been shared, the types of sharing formulas used, and the supplier's willingness to enter into such agreements.

- *How have the supplier's actual billing amounts met with the company's expectations?* The company should find out if the cost of using the supplier is roughly equivalent to the customer's cost expectations before it entered into the contract with the supplier.

- *How has the supplier dealt with the cost of out-of-scope services?* The company should find out the amount of costs charged for out-of-scope services, if these amounts are considered by the customer to be excessive, and if the supplier tries to move services from the baseline costing category into the extra (and higher) cost category.

- *Were there other disputes not covered by the previous questions?* The company should find out if there have been other disputes with the supplier, the nature and seriousness of these disputes, and if legal counsel was required to assist in resolving the problems.

- *Would you hire the supplier again? Why?* The company should find out if the customer would hire the supplier again, and specifically why this supplier is better than its competition.

The above questions cover the initial transition to the supplier, the treatment of former company employees by the supplier, the adequacy of service levels, complaint handling, the supplier's level of expertise, and costs. Though these questions are not sufficient to cover all aspects of a specific function, they can be used as the basis for a set of review questions, with additional questions added that deal with function-specific topics.

Most of this section has covered the steps needed to correctly evaluate a potential supplier. It is equally useful to be aware of problems in the process that may lead to an incorrect evaluation. One problem can be an inadequate time budget for the evaluation. If the selection team has insufficient time, it may not pick the appropriate group of initial candidates, create a sufficiently detailed request for proposals, or conduct reference checks. Another problem can be the scope of work noted in the request for proposals. If this scope statement is too vague, suppliers may make incorrect bids or bid on services that are not required, which may result in considerable renegotiation of the contract once the supplier that has been selected has gone through its due diligence work. Also, there may not be a sufficient definition of the costs of services in supplier bids. If a supplier is picked whose bid costs are too vague, the selection team may find that the actual costs are higher than expected, and will then have to reopen the bidding process to find another supplier. Finally, the selection process can be very political. The selection team should be aware that suppliers may go around them and appeal to higher levels of management for favorable treatment, so that the team's selection may be voided and another supplier hired without their recommendation. It is important to be aware of such problems in advance, so that the selection team can avoid them.

This section gave an overview of the information to be included in a request for proposals, the various criteria to be used in reviewing bids received from suppliers, and the information to obtain while conducting reference checks on supplier finalists. The most important point to remember after reading this section is that picking a supplier based on the bid price is one of the least important factors—it is much more important, due to the long-term nature of the relationship, that the selection be based on such factors as the operating style of the supplier, its compatibility with the company's staff, and its reputation for excellence.

2.3   COST OF THE OUTSOURCING RELATIONSHIP

This section contains a number of general observations regarding the cost of an outsourcing relationship, ranging from how a supplier can offer lower prices than the company can support internally, through how a supplier makes most of its profits from an outsourcing contract, and ending with reasons why an excessively low bid should not be taken. This section is intended to give the reader some idea of where the costs and profits are found in an outsourcing contract, and what to do if a supplier's bid price appears to be incorrect.

A supplier can save costs for a company in two ways. One is that it can purchase assets from the company as part of an outsourcing deal, and then lease them back. For example, a computer supplier can purchase a company's data center and then include the lease for that center in the company's payments to it for services rendered. This gives the company a large infusion of cash at the start of the agreement, which can be useful in terms of the company's reported return on assets, as well as if the company is in a poor financial position and needs a cash infusion. It is also an alternative form of debt financing that can be used if the company needs the cash for other purposes, such as an acquisition. The second way in which a supplier can save money for a company is to cluster the facilities needed for a number of companies to achieve economies of scale. For example, a centralized truck-maintenance facility is more cost-effective than having a single smaller shop at each of many company locations, since administrative costs are minimized while the on-site staff of mechanics is more fully utilized. A supplier can save a client company money by purchasing some assets or by using centralized facilities to reduce transaction costs.

If neither of the previously noted cost-saving items are present in a supplier's costing proposal, then it is likely that the company can perform the task just as cheaply itself, and may want to reevaluate why it is considering farming out the work to another company (though there are many other reasons for outsourcing that may justify outsourcing a function for a higher cost than could be obtained internally, such as obtaining better management skill or overall employee expertise, or because the company wants to have the supplier available for high-volume situations when the in-house function is overwhelmed with work). Some companies even use the bidding process to obtain benchmarking information for improving internal operations. When this is the intention, the request for proposals should request itemized pricing that lists the price for each service to be provided, rather than a lump-sum figure for all services. This gives management a more detailed view of the costs of specific activities within the function. Also, management may find that this more detailed bid format allows it to only outsource those functions that are clearly cheaper than what it can provide through internal work, and keep the rest. However, if the company issues a request for proposals with no intention of hiring a supplier, it should be prepared to wait a long time before issuing it again, because suppliers will not want to waste the time to create a bid when they know it is not the company's intention to give its business to anyone. There are only certain situations where a supplier can provide services at a lower cost than the company; itemized supplier bids will allow management to locate those tasks that can be performed more cheaply by the supplier, while retaining all other tasks.

The company should understand how a supplier makes a profit from an outsourcing arrangement so that the company can retain as much of that profit for itself as possible, while still giving the supplier enough of a profit for it to be interested in providing a good level of service to the company. The supplier's first objective when bidding is to win the bid—this means that it must offer the lowest base price. However, it must still make a profit, so the supplier will exclude as many services as possible from the base price and price these services separately at a much higher price. The supplier is assuming that the company will only compare bids based on baseline costs and not on extra service fees; the company can avoid this pricing strategy by ensuring that all bids are compared based on the total cost of services needed. Also, the volume of services may change dramatically over time for specific tasks, which will allow the supplier to charge high incremental fees for those tasks if they are not part of the baseline cost. The company's reaction to this pricing ploy should be to include as many tasks as possible in the baseline price. The supplier can also charge a low baseline price for the first few years and then ratchet up the price later in the contract, thereby deferring all profits for several years. If the company voids the contract early, the supplier charges a steep termination fee to recover its profits at that time. The company can avoid this situation by shortening the length of the contract and negotiating the smallest possible termination fees. Finally, the supplier will attempt to pass through charges directly to the company, rather than absorb the costs itself. These charges may include, for example, software licensing fees or sales taxes. The company can try to have these charges included in the supplier's baseline price for services rendered. Though a number of ways were noted whereby a company can keep a supplier from earning undue levels of profit, it is important to note that the supplier must be allowed *some* profit—otherwise, the supplier has no incentive to provide services to the company, and will probably try to renegotiate the contract or get out of the outsourcing relationship altogether. There are specific contract pricing areas where a supplier tries to generate its profits. By being aware of these areas, a company can reduce its costs at the expense of the supplier.

One rather unusual risk for the company to consider is that a supplier may bid too low to take over the company's functions. This may happen because the supplier has incorrectly evaluated the specifications for the outsourcing contract. The first reaction of a company that receives such a bid is, of course, to take it and hold the supplier to the quoted price. However, the company must remember that two of its objectives when outsourcing are to find someone else who can provide quality service and to reduce the amount of management time needed to run that function. If a supplier is forced into a relationship with the company in which it is clearly losing money, the supplier will naturally try to cut costs by reducing the level of service, which will require more management time by the company to avoid. Thus, holding a supplier to an obviously incorrect bid amount is not in the interests of the company in the long run. It is better to notify the supplier that there may be a pricing problem in its bid, and request a revised bid that truly reflects the supplier's actual costs and expected profit margins.

This section noted how a supplier can save money for a company through an outsourcing arrangement, why a supplier cannot provide cost savings in some situations, and how a supplier makes its profits from an outsourcing deal. In addition, what to do when an excessively low bid is received was discussed. A company can handle a supplier better if it knows how the supplier can offer lower prices than the company, and how it makes a profit from an outsourcing arrangement.

2.4   KEY LEGAL ISSUES

A company that is new to outsourcing is already in a losing position, because it does not know what terms in an outsourcing contract may cause problems as the relationship with the suppliers matures over time. It is also not sufficient to rely on articles or this book for information about how to finalize a legal agreement—these documents give the reader a general idea of what contract clauses may cause trouble, but every contract will have detailed issues that cannot be anticipated by an author who does not see each contract. Instead, it is mandatory that the company retain a qualified lawyer who is in the business of reviewing outsourcing contracts. Only by this means will the company be assured of having enough expertise on its side to compete against the outsourcing company's lawyers in designing an appropriate outsourcing agreement. They deal with outsourcing contracts every day, since that is the supplier's business, whereas the company will only deal with a small number of suppliers even if it outsources every function. There is just no way to obtain enough legal knowledge of outsourcing agreements internally—the company must retain outside counsel.

Before getting to specific legal clauses that the company should include in or exclude from the contract, the company should look for the presence of any language in the supplier's proposed contract saying that some issues will be deferred for post-contract resolution. This is a major warning flag, because the supplier can then lock the company into an agreement and then work on obtaining more beneficial terms for itself at a more leisurely pace. If this clause is present in the contract, the company should seriously consider stepping back to the selection phase and finding a different supplier. Any contract language that defers certain agreements until after the base-level outsourcing agreement has been signed should be avoided.

Once the previous steps have been completed, the legal team assigned to negotiating a contract on behalf of the company should consider throwing out the supplier's contract and creating a new one from scratch. The reason for this is that the supplier's contract is written exclusively for the benefit of the supplier; there are so many clauses in it that are slanted to the supplier's benefit that it may be a more effective use of the legal team's time to simply start over and construct a new agreement rather than negotiate a change in the wording of every clause in the supplier's proposed agreement as well as add any clauses beneficial to the company that are absent from the supplier's proposed contract. Throwing out the supplier's contract and creating a new one may be an effective approach to gaining a contract that fully addresses the company's needs.

The single largest problem that will arise in most outsourcing relationships is that the services to be provided have not been clearly defined in the formal agreement. This leads to frustration on both sides, since the company feels that the supplier is not providing a sufficient level of services, while the supplier feels that the company is demanding more than is called for in the formal agreement. The best way to avoid this problem is to review all of the tasks being conducted in-house for the function to be outsourced, and verify that all of these functions are itemized in the formal agreement, either to be completed by the supplier or to be retained by the company. A good way to obtain this information is to review all of the job descriptions in the department to be outsourced—the summary of all tasks listed in the job descriptions should be a fair representation of the function's total number of tasks. It is equally important to itemize those functions that will *not* be included in the outsourcing agreement, since this formalizes the company's agreement to continue to provide these services. Be sure to list in the agreement all functions that the supplier has agreed to perform, and all functions in the outsourcing area that the company will continue to support.

Another issue is that the supplier will try to narrow the scope of baseline services. Baseline services are those core functions that the supplier will provide to the company. The prices of these services are typically subject to the most negotiation, and are also used by the company to decide on which competing supplier bid is the cheapest. Thus, the baseline price tends to be very cheap. For the supplier to make money on the contract, as many services as possible must be excluded from the baseline services category and included in an "other" category, which typically costs much more per service rendered. It is the job of the company's negotiating team to move as many supplier functions into the baseline services category as possible to keep the company's total cost as low as possible.

The contract should include some language that allows the company to force the supplier to replace the account manager assigned to the company's account. This is important because services provided to the company may suffer if the account manager has inadequate management skills. There may also be personal friction between the account manager and the company's management, which may necessitate a change even if the account manager is competent. The reverse situation is also possible—if the company finds during the discovery phase that it prefers a particular manager on the supplier's team, it can even name that person in the contract as the account manager. This clause is unusual, since a supplier normally wants the freedom to reassign its employees elsewhere, but may be palatable if the named employee is assigned to the company only for a limited time. Having the ability to remove and assign the supplier's account manager should be written into the contract.

The contract should discuss the transfer of facilities, employees, and assets to the supplier. This should include the price to be paid for all transferred assets, as well as how this price will be paid by the supplier—as a lump-sum fee, incremental payments, or as a reduction in the fees paid by the company for the supplier's services. The supplier will probably want to review the facilities, employees, and assets in advance to pick what it wants, so the company must build into the contract schedule a period of time for this review to take place.

If the function being outsourced involves the transfer of or access to information that the company considers to be critical to its competitiveness in the market, then a confidentiality agreement should be an integral part of the contract. This agreement requires the supplier to not disseminate any information about the company, its products, or its processes to other companies, or to distribute this information to the public through any publications, speeches, or discussions. The agreement normally allows the company to break off the outsourcing agreement at once if it can be proved that the confidentiality agreement has been broken, and to pursue punitive damages in court. Examples of functions where a confidentiality agreement is needed are engineering, computer systems, and marketing. Areas where the agreement would be less necessary (since access to critical information is less likely) are the janitorial, maintenance, and customer service areas. Adding a confidentiality agreement to the contract creates an incentive for the supplier to keep from disseminating information about the company.

The company may want to reserve the right to have a third-party auditing firm review the work the supplier is performing for the company to ensure that all tasks are being completed properly, and that billings to the company accurately reflect the work being performed. A clause that reserves this right should be included in the contract. In practice, the use of an audit is limited to those situations where a dispute has arisen—in these cases, relations with the supplier may be at a low point, and the supplier may not allow an audit team on its premises, so a legal requirement to bring in an audit team may be quite necessary.

One of the greatest dangers of switching a knowledge-intensive function such as computer systems or engineering to a supplier is that the supplier may take the best of the company's staff in those areas and move them to other clients, which results in a net loss of talent for the company. To counteract this problem, the contract can be modified to force the supplier to retain all transferred employees on the company's account for some period of time, such as two years. After that time, the supplier will be allowed to shift staff to other clients, where they may be better suited to the supplier's needs due to their skill sets. This clause ensures that the experience level of the supplier's staff working for the company will remain high, while the supplier still has an option to change its staffing mix in the long run. An alternative is to specify in the contract that the supplier's staff must have a minimum average number of years experience. This provision ensures that the supplier does not overstaff the project with new hires, but is difficult to track, and is also open to some interpretation regarding what constitutes "experience"—total years of experience, years subsequent to college, or years of experience in just the specific application in which the employee is not being used?

A variety of issues must be covered that relate to the costs to be charged to the company. These can include such diverse issues as inflation escalation clauses, cost caps, splitting of cost savings, and unit costing versus fixed-fee costing. These issues are discussed in the following bulleted points:

- *COLA adjustments.* The ideal contract for the supplier is to have the contract allow it to automatically raise its prices every year by the amount of the annual inflation rate. The company may be forced to agree to this clause, especially if there is limited competition for the outsourcing contract, if the supplier obviously provides better service than its competitors, or if the term of the contract is so long that some relief for the supplier is needed to protect it from long-term increases in the inflation rate. If it becomes necessary for the company to agree to this clause, it is prudent to include a cost cap, so that the inflation rate adjustment can be no higher than a specified percentage. This protects the company from the effects of very high inflation rates, though it also means that the supplier will have to absorb the excess amount of inflation, which may lead to reduced service levels as the supplier tries to maintain its accustomed level of profitability.

- *Milestone awards.* It is useful to include incentive clauses in the contract that will award the supplier for reaching specific milestones, usually ones that save the company more than the amount of the award. For example, awards could be given for having an engineering group complete work on a major new product design ahead of schedule, which allows the company to increase revenues by beating its competition to market. It is important not to grant awards for non-profit-generating items, since the company is not experiencing a demonstrable profit improvement in exchange for paying the award.

- *Termination fees.* The supplier will probably demand the payment of termination fees if the company chooses to back out of the outsourcing arrangement prior to the termination date noted in the contract. The company should only agree to this if the supplier will actually incur losses as a result of the early contract termination. These losses may be caused by the supplier having purchased some assets from the company that are now of no use, or because the supplier hired a number of employees from the company that must now be given severance payments. In either of these cases, the company should negotiate a gradual reduction in the amount of severance payments as time passes, since the supplier will gradually recoup its costs through the continuing payment of monthly fees to it by the company.

- *Payment for unearned profits.* If the company elects to terminate the outsourcing agreement, the supplier may want to be paid for some portion of its unearned profits that were supposed to occur in the later years of the contract. The company should only agree to this if it has specifically arranged with the supplier to be charged an unusually low price early in the contract—a price that keeps the supplier from earning a profit. Otherwise, if there is no demonstrable difference in the supplier's beginning price from that of other competing suppliers, there should be no reason to accede to this demand.

- *Cost caps.* There may be a number of escalation clauses built into the contract that may force the company into extremely high cost categories that were not anticipated at the beginning of the outsourcing relationship. A good way to mitigate these problems is to add a cost cap to every escalation clause, so that some cost movement is possible, but with an enforced upper limit. For example, a computer services contract may stipulate that an extra $25 will be charged for every additional copy of a computer report distributed to company employees, with a cap of $500, no matter how many copies are delivered. This keeps the company from paying a prohibitive amount if it has a sudden need for a large number of computer reports.

- *Variable pricing.* It is of interest to both parties to use pricing that varies by transaction volume. For example, the company wants the prices it pays to go down if its transaction volume declines, while the supplier wants the prices it charges to go up if the company's transaction volume increases. Thus, it is reasonable to move away from fixed fees and toward a pricing structure that varies directly with volume. For example, janitorial services can be charged based on a price per square foot cleaned, rather than as a single price for an entire company location.

- *Pricing scale based on volume.* The previous item noted that prices should change based on the volume of transactions. This can be taken one step further to include changes in the per-transaction price depending on the total number of transactions. For example, a manufacturing supplier should rightfully charge the company a large amount per unit produced if only a small number of units are requested—its costs per unit will be high because of high setup and administrative costs. However, if greater volumes are requested, these over-head costs will be spread over more units, resulting in lower per-unit costs that should be passed along to the company in the form of lower prices.

- *Value-based payments.* A few companies are arranging with suppliers to only pay them if the company experiences an increase in profits as a result of the supplier's services. This type of agreement requires very specific contract language to define exactly how an increase in profits is defined, and how the supplier is to be paid based on that increase—otherwise, arguments over payments are likely. For example, a tea manufacturer recently agreed to pay a product-design firm a percentage of any profits earned from designs created by the supplier that were eventually converted into actual products. An alternative example that focuses on cost savings rather than on revenue increases is the freight audit company that is only paid if it can find verifiable reductions in a company's freight bills.

Some suppliers will try to raise prices if transaction volumes increase above a baseline amount. The supplier will want to base prices on an average baseline volume that was determined during a few months of data collection at the beginning of the contract, with an average volume during this period being the baseline. All transaction volumes exceeding this baseline will then incur extra fees or perhaps even fall into a "step costing" situation where the pricing structure is higher. The problem with this pricing methodology is that the company will exceed the baseline one-half of the time (after all, the baseline is an average, so the company is below the average 50% of the time and above it 50% of the time); this allows the supplier to charge extra fees one-half of the time. A better approach is to throw out the baseline system as a basis for changing prices and instead use a pricing structure that is based on a higher transaction volume, perhaps one that the company only exceeds 5 to 10% of the time. By avoiding pricing changes based on a baseline and using a higher basis, the company can avoid extra charges by the supplier.

No matter how clear the contract may be, problems are likely to arise that were not foreseen at the time the contract was written. Though the parties may be able to resolve such situations peaceably, there may be times when matters cannot be re-solved. For such situations, the contract should contain a clause that allows the par-ties to go to arbitration, and requires them to be bound by the judgment of that party, so that all disputes can be resolved relatively quickly and without the expense of un-dergoing legal representation in the court system.

After an agreement with a supplier is signed, the company may want to bring in other suppliers to provide specialized services within the general functional area being covered by the supplier. For example, within the computing function, the com-pany may want to have different suppliers handle the help desk, data center, and net-work maintenance. However, bringing in additional suppliers to work alongside the original supplier can make the original supplier rather testy—it may have assumed that all services within that functional area would be given to it. To avoid such problems with the supplier, a clause should be included in the contract that allows the company to obtain the services of other companies to provide additional services within the general functional area being serviced by the supplier.

Performance metrics must be included in the contract. These metrics usually specify how fast functions will be performed by the supplier. For example, a contract could state that all inquiries by company staff will receive a complete response within one day of the inquiry for 90% of all inquiries. When this type of metric is included in the agreement, be sure to specify how much time is allowed for those instances where the supplier is not able to fulfill the metric. For example, the previous example could be continued to state that the remaining 10% of requests must be completely responded to within three days of the original request. This extra contract clause does not allow the supplier to not perform at all—some performance may be delayed, but it cannot be ignored.

Once the performance metrics have been set up, penalty clauses should be inserted in the contract that specify charges to be levied if the metrics are not met. The amount of each penalty will obviously be a hot negotiating topic, since the supplier will want the lowest possible, while the company will want the reverse. In determining an appropriate penalty amount, one must consider the reason for the penalty—it is not to be so punitive as to put the supplier out of business, but it must be large enough to get the supplier's attention. For example, if an accounting services supplier misses paying a payable item early enough to take a discount on it, a penalty of $10 probably will not attract much attention, and the problem will not be addressed. However, if the penalty is $1,000, the supplier is much more likely to fix the problem immediately, so that no further instances of the issue are likely to occur.

Another issue to be covered is terminating the outsourcing agreement. Termination can be a wrenching experience, since the company must take over or resource a function that it may have invested a large amount of time in transferring to the supplier. However, if it is necessary, there are a large number of issues that must be included in the contract that will ensure a relatively smooth shutdown of the working relationship and a return of conditions to their pre-outsourcing state. The following items relate to terminating the outsourcing arrangement, and should be included in the contract:

- *Types of termination.* There should a variety of reasons written into the contract that allow either party to back out of the outsourcing arrangement. One is *termination for convenience,* which allows either party to walk away from the contract with minimal notice and for no reason. This type of termination is useful for those outsourcing deals where few assets or employees have been exchanged, or where the service being provided can be readily taken over by the company or by a competitor. Another version is *termination for bankruptcy or nonpayment.* Obviously, either party will want to walk away from the outsourcing arrangement if the other party is no longer a going concern and cannot guarantee its day-to-day existence. There is also *termination upon the sale or merger of the company;* the new owner of the business may not want to be involved in an outsourcing relationship that may still have a legal obligation to run for many more years, and this clause gives the new owner an option to get out of the contract. This clause is especially useful if having an outsourcing deal may prevent a prospective buyer from purchasing the business. A less-used clause is *termination based on a change in the technology.* For example, a computer outsourcing agreement may be for maintenance of a company's mainframe computing facility. However, if the company decides to switch to a minicomputer-based client-server computing environment, the supplier may have no experience in that environment; in this case, the company must have the option to terminate the outsourcing arrangement and shift its business to some other supplier that is more technically qualified to assist the company. Finally, and most commonly, there is *termination for cause.* A variety of reasons may be included in the contract that will allow either party (usually the company, not the supplier) to back out of the contract, after giving the other party a reasonable period of time to correct the problem under dispute. Examples of items that might cause termination would be insufficient cleaning for a janitorial supplier, excessive computer downtime for a computer services supplier, recurring difficulty in meeting design milestones for engineering suppliers, and not being able to connect customers after a specified number of rings for a customer service representative supplier.

- *Require supplier to assist in the conversion.* If a supplier is terminated, it will not be happy about losing the company's business, and may obstruct the process of bringing the relationship to a close and moving it either back to the company or to a different supplier. However, if the contract includes a clause that requires due diligence in returning assets and documents, training someone else to take over the services, and providing support services during the transfer, the supplier can be forced to assist in the process. Other supplier assistance may include helping to create a transition plan to move the service away from the supplier, and writing procedures for the daily operation of the function. Of course, if it is specifically stated in the contract that the supplier will be well paid to provide these termination-related services, its help may be more forthcoming.

There are usually some appendices to the contract. These typically include lists of all assets and facilities being transferred to the supplier, which should include some form of identification, such as part numbers or serial numbers, as well as transfer prices for each item. Another appendix may be a complete list of training topics that must be given by the company to the supplier's staff to make it knowledgeable in the company's function that is being outsourced; it is helpful to include a training schedule with this information, since it forces the company to finish the training program at the earliest possible date. Yet another appendix can be a complete list of baseline reports that the supplier is to send to the company, along with complete descriptions of each report and the number of times per month that these reports are to be delivered. Another appendix should itemize all baseline services that the supplier is committed to provide to the company; these should be described in detail, so that arguments over what constitutes a baseline function will be kept to a minimum. Finally, an appendix should include complete descriptions of all performance measurements that will be used to rate the supplier's performance, along with any formulas that will be used to award the supplier with more compensation or penalize it based on the results of those performance measurements. All of these appendices are necessary to provide detailed backup to the issues noted in the main body of the contract, which reduces subsequent arguing over what is meant by various contract clauses.

A final issue regards the timing of signing the contract. The company should wait until the supplier has completed all steps of its due diligence work before having anyone sign the contract. This is because the supplier has an interest in having a preliminary agreement signed, which automatically forces the company to drop all other suppliers from contention for the company's business. In addition, the supplier will usually insist on adding a clause stating that the contract's prices may be changed subject to conditions found during the due diligence phase—this allows the supplier to form an argument for raising prices subsequent to signing the contract. In short, the company should not sign the final contract until the supplier has completed its due diligence work, because this gives the supplier one less reason to argue for raising its prices, while keeping other potential suppliers in the competition until the last moment.

One of the primary steps in the process of outsourcing a function is the negotiation of the contract with the supplier. This section discussed many of the key points that should be part of an outsourcing agreement, such as the scope of baseline services, transfer of assets, confidentiality, audits, cost-of-living increases, cost caps, variable-rate pricing, termination conditions, arbitration, and performance metrics. Including these points in a contract will help to keep a company from falling into a disadvantageous legal position against a supplier. However, each outsourcing situation will require additional contract clauses, which will vary depending on the function being outsourced. Consequently, it is mandatory that outside legal representation that is expert in the negotiation of outsourcing contracts be retained to assist the company. The additional cost of bringing in outside legal assistance will be more than made up for by the cost savings that will result from having a contract without any unfavorable clauses.

2.5 CHANGING THE ORGANIZATIONAL STRUCTURE

If outsourcing is used for several functional areas, a company should consider changing its organizational structure so that the outsourced functions can be managed in the most effective manner possible. This section discusses the need for functional coordinators and support staffs, as well as the reasons for creating long-term relationships with outside legal firms that specialize in outsourcing issues, and creating an internal outsourcing advisory committee to provide support services to the managers of functions that are being or already have been outsourced. By making these changes, a company will find that it is better able to manage those functions that have been outsourced.

It is extremely important that the company retain enough internal talent to exercise proper control over any outsourced function. This is because the company cannot rely upon the management of the supplier to manage the outsourced function in a manner that is beneficial to the company—the supplier will only manage that function in a manner that is beneficial to the supplier, because the supplier is going to look out for itself first. Thus, when the company outsources a function, it must retain an experienced manager who is capable of continually reviewing the supplier's activities to ensure that it is performing the outsourced function correctly.

This manager is called a coordinator. For example, if the manager oversees all janitorial functions performed by a supplier, he is the janitorial coordinator. This person should have enough experience to spot any problems with the way in which the supplier is either taking over or managing its function on an ongoing basis. In addition, the coordinator should have very good people skills and be able to use them to address problems. For example, the coordinator must be able to pass along all complaints regarding services provided by the supplier, negotiate with the supplier regarding how those problems will be fixed, and then oversee the resolution of those issues. In addition, the coordinator must be able to deal firmly with all proposed extra services that the supplier would like to give the company, since most suppliers make the bulk of their profits by charging high fees for these extra services. The coordinator must also supervise the measurement of various aspects of a supplier's performance and follow up with the supplier if these measures indicate substandard performance. Also, the coordinator may have to schedule the work of the supplier, which requires planning skill—for example, the coordinator for the engineering function must decide which product flaws must be redesigned by a supplier, and the priority of the work on each design flaw. This requires considerable tact in dealing with the supplier's management, since the coordinator will usually contact the supplier to discuss issues that are not being performed properly, rather than the reverse. The coordinator must also be able to deal with those company employees who may be having difficulty with the supplier. Also, since relations with the supplier may go on for years, it is important for the coordinator to build trust with the supplier team so that it will want to work with the company. The primary criterion for the coordinator's job description is management, not experience. As long as the coordinator's skills in the area of negotiation, oversight, and teamwork are strong, any weakness in his or her knowledge of the function being outsourced can be supplemented by additional staff who report to the coordinator.

The amount of staff required to assist the coordinator for each function is highly dependent on the size and importance of the function. For example, an outsourced engineering function is so important that the coordinator should receive a sizable staff to assist in controlling the function, whereas janitorial services, which are not critical to the company, may require only a part-time coordinator to oversee the work at even a large facility. For smaller functions, it may make sense to utilize the unique outsourcing experience of the company's coordinators by having each of them oversee several functions, rather than have a single manager with less experience fill the coordinator role for each outsourced function. This gives control over outsourced functions to those in-house staff with the greatest management experience, and also gives suppliers the benefit of dealing with the coordinators who know how to deal with them. In short, the company must give a sufficient number of support staff to its coordinators, while giving a single coordinator several functions to manage if the functions are small enough.

A properly organized company that makes heavy use of outsourcing should make continuing use of the services of a legal firm that specializes in the outsourcing function. Such a firm will have far more experience than any internal legal group in the intricacies of negotiating contracts with suppliers, as well as for subsequent disputes, since it handles this issue for many companies and has gained a considerable amount of experience. Integrating an outsourcing law firm into a company's organizational structure is a necessary task in creating an organization that properly utilizes outsourcing.

If a company wants to outsource a large number of its functional areas, it is useful to create an advisory group within the company that is knowledgeable in the process to be followed in finding potential suppliers, issuing requests for proposals, selecting suppliers, negotiating contracts with them, transitioning functions to them, and managing the ongoing relationship with them. The committee can also collect information about outsourcing experiences in one part of the company and disseminate it to other departments if the information may be useful elsewhere. With this knowledge stored in one group and available to all functions being outsourced, the company will experience fewer problems in making the transition to outsourcing, since problems in the process will not be repeated—the outsourcing advisory committee will help to steer managers away from potential problem areas as functions are shifted to suppliers. The members of this committee should include employees who have already managed the transition of some functions to suppliers, and who are skillful in passing along this knowledge to other employees. Specific committee skills may include human resources (for handling employees who are being moved to suppliers or laid off), financial analysts (to create ways to measure the performance of suppliers), lawyers (to assist in negotiations with suppliers), and managers (to advise new functional coordinators in how to deal with suppliers on an ongoing basis). It can be very effective to create an outsourcing advisory committee to smooth the transition of functions to suppliers, as well as to advise functional coordinators on how to deal with suppliers.

This section noted the need for a strong coordinator for every function that has been outsourced, to ensure that suppliers do only those tasks they are supposed to do, and that those tasks are completed on time and within budget. Depending on the size of the outsourced function, a coordinator may need a large support staff to assist in monitoring the supplier's activities. Also, the company should retain the services of an experienced outside legal firm that specializes in outsourcing issues, in order to have the best possible advice available for reviewing contracts with suppliers, as well as for resolving any subsequent legal issues. Finally, an outsourcing advisory committee should be created that collects information about how to outsource a function and manage the supplier once it has been outsourced, as well as how to resolve any other outsourcing-related issues—and then pass this information along to all parts of the company, so that managers of individual functions can benefit from the outsourcing experience of the entire company. By implementing these changes, as shown in Figure 2.1, a company can more effectively manage the transition to outsourcing, as well as its ongoing relationships with suppliers.

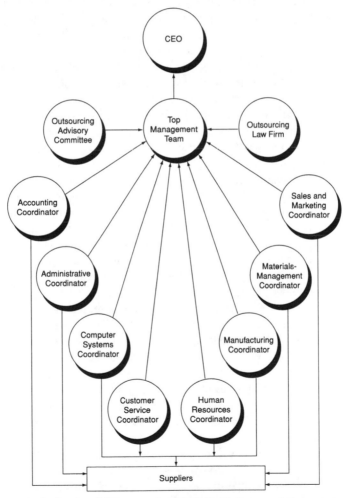

Figure 2.1   Organizational Structure for a Totally Outsourced Company

2.6   PERSONNEL ISSUES

Many people consider outsourcing to be an inhumane practice, for it uproots large numbers of employees either by shifting them to a supplier or by laying them off. This is true. The manager who initiates a move to outsourcing will not be popular—some companies even hire consultants to recommend the decision to them, so that they can blame the consultants for the decision to outsource! There are ways to mitigate the strain on employees during the transition period when suppliers are being selected and functions and staff are being transferred. Those methods are discussed in this section. In addition, the benefits of moving the more talented staff to suppliers are noted, as well as the cost to the employer of laying off staff.

Some companies tell their employees as soon as possible that they are looking into the outsourcing option. This approach is based on the desire to be as fair and open with employees as possible. This is an incorrect approach, for several reasons. First, the request for proposals and selection process may take a very long time—time when employees will be concerned about their jobs and vastly less productive than usual. As long as the outsourcing decision is pending, morale will be low. After all, the company has indicated that it has no faith in a department's ability to do its job, so it is getting rid of the department. Finally, after going through the selection process, the company may find that it wants to keep the function in-house because the outsourcing bids received were not good enough to warrant making the change. In this case, making the staff nervous by telling them about the outsourcing decision has only made them realize that their job security is not as good as they had thought. Staff losses are likely even though there will be no outsourcing, because the company has told its employees that, given the right deal, it is willing to let them go. In short, a company should not tell its employees that it is pursuing the idea of outsourcing until the time when it has settled upon a supplier and is finalizing the contract—informing the staff any sooner will cut into morale and possibly lead to the loss of employees in a period when the company is not even sure if it will go ahead with the decision to outsource.

Once a supplier has been identified who will take over a specific company function, the company must announce the decision to all employees who will be affected by the decision. The announcement must be made at this point because the prospective supplier will need to conduct a due diligence review of the company's operation and staff, so word of the decision will be all over the company as soon as the supplier's review team arrives at the company's location. When the decision is made, the company must be as complete as possible in discussing the outsourcing move with its employees. There are several reasons for having a thorough discussion at this time. One is that employees from whom information is hidden will suspect that there is a cover-up of information, and will immediately begin a search for new jobs, meaning that fewer employees will be available to be transferred to the supplier. Another reason is that employees in other company departments will be interested bystanders—after all, their departments may be next in line for outsourcing, and they will want to know how well the company treats its staff. If it appears as though the company is not being fair to the outsourced staff, this may have the unwanted impact of causing the departure of employees from other departments. It is in the company's best interests to be as open as possible with all employees to be involved in an outsourcing move, not only to keep their trust, but also the trust of all other employees.

When the employee meeting occurs, the company's team should be accompanied by a team from the supplier who will be taking over the function. This gives the staff a chance to meet its new employer. The meeting should last as long as anyone wants to ask questions, so that there will be no reason for anyone to question the company's desire to provide information to its employees. The team that will make the announcement should role-play the meeting in advance and ask itself the most uncomfortable questions, so the team will be more comfortable with how all questions will be answered. The topics that should be covered during the employee meeting include severance payments for those employees who will not be hired by the supplier or retained by the company, as well as employment contracts or guaranteed periods of employment by the supplier. In addition, any union negotiations that have been conducted should be mentioned, as well as whether the transferred employees may be required to join a union at the supplier. Other discussion topics include job functions that may change, the transfer of pension or 401(k) funds to supplier funds and how vesting in these plans will change, the possibility of having to relocate, and any changes in salaries and benefits. Obviously, some of this information is private and not to be mentioned in a group meeting, so the company should schedule one-on-one talks with all affected employees after the group meeting so that employee-specific information such as pay rates or severance or employment offers can be made. These individual sessions should be completed as soon as possible so that no employees are forced to wait an unreasonable period of time. The company should team with the supplier to make a thorough presentation to employees regarding any changes to their status. This discussion should include separate meetings with each affected employee to discuss each person's concerns.

Outsourcing can be a good deal for those of a company's employees with good skills and ambition, because they will have an opportunity to work for a company that specializes in their line of work. For example, a computer programmer who works for a company with many in-house functions will only have a limited opportunity to obtain additional training or be promoted within the company. However, if that person were to be transferred to a supplier who specializes in computer systems, such as Arthur Anderson or Electronic Data Systems, it will be in the interests of the supplier to ensure that the employee receives continuing training in the latest skills. The supplier must do this because it must be able to convince prospective clients that its staff is at the leading edge of technical innovation in its field in order to acquire contracts to provide services to those companies. Also, the supplier is likely to periodically move its employees to different client projects so that it obtains the best skill mix for each client. This is also good for the supplier's employees, since they will gain experience through working with different systems. On the other hand, it can be stressful for supplier employees to be forced to periodically move to new client locations. In short, being employed by an outsourcing supplier can be a very beneficial experience for an ambitious company employee.

It is possible that a large number of employees in the function to be outsourced will not be reemployed by the supplier. The supplier may already have a sufficient number of staff on hand to deal with the work required by the company, or may consider the company's staff to not have enough experience to be worth hiring. In either case, the company will be faced with having to lay off large numbers of employees. Though some companies give no severance, most will make a modest payment to the departing employees, such as a week of pay for every year of employment with the company. Other related costs may include the cost of providing counseling, retraining, or temporary office space to the laid-off employees. If the company decides to make severance or other payments, it is possible that this added cost will counterbalance any savings that the company was anticipating by outsourcing the function. The company should consider the cost of severance payments to departing employees as a significant cost of switching to outsourcing.

In summary, it is better for a company to keep quiet about any plans to outsource until it has selected a supplier and is willing to sign a contract with it. The company should then announce all details of the outsourcing deal to employees, and should have the supplier's representatives meet with its staff. Outsourcing may prove to be a career enhancer for the more talented of a company's employees who are transferred to a supplier, since they have the chance to work with a number of companies in their area of specialization. Finally, a company must consider the personnel cost of switching to outsourcing, as the cost of paying severance to employees who will not be hired by the supplier may negate any savings that would otherwise accrue from the outsourcing deal.

2.7   TRANSITION ISSUES

The process of moving a company function to a supplier has many common elements, irrespective of the type of function being moved. These common transition steps are noted in this section. Other, more specific steps that are only needed for the transition of certain functions to suppliers are noted in the chapters devoted to those functions.

The following bulleted points show the approximate sequence in which a transition to a supplier should take place, assuming that the transition takes place immediately after a potential supplier has been selected. Some of the simpler functions, such as janitorial services, will require fewer steps, while other, more complicated functions, such as computer services and engineering, will require all of the steps. For the more important functions, it is very important not to rush the transition process. If a critical function such as computer services is transferred too quickly, it is possible that some crucial functions will fail during the transition, which may severely impact the company's ability to operate. Also, a fast transition does not give the supplier enough time to review the company's operations, and may result in an incorrect bid price that either party may have to renegotiate to make more equitable. To ensure that both parties are comfortable with the completion of a step before moving on to the next process step, it is useful for both parties to formally sign off on the step just completed; if one party is not willing to do so, then more time must be spent on the completion of that step. The steps to be followed during the transition process are as follows:

- *Select a functional coordinator.* The company must select an employee with considerable management skill to be the functional coordinator. This person will be in charge of all relations with the supplier, and, in this role, is responsible for final contract negotiations. For this reason, the coordinator should be appointed before the final contract terms are agreed to by both parties.

- *Create an experience database.* The company should compile a database containing the levels of experience of all employees who are likely to be transferred to the supplier. This information is needed by the supplier to determine the staffing mix required to serve the company's needs. Some companies accumulate this information very early in the outsourcing process, but this is not necessary—the company may choose not to outsource with anyone, so it is better to save this step until after a prospective supplier has been chosen.

- *Sign a confidentiality agreement.* Once a possible supplier has been selected, it must review the company's functions to see how its initial contract proposal must be modified to match the actual scope of work required. This review process may reveal trade secrets to the supplier, so this is an appropriate time to have the supplier sign a confidentiality agreement.

- *Interview the staff.* One of the primary early steps for the supplier is to interview the company's staff in the area to be outsourced. These interviews, when matched with the company's previously prepared experience database, gives the supplier a good idea of which personnel it wishes to hire. The interviews are also useful for reviewing the procedures used to generate required outputs.

- *Review ongoing work functions.* The supplier should then review the work functions to be transferred to it. This usually involves a "walk-through" of each function, accompanied by any additional interviews needed to clarify the function.

- *Review documentation.* The supplier should then review all documentation related to the function. This documentation may be policies and procedures, reports, or input forms—essentially every document needed to show how information flows through the function and is used to create the desired output.

- *Revise supplier tasks and pricing.* The supplier will use the information collected during its due diligence work to modify its proposal to match the actual services noted. These modifications are most commonly needed when the request for proposal, which should have contained this information, did not accurately reflect the actual state of affairs.

- *Finalize contract.* The functional coordinator should work with the company's legal staff to negotiate changes to the modified proposal presented by the supplier following its due diligence investigation.

- *Announce contract to staff.* Once the contract has been finalized, the functional coordinator and representatives from the supplier should meet individually with those employees who will be impacted by the outsourcing arrangement. This meeting should cover all issues that relate to the employees, such as who will be transferred to the supplier and who will be laid off, salary adjustments, changes in benefits, pension plan modifications, and like matters. Since much of this information is confidential, the meeting should be in two parts—a general meeting with all affected employees, and a series of smaller, one-on-one meetings to go over individual arrangements with each employee.

- *Copy and transfer documentation.* The supplier will need copies of all policies and procedures, forms and reports, meeting minutes, and project schedules related to the function being transferred. The company should send all of this information to the supplier while retaining copies of all documents in case the arrangement with the supplier does not work and the company is forced to take over and manage the function once again.

- *Transfer assets.* Part of the agreement with the supplier may be for the transfer of assets to the supplier. If so, the company must assist in packing and moving the assets to the supplier so that the assets are not damaged. If the assets happen to be data (e.g., computer files), the company is responsible for promptly sending copies of these files to the supplier in a supplier-readable format.

- *Transfer staff.* Transferring staff to the supplier is one of the most important transition steps. The company and supplier should work as a team so that all paperwork for each employee can be handled in one meeting. The information covered should include (depending on each employee's situation) severance payments, paperwork for the disposition of pension payments, payment for accumulated vacation time, and payroll and medical benefits enrollment information with the supplier. A smooth transition in this area helps to reduce staff problems associated with moving to a new employer.

- *Dispose of remaining assets.* The supplier is only likely to acquire those company assets that it can use—the remaining assets the company had used for the now-outsourced function will be useless. The company should act quickly to dispose of these assets before their resale value depreciates further. In particular, computer equipment loses its market value very quickly. Disposal options can include junking the assets, selling them, distributing them to other functions if there is a use for them, or donating them to a tax-exempt organization, which gives the company a deduction on its tax return.

- *Dispose of excess office space.* Depending on the function being outsourced, there may be a considerable amount of office space that is no longer needed once a function has been outsourced. If this space is scattered throughout the company, it may be better to rearrange offices so that a single area can be segregated for rental or sale. It is likely that some space will not be readily converted to other uses, such as specialized maintenance or manufacturing facilities, so the company should be prepared to continue incurring expenses for the upkeep of these facilities.

It may be difficult for the company to accept a supplier, especially when it functions in a manner that is radically different from the company's normal way of doing business. Suppliers may have different policies in regards to standard working hours, operating policies and procedures, and ways of dealing with customers that strike company employees as being wrong. This sort of supplier should have been screened out during the selection process, but if the supplier was considered acceptable for other reasons, the company can insist that it use the company's policies and procedures manual, with appropriate modifications being approved by the functional coordinator, when performing work for the company. By using the company's own guidelines for completing tasks, the supplier will be forced to deal with issues in a manner that is similar to what the company's other departments are used to, which will ease the transition phase for both parties.

One of the biggest mistakes a company can make when transitioning a function to a supplier is to try to convert all possible aspects of that function at once. When this happens, the supplier must try to make a large variety of services operational at the same time. This is difficult, because some services may be based on the correct implementation of other services, and if the first set of services is not operating properly, the additional services will not function either. For example, many companies use outside services to process their payroll. When converting to such a payroll service, it is best to verify that all information on each paycheck, including the hourly or salaried pay rate and address, is accurate. Once this has been verified, other services can be added, such as payment by electronic transfer, automatic calculation of vacation and sick time available, and direct mailing of paychecks to various company locations. A common occurrence with conversions to payroll suppliers, however, is that all of these services are implemented at once. Because of the large amount of information involved in this conversion, a large number of data items will probably be incorrect, resulting in user complaints and possibly the discontinuance of the payroll service with the supplier. In short, it is best to implement just the baseline services first and verify that they are performing correctly before adding additional services.

This section noted the general steps that the company and its new supplier should go through following the initial selection of the supplier, so that a function can be safely moved to the supplier without any loss of services to the company, while giving the supplier enough time to properly evaluate the tasks it is expected to perform.

In particular, the need for written procedures to be followed and a step-by-step, gradual transition process was emphasized.

2.8   RELATIONS WITH THE OUTSOURCING PARTNER

Once a function has been turned over to a supplier, the company should set up a formal review process that allows the two parties to meet regularly and go over any problems that have arisen. This section covers the timing and structure of these meetings, as well as the types of problems that are likely to be addressed during the meetings.

The company should schedule periodic performance-review meetings with the supplier. These meetings are necessary for providing formal feedback to the supplier regarding its performance measurements, how it is doing in achieving any bonus payments under the terms of the contract, personnel issues, and other concerns. This is also a good time for the supplier to bring up the problems that it is having with the company. Even if there are few issues to discuss, it is important to continue to have these meetings so that the managers from both parties can meet and gain a comfort level with their counterparts. The attendees should, at a minimum, be the supplier's account manager and the company's outsourcing coordinator for that function, with a scribe available to take meeting minutes. The meeting minutes should be distributed and signed by both parties as soon after the meeting as possible, so that both sides have an opportunity to review the minutes and protest any items that appear to be inaccurate. The company should retain the final version of all meeting minutes in case they are later needed to resolve disputes. At a higher level, the company and its supplier should meet once a year to discuss how their relationship has progressed, and how any necessary changes should be implemented. This annual meeting should involve senior management from both parties. Because of the extreme importance of communications, both the company and the supplier should make an effort to have the same managers act as the primary contacts for as many years as possible—changing these personnel too frequently will likely lead to a reduced level of understanding of the opposing party, which will result in conflicts. Having regularly scheduled performance-review meetings with the supplier is a necessary part of managing an outsourced function.

Once an outsourcing agreement is finalized, company management must add a task to the range of reviews conducted by its internal audit staff, which is to review the monthly billings sent to the company by the supplier. Supplier billings are very likely to contain errors, since there is always some question as to which services performed for the company were covered as baseline services and which were extra services for which the supplier may charge extra. Especially in the early part of the relationship, there will be a number of gray areas that could fall into either category. When the internal audit team finds these items, they should be brought to the attention of the coordinator in charge of that function, who may have to add a clause to the contract to cover them. It is also useful if the same audit team members can review the billings every time, since those auditors with some experience in the types of services provided will be of most use in spotting problems with the billings. A monthly review of supplier billings is necessary to spot any overbilling problems.

There are a number of areas in which conflicts frequently occur. By being aware of these areas in advance, both the company and the supplier can be on the lookout for developing problems and resolve them before they become severe. The most common problems that can impact relations are as follows:

- *Substandard performance.* The most common problem will be perceived substandard performance by the supplier. This issue requires ongoing review of the standards by which the supplier is judged, the method of calculating the performance levels, and the size of penalties to be applied to the supplier. This is obviously a touchy subject for the supplier, since it impacts the supplier's profitability, so the issue should be handled with a view towards the long-term relationship and how not to alienate the supplier while still ensuring improved levels of performance.

- *Excessive overhead charges.* Part of the costs to be charged to the company will probably include a portion of the supplier's overhead costs. These costs, by definition, cannot be identified directly with any work being done for the company, and so an allocation must be used. It is in the interests of the supplier to charge as much overhead cost as possible to the company, so that it will not have to bear this cost itself. The functional coordinator must regularly review the overhead costs being charged to the company to see if there is an upward trend in the total cost, and if the formula being used to charge the cost is appropriate.

- *High incremental charges.* The supplier may attempt to charge exorbitant fees for additional services requested by the company that were not included in the original contract. In these cases, the company must be careful to obtain a signed quote for the services requested, with the proposed fee noted in the quote. If this is not obtained in advance, there will be continuing problems between the two parties over the appropriate fee structure.

- *Tight definition of baseline services.* The supplier will attempt to tighten the definition of baseline services even after the contract has been signed. This is because new situations will continue to arise, and the supplier will want to list these situations as extra services (with a higher fee attached), while the company will want to itemize them as baseline services, which have a much lower price. Continual negotiations will be needed to redefine baseline services—this is a good task for outside legal counsel.

- *Time required to replace departed staff.* The supplier may take too long to replace departing staff, because the replacements must be pulled from other jobs where they are working for other companies. There is no easy solution to this problem; the company's best recourse is to continually bring the problem to the attention of the supplier, and to charge penalties against payments to the supplier if the reduced headcount is contributing to a reduction in service levels that have penalty clauses attached to them.

*   *Promotion of underqualified staff.* The supplier will want to promote any staff working on company services, since higher hourly fees are normally associated with higher-level staff positions. The company should request a resume showing the level of experience of anyone who is promoted, and should contest the fees being charged if the level of experience appears to be insufficient.

Once the decision to outsource has been made and a supplier selected, it is in the interests of both the company and supplier to ensure that regular communications are set up. There should be periodic, formal review meetings that cover any problems that have arisen since the last meeting, as well as how previous problems have been dealt with. In addition, the internal audit staff can be used to investigate the supplier's activity and bring any problems to the attention of the functional coordinator, who can resolve these issues at one of the formal review meetings. Finally, there are a number of issues that commonly cause problems between the two parties—these issues were noted so that the company can deal with them before they become serious issues. By creating a formal review process and being aware of probable areas of contention, the company and supplier have a much smaller chance of having serious problems over the course of the relationship.

2.9 MEASURING THE SERVICE LEVEL OF EACH OUTSOURCED FUNCTION

This section covers what general types of measurement should be made for each functional area to be outsourced, and how the information should be collected, but does not cover detailed measurements for each function—that information is noted in the chapters that are specifically targeted at each functional area of a company. Measurements are also summarized by functional area in Appendix B.

The performance measurements selected for the review of each outsourced function should be split into measurements that are used by the company to monitor the supplier's performance and measurements that are used to alter payments to the supplier. As examples of the first type of measurement, a company can measure the ability of an engineering team to meet its project milestones, the number of rooms not cleaned by a janitorial team, or the ability of a fleet maintenance supplier to complete regularly scheduled maintenance on trucks within 2,000 miles of the scheduled maintenance mileage. As examples of the second type of measurement, a company can measure a supplier's ability to improve the cycle time of a function, reduce the number of defects in a delivered product, or reduce the cost of delivered services.

The difference between these two types of measurements is that the first involves "maintenance" measurements (e.g., the company wants to make sure that the performance level of a function is not degrading), while the second involves items that will lead to either revenue increases or cost reductions by the company, which allows it to pay the supplier more for its services. An important point here is that the company should not set up a compensation agreement with a supplier that pays the supplier more money for its continuing ability to meet a "maintenance" type of measurement, since this does nothing to improve a company's profits. Only by tying increased payments to those measurements that will also save the company money will the company realize enhanced profitability. In setting up a performance-measurement system, the company must distinguish between those measurements that only allow the company to monitor the progress of the supplier and those measurements that lead to direct profit increases.

The company should spend a considerable amount of time measuring all activities in the functional area to be outsourced prior to outsourcing it. This gives the company a solid baseline of information to use in comparing the company's performance of the function to the supplier's performance. It may be useful to show this information to the supplier, or to even have the supplier sign off on a document containing these baseline measurements—the supplier will then have no excuse to later lambaste these measurements (which may happen if the supplier ends up with worse performance based on the same measurements) on the grounds that they used incorrect data-collection or calculation methods. Creating baseline performance measures is useful as a basis for judging the supplier's performance.

Most measurements should be made at least once a month, and sometimes more frequently. When taken, each measurement should be recorded as the latest addition to a trend line. The functional coordinator can use this trend line to spot spikes in performance in comparison to the trend, and immediately follow up with the supplier to see if there is a problem that caused the spike in the measurement trend line.

The method used to collect measurement information and perform the associated calculations is of some importance. If possible, do not have the supplier collect any information or perform calculations—this is because the supplier has a vested interest in skewing the measurements in its favor, especially when payments to the supplier may vary based on the results of the measurements. If the company must have the supplier do this, then at least have the company's internal audit team periodically review the method of calculation and information collection. A better approach is to have a person on the functional coordinator's staff do the measurement work. This gives the company a more honest appraisal of the supplier's performance. In case the staff person is creating incorrect measurements, it would still be useful to schedule the company's internal audit team for an occasional review of this information. By keeping the measuring function in-house, a company will receive better measurement information.

A company should create measurements that track a supplier's day-to-day performance, as well as measurements that can be used to pay the supplier more (or less) money based on how it improves the company's revenues or reduces its costs. A baseline set of measurements should be calculated before a function is moved to a supplier, so that the company will have a set of measurements to use to compare the supplier's performance to its own. Once a function has been outsourced, measurements should be stored in trend lines, so that sudden spikes in the measurements can be investigated to see if problems are occurring. Finally, the company should have its own staff collect measurement information and perform the calculations in order to obtain measurements that are not skewed by suppliers who want to show the best possible results.

2.10   SUMMARY

This chapter gave the reader a grounding in the techniques needed to locate a list of potential suppliers, pick the right one, determine the cost to outsource, negotiate a reasonable contract, and change the company's organizational structure to accommodate the supplier. In addition, the chapter noted a variety of personnel issues related to outsourcing, as well as several ways to make the transition to the supplier go as smoothly as possible. Finally, it showed how to create a structure for maintaining relations with the supplier over time, and how to measure the supplier's performance. The issues discussed under all of these topics were only such that they would be relevant for all functions being outsourced. For more detailed information about specific functions, the central part of this book covers the same topics, but for individual functional areas such as computer systems, engineering, and materials management. When outsourcing a function, the reader should consult those chapters as well as this one to obtain a complete set of information about how to outsource it.

CHAPTER THREE

Accounting for the Outsourced Company

The cornerstone of operations for most companies is the accounting department. It pays the bills, issues invoices to customers, monitors cash flow, pays employees, and keeps track of assets. It provides services to every functional area of the company. Without an accounting department, a company would not be able to function for more than a few days. What happens to the accounting department when a company outsources all of its functions? This chapter explores the changes that the accounting staff must deal with. These changes are divided into sections. The first is the impact on data collection. Since all activities will be conducted at supplier sites, the accounting staff must find new ways to obtain the information it needs. The next section is financial reporting. The accounting staff will find that outsourcing has an impact on the format of both internal and external financial statements (as well as on the accompanying notes to the statements), the accruals it uses, and even the layout of the chart of accounts. The following section covers changes to control systems, which are primarily based on supplier contracts. The next section is performance measurements. Outsourcing eliminates the need for some measurements, requires the use of new ones, and changes the results of others. The final section covers transactions, which will be fewer in number and easier to manage when outsourcing is used. This chapter provides an overview of how outsourcing the corporation impacts the functions of the accounting department.

3.1   IMPACT ON DATA COLLECTION

When a company switches to outsourcing, the accounting department will find that its primary sources of data switched from being employees within the company to employees of suppliers. This presents a few problems that are covered in this section.

The first issue is communications. The accounting staff will find that it is now relying on a small number of suppliers for most of its data needs, and must work with them for a number of years. In order to get the information it needs, it is a good idea for the accounting staff to develop close ties with its accounting counterparts at the suppliers, so that everyone will know who to talk to in order to get the required information. One way to do this is to pass all information requests through the functional coordinator who manages each supplier, but information requests from the accounting staff will not be of sufficient importance to justify taking the time of the coordinator on an ongoing basis. Instead, the coordinator should only be used up front to set up links between the supplier and company accounting staffs—after that, the functional coordinator does not have to be involved. Also, one person on the accounting staff should become the primary contact with each supplier. This person should travel to his or her designated supplier and get to know the personnel in that company's accounting department. This personal relationship is good for getting a more rapid response from the supplier if there are problems with the accounting information being sent to the company. Sometimes these personal relations between accounting staffs do not work out, and the company's accounting employees must appeal to the functional coordinator in order to have something done, but this is the exception rather than the rule. Thus, establishing close relations with the supplier's accounting staff is the first step in achieving quality data collection from a supplier.

The next step in achieving good data collection is to review the format of information received. This may be a sample billing, or the accounting staff may wait for the supplier to send its first billing before taking action. This billing should be reviewed to see if it has a sufficient level of detail for the control purposes of the accounting department. For example, a payroll supplier should break down its billing to show the amount charged per person for paycheck printing, so that the accounting staff can compare this per-person rate to the contractual rate. Similarly, a production supplier's billing should reveal the number of units produced as well as the per-unit charge—once again, so that the accounting staff can compare the per-unit costs to the contract. An engineering supplier must split its billings into pieces for each contract that it is working on, as well as show the number of hours worked by each position and the billing rate for each position. If this level of detail is not available, the accounting staff should work with its counterparts at the supplier to ensure that changes are made that give the accounting staff the information it needs. It may also be possible to list a sample of the desired reporting format in an appendix to the contract with each supplier, so that the supplier is legally required to make the necessary changes. Altering the supplier's billing format is usually necessary so that the accounting staff can compare various elements of the billing to the supplier's contract.

Suppliers may have billing periods that do not match the company's financial reporting period. This is a problem if a billing arrives that covers only a few weeks of activity within a reporting period, requiring the accounting staff to guess and make an accrual for the remaining period of the month that was not billed. Alternatively, the supplier may send out billings less frequently than every reporting period, so that the company's financial statements will oscillate between having no expenses for each supplier and having expenses for multiple periods. The best way to avoid this problem is to have the accounting person assigned to each supplier be responsible for getting a billing from his or her assigned supplier that covers the company's reporting period. This involves tracking the receipt of billings and the time period covered by each one, and continually getting back to the supplier to improve the billings if the billings are for partial or multiple periods. If this approach does not work, the next approach is to make the person responsible for each supplier keep track of the average expenses being billed by his or her assigned supplier, and create an accrual for any missing time periods that is based on this average expense. Alternatively, the controller or an assistant may be in charge of this accrual tracking activity. Yet another approach is to list the billing period in the contract, so that the company has a legal reason for forcing a supplier to comply with its wishes in this matter. A company has several methods available to ensure that supplier billings match its financial reporting period.

There are several methods of data collection available to a company that uses outsourcing. These begin at the most primitive level—that of sending information by mail—and extend through several forms of electronic transmission. Most suppliers start by mailing billings and any other information to the accounting staff. This approach is slow and information may be lost if the postal carrier loses the document, or (even more likely) if the document is misrouted within the company after it has been received through the mail. If company management chooses to speed up the transfer of information, a faster approach is to fax this written documentation to the company. Faxing is not a perfect approach, for the fax may be lost or the transmission interrupted, and the recipient will never know that the fax was sent. If this approach is not sufficient, another rapid approach is to send an electronic transaction. This can be either a free-form electronic mail message or an electronic data interchange (EDI) message that uses a strict reporting format. In either case, the information can be retrieved by the recipient whenever he or she logs into the electronic mail system (which may be more or less frequent than the transfer of information when using a fax). This electronic transfer can be greatly enhanced by including automated interfaces at both ends of the transmission, so that information is automatically sent to the recipient by the computer of the originating company and received and routed by the receiving computer. This approach has the benefit of avoiding any risk of data-entry errors, since there is no data-entry staff involved.

The final variation on data collection is to not have the supplier send any information at all, but instead install a terminal at the company that gives it direct access to the supplier's computer system, so that the company's accounting department can go into the supplier database and find the information it needs. This approach is not frequently used when there are many suppliers, since the accounting department would require a large number of dedicated phone lines and terminals to access all of the supplier databases.

A company usually chooses a mix of these methods based on the urgency or importance of the information it is trying to collect. For example, the monthly billing from a maintenance supplier is not critical information, so it can be sent by mail.

However, the mail from a foreign supplier may not arrive in time, so that supplier sends information by fax. Alternatively, a company needs up-to-date information from its manufacturing supplier, such as quantities shipped every hour, so an automated EDI data exchange is used. If the information must be transferred soon but does not warrant the cost of programming an EDI interface, then a data-entry clerk can be inserted between the computer and the communications line. An example of the variety of possible data-collection methods is shown in Figure 3.1. In short, there are many data-collection methods, ranging from slow and unreliable to fast and automated. Different collection methods are used based on the company's need for up-to-date information.

This section covered the need for close contacts between the accounting staffs of the supplier and company, since they will be working together for several years. Also, the format as well as the timing of the billing statements sent to the company from its suppliers must be sufficient for use in verifying unit costs as well as volumes, and must be sufficient to ensure that all of the expenses incurred during a financial reporting period have been billed. Finally, this information can be sent by a variety of methods, depending on the company's need for fast and reliable information.

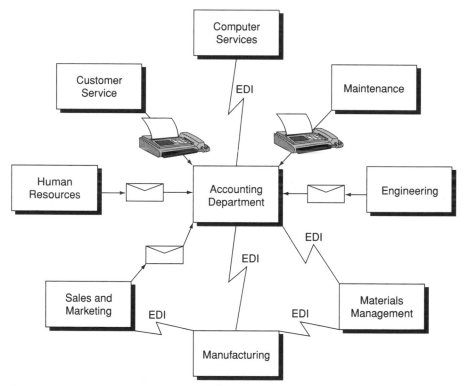

Figure 3.1   Various Forms of Data Collection

3.2 IMPACT ON FINANCIAL REPORTING

The internal and external financial reporting that the accounting department is responsible for producing is impacted in several ways by the use of suppliers for outsourcing. This section discusses those changes.

The chart of accounts of a typical corporation is fairly lengthy, since it must include all necessary expense categories that can be used by each in-house functional area. These expenses typically include, at a minimum, separate line items for payroll, payroll taxes, benefits, travel, entertainment, phones, utilities, office supplies, office equipment, depreciation, autos, corporate allocations, and miscellaneous expenses. Some companies use far more accounts to ensure that they can track every conceivable expense that may occur. When a company switches to outsourcing, however, the chart of accounts no longer needs to be so detailed, since most of the expenses are now being absorbed by the suppliers, who summarize their costs and send it all to the company in just one billing—and that can be recorded in one line item. This allows the chart of accounts to be dramatically reduced to one line item for each functional area, plus a few line items to cover the payroll and travel costs of the functional coordinators and their staffs. Other expenses are so small that they can be easily rolled into a miscellaneous expense account. Asset charges are usually dispensed with, since most of the assets were transferred to suppliers. Since the in-house functions are now so small, there is no need for a corporate allocation account—it is not worth the time to calculate the allocation. A sample of expense account line items is shown in Figure 3.2, showing how few line items are needed once outsourcing is used.

These changes to the chart of accounts should be thoroughly documented, showing which line items have now been merged. This documentation is necessary for the external auditors, who frequently run comparisons of the larger expense accounts

Figure 3.2 Chart of Accounts When Outsourcing Is Used

Line Item Description	Without Outsourcing	With Outsourcing
Payroll	✔	✔
Payroll taxes	✔	✔
Benefits	✔	
Travel	✔	✔
Entertainment	✔	✔
Automobiles	✔	
Telephones	✔	
Office supplies	✔	
Office equipment	✔	
Depreciation	✔	
Miscellaneous expenses	✔	✔
Asset charge	✔	
Corporate allocation	✔	
Outsourcing charges		✔

from year to year to see if there are unexpectedly large changes in the accounts that could indicate improper accounting methods. These changes would make it difficult for the auditors to do this comparison in the year when the chart of accounts is converted to the new layout. However, the external auditors are primarily concerned with changes in the accounts that roll up into the balance sheet, and that document will remain largely untouched by any changes caused by outsourcing. If the accounting staff does need to change an asset or liability account, it must be aware that such a change will not make the financial statements comparable to the statements of previous years, so the external auditors will have to charge extra to restate the format of previous years' financial statements to match the new reporting format (since the current financial statements are usually shown alongside the results from one or more previous years).

The notes to the financial statements must also be modified when outsourcing is used. This is not required by law, which is more concerned with the concentration of a company's sales with a small number of customers than with the concentration of its operations among a small number of suppliers. Nonetheless, it is very useful for the management team to have a handy reference that lists the start and termination dates of all outsourcing contracts, baseline pricing, volume changes that impact pricing, and maximum payment amounts. These notes are not intended to be an extensive reiteration of each contract, just a brief summary of the relevant facts that management can easily reference.

The previous section, covering data collection, noted that there may be problems with having to accrue supplier billings as well as getting them to bill for the same time period used by the company as its financial reporting period. These problems can impact the accuracy of the financial reports, since costs may not be reported in the correct amounts, if at all. As previously noted, these problems can be mitigated by using an accrual procedure that spots all missing expenses, and solved by working with each supplier's accounting staff to have them send billings that match the company's reporting periods. If the supplier simply cannot alter its billing period (as may be the case if the supplier bills on a monthly schedule but the company uses a 13-period year), it may still be possible to have the supplier indicate on its billing the weeks in which expenses were incurred, so that the accounting staff can split the billing into the appropriate reporting periods.

Internal management reports are also a major reporting task for the accounting department. When functions are outsourced, the measurements that the accounting staff previously recorded in the management report for those functions are usually eliminated, since there is no need to track the performance of the supplier in any areas besides the cost of their services. There are a number of new performance measures that can be added to the management report for suppliers; these measurements are covered in a later section of the chapter entitled "Impact on Performance Measurement." Some replacement of measurements on internal management reports occurs when outsourcing is used.

In short, the chart of accounts may be altered as a result of using outsourcing, which may have an impact on the year-to-year reporting of the income statement.

This should have no impact on the balance sheet. The accounting staff must be sure to account for the timing of all expenses billed by suppliers to ensure that they fall into the correct reporting period. Finally, internal reports must be modified to exclude measurements that have been outsourced, while including new ones to track supplier costs. Outsourcing has a moderate impact on a company's external reporting, and a major one on its internal reporting.

3.3   IMPACT ON CONTROLS

A company controller has full control over the financial control systems of a company. However, many of these controls go away when functional areas are given to suppliers. What should the controller do?

The key to keeping control over the financial systems of a company that has been largely outsourced is to work with the billing statements and contracts of the suppliers. Other tasks, such as auditing, can augment and support the information shown on the billing statements and contracts, but these documents are the keys to control. The following examples show how the supplier billing statement and contract can be used to provide adequate financial control over the functional areas being run by suppliers:

- *Computer systems.* Computer systems suppliers issue billings based on a mix of fixed (or minimum) fees and volume-based fees. The fixed fees can be compared to the supplier contract to determine their accuracy, while the volume-based fees are somewhat more difficult to verify. One of the more common variable fees is the amount of computer-processing time taken up by the company. To verify this, the company must send an audit team to the supplier to verify from computer records that the amount billed was the amount of time actually incurred.

- *Customer service.* Customer service providers usually bill based on the number of calls taken, with rate changes based on the total number of calls. The rate per call can be compared to the contract, while an audit team is needed to examine supplier records to verify that the number of calls received equals the number billed.

- *Engineering.* Engineering billings are either on a time-and-materials basis or fixed fee. In either case, the accounting staff can compare the billed rates to the contract, either to ensure that the hourly rates billed are the same ones noted in the contract or to verify that the cumulative amount billed is equal to or less than the maximum amount authorized in the contract. An audit is useful in a time-and-materials situation for verifying that the time as shown on engineer time cards is equal to the time charged to the company.

- *Human resources.* To verify that the medical insurance billing forwarded by the human resources provider is accurate, the accounting staff should compare the list of employee names on the billing statement to its list of employees who should be receiving insurance, and also compare the billed per-person rate to the rate listed in the contract with the supplier.

- *Maintenance.* Maintenance fees are based on the number of rooms or square feet cleaned, or are on a time-and-materials basis for equipment repairs. The janitorial fees can be compared to the square footage of the area cleaned and the rate per square foot, as shown in the contract. The time-and-materials billings can be compared to the contract to verify the hourly rate, while the number of hours charged can be audited by reviewing supplier time cards.

- *Manufacturing.* Billings are usually based on the number of products shipped to the company or its customers. The rate per unit can be verified by checking the contract, while the number of units shipped to the company can be verified by checking the company's receiving log. The number of units shipped to customers can be directly checked by auditing the supplier's shipping log, and indirectly checked by seeing how many customers refuse to pay for products supposedly shipped to them, claiming that they were not shipped. The accounting staff can also track changes in the volume of products shipped, which may change the price paid (usually a lower per-unit cost for high-volume situations).

- *Materials Management.* Trucking billings are based on a variety of factors, but can most easily be audited by an outside freight auditing company that is knowledgeable in the area of freight rates. Trailer loading and unloading fees can be compared to the contract with the freight hauler. Warehousing fees are based on square footage of storage space, which can be checked against the contract with the warehouse supplier.

- *Payroll.* Payroll billings are a mix of fixed fees and (mostly) per-person fees based on the number of paychecks issued. It is an easy matter for the accounting staff to compare the fixed fees to the contract with the supplier, and to compare the number of paychecks cut to the number of employees in the company.

- *Sales and marketing.* Marketing fees can be either fixed fee or on a time-and-materials basis, or a percentage of the advertising fees incurred. In all cases, the rates charged can be verified against the contract, while hourly charges can be audited by reviewing the time cards of the marketing supplier's employees. Sales broker fees are a percentage of the sale price of the products sold; this percentage is easily checked against the contract with the sales broker.

The above list of controls over all outsourced functions is monotonous—compare the billing to the contract, look for maximum payment limits and audit supplier time cards. It is apparent that these controls can be consistently applied to all functional areas. The reason why the billing statement and contract are such key control factors is that they are frequently the only documents the accounting department has to work with on a regular basis. The accounting staff cannot go to supplier locations to root through supporting documents, for this is too expensive and time consuming, and also gets in the way of the supplier's activities. Thus, the billing statement and contract form the core of any control system over suppliers.

The most significant other control is requiring approvals by functional coordinators for all billings received from suppliers. This is because the functional coordinators are the in-house managers who are directly responsible for the activities of each supplier, and they are therefore the only employees who will know if the billings submitted by suppliers are reasonable. Of course, the coordinator should be made aware of any pricing problems already noted by the accounting staff when they compared billed prices to contract prices, but the coordinators must still sign off on the supplier invoices.

Though it is not a direct control point, the accounting staff can also prepare a simple report for each functional area that details the amounts invoiced in the past month, the total amount invoiced for the contract to date, the maximum amount that the supplier is allowed to bill the company, and any variances noted by the accounting staff from the contractual rates. This information is needed by the functional coordinators during their meetings with their counterparts at the supplier companies, when they will discuss performance against the contract, contract renewals, and any variances from the contractual rates. An example of such a report is shown in Figure 3.3.

An item that was constantly referred to earlier was the need to conduct regular audits of the supporting documentation of suppliers. However, this control point is not always under the control of the accounting department. Instead, it is most commonly under a review group that reports directly to the board of directors or the chief executive officer. Since it reports elsewhere, the controller is put in the position of only persuading the audit staff to review the activities of suppliers (which they will readily do, if they see a control risk in this area). Some of the audit program topics

Figure 3.3   Supplier Invoicing versus Contract Report

Month	Monthly Billing ($)	Cumulative Billing ($)	Contractual Maximum ($)	Variance Comments
January	85,000	85,000	1,750,000	All time cards missing
February	175,000	260,000	1,750,000	Partner rate too high ($285)
March	225,000	485,000	1,750,000	Drafter rate too low ($85)
April	210,000	695,000	1,750,000	Passed through overtime
May	180,000	875,000	1,750,000	Extra charge for travel
June	125,000	1,000,000	1,750,000	No comments
July	175,000	1,175,000	1,750,000	No comments
August	210,000	1,385,000	1,750,000	No comments
September	125,000	1,510,000	1,750,000	Retroactive designer increase
October	80,000	1,590,000	1,750,000	P. Smith time card missing
November	75,000	1,665,000	1,750,000	No comments
December	85,000	1,750,000	1,750,000	Passed through vacation charge

that the controller should suggest to the internal audit group as being worthy of review are as follows:

- *Time cards.* Compare hours noted on supplier time cards to the hours billed to the company. The objective is to ensure that the supplier is correctly tracking time charged to work for the company, and that these hours are correctly transferred to the company billing.

- *Hourly rates.* Compare the hourly rates charged on the company billing to the rates agreed upon in the contract for each position working on behalf of the company. The objective is to ensure that the supplier is charging hourly rates that match the amounts noted in the contract. This audit must also account for the timing of billings when supplier employees are promoted. For example, if a person is promoted at mid-month to a position that is charged to the company at a higher rate, then there should be two line items in the monthly billing for that employee, one at the older, lower rate and one at the higher, newer rate.

- *Units billed.* Compare the production units produced or shipped to the number of units listed on the company billing by comparing the quantity on the billing to the quantity shown in the supplier's production or shipping records. The objective is to ensure that the company is only billed for those units actually produced or shipped.

- *Unit costs.* Compare the price of units produced to their contractual rates to see if the billed per-unit costs are incorrect. The objective is to ensure that the company is not overbilled for units produced.

- *Incidental costs.* Compare the incidental costs billed to the company to the actual costs incurred by the supplier by comparing the billed amounts to detailed expense reports. The object is to ensure that the supplier has backup for all expenses billed, and that the supplier does not add a markup to the expenses passed through to the company.

The above audit objectives are among the most important that audit teams should review when investigating controls over suppliers.

The cost of goods sold becomes very predictable when manufacturing is outsourced, for there are no labor or material variances—there is just a single unit cost for each product manufactured by the supplier, as noted in the original contract, which may be subject to escalation clauses or extra fees for variations to the products. This means that there should be a mandatory review of the cost of goods sold and sales accounts if the gross margin percentage is off by even a fraction of a percentage, since it indicates that the number of items billed to customers does not match the number of items that the company purchased from the supplier. If the company is purchasing products and placing them in stock, then the number of units billed will not always match the number of units purchased from the supplier, but this can still be cross-checked against inventory levels to find errors. In short, the fixed per-unit cost of goods sold makes it easy to verify the accuracy of the gross margin percentage as reported on the financial statements.

This section covered the major accounting controls over suppliers, which are based on a careful and continuing comparison of billed costs to contract costs. This comparison should be accompanied by a periodic audit of the detailed records used by suppliers to create their billings. The accounting staff should also issue periodic reports to the functional coordinators, showing them the ongoing billings of the suppliers for which they are responsible, as well as how these costs compare to contractual rates, and accompanied by any notes on variances that the accounting staff has discovered. This system allows a company to have adequate financial control over its suppliers.

3.4   IMPACT ON PERFORMANCE MEASUREMENT

Many of the measurements used by a company that keeps all of its functions in-house are no longer needed by a company that outsources all of its functions, while there are very few new measurements needed. Also, there will certainly be a change in the results of measurements that are tracked before and after outsourcing is implemented, and there should be a change in the emphasis on certain measurements. All of these issues are discussed in this section.

When a company outsources its functions, many of the measurements that were used to monitor the performance of those functions can go away along with the functions. These measurements are as follows:

- *Asset tracking.* Most assets are shifted to suppliers, so there is no great need to track the company's investment in assets in a particular area. The bulk of the assets for most companies are in the manufacturing area, and once that function goes to a supplier, there will not be very many assets left to track. Similarly, the accounting department is commonly put in charge of physically tracking the locations of all fixed assets in the company. Once outsourcing has been completed, there may be so few assets left that the accounting staff can eliminate this task, or only perform it infrequently for the most expensive remaining assets.

- *Square footage.* Many companies track the square footage used by each functional area, partially to see if the functions are taking more space than benchmark figures indicate, and partially so that the accounting staff can allocate some overhead costs to those functions based on square footage (utility costs being the most commonly allocated by this means). When functions shift to suppliers, there is so little space left that there is no substantial reason to track who is using how much of it. Allocations based on square footage may also not make much sense when the only offices remaining are those of functional coordinators and their staffs, who are monitoring the activities of suppliers.

- *Head count.* Accounting staffs are frequently called upon to track the head count by functional area, and to track sales by head count. This measure becomes irrelevant when the bulk of the head count has been moved to suppliers, leaving only a few company employees in each functional area. Sales and profit per person are also not worth tracking, since all of the people have been moved to suppliers.

- *Inventory accuracy.* If the manufacturing supplier owns all of the inventory and only sells it to the company when completed products have been shipped to customers, there is no inventory. This means that the accuracy of the inventory is the supplier's problem, and is not an issue for the accounting staff to monitor. However, if the company maintains finished-goods inventories in supplier warehouse locations, inventory accuracy is still an issue.

- *Labor-routing accuracy.* In a traditional manufacturing environment, the accounting staff is very concerned about the accuracy of labor routings, for they are used to derive work-in-process costs. However, when a supplier has taken over the manufacturing function, the accounting staff is only concerned that the price per unit billed matches the contract price—the labor routing accuracy has become irrelevant.

- *Production scrap.* When manufacturing is moved to a supplier, the amount of scrap becomes the supplier's problem. The company will pay the same per-unit fee for each unit the supplier manufactures, irrespective of the amount of scrap, so there is no need for this measurement. If the company is sending engineers into the supplier's facility to help it cut costs, this may be a different matter, but the company's accounting staff is in no position to collect scrap information even in that situation.

- *Labor efficiency.* A company pays its manufacturing supplier the same amount per unit produced, no matter how efficient the supplier's labor force may be, so there is no need to track labor efficiency. Even if the company is assisting with cost reductions at the supplier location, there is still no way for the accounting staff to collect labor efficiency information from the supplier.

Different measurement results can be expected in many measurement areas. The previously noted measurements would experience radical changes (such as sales per person, which would increase logarithmically), but, since it was already recommended that they be eliminated, they will not be included in this discussion. A number of accounting measurements are noted here that should still be measured, but these will change as a result of the outsourcing. The likely direction of each change is also noted. The measurements are as follows:

- *Break-even.* One of the primary reasons for moving a function to a supplier is to get rid of its fixed costs. When this happens, the company break-even points shift downward. The only case in which this would not happen is when a company outsources a function but retains many of the fixed costs. It is an unlikely circumstance, but can happen if a company is left with a large facility that it cannot dispose of, but must continue to expend funds on to maintain.

- *Leverage.* Another of the primary reasons for switching to outsourcing is to have the new supplier pay the company for assets or facilities transferred to the supplier. These funds can then be used to pay down debt, which reduces the amount of leverage. However, this is a one-time benefit, so the leverage ratio may increase after the initial reduction.

- *Working capital.* The impact on a company's working capital is similar to the impact on leverage—if assets are sold to a supplier, this gives the company a cash infusion, which increases the amount of working capital available. Cash can also come in when production is moved to a supplier and the supplier takes over the company's raw materials and work-in-process inventory. However, if the company chooses to use the extra cash for non-working capital purposes, such as buying back stock, then the amount of working capital will return to its pre-outsourcing level.

- *Inventory turnover.* When the manufacturing function is outsourced, the company may continue to own the raw materials and work-in-process inventory, in which case the inventory turnover measurement will not change. However, the supplier may purchase this inventory, which reduces the amount of inventory to just finished-goods stocks. Since sales should stay the same, this reduction in inventory should result in an improvement in the inventory turnover ratio. If a company has no finished-goods stocks (i.e., if it ships straight to customers without any storage), there will be no inventory at all, and it will not be possible to calculate the inventory turnover ratio, since there will be a zero denominator in the turnover calculation.

- *Accounts receivable turnover.* Using a collections agency should bring about a moderate reduction in the amount of accounts receivable outstanding, but only if the collection agency is noticeably more effective than the in-house collection staff.

- *Salaries and wages to net sales.* Many industry trade groups track the proportion of salaries and wages to net sales; this measurement is intended to tell member companies if they have too much staff compared to the industry average. When a company outsources its higher head count areas, such as production, the salaries and wages figure will plummet while sales will stay the same, which will make the company look great compared to the industry average.

- *Average annual salary.* Many companies calculate their average annual salary, sometimes by department, and compare this information to an industry average. However, when outsourcing occurs, only the most experienced personnel are retained, along with a functional coordinator who tends to be at the top of the pay scale. Consequently, the average annual salary will jump to a level well above the industry average.

- *Purchase discounts to purchases.* When the manufacturing function is out-sourced, the company is no longer making bulk purchases of materials for cost-of-goods-sold items. This is the primary source of purchase discounts, and where the purchasing staff concentrates its efforts on negotiating better discounts. When the function is gone, the purchasing staff may disappear with it, which cuts into the company's ability to obtain discounts in other areas. Also, the company's purchasing volume will drop with most suppliers, so that it will not be eligible for discounts. However, discounts related to early pay-ment are available through many suppliers, so these discounts can still be taken. In general, due to the loss of materials-purchase discounts, the propor-tion of purchase discounts is likely to drop when outsourcing is used.

A number of the measurements tracked by the accounting department will not change as a result of using outsourcing. These are measurements that have nothing to do with head count, square footage, assets, or manufacturing. These tend to be the "pure" financial measurements. For example, revenues are not likely to change, espe-cially if a company is in a mature market where its market share is relatively unchang-ing. Another measurement is gross profit; this percentage may change over time as a company works with its suppliers to reduce their costs, but this change may occur only over a long time interval. Another area is profitability, where cost reductions from sup-pliers are not assured; many companies can perform their functions more cheaply in-house, since suppliers have other costs, such as profits and sales and marketing costs, that they must charge through to companies, and that those companies would not have to incur if they kept all functions in-house. One other measurement that will not change, but which must be kept in-house, is the accuracy of bills of material. This mea-surement is not normally tracked by the accounting staff, but it is mentioned here be-cause it is so important. The bill of materials for every product must be kept accurate so that products will be produced correctly by the manufacturing supplier; if it is inac-curate, products will have poor quality, not work at all, or be produced well behind schedule. Thus, the revenue, margin, and profitability measurements, as well as the bill of material accuracy, are not likely to change as a result of outsourcing.

Two new measurements will be necessary as a result of using outsourcing. One is only needed in the short term, while the other will be required on an ongoing basis. The measurements are as follows:

- *Gain or loss on sale of assets.* One measurement that will go away shortly after outsourcing is completed is the gain or loss on sale of assets no longer needed as a result of the outsourcing. A company may have many facilities and a large amount of equipment, perhaps in the manufacturing, computer services, or maintenance areas, that its suppliers did not want to purchase at the time of outsourcing and which it no longer needs. If the cost of these items constitutes a large part of a company's assets, selling them at a substantial gain or loss could have a very large impact on the company's reported profits, perhaps ex-ceeding or eliminating its regular amount of profits. Since it may have a significant impact on short-term profits, this gain or loss must be carefully tracked during the period when the assets are being disposed of.

- *Transaction volumes.* It is extremely important that the accounting staff tracks the number of transactions processed by each supplier. This is because supplier billings in most functional areas are largely based on the transaction volume. If the supplier uses an incorrect transaction figure, it will bill the company for an incorrect amount. Examples of these transaction volumes are the number of units produced by the production supplier, the number of employees who are provided medical insurance by the human resources supplier, the number of trucks maintained by the maintenance supplier, the number of invoices issued by the accounting supplier, and the number of rooms cleaned by the janitorial supplier. Very few companies track these transactions volumes if they keep all of their functions in-house, so new measurement systems are required for most companies to track this information.

Many of the measurements that an accounting department derives for perusal by management are listed alongside industry averages. These averages are collected by trade associations from member companies, summarized, and sent back to the members once a year. Many of the previously noted measurements are among the ones tracked by these trade groups. An interesting problem that will arise as more companies use outsourcing is that, once enough of them are using it, they will skew many of the measurements so dramatically that the average measurements will be far away from the measurements submitted by those companies who have not considered outsourcing. If they notice how far their measurements are from the industry averages, they may investigate, resulting in even more companies converting to outsourcing. Thus, once the number of companies using outsourcing reaches critical mass, more companies will be attracted to the concept, accelerating the trend.

This section covered how outsourcing impacts the performance measurements tracked by the accounting department. A number of measurements—primarily in the areas of head count, assets, and square footage—are no longer necessary, while others—mostly in the areas of revenues, costs, and profits—will probably not change at all. Other measurements, such as the gain or loss on sale of assets, as well as transaction volumes, are new measurements for the accounting staff to track. Other existing measurements, such as break-even, leverage, and inventory turnover, should still be tracked, but are likely to yield different results when outsourcing is used. In short, outsourcing has a profound impact on the measurements tracked by the accounting department.

3.5   IMPACT ON TRANSACTIONS

Using suppliers to take over a company's functional areas has a major impact on the transactions that reach the accounting department. This section details those changes, which range from a reduction in transaction volume to off-site customer billings and smaller computer systems.

There are only a few sources from which a company receives cash in payment for accounts receivable. One is directly from customers for on-the-spot payments, such as in a retailing environment; another is from a bank in exchange for a credit card authorization from a customer; and another is a mailed-in payment from a customer, which can come straight to the company or through a lockbox. When collections are outsourced, this creates another source of cash payment. Under this scenario, a collection agency will have customers send delinquent payments to them instead of the company. The collection agency will then take a percentage of the payment as compensation for its services and send the remainder of the payment on to the company. The problem for the company is that it takes more time to log this kind of payment into the computer system. This is because the accounts receivable clerk must enter the cash receipt against the delinquent accounts receivable and then issue a credit for the portion that the collection agency took from the payment. This more complex transaction is frequently routed to a more experienced clerk to ensure that it is performed correctly. Cash receipts from collection agencies represent a new and more complicated cash receipt transaction.

The volume of accounts payable transactions is reduced when a manufacturing supplier is used, for a very large proportion of a company's billings from suppliers are caused by the cost of goods sold. All of the billings that were sent to the company for raw materials, components, sub-assemblies, shop supplies, and maintenance will now go to the manufacturing supplier. A good way to get a grasp of the number of these supplier invoices is to go to the accounts payable register and note the proportion of line items that are charged to the cost-of-goods-sold, maintenance, and shop supplies accounts. As a result of this dramatic drop in transaction volume, the company may be able to eliminate several clerical positions—not only the accounts payable data-entry function, but also the functions for filing supplier invoices and matching these invoices to purchase orders and receiving documentation. Switching manufacturing to a supplier has a major impact on the number of people needed in the accounts payable department.

Other kinds of accounts payable transactions besides those related to the cost of goods sold will also drop. This is because outsourcing other functions than manufacturing will bring about a drop in head count, and the fewer employees, the fewer purchases the company will make. For example, there are purchase transactions for the office supplies, computer equipment, furniture, business cards, and telephones for every person hired into a company. If many of these people go to work for a supplier, these transactions will go away with them. In fact, there will be a long and deep dip in transaction volume after an outsourcing contract is completed, for the employees who are transferred to the supplier will leave behind a large amount of equipment and materials that will be spread among the remaining employees, and who will therefore not need to purchase anything until the surplus is used up. This dip in accounts payable transaction volumes may lead to a further reduction in the accounting staff used to process these transactions.

A company can use electronic data interchange (EDI) to automate some portions of its accounts payable and receivable transactions. The EDI system is usually only used by those companies that have longstanding business relationships with large transaction volumes, which fits perfectly into a long-term outsourcing arrangement. The reason for this limited use is that EDI takes a fairly large investment in time and money to install, so companies with infrequent business contacts prefer not to use it. The simplest EDI arrangement is for a company to enter a transaction into a computer at its location, using a standard EDI transaction format. The company then transmits this transaction to a value-added network, which is run by a third-party provider who maintains a mainframe computer that acts as a large electronic mailbox. The corresponding company then accesses its electronic mailbox from time to time, collects the electronic transactions, and translates them into a format that is readable by its own computer system. This process is shown in Figure 3.4. The system is difficult to install because it requires programming to create interfaces between the computer

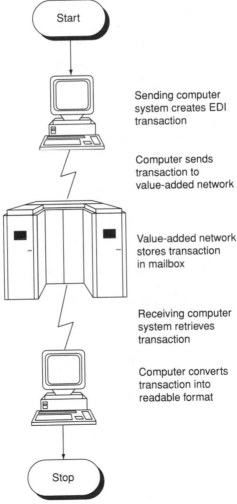

Start

Sending computer system creates EDI transaction

Computer sends transaction to value-added network

Value-added network stores transaction in mailbox

Receiving computer system retrieves transaction

Computer converts transaction into readable format

Stop

Figure 3.4   Electronic Data Interchange Transaction

system of the supplier and company, so that transactions are automatically exchanged without the need for any manual data-entry work. However, if there are many transactions or they are time sensitive or subject to data-entry error, this is a rewarding project, for it allows an accounting department to bypass all data-entry labor when dealing with EDI-equipped suppliers. In short, using EDI with its suppliers gives a company the ability to automatically process selected transactions through its accounting and manufacturing computer system.

Though it is not an accounting function, it is important to note that manufacturing outsourcing will also have a major impact on the purchasing department. This area is primarily concerned with the purchase of materials for manufacturing, so if that function goes to a supplier, it is likely that the purchasing area will be stripped to a skeleton crew to handle all remaining purchasing tasks.

The transaction volume for payroll will experience a sharp decline if the manufacturing function is outsourced, and a lesser decline if other functions are outsourced. The manufacturing function contains the majority of all direct labor personnel in most companies. These employees use time cards, and the information on these cards must be input into the payroll system. This labor is the largest amount of transaction work in the payroll area, for there is no payroll work to be done for salaried personnel—the payroll system just creates a new paycheck for a salaried person without any prompting from the payroll staff. Thus, there is a major drop in transaction volume if the manufacturing function is outsourced, but a minimal one if other areas, where more salaried personnel reside, are outsourced.

It is also possible to have a manufacturing or materials-management supplier create invoices for a company's customers, which it can send to them along with their product deliveries. This is a very useful item, for the company can get invoices to customers more quickly, which speeds up its cash flow. There are several ways to accomplish this. One is to have the supplier create invoices through its own computer system and then send this information to the company, which re-enters it into its own computer system for collection purposes. Another approach is for the company to set up a terminal and printer in the supplier's location that is linked to the company's computer system; when invoices are printed off this terminal, the information automatically updates the company's database. The problem with this approach is that the company must maintain a leased phone line for continual access, or it must poll it under a client–server arrangement, which may require special programming. Some companies want control over the invoicing process, and prefer to do this work themselves. In these cases, the supplier must send shipment information to the company as frequently as possible, so that invoices can be created and mailed by the company in as timely a manner as possible. Under this approach, the controller must verify that the information sent by the supplier is sufficient for use in completing a customer invoice. From the perspective of the accounting department, the transaction information will arrive in the same old format—it will just be coming from the supplier instead of the company's shipping department. Thus, there are several alternatives available for handling customer billing transactions, ranging from having the supplier do it to having the company do it.

When the number of transactions drops, it is possible that a company may be able to reduce its accounting software requirements in several ways. For example, a reduction in the number of payroll, accounts payable, and accounts receivable transactions will require fewer people to input transactions into the computer, so the company may be able to revert back to a smaller number of user licenses for the computer software, which can be much less expensive. Another possibility is no longer paying update fees (which are frequently 15% of the purchase price) for software modules that are no longer needed. For example, outsourcing manufacturing may allow a company to eliminate its manufacturing resource planning software, while outsourcing engineering may allow it to get rid of its bill of materials software. Also, if the number of users shrinks enough, the company may even be able to shrink its computing platform down to a smaller and cheaper computer, with fewer (and cheaper) storage and maintenance requirements. Finally, the company may no longer need such complex accounting software at all, and can downgrade to a smaller and cheaper software package that does not have the in-depth level of functionality that was necessary when the company kept all of its functional areas in-house. If the company has a customized software package, then it can reduce the maintenance budget on that software by stopping or reducing the number of programming changes—these changes are usually to improve the functionality of the software, which is no longer necessary. Thus, using outsourcing can lead to a smaller number of software user licenses, fewer software modules, a smaller central computer, and perhaps even a smaller software package.

Finally, there is some new error checking to use when the above transaction changes are implemented. These error checks are intended to reduce the risk of incurring extra expenses or of operating on incorrect information. The error-checking procedures are as follows:

- *Use a checklist.* There will frequently be a single large invoice coming from each supplier each month, so there should be a checklist for each supplier that the controller uses to ensure that an invoice was received each month from each one—otherwise, the financial statements will be missing key costs. The checklist should also include an average invoice amount, so that the controller can compare the list to actual invoice amounts and call suppliers about any invoices that appear to vary significantly from the norm. This added error check prevents last-minute scrambling to fix problems when the financial statements are released with unusual cost variances.

- *Review medical insurance bill.* In the human resources area, the largest cost is for medical insurance for each employee. To ensure that there are no errors in this cost, someone should compare the insurance supplier's list of covered employees to the company's payroll listing every month to ensure that all employees are covered, and that employees who have left the company are no longer covered.

- *Use confirming EDI messages.* When EDI is used, the system must include the transmission back to the sending party by the receiving party of a confirmation message, letting it know that the original transaction was correctly received. If this confirming transaction is not received within a reasonable time period, the originating company must send its original transaction again. This process ensures that electronic messages are not lost in transit.

- *Review shipping log.* The largest supplier invoice each month will be the one from the manufacturing supplier. If this invoice is incorrect, the company may incur a very large extra charge that it does not deserve to incur. The best way to ensure that this invoice is correct is to have an audit team compare the number of production units billed to the number of units shipped, as listed on the supplier's shipping log. The audit team can go to the supplier location to do this, or the supplier can send a copy of the log to the company at the end of each month. Another possibility, if the supplier sends all of its production straight to the company for final distribution, is to compare the billing to the company's receiving log. This is a more reliable approach than reviewing the supplier's shipping log, since a dishonest supplier could modify its shipping log.

This section covered any changes to accounting transactions that occur when outsourcing is implemented. Those changes include a new source of incoming cash payments, reduced accounts payable transaction volume related to cost of goods sold and overhead purchases, minimal manual data entry, greatly reduced payroll transactions if manufacturing is outsourced, customer billings by suppliers, and reduced software needs. All of these changes point in one direction: reduced transaction volume for the accounting department.

3.6   SUMMARY

This chapter covered several topics that are of importance to an accounting department that must interact with suppliers who have taken over outsourced functions. The topics include data collection from the suppliers, the impact of outsourcing on the format of the company's financial statements, and the need for changes to existing financial controls. Also, outsourcing will change the results of some financial measurements, while reducing the need for some measurements and requiring the addition of others. Finally, transaction volumes are heavily impacted by outsourcing, especially when the manufacturing function is handed to a supplier. An accounting staff must be knowledgeable regarding these issues if it is to operate efficiently and effectively in an outsourcing environment.

The accounting staff must manage the transfer of accounting information to it from each outsourcing supplier. This calls for the creation of personal contacts between the accounting staffs of both organizations, as well as an agreement that the supplier will issue billings in a format having sufficient detail for the company's accounting staff to review it for accuracy. The billing period must also correspond to the company's financial reporting period, so that no accrual estimates are necessary.

Finally, there are several ways to transmit key information to the company—the correct method must be picked based on how critical the information may be.

The accounting staff must modify the income statement to accommodate an altered chart of accounts, which is reduced in size when outsourcing is implemented. Internal management reports should be much more drastically altered to exclude measurements for functions that have been moved to suppliers, while adding new measurements to monitor supplier pricing against contract rates. Notes should also be added to the financial reports that give the most important details of each outsourcing deal. The financial reports, both internally and externally, will change as a result of using outsourcing.

New controls are needed to ensure that the accounting staff has adequate financial control over the suppliers who are handling the company's outsourced services. The best way to do this is by regularly comparing the information on each supplier's monthly billing to the related contractual agreement, looking for pricing discrepancies. This information can be supplemented by periodic audits of each supplier's detailed expense records, and should be summarized into a periodic report for the use of each functional coordinator in fixing any pricing issues with the suppliers. New outsourcing controls are centered on the supplier billing statement and contract.

Many of the measurements tracked by the accounting staff will change as a result of outsourcing. Some related to assets, head count, and square footage will no longer be needed, while others, such as transaction volumes, must be added. Other measurements—such as those covering revenues, margins, and costs—will not change, while others—covering inventory turnover, average salaries, and break-even—will yield radically different results. Outsourcing has an important impact on accounting measurements.

Outsourcing has a very significant impact on accounting transactions. These changes include reduced transaction volume in accounts payable and payroll, minimal data-entry requirements, new sources of accounts receivable payments, several new transaction error-checking procedures, and possibly even a chance to shrink the accounting computer system to something with fewer users, less functionality, and a smaller central processor. Transactions become fewer and easier to manage when outsourcing is used.

In all areas of its operations, the accounting staff will find that outsourcing will alter the way in which it does its work—transactions will come from different places and be fewer in number, and controls must be reconstructed and measurements altered, resulting in different financial statement layouts. The drastic level of changes elsewhere in the company will be reflected in the accounting department.

CHAPTER FOUR

Outsourcing the Accounting Function

The accounting function is among the most commonly outsourced, though this is usually limited to only a few tasks within the function. There are opportunities to outsource a wide array of services in this area, if a company is willing to work with multiple suppliers to achieve this goal. For example, payroll can be outsourced through several large international suppliers, such as ADP, Ceridian, and Paychex. Virtual Payroll, Inc., can even provide full payroll services over the Internet. Collections of accounts receivable can be outsourced through hundreds of suppliers, some of whom are very large, such as Dun & Bradstreet Receivables Management Services. Cash management services are offered by most regional banks. Taxation, financial reporting, and internal auditing services are provided by all of the largest auditing firms, such as Ernst & Young LLP and Deloitte & Touche LLP. For example, Ernst & Young LLP provides internal auditing services to the Whirlpool Corporation. Accounts payable check printing can be outsourced to some of the more technologically progressive banks (such as Chase Manhattan), which only require a computer file from the company containing information about who is to be paid and how much to pay. Some organizations, such as Arthur Andersen LLP, even operate transaction-processing centers that efficiently handle a company's general ledger, accounts receivable, and accounts payable tasks. A good example of this is Andersen's handling of the accounting chores for Conoco's United Kingdom drilling and piping divisions. There are also suppliers who specialize in taking in cash receipts on behalf of companies (usually utilities) and forwarding the receipts to the company's bank account along with a collection register detailing who paid the money. Thus, there is a wide array of suppliers available who can take on most of a company's accounting tasks.

This chapter describes the advantages and disadvantages of using outsourcing for a variety of accounting services, with particular attention paid to the most controversial topic, the outsourcing of internal auditing. There are also several points regarding contract clauses that the reader should know about before signing any contracts with suppliers. In addition, a section covers the various transition steps needed to hand over an in-house accounting function to a supplier. Many ways to control and measure the performance of suppliers are also revealed, as well has how this information can be used by the managers of the accounting and treasury functions. Finally, there are a number of issues to be aware of that can cause problems when a company wants to terminate a supplier relationship—these issues are described, along with possible solutions. After reading this chapter, the reader should have a good grounding in the fundamental issues surrounding outsourcing the accounting function, and will know how to negotiate contracts with suppliers, transition tasks to them, measure their performance, manage them, and sever the relationships if necessary.

4.1 ADVANTAGES AND DISADVANTAGES

This section presents a series of advantages and disadvantages for outsourcing many of a company's accounting functions. Areas covered include accounts receivable collections, internal auditing, payroll, taxation, financial statement reporting, pension administration, transaction processing, and cash management. Each area covered places both the advantages and disadvantages in close proximity, so that the reader can compare and weigh the benefits and associated problems of using outsourcing. The two areas covered most heavily in this section are payroll and internal auditing. Payroll has the longest history of outsourcing and is the most successful, so there is a long list of reasons for using it. Internal auditing is the most controversial outsourcing topic in the accounting area, and is vigorously denigrated by internal auditors (who want to keep their jobs) and advanced by external auditors (who want the business).

Several points in favor of outsourcing are not covered for each of the accounting topics, since there would be considerable duplication. Those points are that many of these accounting areas are clerical or subject to automation—such as transaction processing, pension administration, and payroll—and are therefore nonstrategic. Since they are not of importance to the company's strategic direction, they should be outsourced so that the company can concentrate on more important tasks that will impact its profitability or position in the marketplace.

The best reason for outsourcing the collections function is that the supplier may pursue those customers who refuse to pay with greater energy than would the in-house collections staff. Particular skill is required in persuading companies to pay for old invoices, and good collections suppliers have many people of this kind. The downside of using collections companies is that they can be so aggressive with the company's customers that the customers will refuse to ever do business with the company again; however, since the company had to refer the customer's account to collections anyway, the company may not want to do business with the customer again. Also, a collections supplier is typically paid a large percentage of each bill collected, normally about one-third of the total. However, a company usually passes along a bill to a collection supplier at the point when it does not believe it can collect the bill itself, so any collection, even if not for the full amount, is better than what the company had before. Furthermore, many companies write off accounts receivable that must be handed over to collection suppliers, so it is apparent that there is no expectation of ever collecting the money. Also, a company can sometimes work with collection suppliers who are willing to be paid by the hour rather than on a percentage basis. This payment scheme reduces the high cost of collection, but also converts the collections cost from a highly desirable variable cost to a fixed cost. It is very useful to switch the most difficult accounts receivable collection items over to a collections supplier, since they are better at persuading companies to pay their bills; this service is worth the high prices paid when collection efforts are successful.

Some companies are now outsourcing their internal audit functions. There are a number of good reasons for doing so, and those reasons are noted below. However, these points should be compared to the list of disadvantages that follows in order to fully understand the ramifications of taking the step to outsourcing. The reasons in favor of outsourcing the internal auditing function are as follows:

- *Mix of skills.* There is a big advantage for the company if the auditing firm is a large one, for the auditors provided can be changed for each audit, only using those people who are most skilled in the requirements of each audit.

- *Staff quality.* The quality of auditing staff supplied is usually quite high, especially if the supplier used is one of the prestigious "Big Five" accounting firms. This allows the company to have confidence that audits will be in-depth and thorough.

- *Management ability.* The supplier can manage the audit for the company; since this is all the supplier does, it is very good at managing audits, and can probably do so better than the company's in-house staff.

- *Knowledge of best practices.* An auditor who reviews the functions of many companies will build up a knowledge base of how processes can be performed most efficiently and effectively, or has access to that knowledge through other auditors at the firm, and can therefore recommend changes to the company. Many internal audit staffs have been with their companies for years, and have not acquired this same range of knowledge of processes due to a lack of exposure to other businesses.

- *Variable cost.* The company only pays for audits performed by the supplier, so the auditing cost can be switched from being a fixed one for an in-house staff to a variable one for an outside staff.

- *Quick access.* The company has the option to quickly bring in an experienced audit team if it acquires a new business in a foreign location that is inconvenient for its internal staff to reach.

- *Reduced travel costs.* The company must fly its internal audit staff to any company location that needs an internal audit, whereas a large auditing firm can assign staff from its regional offices to go to those locations, thus avoiding the excessive travel costs incurred by the internal audit staff. This cost reduction only works if the auditing firm has regional offices near the company's locations, so this proximity should be investigated prior to hiring the audit firm to ensure that costs can be saved in this area.

- *No downtime.* Bringing in an audit team only for specific tasks allows the company to avoid the kind of nonproductive downtime that sometimes occurs with an in-house staff, such as the interval between the end of one audit and the beginning of the next.

- *No hiring and training costs.* The company can avoid the substantial hiring and training costs needed to staff and retain a top-of-the-line in-house audit team.

There are several important reasons why the internal auditing function should *not* be outsourced in some circumstances. Management should be aware of these reasons before making the decision to outsource. Some of the concerns with outsourcing are as follows:

- *Cost.* One downside of using an outside auditing firm for internal audits is that they are substantially more expensive than an in-house staff, since the hourly cost of this service includes the very substantial overhead of the firm, as well as its profit margin. There may be an additional concern that fees will be low-balled until the company has disbanded its internal auditing staff and has become reliant on the supplier for all audit work, at which point the supplier will increase its fees. However, this cost can be lowered through negotiation—the auditing firm wants this kind of business because it keeps its staff busy during the slow times of the year, and because it is also less risky than its typical line of work (i.e., no audit opinions are required). An internal audit supplier can match auditor skills to the needs of each audit, and allows the company to only pay for audits performed, but is more expense on a per-hour basis than an in-house staff.

- *Training.* A real concern when moving the audit function to a supplier is that some companies use the internal audit function to train their managers (since the job gives a good knowledge of how the company functions); by taking away this function, the company loses its training ground for the future managers of the company. One solution is to retain a stripped-down version of the in-house auditing function, and team these remaining personnel with the audit teams provided by the supplier, so that some training is still available by this means.

- *Experience.* The perceived quality of the auditors provided by the supplier may be lower than anticipated, since most auditing firms have very high turnover and also like to bring in employees with lower levels of experience in order to give them experience with different accounting systems. This problem can be avoided by previewing the qualifications of every person the supplier wants to bring onto an audit job. A more serious concern is that internal and operational audits are not the same as financial audits, and the audit firm's employees may not be as well trained in these areas as in financial auditing. Certainly, a company contemplating outsourcing its internal auditing function would want to interview prospective suppliers to see what kinds of audit programs they have created in these areas. One way to mitigate this problem is to add some members of the in-house audit team to the outside audit team, which brings in a knowledge of the company's procedures, personnel, and politics, and eliminates the time the outside audit team would need to become familiar with these issues.

- *Responsibility.* Management must still realize that it is responsible for the establishment and maintenance of internal controls and the audit of those controls. If the company is sued over a lack of controls, it cannot point to the internal audit supplier as the culprit—management is still responsible, and can even be jailed for certain violations.

- *Independence.* An auditing firm is supposed to create "walls" within its own company that keep its internal audit work from interfering with the independence of its financial statement audit work. This is possible for a large firm, where there are many employees who can take part in one activity or the other, but not both. However, a small audit firm may have to use the same employees for both activities, which may interfere with the real or perceived independence of the audit firm's review of the company's financial statements. A related problem is that an audit firm may have a lucrative practice in conducting internal audits for a company. What if the audit firm cannot issue an unqualified opinion on the same company's financial statements? Will it be tempted to issue an unqualified statement anyway rather than run the risk of angering the company and losing its internal auditing work? This is a concern for those entities who rely on the audit firm's opinion of the company's financial statements.

The most commonly outsourced accounting function is payroll. There are a variety of good reasons for outsourcing it, which has led to well over one hundred thousand companies having taken advantage of the services of suppliers in this area. Some of the advantages of outsourcing are as follows:

- *Avoid filing tax payments.* One of the primary reasons for doing so is to avoid having to file payroll tax payments on time. The government has begun requiring increasingly rapid tax filings, and has imposed stiff penalties if taxes are not filed on time. For those companies with a chronic tax-filing problem, handing over this task to a supplier may save the company more money in tax penalties than the cost of having the supplier handle the payroll.

- *Avoid paying for software updates.* Companies do not want to pay their software providers for new tax tables every year so that they can correctly calculate payroll taxes through their in-house software packages. Since there are some incremental tax rate changes somewhere every year, a company that runs its payroll on an in-house software package must incur this expense every year in order to stay current.

- *Avoid creating W-2 forms.* A payroll supplier will accumulate all annual payroll information into W-2 tax reports and even mail them to employees for the company. Otherwise, the in-house system would produce these documents and send them to employees.

- *Avoid printing paychecks.* A payroll printing can tie up a printer for a long time if a company has a large number of employees, and this printing must be monitored by an employee to ensure that there is no jamming. When the function is outsourced, the company can use both the printer and the employee for other purposes.

- *Use direct deposit.* Many in-house payroll systems do not allow direct deposit, since this requires a software interface that can be read by the local bank. All major payroll suppliers, however, offer direct deposit. This is a major advantage for those companies whose employees are constantly traveling and who are frequently not on-site to pick up and deposit their paychecks. There is always a fee associated with direct deposit, so this is not a cost-saving feature, but it is very good for employee relations.

- *Use check stuffing.* A further convenience is for the supplier to automatically stuff all checks into envelopes for delivery to employees, which eliminates a clerical task for the accounting staff.

- *Use check delivery to multiple locations.* Though most payroll services will not mail checks to individual employees, they will send batches of checks to multiple company locations for distribution to employees. This eliminates the risk that the company will forget to distribute checks, which can easily happen if the person responsible for this distribution is on vacation or sick.

- *Stamp signatures on checks.* Some company officers are burdened with the task of signing a multitude of checks every payday. Ostensibly, this is necessary so that someone reviews all checks prior to delivery to the employee. However, since checks can easily be reviewed subsequent to distribution by perusing the accompanying payroll reports provided by the supplier, it is easy to correct payroll errors in the next payroll. Taking this view allows a company to deliver signature samples to the payroll supplier, which automatically affixes a signature to each check and saves an officer the trouble of doing so.

- *Use custom and standard reports.* Most payroll suppliers provide a plethora of reports that cover the needs of most companies. For special reporting needs, there is usually a custom report-writing tool available that allows the company to create any additional reports that it needs, without any special programming.

- *Link to 401(k) plan.* Some suppliers are even offering to make automatic deductions from paychecks and deposit this money into 401(k) accounts for the company, which greatly reduces the paperwork associated with this function.

Despite the formidable array of advantages previously noted, some companies do not outsource their payroll functions. There are a variety of reasons for this, ranging from inertia to company politics. The two most legitimate complaints are excessive costs and the difficulty of converting the more complex payroll systems to a supplier's system. Some of the more realistic disadvantages are as follows:

- *Cost.* Payroll suppliers can be quite expensive if all possible payroll services are used. The most typical supplier ploy is to initially charge very low rates for the basic service of printing paychecks. This is done to keep the company from going with the services of a competitor. However, once the company has signed on with the supplier, it will find that additional services may easily exceed the cost of the basic service. For example, additional fees will be charged for automatic signature printing, check stuffing, delivery to multiple locations, access to custom reporting software, and direct deposits. A very large company that represents a major portion of a supplier's business has more sway in negotiating prices than will a small company.

- *Conversion problems.* There are a number of data items that must be properly converted over to the supplier's software to ensure that employees will continue to receive paychecks in the correct amounts and with accurate deductions. If the conversion does not go well, the company may become so disenchanted with the supplier that it will convert back to an in-house processing solution. Conversions can be a problem because many companies want to convert to a supplier at the beginning of each year, which creates a considerable work overload for system-conversion employees of the suppliers. This problem can be avoided by conducting a gradual conversion to the supplier, so that only the most basic payroll features are moved to the supplier first and debugged before additional features (such as direct deposit, check signing, and envelope stuffing) are added. However, some highly complex payroll systems must be converted at once, so that employees see no difference in the payroll services provided to them; in these cases, the risk of high error rates and company dissatisfaction is high.

- *Create manual paychecks.* Some companies complain that they cannot easily determine the correct tax rates to charge when cutting a manual paycheck for an employee. This is most commonly needed when an employee is being released, and government regulations require that final payment be made to the employee at once, rather than when the next payroll-processing period arrives. However, several payroll suppliers now allow companies to dial up the database of information on each employee, plug in the special payment amount, and have the system immediately tell the company the appropriate amount of taxes to deduct from the paycheck.

- *Must send in payroll information.* The payroll supplier does not collect payroll information. The company must still collect payroll information from a variety of sources, organize this information, and input it into the supplier's system, usually through a software program that uploads the information to the supplier via a modem link. As this may be the primary source of clerical time in computing payroll, some companies may not see how they are saving costs by shifting to a supplier to perform the remaining payroll tasks. This is less of an issue for companies with mostly salaried staffs, since there is little data collection to do. Also, companies can pursue automated options to reduce their data-collection labor, such as bar-coded time clocks that calculate the total time worked for each employee; some of these clocks even link to the payroll supplier's systems to further reduce the work of the in-house staff in sending data to the supplier.

Some in-house payroll-processing functions are responding to the threat of outsourcing by providing more service to employees. For example, the HR Access software sold by IBM allows employees to access their payroll files from their desktops or over the Internet, so that they can change their own addresses, deductions for various benefits, and W-4 form tax deductions. Employees frequently prefer this access, since they can be assured that the changes they want have been made.

Taxation can be outsourced when a company is not big enough to support the full-time services of a tax department of its own. This is frequently split into two pieces, with state and federal taxation reporting going to a supplier and local taxation being kept in-house. The reason for this split is that many taxation firms are experts at state and federal issues because they have their own teams of experts who advise them on these issues and know how to save money on taxes in these areas; however, they have no experts who specialize in local taxation issues such as enterprise development zones. Thus, many companies find that taxation firms can help them to file tax returns for state and federal taxes and can save them money while doing so, but that they have little knowledge of local taxation issues, which are therefore kept in-house.

A company has a supplier create financial statements for it when its in-house accounting staff is not large enough or experienced enough to do so correctly or in a timely manner. This can be a good idea if the accounting firm used is a large one, for its staff will have an excellent knowledge of all reporting requirements needed for financial statements, especially for all required notes that must go along with the financial statements. A popular variation on this approach is to have an outside firm verify the accuracy of the financial statements that were produced by the in-house staff, which is very helpful if the company is a public one and is not sure that its 10-Q or 10-K reports to the SEC are correctly presented. The downside of this approach is that accounting firms usually charge high rates for this service. Thus, a company must decide if the improved reporting format of its financial statements is worth the additional cost.

The advantage of using a supplier to handle a company's 401(k) plan includes reducing the paperwork associated with tracking investments for employees, and of changing the cost of this function from the fixed cost of an in-house staff to the variable cost of having a supplier do it. This becomes a variable cost because the pricing structures of most suppliers are on a per-person basis. For example, there is a per-person setup fee, an annual per-person maintenance fee, and a per-person fee to remove someone from the plan. If the company's head count changes, the cost of the supplier will vary with the head count level. The primary disadvantage of this approach is the risk of hiring a bad supplier who does a poor job of accurately investing funds or tracking investments for each employee. This problem can be partially mitigated by requesting references for the supplier and contacting all of them for detailed information about the supplier's performance. Thus, using a supplier reduces a company's paperwork requirements while converting the 401(k) administration cost from a fixed to a variable cost, though there is a risk that the supplier will botch the administration of the plan.

One of the more recent accounting tasks to be outsourced is transaction processing, mostly of accounts payable and receivable. So far, outsourcing this function has been confined to a small number of large companies, but it may extend down to smaller companies as more suppliers begin to offer this service. One advantage of outsourcing transaction processing is that the supplier may have a better knowledge of world-class processes that allows it to complete transactions faster than the company's in-house staff. Also, if the company has a widely dispersed transaction-processing function, a supplier can consolidate all of these locations into a single, highly efficient location to reduce costs. In addition, a company may be able to replace poor in-house management with the (presumably) top-notch management of the supplier. The downside of outsourcing transaction processing includes the cost of doing so; unless they can use their greater knowledge of processes to cut costs, suppliers will be more expensive than the in-house function, because they must include a profit as well as their sales and marketing costs in their pricing structures. Another problem is that transaction processing is usually maintained by the largest number of employees within the accounting function. Some controllers base their power within the company on the number of employees they supervise, so losing transaction processing to a supplier will, in their eyes, reduce their power within the company. The only way to outsource transaction processing in these situations is to fire the controller and bring in someone with a less power-hungry attitude toward the job.

The cash-management function is also a good area for outsourcing. One reason is that a company manually moves money between accounts and manually records this information. On the other hand, a bank can automatically consolidate the cash in various accounts and sweep it all into an interest-bearing account without any manual interference at all. This allows a company to reduce the fixed cost of the in-house staff it uses to track the flow of cash through its accounts in exchange for a per-transaction fee from the bank for performing the same service. Also, since the bank can fully automate this work, the company has a much lower risk of having any errors in moving funds between accounts. The only disadvantage of this approach is that the company is forced to use the same bank for all of its accounts, which does not allow the company to use the services of multiple banks and have them compete against each other in offering the best prices to the company. Switching cash management to a bank improves the automation of this error-prone function while replacing some fixed costs with variable costs.

This section covered the advantages and disadvantages of using outsourcing for all of the accounting functions. Particular attention was paid to internal auditing, which is one of the most controversial areas, and payroll, which is the most outsourced of all accounting tasks. Many of the accounting tasks—such as payroll—are highly clerical and subject to automation, and are therefore most likely to be outsourced. Others, such as internal auditing, require more expertise or have strong internal constituencies, and are therefore less likely to be outsourced. Given the large number of solid reasons for outsourcing some of the accounting tasks, it is likely that even the most conservative accounting organization will find good reasons to outsource several of these functions.

4.2   CONTRACT-SPECIFIC ISSUES

This section covers a variety of contract-related issues that a company should be aware of before signing a contract with a supplier to take over an accounting task. This section is shorter than in other chapters, for there are fewer points of negotiation for accounting contracts than may be found for other functional areas. However, there are a number of lesser points to consider before signing a contract, and this section covers those items.

A contract for payroll services will only be negotiable on prices. This is because a payroll supplier has thousands of clients and prefers to use a standard contract for all of them—it cannot hope to track slight contract changes for all of those companies, and so it does not allow them. However, suppliers have modified their computer systems to allow for different prices for each company, so this one area is subject to negotiation. Pricing is typically on a per-person basis, plus a fixed baseline fee for various services. Each of those fees can be changed. A company has the most negotiating power if it has a large number of employees to put on the supplier's payroll system; the prospect of losing all of that revenue will normally elicit price cuts by the supplier. A small company will likely have no luck in negotiating reduced prices, for it has no basis for demanding a price reduction. The one exception to this rule is that a payroll supplier will sometimes grant a price cut if the company employee who is sponsoring the supplier has brought the supplier into other companies as well—this loyalty to the supplier can be worth a small discount. Payroll suppliers allow no contract changes, but price alterations are possible if the company has a large payroll.

A contract for tax work is negotiable on prices and supplier staff to be used. Any tax supplier charges a basic hourly rate for work performed, and then discounts this rate for any number of reasons. Most companies can reduce this per-hour rate with enough negotiation time, or can convert the tax work to a fixed fee for work performed, with an hourly rate to be charged for any additional work that falls outside of the deliverables noted in the original contract. If the company finds that a specific supplier employee does especially good work, then it can specify that all work will be done by that person, or at least that the company can reject supplier personnel whom it feels are unsuitable for doing any of its tax work. Thus, a company seeking quality tax work has some room to maneuver on prices and supplier employees to be used.

A contract for cash-management work is sometimes not even negotiable on price, and certainly not on any other contract points. This is because these services are offered by banks to thousands of customers; given the volume of customers, the bank cannot keep track of slight variations in contracts, and thus offers no negotiation options at all. Pricing also tends to be highly fixed; this is because cash-management services do not generate an enormous amount of profit for the bank from a single customer. However, if the volume of cash-management services is very high, as would be the case for a very large company receiving thousands of check payments every day, the bank could be persuaded to cut its pricing structure (especially if another bank were brought in to compete with it for this business). However, for most companies, cash-management contracts are unalterable.

A contract for collections work focuses on reimbursement. A typical collections agency wants to keep a large percentage of all money it collects on a company's accounts receivable. This percentage typically varies between one-quarter and one-third of the amount collected. If a company gives a large dollar volume of its business to a collections agency, it may be possible to negotiate this number down. If a company does not want to pay so much money to the supplier, it can ask a law firm to collect the largest receivable debts in exchange for per-hour compensation. The only other negotiation point is whether the collections agency should be allowed to finish collecting any accounts receivable it has in its possession at the time when the company decides to stop using the agency. In most cases, the collection agency is allowed to finish the collections work, since it may have already invested a large amount of time in trying to collect those items. If the collections agent is a law firm working on an hourly basis, then the company can take back all accounts receivable at any time; after all, the lawyers have already been paid for every hour worked, so they have no right to retain the accounts receivable until collected. In short, a company can outsource its collections work to either a collections agency or a law firm depending on the type of compensation it is most comfortable paying, and has some contract points to negotiate regarding the disposition of receivables if the relationship is terminated.

A contract for internal auditing must target hourly fees, the specific staff to be used, and the methodology that will form the underpinnings of all internal audit work. The hourly fees are subject to considerable negotiation, with price cuts based on the anticipated number of staff hours to be used, as well as on the time of year when the company will use a supplier's staff. Since most suppliers who provide internal audit work are also auditing firms, they have poor staff utilization during the summer and fall periods, and are most likely to accept lower pricing during those periods. A company may have developed its own detailed internal auditing methodology and wants the supplier to continue to use it—this is rarely a problem for the supplier, since there is no legal risk in doing so. A typical contract clause addressing this issue should, however, allow the supplier to recommend changes that will bolster the methodology to help provide more complete audit results. Finally, it is not wise to specify in the contract which supplier employees will be used on internal audits (since they will eventually leave the supplier, rendering that part of the contract invalid), but it is desirable to require that the company can request or reject supplier personnel. Thus, internal auditing provides a greater range of contract negotiation than other accounting areas—in pricing, staff selection, and audit methodology.

A contract for pension management tends to have rigid pricing, but does allow some movement on the types of investments offered to employees. Pricing normally includes both baseline fees and per-person fees that are not negotiable unless the company has a large pension plan that can be highly profitable for the supplier. The more common point of negotiation is in having the supplier create a mix of investment vehicles, normally ranging from conservative to speculative, that the company's employees can select from. There will be a limit to the number of investment choices, usually being no more than a half-dozen. Typically, there is no need to press for more types of investment, since a half-dozen choices is sufficient for most people. However, not having a complete range of conservative to aggressive investments is of great concern to those employees who need a full range of options, so considerable negotiation time should be targeted at this issue. Consequently, contract changes for pension management focus less on pricing and more on the mix and number of investment vehicles offered.

A contract for transaction processing has the largest number of clauses that can be negotiated. One point is that the company should push to have as many services as possible covered by the baseline or per-transaction fee. Otherwise, the supplier will charge much higher add-on fees for any extra services. Also, if the company's staff is being transferred to the supplier, the contract should specify the minimum time period for retaining these employees (in order to give them some job security), or at least the minimum percentage of employees who will be kept by the supplier. The contract should also specify a minimum time period during which the supplier must keep key personnel working on company business; otherwise, suppliers may take the best of the transferred staffs and move them off to work on projects for other clients. Another issue is that the company should have control over the implementation of new efficiencies by the supplier that will achieve greater efficiencies. This may seem like no control is required—just do whatever it takes to cut costs—but there may be political reasons within the company for keeping the methods of transaction processing the way they are. If this control is proving to be a difficult negotiation point, then a fallback position is to require company approval over any transaction-processing changes that impact other areas of the company, thereby retaining control over those changes that may result in some political fallout. It is apparent that transaction-processing contracts can be negotiated to a far greater extent than other accounting tasks, including pricing, employee retention and transfers, and process changes.

This section covered the contract-related issues that arise when outsourcing the accounting function. Many supplier contracts are not negotiable, or are negotiable only on pricing, while others—such as internal auditing and transaction processing—can be substantially modified by the company.

4.3 TRANSITION ISSUES

This section covers the specific transition issues associated with each of the accounting tasks that can be outsourced. There is not a Gantt chart showing the sequence of transition steps, as there is for the functional areas discussed in most other chapters. This is because there are many tasks within the accounting function that may be individually outsourced—there is no sequence of events for outsourcing all of the accounting tasks, because no one does it that way. Companies outsource small pieces of the accounting function at one time, so there is no need for a complex, multi-layered Gantt chart. Also, the contract-negotiation step is not itemized as a transition step, because there is very little negotiation to be done for the accounting tasks, outside of some limited price negotiation. In addition, it is assumed that the company will discuss performance measurements and associated penalties and bonus payments for all of the accounting tasks that are outsourced, so this item is also not mentioned for each of the accounting tasks.

One key task for other functions that is not necessary in the accounting area is the selection of a functional coordinator to manage the activities of suppliers. A coordinator is rarely selected in this area because the controller and treasurer normally manage the suppliers who take over outsourced functions. The reason for not having a coordinator is that only pieces of this functional area are usually outsourced, so that the original managers of the function (i.e., the controller and treasurer) are always on-site, managing the remaining functions. Since they are already available and they are familiar with the functions being outsourced, it is logical that they be retained to manage the outsourced functions. Thus, there are no transition steps listed here for selecting a coordinator.

For the payroll function, the first transition step is to meet with the supplier about one month in advance of the conversion date (or earlier if the payroll system to be converted is especially large or complex). This meeting should cover all key conversion dates and who is to perform which tasks by those dates. Since the payroll function must usually be brought on-line with the supplier as of the first day of the year, this is a very time-sensitive process, so the initial meeting with the supplier is especially important. If various extra payroll features, such as automated check signing, are to be added to the payroll later on, these dates should also be agreed upon by both parties during the meeting. The next transition step will be to transfer all payroll information for all employees to the supplier at the end of the year or slightly prior to that date. This may require either the conversion of existing computer data to a format that is readable by the supplier's computer system, or a large rekeying effort by the company's payroll staff. It is particularly important during this step to provide time and personnel resources to review all rekeyed information to ensure that it is correct. There must also be enough time to adequately train the staff who will be inputting information into the payroll system on an ongoing basis. Supplier representatives should be on hand during the first few data-entry sessions to ensure that all problem areas are adequately addressed. In short, there is a tight sequence of events that must be followed when converting the payroll system to a supplier, which is made more difficult by the need to convert accurate payroll information to the supplier's computer system.

The transition of cash management to a supplier begins with a review by the cash-management consulting division of the bank to see where lockbox accounts should be set up. The company then has the bank create these accounts, and the bank sets them up to automatically sweep cash receipts into a single account that provides interest income. The company should then create an audit program for periodically reviewing the contents of each account to ensure that cash balances have indeed been shifted to the investment account. Once all of these steps have been taken, the company must send a mailing to all customers, informing them of the address of the lockbox nearest to them to which they should send remittances. Finally, the company should have a procedure in place for reminding companies of where to send their payments, since many will ignore the request to send cash to a lockbox, and instead will continue to send it to the old remittance address. An additional note is that many companies hand this business over to their existing banks without any search for an alternative, because loan agreements require that all banking business be conducted through the current bank, or because the company does not want to go through the difficulty of switching its accounts to a new bank. However, the company may find that the existing bank does not have enough branch locations to provide a sufficient number of accounts in all of the geographical locations that the company needs, so switching to a new bank may be the only option for having a supplier take over the cash-management function. Thus, transitioning cash management to a supplier may include bank selection, lockbox-location selection, setting up sweep accounts, notifying customers, and auditing the results.

Handing over the financial-reporting task to a supplier is one of the easier tasks to transition. A quality accountant can produce a financial statement directly from a general ledger report, and can add notes to the financial statements based on periodic interviews of company management. The only transition steps required here are to go over with the supplier how individual accounts are to be rolled up into financial statement line items, and to then monitor the supplier's financial reports for several months to ensure that the reporting is being completed properly.

The internal audit function requires several extra transition steps to complete. Since the quality of the supplier's audit staff has a strong impact on the speed and in-depth analysis that will characterize each internal audit, the controller should carefully review the qualifications of all auditors proposed by the supplier, and feel free to reject any who appear to have too little experience. Next, the supplier's staff should be thoroughly trained in the company's policies and procedures, meet key employees, and be set up in permanent offices with ready access to office equipment (assuming that the auditors will be on-site at one location for a large proportion of the year). This step is necessary to ensure that the auditors start off as efficiently as possible; if not, there may be charges within the company that the new auditors are not as good as the in-house internal audit staff, and there may be pressure to return to the in-house auditing arrangement. Next, if the company wants to continue with its own internal auditing methodology, it can train the supplier's staff in using it. This is of particular use in those industries where a standard audit program would not work. For example, the gambling industry requires intensive and frequent reviews of all controls over the cash function, whereas most other industries would pay far less attention to this audit area. The controller and the supplier's management must then agree upon an audit program for the upcoming year. The controller has primary control over the contents of this plan, but the supplier is certainly welcome to recommend changes that will give a more rounded review of as many control points as possible, or which will take advantage of the particular skills of the supplier's staff. It is also helpful to arrange for periodic review meetings in which the supplier's audit staff goes over the findings from each of its audits and in which the controller asks for further reviews based on these findings, or modifies the schedule of remaining audits based on time or cost constraints. The final transition step for internal auditing is to arrange for other means of training future company managers if this function had previously been used for that purpose. One option is to retain a small in-house staff to act as a vehicle for training, while the company could also have these people work with the supplier's staff to gain some experience in that manner. Thus, considerable transition work must be completed before a company has successfully moved its internal auditing function to a supplier.

Turning over the taxation function to a supplier is one of the easiest accounting tasks to outsource. The supplier who normally takes over tax-preparation work is the company's existing external audit firm. The company merely needs to authorize the audit firm to begin tax work, and that is about all that is required; nearly all of the information the supplier needs can be gleaned from the audit workpapers that it already has in its possession. However, if the company has chosen a supplier other than its auditor to do the tax work, then the company must send written permission to the auditor to copy audit files and send them to the tax preparer (frequently for a copying fee). Finally, though most tax preparers are too expert in their field to make any mistakes, most companies will review the tax forms they have prepared prior to sending them on to the government. Outsourcing tax work can be the easiest accounting task of all to outsource—just authorize the company's auditor to do it based on existing audit workpapers already in the auditor's possession.

The most difficult accounting task to outsource is transaction processing. This is because the task may involve large numbers of employees, custom software, supplier training, and a risk of task interruption. However, if the transition of this task is properly carried through, the company's customers will notice no change in the accounting function's service to them. The first task in this area is to transfer the company's staff to the supplier. Since the supplier may not have chosen to hire all of the existing staff, it may also be necessary to train new staff in how to run the company's transaction-processing (mostly accounts payable and accounts receivable) systems. This training task may extend to the supplier's management team, who may not have hired the company's management team to oversee the area. Also, if the supplier decides to set up an off-site facility, then the company's existing hardware and software may have to be moved to that location. An alternative is to just load the company's software and related database of information into the supplier's computers at a pre-existing location. In either case, the company will have to transfer the software license for the software it uses to process transactions from the company to the supplier—this may involve a substantial payment to the software provider. Once all of these steps have been taken, the supplier should run through a set of sample transactions to ensure that the system is operating properly, prior to processing any real transactions. If all goes well at this point, the transition of transaction processing to the supplier will be complete.

The transition process for pension management starts with sending all account information for each participant to the new supplier. Since the current supplier may have the most up-to-date form of this information, written permission may be needed for its release to the new supplier. This information must be loaded into the supplier's database and checked for accuracy. Next, the company must transfer all fund balances to the supplier. Sometimes, the money is invested in specific stocks or third-party funds, so simply transferring the power to invest this money to the new supplier is a sufficient way to transfer the funds, which do not really move from where they have been invested. However, if the new supplier has its own funds in which pension investments are to be made, then the money must be extracted from the original supplier and given to the new supplier for reinvestment. In this second case, the company must have all plan participants choose new investment vehicles in which to investment their funds—assuming that the pension plan is a 401(k) plan, where employees make their own investment decisions. This paperwork must go to the new supplier, who uses it to apportion the transferred funds to its funds. Also, the company's in-house human resources personnel must be given adequate stocks of the supplier's investment forms, and be instructed in their use. These forms are needed on an ongoing basis to allow employees to enter or exit the plan, or (depending on the type of plan) to alter their mix of investments or amounts of funds invested. Also, the supplier commonly has its own proprietary software that it gives to the company to input new pension-contribution information for each employee following each pay period; the employees who will do this inputting must be trained in how to use the software, and allowed practice sessions with test data. After all of these tasks have been completed, the company will have completed its transition of the pension-management task to a new supplier. However, given the sensitive nature of the information transferred, it is advisable to continue to closely review all pension statements for each employee following the first few months of the transition, to ensure that all information was correctly converted to the new supplier. After all, there is nothing worse than an irate employee whose funds have been placed in the wrong investment or who finds that some pension funds have disappeared.

This section covered a large number of transition issues, spread across a wide range of accounting tasks. The transition steps were not presented as a unified and sequential cluster of events, since that would assume the conversion of virtually all accounting tasks at once to one or more suppliers. In reality, the accounting function tends to be outsourced in pieces, with few companies ever attempting a complete outsourcing of all functions. Also, it was assumed that the appointment of a functional coordinator would not lead off the transition steps—this is because the controller and treasurer usually shoulder the outsourcing management tasks due to their continued presence at the company. When the transition steps noted in this section are followed, a company has a much greater chance of success in converting accounting tasks over to a supplier.

4.4   CREATING CONTROL POINTS

This section covers the variety of control points that are available to a company that wants to ensure that suppliers are completing their designated accounting tasks as efficiently and effectively as possible. Most companies will not have the resources to implement all of the controls noted in this section, but a mix of selected controls should be sufficient to maintain adequate control over accounting suppliers.

The primary control point is the internal audit. The internal audit team should follow an audit program that takes it through a review of each supplier's activities regularly enough for the suppliers to know that they will be undergoing an audit at least once a year. There are many items that the audit team can review. A few of the more common audit objectives are as follows:

- Verifying that supplier invoices have an attached approval signature or purchase order.

- Verifying that expense reports are approved and have supporting documentation for expenses of $25 or more.

- Verifying that all accounts receivable credits have been approved.

- Verifying that appropriate tax amounts were charged on invoices.

- Verifying that invoices are mailed in a timely manner.

- Verifying that payroll taxes are being deposited.

- Verifying that tax returns have no material errors.

- Verifying that the financial statements and accompanying financial notes have no material errors.

- Verifying that the cash in all lockbox accounts is being swept into an interest-bearing account.

Once the audit team has completed its audit program for a supplier, it should go over its findings with the management of the supplier to verify that all audit findings are accurate, and then meet with company management to present its findings and recommendations. A key consideration when using an audit team is whether it should be outsourced. If the company has an outside audit firm take over this key function, that firm should not be allowed to take over any other accounting tasks—otherwise, the audit team will be auditing the work of its own supplier, which may not result in a clearly independent review of operations. In short, the internal audit function is the most valuable control tool available for the accounting area.

Bonuses and penalties are one of the more effective ways to control suppliers. To begin, the company must create target goals for suppliers to achieve. The suppliers must sign off on these goals in advance, so that there is no conflict over the nature of each goal, how it is to be measured, who is to measure it, and the size of the penalties or bonuses that will result from the measurements. The company must track the measurements, and not the suppliers, so that suppliers will not be tempted to skew the results. If the penalties or bonuses tied to these measurements are large, then the measurement results should be given to suppliers during formal meetings, so that they can defend the measurement results. When suppliers can gain or lose significant amounts of money through performance measurements, their performance will improve dramatically.

There should be a separate line item in the budget that shows the cost of each accounting supplier. When this information is listed in the monthly financial statements alongside actual costs, company management gains a clear understanding of the cost of each supplier, and how that cost is changing in comparison to the budget. If there are significant cost overruns showing in the financial statements, management can take action to reduce those costs, either through negotiations, less use of the supplier's services, or by switching to a new supplier.

The final control area is the scheduled review meeting. This is useful for going over the results of internal audits, reviewing progress towards predetermined goals, and discussing any problems that have arisen since the last meeting. An agenda should be distributed in advance and strictly followed to ensure that all major areas are addressed. The company should have a meeting secretary record the minutes of each meeting, distribute them to all participants, and require that the chief representatives from each side sign off on the meeting minutes as being accurate (or modify them as necessary and then sign off). These minutes should be kept on file in case there are questions later on about what was agreed upon during meetings. The number of meetings per year will vary greatly with the type of accounting function being reviewed. Some of the more automated accounting tasks, such as payroll, need as few as one review meeting per year, though many more may be required while the area is first being implemented. Other areas that require constant interaction between the staffs of the company and supplier, such as internal auditing, may need monthly review meetings. Areas that do not have a major impact on company operations, such as pension management, can easily be limited to quarterly or even semiannual meetings. The one area that must be reviewed frequently is transaction processing, because problems in this area that are not quickly addressed will cause problems with the company's accounts payable and receivable, which can irritate customers or suppliers. Review meetings are useful for going over problems and reviewing progress toward performance goals.

A company can ensure adequate control over its accounting suppliers by scheduling frequent audits of the areas they are administering, tying bonuses and penalties to their performance, tracking the cost of their services against a budget, and meeting with them regularly to go over problems. A judicious mix of these controls can provide adequate control over accounting suppliers.

4.5   MEASURING
THE OUTSOURCED FUNCTION

Given the great number of tasks within the accounting function that can be outsourced, there are a large number of measurements needed to properly keep track of all of them. In this section, the measurements are listed in alphabetical order by task. Each measurement description includes the reason why it is necessary, any pitfalls associated with using it, and how it may be measured.

CASH MANAGEMENT

- *Earnings rate on investments.* Banks can differentiate themselves by offering higher investment rates on various investments, which they do by keeping less profit on these investments for themselves and giving the forgone profits to the company. Though there is not normally a large-basis points spread between the investment rates offered, a company could still realize a considerable increase in investment income if it has a large cash balance to invest. Thus, the average earnings rate on investments can be an important measure of a bank's performance. This measurement can be derived from the monthly bank statement, where one can take the total investment income for the month and divide it by the total average balance invested to come up with the earnings rate on investments. One concern here is that the company may try to improve its income by investing in more risky investment vehicles; this measurement does not factor in any element of investment risk, so the company should adopt an investment policy that restricts investments to only specific areas that have limited and acceptable levels of risk.

- *Transaction fees.* A bank will charge a per-transaction fee for every transfer of cash between accounts. Though this fee may be absorbed by credits earned from having excessive cash balances, the fee is still charged, and should be tracked in case the company decides to eliminate its excess cash balances, which would result in these fees actually being charged. The information for the measurement is easily collected from the bank's monthly reporting statement. It is more important to track the per-transaction fee than the total fee, since the total fee will be skewed by the volume of transactions.

COLLECTIONS

- *Percentage collected of dollar volume assigned.* The primary performance measure for any collection agency is the amount of money collected out of the accounts transferred to it. An ineffective agency is one that cannot collect at least a portion of each account receivable turned over to it. Since the company wants to work with only those agencies that can convert the highest possible proportion of accounts receivable into cash, this is the primary measurement to use. The calculation is easy: Divide the total cash received from the agency by the total amount of accounts receivable turned over to it for collection; since there may be a large time gap between when the agency receives the account and when the cash comes in, it is better to annualize this measurement in order to match inflows and outflows in the measurement.

FINANCIAL STATEMENTS

- *Accuracy of accruals.* Most suppliers of financial statements only take a set of reports supplied by the company and use them to construct financial statements—they do not get into any journal entries, such as accruals. However, for those that do, it is important that accruals be made correctly. Incorrect accruals lead to inaccurate financial statements, not only for the month in which the accruals are made, but also for the month when the accruals are reversed. This measurement is derived by having the internal audit team periodically review the calculations used for each accrual, and then come up with its own accruals. The net variance between the two sets of accruals is the percentage by which the accruals are inaccurate.

- *Number or percentage of material irregularities.* A supplier must be able to restate a company's reports into an accurate set of financial statements. Any material irregularities in the numbers or accompanying financial notes may cause problems with the company, since lending, investment, and regulatory bodies rely on this information. This can be a difficult measurement to derive. The internal audit team should periodically review the statements for material irregularities, wade through the claims and accusations between the supplier and company regarding how the irregularities occurred, determine the amount by which the financial statements are incorrect, and derive a percentage of inaccuracy based on how far off the profits are from what they should have been. If the problem lies in the accompanying notes, then the measurement is purely qualitative, and should be reported as a discussion of how the notes are incorrect.

- *Time to release statements.* A supplier may take its time in preparing and mailing out a company's financial statements. This can be a major problem for the

SEC, banks, and investors, who require this information by specific deadlines. Banks frequently require that financial statements be delivered by specific dates—no financial statement, no loan. It is easy to measure this item. Just designate to whom financial statements will be sent by the supplier, and have that person record the number of days lag between the end of the reporting period and the receipt date.

INTERNAL AUDITING

- *Percentage of audits completed.* When a company brings in a supplier to conduct a series of internal audits, it usually starts with a plan of audits to be conducted over the upcoming year. If the supplier cannot complete all of the audits that it agreed to, the supplier is not being very efficient, and could be replaced in favor of someone else who can do the required number of audits. This item can be measured by dividing the total number of completed audits (defined as having been signed off on by all parties) by the total number of audits listed in the annual audit plan.

- *Cost per audit.* Suppliers of internal audits, such as the Big Six audit firms, are usually much more expensive on a per-hour basis than an in-house staff. However, this should not be the way to measure the cost effectiveness of an internal audit supplier. Due to the exceptional experience and training of many supplier employees, they may be able to conduct an internal audit engagement faster than an in-house team, and also come up with more suggestions for improvements. Since suggestions for improvements are difficult to quantify, it is better to measure the supplier based on the cost per audit, which can usually be extracted directly from the supplier's billing statement.

INVESTMENTS

- *Accuracy of trades.* If the company has a supplier handling all investment trades for it, the company wants some assurance that the trades are being handled properly. For example, authorizations to purchase or sell specific bonds or stocks should be carried through with total accuracy. The company's internal audit team or a staff person can regularly measure this by comparing the company's records of what it authorized for trades to the supplier's periodic statements showing what it actually did. Any problem trend should prompt a discussion with the supplier, if not the firing of the supplier—the company cannot run the risk of having its money incorrectly stored in improper investment vehicles.

- *Brokerage fees as a percentage of the amount invested.* A company conducting large numbers of trades should be able to negotiate very good brokerage rates from its supplier. Companies with smaller trading volumes may pay higher rates, since the supplier has no incentive to offer low prices to retain their business. Brokerage fees are usually located on the periodic brokerage billing statements. If not, the supplier may be hiding excessive fees. If the supplier is unwilling to change its statement format, the company may be better served by switching its business to a more open supplier.

PAYROLL

- *Timeliness in paying payroll taxes.* One of the primary tasks of the supplier is to pay all payroll taxes on behalf of the employer. This greatly reduces the labor and risk of penalties for nonpayment by the supplier. It is a very easy measurement to track, for the government will notify the company of any late payments. If there are no notifications, then the supplier has filed tax payments at the appropriate times. The measurement is to divide the total number of missed tax payments by the number of payrolls per year to determine the average timeliness in paying payroll taxes.

- *Transaction fees per person.* A payroll supplier's services are billed as a mix of per-person costs and fixed costs that are not linked to head count. The bulk of these fees are based on per-person costs, however, and are therefore an excellent way to determine the per-unit cost of this service. Most payroll providers send out highly detailed billing statements after each payroll, so the information used to derive this measurement is usually easily obtained. To calculate it, summarize all costs per payroll for each person for whom a paycheck was created. This may include fees for check preparation, stuffing, extra calculations for vacations or 401(k) deductions, and wire transfers. All of these per-person fees should be compiled when deriving the transaction fee per person. The total fees are then divided by the total number of employees paid in the period to come up with the per-person amount. If a company has different payrolls of different lengths (e.g., once a week or twice a month), the costs should be annualized to properly account for the costs of all payrolls.

- *Proportion of fees for extra services.* A payroll supplier likes to gain business by charging low fees for basic payroll-processing services, since companies make the decision to use suppliers based on these initial fees. The suppliers then charge exceedingly high rates for all additional services, which companies ask for after they have enrolled with the supplier and are "locked in." A company should separate these extra fees from the baseline fees to gain an understanding of incremental costs. The calculation should be the total additional fees per reporting period, divided by the total fees during that period.

- *Proportion of payrolls delivered to correct locations.* One service provided by payroll suppliers is guaranteed delivery of payrolls to the company's various locations by payday, usually using overnight mail delivery. If a payroll is sent to the wrong location or lost, this causes major personnel problems (since employees are not being paid), and therefore should be measured. The measurement is to summarize all instances when payroll was incorrectly delivered and to divide this by the total number of payroll deliveries in the reporting period. There is never a problem with collecting the information for missing payrolls—company employees will bring this problem to your attention very quickly.

PENSION

- *Investment return.* A typical pension plan will allow a participant to choose from a variety of funds, each of which has a different level of return and risk. To a large extent, the desired return is up to the participant and not the supplier. However, the supplier may do a poor job of managing the funds or extract too large a portion from each investment in the form of management fees, resulting in low returns. If so, it may be time to try a new pension supplier. This is measured by having the supplier provide a quarterly statement of investment return for each fund in the pension plan.

- *On-time release of funds.* Pension suppliers are in charge of disbursing funds to plan participants. These payments normally go straight from the supplier to the participant, so it is difficult for the company to determine if there are any problems with the release of funds on time. However, if there is a pattern of employee complaints in this area, there may be grounds for further investigation.

- *Release of statements on time.* Most pension suppliers issue investment statements to plan participants once a quarter. The in-house pension coordinator will receive many employee complaints if these statements are not released on time, since employees want to know how much money they earned in the last quarter. Also, any supplier that cannot get this simple report out on time may have other administrative problems related to tracking the investments, so not being able to release statements on time may be a sign of other problems at the supplier. This measurement is tracked by comparing the date when statements are received to the date when they are due.

TAXES

- *Absence of penalties.* One of the main reasons for employing someone else to prepare a company's taxes is to avoid tax penalties. These penalties can be caused by either filing tax returns too late or by filing incorrect returns. In either case, the company pays for the penalties. This measurement is simply the total of all penalties and related charges paid to tax authorities in a given time period. If company management finds that the tax preparer's fee plus the tax penalties sum to more than the company was spending internally to prepare the tax returns, it may be time for a new supplier.

- *Timeliness of filing.* A tax preparer must be able to file all tax returns on time. This is a large chore if the preparer is filing returns on behalf of the company for a large number of states, perhaps including quarterly returns of various kinds, as well as those tax filings sent to the federal government. Nonetheless, despite the volume, it is the tax preparer's responsibility to send out all tax returns on time. Otherwise, the company may have to pay penalties for late filings. This measurement is easy to track, since the company will be notified by the various government authorities whenever a filing is late—usually by sending a penalty notice. The number of these late filings can be divided by the total number of tax filings to determine the proportion of late filings. One consideration here is that a tax preparer may be late with a variety of inconsequential tax filings but on time with the more important income tax returns. In these cases, due consideration should be made for the importance of the filings that are late.

TRANSACTIONS

- *Average employee expense report turnaround time.* One of the most sensitive accounting issues is the review, approval, and payment of employee expense reports. If payments are made incorrectly or late, employees will be more irate than if the accounting function were to have problems in any other area—after all, it is their money. This problem can be avoided by periodically reviewing the time required to pay employees after they submit expense reports. The sampling method can be to either submit sample expense reports and track the time required to receive payment back, or to have an audit team review the supplier's payment records to determine the average turnaround time.

- *Cost per transaction.* The cost of a transaction-processing supplier can vary dramatically based on the volume of transactions processed. During a month when there are many invoices to process or bills to pay, the apparent cost of the supplier increases dramatically. However, it is misleading to look at the total cost of such a supplier, since the cost of using one is so dependent on processing volume. Instead, the cost per transaction should be used. This cost does not vary much, unless there is a contractual agreement to alter the cost per transaction if there is a significant change in the volume of transactions. This cost is easily obtained from supplier billing statements, and should be tracked on a trend line to spot any changes to the per-unit cost.

- *Error rate on processing.* It is very expensive to use staff to research and resolve any problems caused by incorrect transaction processing. It can also anger customers who may be incorrectly billed, or suppliers who are incorrectly paid. To determine the extent of this problem, the company should schedule periodic audits of all processed transactions to determine the percentage of errors in such areas as billing addresses, accounts payable matching, and tax rates on billings.

- *Average time to resolve errors.* Once an error is found, it is important to fix it as soon as possible. Otherwise, the paperwork associated with it is relegated further back in the archives area and is more difficult to research and correct.

Also, there may be problems caused by an error that will magnify over time and cause considerable effort to correct—angry business partners certainly being the greatest danger to avoid. This is a difficult measurement to derive, since a transaction-processing supplier can easily hide the existence of mistakes or mask the element of time it took to handle them. The best approaches are either to rely on the supplier to track this measure or to send in an audit team. The audit team can find evidence of error correction by looking for journal entries or debits or credits in the accounts payable or receivable journals—these are normally added to the records to fix a previous problem.

- *Timeliness of processing.* Some transactions must be processed on time, or they impact company cash flows. A prime example of such a transaction is billing, which should be conducted every day to avoid a reduction in the inflow of cash payments from customers. An internal audit team can measure this item by comparing the arrival of paperwork at the supplier to initiate the transaction processing (with the date of receipt presumably being stamped on the document by the supplier) with the date when the transaction was completed.

- *Percentage of payment discounts taken.* Any supplier who takes over the accounts payable function should certainly be able to process payments fast enough to take all early-payment discounts. If not, the company may be losing more money in discounts lost than it is saving by using the supplier. The easiest way to measure this item is to have the supplier generate a monthly report listing all payments made and those for which discounts were taken. An audit team can then sample the payments listed on this report to verify that all discounts were taken, as well as to verify that all payments made during the month are listed on the report. This review can verify that the reported percentage of payment discounts taken is correct.

This section described many measurements that can be used to monitor the performance of most accounting tasks that may be outsourced, including cash management, collections, financial statements, internal auditing, investments, payroll, pension administration, taxes, and transaction processing. The measurements focus on the timeliness, accuracy, and cost of each task—the same items that are of concern for an in-house accounting department. Though using all of these measurements at once would be quite a data-collection and analysis burden, a blend of some portion of the measures would be an effective means of monitoring the outsourced accounting tasks.

4.6   MANAGING THE OUTSOURCED FUNCTION

The accounting function is unique in that no functional coordinator is appointed to review the activities of suppliers. Instead, the controller and treasurer usually take on this added task. This section discusses why there in no coordinator, how outsourcing-management duties are shared between the controller and treasurer, additions to their job descriptions, and how to train them in handling supplier activities.

Outsourcing of the accounting function almost always occurs in a piecemeal fashion, with one task going to a supplier, followed by a lengthy evaluation period, followed by outsourcing another task. Rarely does an accounting function ever reach the point of being totally outsourced. Instead, a number of key functions, such as cost accounting and financial analysis, are always kept in-house. This means that a controller must also be kept to manage the remaining functions. Since the controller is quite knowledgeable in the duties of the suppliers for those functions that have been outsourced, this means that this person almost always takes the place of a functional coordinator. Also, since some of the "accounting" tasks noted in this chapter, such as cash management and pension management, are actually treasury functions, this same logic applies to the treasurer, who is expected to manage the suppliers of all treasury functions. Even with many treasury functions outsourced, there is still a need for a treasurer, since in-house personnel should still be involved in the equity-planning and debt-management tasks. The reporting relationship between suppliers and the controller and treasurer is shown in Figure 4.1.

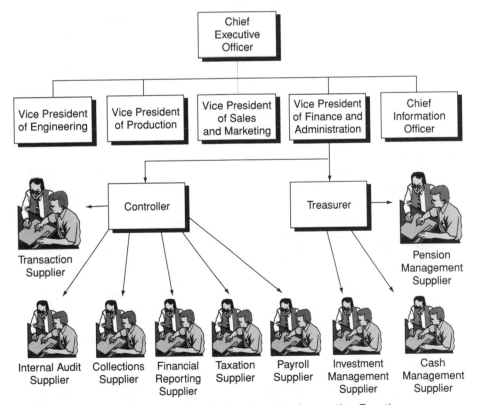

Figure 4.1   Organization Chart for Outsourcing the Accounting Function

If a company is small enough not to need a treasurer, the above reporting structure would be consolidated to have all suppliers for both the treasury and accounting functions report to the controller, with no treasurer present. An extremely small company also might not have a vice president of finance and administration, so the controller may report straight to the chief executive officer. A final variation on the reporting relationship is that, in some companies, pension management is not controlled by either the treasurer or the controller—instead, the human resources department is responsible for it. This is fine, as long as a knowledgeable human resources coordinator can properly manage the supplier. In short, the controller and treasurer should manage the suppliers of any accounting tasks that are outsourced, with some variations based on the size and structure of the company.

The job descriptions of the controller and treasurer must be altered to reflect their management of suppliers. In the example shown in Figure 4.2, the additional tasks for both the controller and treasurer are listed under the controller's job description, on the assumption that the company is small enough to merge both functions into the supervision of the controller. The responsibilities are similar to those for a department where all of the functions are kept in-house, except that there is a greater need to review the work products of the more important functional areas, such as financial statements, tax returns, and internal audits.

If the controller and treasurer are not accustomed to dealing with suppliers who have taken over outsourced functions, the company has several options to remedy the problem. One is to send these managers to training classes that will educate them in the basic techniques of selecting suppliers, negotiating with them, and monitoring their work. Another option is to have a consultant or an in-house expert train them or

Figure 4.2   The Outsourcing Portion of the Controller's Job Description

Employee Title: Controller
Reports to: Vice President of Finance and Administration
Responsibilities:

- Sign off on all agreements with the various accounting suppliers.
- Authorize the release of funds for payment to suppliers.
- Compare actual costs charged to costs listed in contracts to determine the causes of variances; follow up on these variances with suppliers.
- Measure service levels for all accounting areas and resolve any problems.
- Authorize the movement of cash between accounts.
- Approve the transfer of large accounts receivable to collection agencies.
- Review and approve supplier-generated financial statements.
- Review and approve supplier-generated tax returns.
- Approve the annual internal audit program, and review the findings of completed reviews.
- Approve investment criteria.
- Manage the transfer of functions from the company to suppliers.
- Manage any tasks within the accounting function that have been kept in-house.

at least be available to them for advice. Either option is acceptable, as long as these managers have access to the information they need to manage supplier activities.

Some functional coordinators, especially in the areas of engineering and computer services, require large support staffs. However, the accounting function, even when largely outsourced, requires less in-house support staff. The reason is that other functions are so diverse that the functional coordinator cannot be expected to have the technical knowledge to closely monitor every aspect of the function, whereas there are degree and certification programs in the accounting and finance areas that give controllers and treasurers an adequate knowledge of all tasks within the accounting and finance area. However, there will still be a need for financial analysts who can support the controller and treasurer in monitoring the activities of the various suppliers. If the company is a large one, there may be quite a few analysts on the company's payroll. Consequently, though controllers and treasurers who manage outsourced functions may have the usual need for analysts to help monitor suppliers, their need for technical specialists to explain the more abstruse topics is much reduced.

To summarize, the management of accounting suppliers typically falls on the controller and treasurer, rather than a functional coordinator, as is common with other functions. These managers supervise both the suppliers and all remaining in-house accounting activities. They can be trained to take on this additional role, or experts can be made available for consultation on key items. Finally, a core team of analysts is needed to support the controller and treasurer in managing the suppliers, but technical experts who supply information about the more complex topics are usually not needed.

4.7   POTENTIAL CUSTOMER SERVICE ISSUES

There are several customer service issues that may arise if accounting tasks are outsourced to suppliers who do not do a good job of performing the functions given to them. These issues can cover both internal and external customers.

One of the primary customer service problems is when customers are not correctly invoiced. This does not just irritate the customer's accounts payable staff, but also whomever is approving the invoice at the customer. This may be a manager who purchases large amounts of product from the company, and who will not do so if the invoicing is incorrect. Incorrect invoicing can take several forms—inaccurate prices, incorrect taxes, late billings, missing purchase order numbers, wrong bill-to addresses, or (worst of all) invoicing when the customer has already paid in advance. Any of these problems, especially if they appear on multiple invoices, can be grounds for pulling business from a company.

Another accounting problem that many customers consider to be serious is in the area of collections. Payments received must be correctly applied to accounts receivable balances, or else the company will assume that a customer is not paying its bills on time. This will result in collections activity that should not take place, since the customer has already paid for the invoice and will resent any collections calls. This matter will be worsened if the collections are done by an aggressive collections agency that hounds the customer. An overly aggressive collections person is one of the surest ways to permanently lose a customer's business. To avoid this problem, cash-application efforts must be reviewed from time to time to ensure that cash is being applied correctly, while collection agents should be fired if there are too many customer complaints about their actions. Thus, improper attention to how customer payments are posted and overly aggressive collection efforts can alienate customers.

If the customer is defined as the investment community, then the accounting department can also cause problems with this group of people by issuing inaccurate financial statements, or issuing them very late. The best way to avoid this problem is constant monitoring of the timing of financial statement releases by the supplier, as well as periodic audits of the accuracy of the statements.

If the customer is defined as the company employee, then payroll and pension management can be problem areas, since they impact all employees. Problems in this area can include incorrect pay rates, inaccurate vacation accruals, posting of investments to the wrong investment accounts, and late issuance of paychecks. Continuing problems in this area are typically dealt with by replacing the supplier. This usually happens quickly, since employees will not tolerate continuing problems with how they are paid.

The primary customer service areas within the accounting function are accounts receivable cash application, collections, financial statements, payroll, and pension administration. The best way to monitor the effectiveness of a supplier's performance in any of these areas is to have the internal audit staff regularly conduct a review. If there continue to be problems no matter how many suppliers are used, the company can always bring the function back in-house so that it can keep a close eye on them. However, many of the problems with suppliers can be fixed, given enough time, resulting in better customer service. For example, payroll problems are usually caused by a poor setup when the function was first passed to the supplier. By correcting pay rates and deduction information, payroll errors will disappear over time. Also, if suppliers know that an internal audit team will be checking on their performance from time to time, they will usually improve their customer service. In short, customer service problem areas can be monitored and brought back in-house if problems persist.

4.8   GETTING OUT OF THE OUTSOURCING ARRANGEMENT

With a few exceptions, a company can remove itself from an accounting outsourcing arrangement quite easily, since there are minimal supplier investments involved and the transfer of staff and fixed assets is minimal. This section points out the areas where this is not so easy, as well as the issues to deal with when this is the case.

One of the more difficult tasks to take away from a supplier is pension management. This is because it is costly for the supplier to enroll employees in investment funds and to set them up in their computerized asset-tracking systems. If the company pulls its business away from the supplier after a short time, the supplier will probably not earn any profit at all, since it earns its profit after start-up costs have been covered by a number of periodic maintenance payments. It may take much more than a year before profits begin to flow in for the pension supplier. Thus, in this case, suppliers like to charge per-person and lump-sum exit fees to keep a customer from pulling out, and also to recoup their costs if companies pull out despite the exit fees.

If a company wants to pull its business away from a collections agency, it is customary to let the agency finish collections work on any accounts receivable that the company has already given to it. This prevents the collections agency from complaining that the company is trying to avoid paying collection fees on any accounts receivable that the collections agency was on the verge of receiving. If the company feels that the collections agency must stop all collections work on behalf of the company at once, then an alternative is to pay the agency a negotiated fee in exchange for handing back any accounts receivable that it has not yet collected. This fee should be included in the initial contract with the collections agency—this avoids any bickering about fees later on. Thus, terminating a collections relationship may take longer as some accounts are collected, or this period can be shortened with a lump-sum payoff.

Canceling an outsourcing contract with a payroll supplier is easy to do, but a company should think through the ramifications before going forward with this step. The main problem involves tax and pay accumulators. If a single payroll supplier accumulates all of this information for a full calendar year, then it will agree to issue W-2 forms to the company for its employees at the end of the year. However, if the supplier is taking over for only part of a year, it will either not guarantee the accuracy of the W-2 forms or—more commonly—will not agree to put out the W-2 forms at all. This means that the company must manually produce all W-2 forms at the end of the year, which can be a considerable chore if there are thousands of employees. The best way to avoid this problem is to only switch payroll suppliers at the end of the calendar year, when payroll and tax accumulations are complete and can be reported as such on employee W-2 forms.

The most difficult area to terminate is transaction processing. This is because the supplier may have hired the company's staff and purchased its computer-processing equipment, and will want to return both. If the company does not want to hire back all of the staff it sent to the supplier, it may have to negotiate payment of some portion of severance payments to them. The company will also need to pay for any equipment previously purchased from it by the supplier; if so, there should be a clause in the original contract stating the prices at which the equipment will be repurchased (presumably reduced by an appropriate amount of depreciation). The company may also need to transfer back the license to any transaction-processing software that the supplier took over. Also, all transaction information must be sent back to the company and closely reviewed to ensure that no accounts payable or receivable transactions are missed. It is clear that terminating a transaction-processing agreement will require significant management time to ensure that all personnel, hardware and software, and data are successfully transferred back to the company or to a new supplier.

Terminating the cash-management services of a bank is much more difficult than a company may initially realize. The problem is that the company has gone to some lengths to notify all of its customers regarding the correct address of the nearest bank lockbox to which they should mail in their payments. When those lockboxes are shut down as part of the termination, customers will find that their payments are being returned to them. The customers must then call the company to determine the new lockbox address. This problem reduces the speed with which cash comes to the company, and may require additional debt to tide the company over the period of lengthened cash flow. There are two ways to avoid this problem. One is to keep the lockboxes open for a substantial period of time after the company has moved its business to a new bank. This keeps payments from being sent back to customers. The other step is to contact all customers well in advance of the termination of all lockboxes, so that they know where payments should be sent. The best approach is to use both options: notify all customers of the new address while assuming that some cash will still arrive at the old lockboxes for some time to come. Thus, the largest problem with terminating a cash-management arrangement is that cash will continue to go to the old lockboxes, despite all company efforts to the contrary.

This section noted several items to consider when contemplating a termination of outsourced accounting services. Most services are easy to outsource, but there are several points to be aware of prior to doing so for pension management, transaction processing, cash management, collections, and payroll-processing services.

4.9 SUMMARY

This section described a number of issues that are of concern to the manager who wants to outsource various accounting tasks. There are many accounting tasks, such as payroll, transaction processing, and financial reporting, and there are different outsourcing problems to consider for each one. A particularly acrimonious debate has been over the need to outsource the internal auditing function—a complete listing of the many points both in favor of and against the outsourcing of this task were noted.

Issues related to contracts focused on the negotiability of prices. Other contract terms tend not to be negotiable in the accounting area, with the exception of major projects like transaction-processing outsourcing, or anything involving outside audit firms—such as taxation, financial reporting, and internal auditing. Even in these areas, the focus of negotiations tends to be only on staffing issues.

There were many transition issues, since there are a number of them for each accounting task, and there are many accounting tasks. The primary difference from the transition steps for other functional areas is that there is no need to appoint a function coordinator, since the controller and treasurer are usually retained to manage all remaining accounting and finance functions, and can manage the outsourced functions as well. Also, some tasks, such as payroll and financial reporting, are date sensitive, and must be carried out at specific times. Some tasks, such as internal auditing, require unusually large amounts of supplier training, and extra time is needed for these transitions. Finally, some transitions, such as for transaction processing, are major undertakings and should not be treated lightly—considerable planning and adequate conversion time is needed to achieve a successful transition. Thus, given the large variety of tasks to be outsourced, the controller or treasurer must carefully plan and implement each one, usually not in parallel, but one after the other, so that each task being outsourced receives the complete management attention that it deserves.

Control over the various accounting tasks is quite possible, and can be achieved through a wide variety of internal audit programs, measurements, regularly scheduled review meetings with suppliers, reward and penalty programs, and separate reporting of the costs of each supplier. The accounting function, given its highly repetitive transaction nature, is easily measured and controlled.

There are a vast array of measurements available for measuring outsourced accounting tasks. These include accuracy measures, to ensure that transactions are properly completed by suppliers. Other measurements cover the timing of transactions, since some—such as payroll, tax returns, and accounts payable—must be completed on time. Still other measurements focus on the cost of each supplier, especially the cost per transaction. When these measures are prudently chosen and carefully tracked, they form an effective means for determining how well a supplier is carrying out its task.

Management of outsourced functions is easier than for other functional areas. This is because there is a controller and treasurer on-site to supervise supplier activities. Also, these managers are usually well versed in the functions of their departments (as opposed to other functions, such as engineering or computer services, that are too specialized for one person to be conversant in all activities), so there is less need for a technical-support staff, though analysts are still needed to assist in monitoring the activities of suppliers. This is one of the least worrisome areas when management is considering outsourcing accounting tasks.

The primary accounting tasks that can impact relations with customers who are external and internal are accounts receivable cash application, collections, financial statements, payroll, and pension administration. By closely monitoring the performance of these areas, management can spot initial problems and fix them either by bringing them to the attention of the appropriate supplier or by changing suppliers.

Terminating the services of an accounting supplier is generally easy, though there are a few exceptions. Two problem areas are pension management and transaction processing, where exit fees may be charged. Another is payroll processing, where termination at any time other than at year-end will cause problems with year-end payroll tax reporting. A final area of concern is cash management, where cash payments may continue to pour into lockbox addresses that have been closed down. Careful attention to contract terms, termination timing, and the use of advance planning can avoid most of these problems.

In short, accounting outsourcing is unique because there are so many functions to outsource—no one supplier does all of them, but everyone does some of them. Tight control and carefully planned, sequential transitions by the controller and treasurer are the keys to successfully outsourcing the accounting function.

CHAPTER FIVE

Outsourcing Computer Services

Over the last two decades, computer services outsourcing has seen the largest volume of outsourcing of all functional areas, in terms of the total dollar volume of contracts signed. Some of the contracts have been immense, easily exceeding a billion dollars in value and stretching over as long as 10 years. The companies that have participated in these contracts are representative of the best and largest of the world's corporations. A sample of the more recent deals is shown in Figure 5.1, listing the name of each company and the supplier who is providing services.

A review of Figure 5.1 reveals that computer services outsourcing has spread through many industries, including software, oil refining, paper production, and brewing. Some suppliers even outsource some of their own functions to other suppliers; for example, Automated Data Processing, the payroll-processing giant, outsources some of its data-processing functions to Acxiom Corporation, while Computer Sciences Corporation (CSC) outsources the maintenance of its computers to the Amdahl Corporation. Based on recent examples, it is clear that computer services outsourcing will fit into any industry.

The lesser number of suppliers involved in these deals is instructive. The computer services outsourcing industry is rapidly consolidating, with only a few suppliers taking the bulk of the business. These include Electronic Data Systems (EDS), Integrated Systems Solutions Corp. (a division of IBM), Andersen Consulting, and CSC. Together, these companies owned more than 80% of the market in 1990. Though the profitability of this area is drawing many new competitors, these few suppliers are continuing to dominate the industry.

There are a number of functional areas within the computer services umbrella that can be outsourced. One of these functions is data center management, in which the supplier frequently transfers all of a company's mainframe-based applications to a large, centralized facility that it operates for a number of companies, and processes all of the company's software applications from that location. Another function is management of a company's voice and data networks, which requires that the supplier have a staff on-site to fix and upgrade these networks, while also maintaining

Figure 5.1 The Names of Participants in Recent Computer Services Outsourcing Deals

Company Name	Supplier Name
Bank of America	ISSC
J. P. Morgan	CSC
LTV Corp.	Andersen
National Steel Corp.	SHL Systemhouse Inc.
Guinness Brewing	CSC
Continental Airlines	EDS
Western Union	EDS
Rank Xerox Hong Kong	EDS
Owens-Corning	Hewlett-Packard
Eastman Kodak	ISSC
Goodyear Tire & Rubber Co.	ISSC
IRS	Dynamics Research Corp.
Mutual of New York Life Insurance	CSC
TRW Steering Systems Ltd.	SHL Systemhouse, Inc.
Rolls-Royce Aerospace Group	EDS
Microsoft	Entex Information Services
Cathay Pacific	Unisys
Campbell Soup	ISSC
Texaco	ISSC
James River Corp.	ISSC

ISSC = Integrated Systems Solutions Corp.
CSC = Computer Sciences Corp.

on-line diagnostics from a remote location to determine how to fix network problems. Another area is the help desk, in which a supplier maintains an off-site staff that answers the queries of company employees regarding problems with their software (either packaged or developed in-house). Another function is maintenance of desktop computers, which requires a skilled team of on-site technicians. Yet another function is legacy system maintenance, in which a supplier is brought in to ensure that a long-term, custom-developed software application that the company depends on continues to operate properly. Finally, there is the applications-development function, in which suppliers have teams of systems analysts and programmers develop new software for a company. A company can either outsource all of these functions or just a few, depending on its needs or concerns regarding moving key functions to a supplier.

This chapter covers the advantages and disadvantages of outsourcing the computer services function, as well as specific contract clauses that relate to computer services. In addition, there are a number of control points to implement, measurements to take, and modifications to a company's organizational structure to ensure that the outsourcing arrangement will work. All of these topics are also covered. Finally, various customer service issues are noted, as well as several points to consider in case the company needs to get out of the outsourcing contract. This chapter is intended to give the reader a solid foundation of knowledge about how to outsource the computer services function.

5.1   ADVANTAGES AND DISADVANTAGES

There are a multitude of reasons why a company should consider outsourcing all or part of its computer services functions. The functions more commonly outsourced are data center and network management, as well as the help desk, while such areas as legacy system maintenance and applications development tend to be retained in-house. Some of the reasons in favor of outsourcing, as discussed below, include reduced capital expenditures, better supplier management and staffing, data center cost reductions, and upgrade management. However, these advantages must be weighed against such problems as possibly losing quality programmers, the potentially higher cost of applications development, and the non-transferability of software licenses to the supplier. All of these considerations and more are noted in this section.

A particularly tempting reason for switching to outsourcing is the reduced need for large capital expenditures for computers—this is especially important for cash-strapped companies. In outsourcing, not only does the supplier purchase and maintain all of the data center computing power, it needs to maintain services to the company, but it may also purchase all of the company's data center computers for up-front cash. The supplier may even be able to consolidate all of a company's data centers (assuming that there are more than one) into one supplier-managed facility, thereby eliminating a large capital investment. This can be a boon for those companies that cannot afford to keep up with the latest and most expensive technology, and who would rather spend their capital funds on functions other than computer services. Reduced capital expenditures attracts many companies to outsourcing.

Another reason for adopting outsourcing is that computer services is one of the most difficult functions to manage. Many companies make the mistake of promoting programmers into management positions that they are not capable of handling. Alternatively, companies may have trouble finding any managers who are capable of competently running the most advanced computer shops. This results in poor efficiency by the computer services staff, inadequate planning, and cost overruns. One way to avoid this problem is to outsource a company's entire computer services function to a supplier solely to make use of its better management team.

If a company has good management for its computer services function, it may have the reverse problem of having supporting staff with an incorrect or outmoded skill set. This is particularly common for those companies that have been in existence for a long time, whose computer services staffs are trained in old technologies, and who may be unwilling to retrain in the latest technologies. By using a supplier, a company with this kind of staff can draw from a much larger pool of personnel who have a much larger skill set, more experience (since they move around among a number of client sites), and better training. Outsourcing to take advantage of the supplier's staff is one of the more common reasons for outsourcing the computer services function.

If a company wants to keep its existing computer services management and staff, but wants to move to a new computing platform, it can use outsourcing to achieve this goal. It can bring in a supplier with enough expertise to transition the company to the new platform, which the company then takes over from the supplier. This process may involve having the supplier take over maintenance of the existing platform while the in-house staff works on the transition to the new platform, or the reverse may occur—the supplier works on the transition while the in-house staff maintains the existing systems, and then trains the in-house staff to take over the new systems. This approach has the advantage of only relying on a supplier for a year or two (or longer, for large system installations). Transitional outsourcing is a viable way to use a supplier to move from one computing platform to another, while ultimately keeping the work in-house.

Some company managers try to strip their organizational functions down to the bare minimum so that they can spend more time concentrating on the most strategically valuable corporate functions. For these managers, there are several functions within the overall computer services function that are not strategic, and can be safely moved to suppliers without the company suffering any loss in its strategic position. These functions are running the data-processing center, managing the voice and data networks, and managing the help desk. Of course, they must be appropriately managed so that services are provided to the company, but it is better for the company to concentrate on maintaining its legacy software systems and developing new applications that will provide a strategic advantage both now and in the future. Using this reasoning, several computer services functions should be moved to suppliers so that company management can concentrate on more strategically valuable functions.

Another advantage is that a company can reduce its data center costs by moving this function to a supplier. A number of studies have shown that a supplier does have lower costs in this one area of computer services, and therefore is able to pass along some of its cost savings to a company. For example, a study by Nolan, Norton & Co. has found that large data centers can run the comparable workload of a small data center for about 20 cents on the dollar. The reason why data centers are cheaper to operate for a supplier is that it can gather a large number of mainframe computers into one location, thereby reducing overhead costs considerably, and run all of the programming needs of a number of companies through this one set of computers, which leads to very high (and cheap) levels of computer utilization. Thus, data center operations are cheaper to outsource than to keep in-house, especially when the data center is quite small and has a large amount of administrative overhead or underutilized computer processing capacity.

A company can also move its computing costs from being largely fixed to largely variable. A typical computer installation requires a large fixed-cost investment in computers, along with salaries for supporting personnel—there are almost no variable costs at all. This is a major disadvantage if the company's transaction volume is declining, since it must still make all of the same expenditures irrespective of the volume of transactions that the computer services function is processing. This situation can be resolved by moving the function to a supplier who only charges the company for the services used. For example, a supplier can charge a company based on the millions of instructions per second (MIPS) that it uses in the supplier's data center computers—if the company's transaction volume declines, so too will its billing from the supplier. Also, if the company chooses to pare its application development activity, it will be charged less by the supplier while also not having to worry about laying off any programmers. Thus, shifting the computer services function to a supplier converts more of a company's costs to variable costs, which allows it to reduce costs as transaction volumes fall.

Another advantage of outsourcing is that the company can save on the space previously used by its in-house application-development programmers. When a supplier takes over these staff, it typically moves them to its own facility. The programmers will still need to meet with company personnel from time to time to go over programming requirements, but there is no need for them to be permanently on-site. Also, the argument that they must be close to the company's computer systems to write programs is no longer valid if the supplier also takes over data center management and moves the computer systems to a new location. This argument also applies to the help desk staff, which performs much of its support work over the phone and can therefore be located anywhere, not just at the company location. This extra space can be leased out to another company, sold off, or used for expansion by other functions. In short, extra floor space should become available as a result of moving some computer services applications to a supplier.

Using a supplier for applications development can be a good idea if a company is bogged down in a development process and needs a way to jump-start the process. A supplier can do this if it has a highly trained staff of programmers and systems analysts, plus better development tools and methodologies than the company. Once a supplier has been brought in to jump-start a development process, this also creates pressure on the in-house development staff, who may respond by either quitting, increasing their efforts, or trying to sabotage the efforts of the supplier's team. The supplier's motivation will be to show up the in-house staff so thoroughly that company management will later decide to permanently outsource the entire function to the supplier. These conflicting motivations will cause some difficulties between the in-house and supplier staffs, and may be a problem for company management to deal with. A supplier can be asked to bring in an applications-development team to jump-start a slow in-house development effort, though this can create personal problems between the two teams.

An administrative problem for a company is tracking when software upgrades should be started and the rollout of those upgrades throughout the company's computer systems. This can be quite a chore for the upgrade of software that is resident on perhaps as many as several thousand desktop personal computers! It is much easier to hand over the task to a supplier who can procure and install these upgrades. Since software licensing and upgrades can hardly be considered a strategically important area for any company, this is an obvious chore to give to a supplier to handle.

One functional area with both advantages and disadvantages to outsourcing is the help desk. It is useful to give this function to a supplier if the supplier has better text search engines or expert systems (e.g., case-based reasoning, decision trees, or neural nets) for finding answers in a text database. Another reason is if the supplier has a more experienced staff, which is especially useful if the company has no help desk at all or one with such junior staff that they can answer only the most basic questions. Alternatively, a company may be staffing its help desk with such senior staff that this is an inappropriate use of their time, which could be better spent on advanced applications-development projects. Another advantage is that many companies have their help desks spread throughout the company—essentially, a few experts whom everyone knows will help them. A supplier can centralize this function and store all problems in a single database, which allows management to see patterns in the problems being fixed, and in turn allows management to anticipate the volume of some types of problems that are likely to arise. It is also good to outsource the help desk if a company only has a small number of specialized applications for which it is not cost effective to maintain an in-house expert. A final reason for using a supplier to man the help desk is that some suppliers are open to calls around the clock; this is most useful for companies with a wide geographic dispersion that covers many time zones. This allows any employee, anywhere in the world, to call and have a problem resolved. However, this multitude of advantages must be balanced against several disadvantages. One is that the company must educate its employees about how to contact the help desk supplier. Another issue is that the help desk is the first line of customer satisfaction with the computer services function—if a supplier does a poor job of dealing with employee problems, the issue may filter up to top management, who may reorganize the function (e.g., fire managers and staff) so that employee needs are met. It is also possible that the supplier will not do a good job of tracking open problems. These are problems that could be resolved during the initial phone call, and which the help desk must research to find an answer. If employees do not receive callbacks on these items, they will be intensely dissatisfied. Finally, company management may not have access to the problem database, meaning that it will not have access to data that would have told it about various computer system problems and how to head them off. In summary, there are many good reasons for outsourcing the help desk, but management must ensure that any supplier of this function will provide top-notch service to company employees while also giving management access to its problem database.

One of the primary risks of outsourcing the applications-development function is that the company may lose its best programmers. Top-notch programmers are attracted to the applications-development function, since this is where they can work with the latest technology while also avoiding the more dreary software-maintenance tasks. If this function is outsourced, these top-of-the-line programmers may leave for a number of reasons. One is that they feel insecure in moving to the supplier, especially if it has a reputation for poor treatment of employees. Another reason is that software search firms, who are always contacting software developers with competing offers, realize that this is a prime time to contact the programmers, who are going through a period of great uncertainty, and who will therefore be more likely to consider competing offers. Finally, programmers may be moved by the supplier to other client sites, so that the company loses the services of the programmers even if they have been successfully moved to the supplier. This last item can be prevented by contract terms stipulating that no transferred staff will be moved elsewhere by the supplier for a specified period of time; however, the first two items cannot be prevented by a contract, so there is a real danger to the company that it will lose some programmers during a switch to outsourcing.

Some companies may have developed customized programs that they consider to be so valuable that it would be risky from a competitive perspective to put them in the hands of a supplier. This is because the supplier may copy portions of the code into programs it is developing for other companies, some of whom may be competitors of the company. This is generally not a valid concern, since competitors could also obtain this code simply by hiring away a few key programmers from the company. It is also possible for competitors to develop similar applications on their own by reverse engineering, which is done by determining what the program is supposed to do and then writing an application from scratch that performs those functions. The company can restrict a supplier from using its program code by including this restriction in the contract with the supplier. Whether it is a valid concern or not, some companies refuse to outsource their data center operations or applications-development functions in the interest of keeping their most important custom programs "under lock and key."

A concern for many companies is that they may have trouble transferring their software licenses to a supplier. Software providers do not like to transfer large numbers of their software packages to a smaller number of suppliers, because the suppliers take advantage of the larger number of users to force the software providers to charge lower per-person license fees. This reduces the overall revenue of the software providers. As a result, there have been a number of lawsuits recently in which suppliers have accused the software providers of not allowing licenses to be transferred to them, while the software providers have accused the suppliers of forcing them to drop licensing fees. This issue has not yet been completely resolved in the courts. In the meantime, it is useful for a company contemplating outsourcing to review its software agreements to see if the software provider has stipulated that extra fees will be paid if the license to use its software is transferred to a third party. If these fees are present, they may be excessive enough to prevent the company from taking advantage of the (otherwise) lower costs of outsourcing.

Another concern in the applications-development area is that the supplier will charge the company more on a per-hour basis for its programmers to develop new applications than it would cost the company to do so itself. This is a valid concern. The cost of an internal development group only includes the salaries and benefits of the programmers, while the cost of a supplier's development group also includes the supplier's profit, which can be a considerable increase. For example, an internal development group may cost $40 per hour per person, whereas a supplier's programmer may be charged out at $75 per hour or more, while senior managers are charged out at more than (sometimes *much* more than) $200 per hour. The best reasons for using a supplier in this area, despite the added cost, are that the supplier has a much better programming staff who can deliver higher-quality work, or that the in-house staff has not proven that it can reliably issue a good work product on schedule. In short, companies usually only incur the added expense of using a supplier's programmers if they cannot get the work done internally.

Many companies are not willing to outsource their legacy systems. This is because a company may spend years developing the systems with its own staff, who are more knowledgeable in the system operations than anyone. Management's reasoning in this case is that bringing in new staff to manage the systems will be less efficient, since the new staff has nowhere near the experience with maintaining the software. This is a valid argument, especially if the existing staff has done a poor job of documenting the systems (which is usually the case—documentation ranks as a low priority with most programming teams). Thus, in some cases, a valid argument can be made for keeping all legacy systems in-house.

Another problem that keeps some companies from considering using a supplier is the sales-oriented nature of the supplier. A supplier's staff is trained to look for additional work opportunities at any company where they are working, and their ability to both find these issues and sell the company on having the supplier fix them are large factors in promotions and pay raises. Thus, there is a valid concern by company managers that a supplier will expand beyond the function that it was originally given into other functions, gradually taking over the entire computer services function. This is a valid concern, but a supplier can only do this if it can prove to a company's senior management that it can do a better job than the internal staff. If the company's in-house staff is doing its job properly, the chance of having any supplier encroachment is greatly reduced; if not, the supplier may find a way to take over more of the computer services function than it was originally assigned.

It is also possible that a supplier's response levels will not be as good as the in-house staff was able to provide to the company. These response levels can involve fixing networks that are down, getting required reports back to company employees on a timely basis, assuring adequate computer uptime, or developing new applications by the specified due dates. The best way to solve this problem is to specify in each supplier's contract that the key response levels will be measured, and that each supplier will be penalized if the response levels are not met. If suppliers still cannot match the required response levels, the company should replace them. However, it is possible that the company was used to extremely high response levels that were achieved only by expending excessive sums on large internal staffs; if so, it is possible that no supplier will be able to match the response levels of the in-house staff unless they greatly increase their prices to the company. In these cases, the company should either keep its function in-house and get used to paying a lot for high service levels, or reduce its expectations in order to take advantage of the lower prices of suppliers. Thus, services levels may drop when outsourcing occurs, but this can be monitored and corrected with penalties or by shifting the work to other suppliers.

A final point to consider for the senior manager who is afraid of outsourcing a company's entire computer services function is that there are many clearly defined tasks within the computer services function, and some of these tasks can be outsourced while others can be kept in-house. This allows the manager to "cherry pick" the function and keep in-house those tasks for which there is some concern about the ability of the supplier to perform with better efficiency or effectiveness. Then, if outsourcing works for the limited number of functions that were given to a supplier, the cautious manager can then give one more task to a supplier and see how that works. It is also not necessary to give all of the computer services function to one supplier. Instead, the manager can also cherry pick the suppliers—for example, giving the voice and data network management task to one supplier, while data center operations go to another and the help desk to yet another. By taking this approach of gradually farming out computer services tasks to a select group of suppliers, a cautious manager can gain some comfort with the outsourcing concept while retaining those tasks for which some of the previously described disadvantages have proven to be overriding concerns.

In summary, there are many reasons for moving at least some portions of the computer services function to a supplier. Data center operations can be moved because of lower costs, while other functions—such as network management and the help desk—can be transferred because of their low strategic value. Other functions, such as legacy systems management and applications development, are more infrequently transferred to suppliers, but can be outsourced to take advantage of a supplier's superior management or staff. Against these reasons must be balanced the possibility of losing quality programmers during the transition to the supplier, as well as risking the spread of knowledge about classified information to competitors. However, despite these problems, it is reasonable for most companies to outsource at least a portion of their computer services functions.

5.2   CONTRACT-SPECIFIC ISSUES

There are several contract clauses that are unique to a computer services outsourcing situation. These clauses need to cover computer uptime, the definition of computer maintenance, termination based on changes in technology, upgrade payments, and a number of other issues that are not unique to computer services, but which must be included in a computer services contract. These issues are discussed in this section.

Part of the legal agreement may need to address the issue of computer uptime. This would apply primarily to a data-processing center, though it could also be used for the uptime for networks or telephone systems. The clause can be written as either a "carrot" or a "stick" approach. A "carrot" clause would reward the supplier for an average uptime that exceeds a base level, while a "stick" approach would penalize the supplier if the average uptime goal was not met. The two approaches can also be combined. In addition, the company may want 100% uptime during regular business hours, so the contract could state that 100% uptime is required during the hours of 7 A.M. to 6 P.M., Eastern Standard Time. A lesser uptime percentage could be written into the contract for hours outside of the company's regular business hours. Of course, if one data center is servicing the needs of a company that has facilities in multiple time zones, the time period that is considered outside of regular business hours will be quite small. For example, this is a very important issue for airline reservation systems, which cannot afford to be down for even a few moments. If computer uptime is of overriding importance to the company, it can even specify the amount of redundant data-processing equipment that will be used by the supplier, and the details of how a disaster-recovery system shall be maintained. However, most contracts will merely specify the desired uptime performance criteria and let the supplier figure out how it will meet those goals. In short, many companies will find it desirable to include uptime objectives in the contract, along with associated penalties and rewards.

One of the chief issues of contention in the computer services area is how maintenance is defined, as opposed to new systems development. "Maintenance" services are typically part of the lowest-cost baseline services, whereas application-development services are usually the most expensive. Based on this pricing structure, the supplier will want to call everything application development, while the company will want to call it maintenance. It is useful to define maintenance in advance to avoid these problems. Activities that are normally considered to be maintenance are any form of error correction, installing any new software releases and updates, complying with any new regulatory requirements, and a variety of small enhancements. A "small enhancement" should be carefully defined, since this will otherwise cause arguments. For example, it can include report format changes or any programming requiring less than two hours of work. Alternatively, the contract can specify a monthly budget of time for maintenance activities without specifying the activities that go into it— once the budget amount is exceeded, all other activities, irrespective of what they really are, can be charged at a higher rate as application-development work. It is in the interests of the company to avoid the monthly maintenance budget, since maintenance may be quite large in some months—exceeding the maintenance budget will allow the supplier to charge much higher prices for maintenance services during these months. If the maintenance budget approach is accepted, the company should at least negotiate for a very large monthly budget. The contract should carefully define maintenance activities, and how they are to be paid for.

If part of the contract includes giving control of the company's data-processing center to the supplier, then it is critical that the contract include a clause covering disaster-recovery planning. This clause is necessary so that the supplier is forced to provide safety and redundant systems that are capable of either keeping the company's computer applications running at all times or of bringing the systems back up after a minimum period of downtime. Terms related to the safety of current systems can include the presence of an inert gas fire suppression system at the supplier's data-processing center, or even the absence of a water-based fire suppression system (which will ruin the computer equipment just as thoroughly as a fire). The most important terms on this topic should require the presence of either on-site or separate redundant computer systems with mirrored data storage. These backup systems should be capable of keeping the company's processing operational even if the primary computer systems crash. It is preferable to require a physically separate computer location, in case a natural disaster such as an earthquake destroys the primary computer facility. Also, the contract should specify the amount of time allowed for the supplier to bring up operations at the secondary facility—this can be fractions of a second for critical applications, or more than a day for less critical applications. All computer services contracts covering the outsourcing of data-processing services should require the presence of backup computer facilities.

A contract clause should allow the company to terminate the outsourcing relationship based on a change in technology. This is particularly important in the computer services area, where a supplier may be brought in to handle a very specific type of technology. If the company decides that it must jump to a new type of computer technology, the supplier may not have the skill to install or maintain it, and therefore must go. Examples of technology shifts are from cable to fiber optic voice and data networks, and from mainframe computers to client/server arrangements. Being able to terminate an outsourcing contract based on changes in technology is a mandatory part of a computer services contract.

There will almost certainly be technology upgrades during the life of an outsourcing contract, given the speed of technological change today. If so, who pays for the upgrades? It is reasonable for the company to pay for upgrades as a separate part of its billing from the supplier, since it allows the company to isolate and investigate the reasonableness of this cost. Alternatively, the supplier can include the cost in its standard baseline fee, and simply spread the cost over a large number of payments. The problem with this second approach is that the company does not know the cost of the upgrades. Thus, a separate billing for upgrades is desirable.

Transferring a company's computer staff to a supplier is a common part of any computer services outsourcing arrangement. If this has occurred and the company wants to terminate the outsourcing relationship, there should be a severance payment clause in the contract. This clause states that the company will fund the severance payments of those former company employees whom the supplier must lay off as a result of the early termination of the agreement. This is a reasonable clause to agree to, since the employees should be taken care of. However, the clause should specify exactly how much money is to be paid out in advance, so that the company can put a cap on its costs. Also, the company can demand a gradual reduction in the proportion of the severance that it pays for each year that the former employee has been located at the supplier. For example, a gradual reduction in its share of the payments over five years is quite reasonable, with many companies negotiating a much quicker reduction on the grounds that former employees will be transferred to other supplier clients within a few years anyway. It is reasonable for the company to pay some share of the severance payments for former employees who were transferred to a supplier if the agreement is shut down early by the company.

The company will want some control over the transfer of its former employees by the supplier to other clients of the supplier. This is a common occurrence, whereby the supplier moves the best staff to other clients, leaving a much lower level of staff person to service the needs of the company. This can be prevented, at least in the short term, by including a clause in the contract that either prohibits the transfer of former employees to other clients for a specific time period, or at least requires the permission of the company before this transfer may be allowed.

A computer services contract term frequently lasts for as long as 10 years. During this interval, there may be ownership changes at the supplier or the company, such as a merger or an outright purchase. To avoid the service problems that may arise as a result of these changes, the contract should include a clause to renegotiate the entire contract in the event of a change in the ownership of the supplier or of the company. This clause protects both parties, for the owners of either one may not be interested in pursuing outsourcing once a merger has been completed. Also, without this contract clause, a long-term outsourcing agreement with mandatory (and large) periodic payments may even drive away potential buyers of the company. Thus, a long-term contract should include a clause that allows either party to dissolve the agreement in the event of a change in corporate ownership.

A related issue is a merger by the company with the company being the surviving entity. The supplier may have some interest in requiring the company to use its services for outsourcing the computer services function at any acquired companies. This constitutes a cheap sale for the supplier, who automatically receives the business of all acquired companies. The company should retain the ability to not outsource for each of these acquired subsidiaries, so it is best to avoid this contract clause. However, if the supplier is adamant about including it in the contract, the company can at least include contract language that requires a reduction in the supplier's fees based on the increased volume of services being purchased from the supplier as a result of an acquisition. Giving the outsourcing business of an acquired company to a current supplier provides the supplier more business while giving the company the opportunity to reduce its per-transaction outsourcing costs.

If the supplier is to take over the applications-development part of a company's computer services function, the contract should cover any joint marketing of resulting programs or services that may have market value, as well as the restriction of these products from sale to competitors. First, the contract should specify who has ownership of any programs, either the supplier or the company. A case can be made in either direction, since the supplier's staff did the programming and the company paid for the programming. Irrespective of ownership, the contract should also note the profit split if any programs are to be marketed to other companies, and who is to pay for the marketing costs (usually the supplier, who does the distribution). The company may opt for a deal whereby it pays the supplier lower prices up front for the initial development of the product, while the supplier takes a larger share of any profits from the sale of the resulting programs. Also, the company should have the right to restrict programs from sale to companies within its industry, or to reject sales efforts to selected companies by the supplier. An advanced example of such a relationship is that of the Big Five firm of Ernst & Young LLP and Farmland, two companies that have formed a joint venture called OneSystem Group LLC, which provides business process and information technology solutions to Farmland and its

Figure 5.2   Extract from a Reports Appendix to a Computer Services Contract

Report Name	Report Title	Report Description	Due Date
AC7002	Payables Due for Payment	Lists all accounts payable for which the due date is earlier than today's date	Every Monday
AC7089	New Suppliers	Lists the detailed payment terms and payment addresses of all suppliers added to the database in the last month	Last business day of the month
AC0042	Discounts Lost	Lists all accounts payable with discount dates that were not paid on time, showing the discount amount lost	Every Monday
AC0003	New Customers	Lists the credit limits and billing addresses of customers added to the database in the last month	Last business day of the month
AC9031	Overdue Receivables	Lists all overdue invoices, sorted by customer, including invoice number and invoice date	Every Monday
AC1309	Inventory Valuation	Lists total cost of all inventory in stock as of the end of the month	First business day of the month
AC8426	Inventory Audit Sample	Lists a random sample of 100 inventory items, along with their descriptions and location codes	Every Friday
AC1357	Fixed Asset Additions	Lists all fixed assets that were added to the general ledger in the last month	First business day of the month
AC3590	Sales Journal	List all invoices, debit memos, and credit memos issued during the last month	First business day of the month

member cooperatives. Both companies add capital and personnel to the joint venture, with the profits being split between the two companies. In summary, including contract terms for the ownership and marketing of new software applications should be covered if the supplier is to provide application-development services.

Pricing levels for various services can be matched to the company's need for the service. For example, desktop computer-repair services can be priced at a low level for stand-alone units or at higher prices for servers or those performing mission-critical functions. An alternative approach is to price services based on the time the supplier is allowed to get on-site and fix the problem. Thus, one set of computers that can be down for some time without any major impact on operations can cost less to repair if the company is willing to wait a few days for the repair work, while the company can pay a premium for rapid on-site support of a smaller number of computers that it cannot afford to have go down.

It is useful to attach an appendix to the contract that itemizes all hardware and software being transferred to the supplier. This is useful in case the supplier needs to know when to make annual software license payments, or if there is a dispute with the company about why software license payments were not made—if the payment due dates are clearly noted in the appendix, then it is clear that the supplier was adequately informed of the due dates. Also, an exact listing of computer hardware items and their costs is necessary if the company later decides to terminate the contract and must purchase the equipment back from the supplier. An accurate list keeps the parties from disputing what hardware was transferred or what it cost at the time of the transfer. A clear itemization of all assets shifted from the company to the supplier is a necessary part of a computer services contract.

Another appendix should itemize any production reports to be sent to the company by the supplier, provide descriptions or one-page samples of the reports, and note the dates or times when they are to be delivered. By itemizing this information in advance, there is little reason for disputes to arise regarding when the supplier was supposed to deliver reports to the company. As an example, an extract from a reports appendix is shown in Figure 5.2.

In summary, this section covered contract issues that were unique to computer services as well as issues that were not unique, but which must be included in a contract for this category of outsourcing. The first set of issues included computer uptime, the definition of computer maintenance, termination based on changes in technology, and upgrade payments. The second set of issues included severance payments to transferred staff, retention of transferred staff, issues related to changes in corporate ownership, ownership of work products, and changes in contract terms in case of a merger. These contract clauses should be included in every computer services contract.

5.3   TRANSITION ISSUES

This section notes the large number of transition steps needed to find an appropriate computer services supplier, as well as to transfer the function over to that supplier. Many of the transition steps are unique to the computer services function, such as setting up remote processing sites, obtaining approval for the transfer of software licenses, and transferring the database. The most important item to consider during this transition phase is that it takes more time to transfer than for most other functional areas. In particular, setting up off-site computer-processing locations requires a significant amount of time, especially to thoroughly test all transferred hardware and software. Since the computer services function is so critical to the company's existence, the full ration of time must be taken during the transition process to ensure that all functions are fully operational once they have been moved to the supplier. In short, do not rush it! The transition steps are listed in numerical sequence as follows:

1. *Appoint a coordinator.* The company should appoint a computer services co-ordinator as early in the outsourcing process as possible. This person will be in charge of managing the activities of all suppliers hired to take over this function, and therefore should be given the opportunity to evaluate potential suppliers and negotiate contracts with them in order to learn as much as possible about them and to work with them. Depending on the size of the computer services operations to be outsourced, the coordinator may require a large support staff—these personnel should be assigned to the coordinator as soon as possible to assist in the selection and transition process.

2. *Obtain third-party consents.* Before a company has fully locked itself into the decision to outsource, it should review all consents needed by third parties— these are the software suppliers, who must agree to transfer the company's software licenses to a computer services supplier. If the suppliers are only willing to do so for prohibitively high fees or will not transfer the licenses under any circumstances, the company needs to know this up front so that it can factor this cost into the outsourcing decision. A difficult software supplier can torpedo the outsourcing decision.

3. *Sign a confidentiality agreement.* Once a possible supplier has been selected, the supplier will want to review the company's computer services operations in detail in order to gather enough information to negotiate a final contract that will cover all aspects of the actual situation and services required. However, since confidential material may be part of that review, the supplier should sign a confidentiality agreement prior to undertaking any phases of the review.

4. *Create a skills database.* A prospective supplier will want to know what kind of staff it is inheriting, so it is important for the company to peruse all employee files and interview the computer services managers to derive a database of all relevant skills for each employee. The supplier can then use this information to determine what kinds of staff it needs to supplement the employees being transferred to it, or, depending upon the circumstances, it can pick only those employees with particular skills.

5. *Identify the lead supplier.* The company may appoint a lead supplier who is paid extra to manage the activities of other subcontractors; this is very common in those cases where the coordinator does not have a sufficient support staff to properly manage all suppliers. This identification should be complete before the supplier contract is finalized, since the added responsibility and related fees should be noted in the contract.

6. *Finalize the contract.* Once the supplier has completed its due diligence phase, it is time to negotiate the final contract with the company. The company should consider the numerous topics noted in the previous section that deal with computer services contracts. Given the great cost of some computer services outsourcing deals, it may be a worthwhile investment to bring in out-

side counsel to assist in the negotiations or to at least review the contract as it is being negotiated.

7. *Test phone lines.* This step is only necessary if the supplier is going to move the data center to an off-site location. The phone lines used to transmit data to and from the new facility should be set up and thoroughly tested as far in advance as possible. They should be tested for downtime as well as for traffic volume, and adjusted accordingly to meet the company's transmission standards. This step is also necessary for the help desk function, where the supplier may only be sent overflow calls that cannot be answered by the company within a minimum time period; alternatively, the phone system may automatically transfer all calls at once to the help desk supplier.

8. *Transfer documentation.* There is a large amount of documentation to give to the supplier. This includes program specifications and related project information for the applications-development area and an inventory of software and hardware, as well as a list of any pending repairs for desktop applications, all operating policies and procedures for the data center, and the help question and resolution database for the help desk. The company should go over this information with the supplier and have the supplier sign a receipt for all documents transferred, so that there will be no question of who has the paperwork. Also, the company should keep copies of the information in case the relationship sours and the company must move the function either back in-house or to another supplier.

9. *Train the supplier.* There will be some supplier training required, no matter what portion of the computer services function is transferred. For example, there will be maintenance training for legacy systems, a detailed review of all ongoing project information for applications development, problem-resolution training for the help desk, and repair training for desktop applications. This step must be conducted before the company lays off any staff, since the employees being let go may be the best trainers.

10. *Transfer hardware and software.* If the data center is being moved to a supplier location, some hardware and software may have to be moved. This can be a lengthy process, especially since the systems must be tested once they are restored in the new location, and all data links on phone lines must also be tested.

11. *Transfer database.* This is listed as a separate step from the transfer of hardware and software, since outsourcing some applications requires only the transfer of the database and not any hardware or other software. The best example of this is the help desk, where the database containing typical problems and how to resolve them must be sent to the supplier.

12. *Transfer staff.* One of the most critical issues is transferring the company's computer staff to the supplier. This step should be handled with proper respect

for the employees, who will be uncertain about the switch to a new employer and perhaps a new place of work. Each employee is deserving of a private meeting with representatives from the company and the supplier—one to go over termination paperwork such as pension and 401(k) benefits, while the other must cover payroll sign-up documents and paperwork for inclusion in the supplier's benefits package. Each employee should be able to take as much time as needed for thorough coverage of all paperwork and to have all questions answered.

13. *Dispose of excess space.* If some functions are moved to a supplier's off-site facility, the company may have enough excess space left to be worth subleasing or selling to another company. However, this may entail consolidating the remaining staff into a new location, which may be more costly than the savings that would result from the move. Also, some computer facilities, such as mainframe computer rooms, are so specialized that there are no alternative uses for the space; these locations may require large expenditures to modify for other uses, or the cheapest alternative may be to let them lie idle.

In summary, the previous list includes both standard transition steps that are common to most functional areas—such as appointing a functional coordinator—and a number of additional steps that are only used for the computer services function, such as installing and testing phone lines to an off-site data-processing center. The transition steps are noted in Figure 5.3. The time intervals noted in Figure 5.3 are very rough—depending on the size of the computer services function, the actual transfer times may vary considerably from those listed here. As noted previously, it is very important to allocate a large amount of time to this transition process; the computer services application is just too important to rush the transfer to the supplier, which may lead to either reduced service levels or no service at all.

5.4   CREATING CONTROL POINTS

A number of suggestions are noted in this section that are useful for maintaining control over the computer services function. A company manager should not just use one of these controls, however, and expect to know how well a supplier is running the function. Instead, a mix of several controls is necessary in most instances, since there are a wide variety of tasks within the computer services function, and a single control is not sufficient for all tasks. The exact mix of controls will vary based on the circumstances. If it appears to be expensive to implement the appropriate number of controls, one should remember that computer services outsourcing can be among the most expensive functions to outsource. Having the proper controls is well worth the price, since they will allow the company to maintain close oversight over the function and keep the supplier from spending too much money on the wrong activities. Good controls pay for themselves.

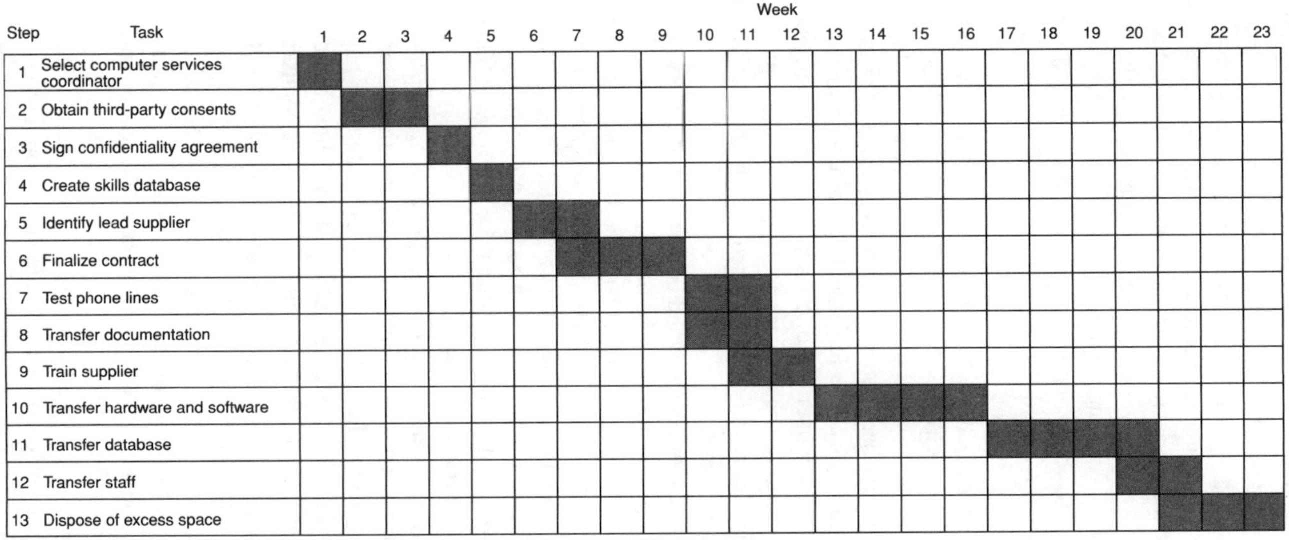

Figure 5.3 Gantt Chart for the Implementation of all Computer Services Transition Issues

119

The principal control is to assign a sufficient number of company employees to support the functional coordinator. The coordinator is responsible for the function but, except for the smallest computer services functions, cannot hope to maintain sufficient control over all activities. Additional personnel are needed to overview the activities of each supplier, of which there may be one for each task within the functional area. Experts are also needed who are well versed in each task, so that they will know if problems are arising as soon as possible; these highly knowledgeable people may be needed to review the voice and data networks, the help desk, legacy systems, applications development (perhaps one for each programming language used), and desktop computing support. No single coordinator can hope to have the vast array of knowledge required to properly oversee all of these areas, so a strong support staff is necessary.

Another control is to use a third-party benchmarking organization. This company periodically measures key activities in the computer services function and compares the results to its database of world-class measures that it has obtained from other companies. It then reports back to company management regarding how well the suppliers are doing their jobs. The functional coordinator can then demand better performance from those suppliers who are not performing well enough, hand out bonuses or penalties based on the measurements, or look into replacing laggard suppliers. A benchmarking organization can be used to audit the performance of the various computer services suppliers.

A key control is the use of penalties and bonuses based on key performance measurements. For example, a supplier can be penalized for poor data center downtime performance, but can receive a bonus if it can exceed the lowest downtime standard. Using bonuses and penalties is a good way to force suppliers to focus on what the company considers to be the most important activities or measurements. However, the company must be sure to clarify in advance how all measurements are to be calculated and who is to calculate them, so that there is no squabbling later on when penalties are imposed or bonuses awarded.

Periodic formal meetings are useful for going over supplier performance. If these meetings are not formalized with an annual list of meeting dates and places, it is likely that they will not be held—review meetings tend not to happen without this formal structure. The agenda for such a meeting should include a detailed review of all performance measurements, the resulting penalties and bonuses, a review of upcoming events, long-range planning topics, and a discussion of any complaints (which can go in both directions—the supplier may be unhappy with the company, and this is a good place to discuss those issues). The meeting minutes should be taken and signed off on by both parties. Accurate minutes are mandatory, since they can head off any arguments over what was decided during these meetings. Periodic review meetings are a useful control tool.

The company should use its internal audit team as a control point. The team can periodically compare the original contract with each supplier to the actual activities of the supplier, and also compare contract prices to the prices noted on the supplier billings. Of particular concern is ensuring that the company is not paying for extra services that it never agreed to in the contract, or is paying more than what was noted in the contract. If there is no internal audit staff, the company can periodically bring in its outside audit firm to handle these tasks. Comparing actual supplier activities and billings to the contract is useful for spotting billing problems.

In the area of applications development, the functional coordinator should keep a detailed log of all change orders, so that there will be proper control over all modifications to the original application specifications. This is important not only to ensure that all changes are made, but also to ensure that unauthorized changes are not made—a common problem is that many company employees will demand that changes be made to programs long after the specifications have been finalized, which can drastically lengthen the programming process and increase the cost of the work. Using change order tracking to control the application-development process helps to keep this work on time and within budget.

The company can also use its own staff or an outside party to compare the initial specifications for the development of an application to the final results. Outside software testing companies specialize in this, and are a good resource for the functional coordinator. If there are differences between the specifications and the final product, the coordinator can force the supplier to modify the program code to include any missing features from the application.

In summary, a company can use a large support staff for the functional coordinator to improve the level of control over its computer services suppliers, as well as reviews by auditors and third-party benchmarking organizations. Other controls are the use of penalties and bonus payments based on key performance measurements, regularly scheduled review meetings with suppliers, and change order tracking for applications-development work. A judicious mix of these controls gives a company a good idea of how well its computer services suppliers are performing.

5.5 MEASURING THE OUTSOURCED FUNCTION

This section primarily covers the tracking of supplier response time to computer problems, system downtime, and the cost of supplier services. There are quite a few more measurements in the section than this brief list would indicate, because there are many types of downtime and cost to track; in addition, there are measurements for specific activities within the umbrella of computer services, such as the help desk, applications development, and desktop computer support. Thus, there are a large number of performance measurements in this section to choose from that are useful for determining the quality of service received from a company's suppliers. The measurements are as follows:

- *Time from update release to installation.* A software company may release an update to its packaged software, but the company's computer systems may not be updated with this new software by the supplier for a long time. This results in reduced productivity by the company, since there may be workflow enhancements in the upgrades that are very useful to the company's operations. It is therefore of some importance for a supplier to update a company's software with new software releases as rapidly as possible. A company can track this by having the software supplier send notices of release dates for new software; then a staff person can determine the date when the upgrade was installed. The difference between these two dates is the time from update release to installation. However, this measurement must be used with some caution, for there may be a good reason for not installing the software on time—rumors of software bugs in the upgrade, a specific request by the company not to install the upgrade, or a diversion of resources at the company's request, so that upgrades are not a supplier priority. These reasons should be considered before confronting a supplier with poor performance in this area. The culprit may be the company.

- *Help desk average response time.* It is useful for the supplier to know how soon a help desk supplier picks up the phone (e.g., how many rings occur); this tells the company how well staffed its supplier's help desk function is, and how prompt those people are in starting problem resolution for the company's employees. This measurement can either be supplied by the supplier, or the company can periodically audit the help desk to determine response time on its own. A more important variation on the call pick-up time is the total time needed before an employee's problem is resolved. This is the better measurement, for the first measurement may only show that the supplier is good at answering the phone, not at fixing problems. Once again, the second measurement can be tracked by the supplier, or the company can perform an occasional audit to derive the information.

- *Mission-critical problem average response time.* There are some portions of the computer services function that cannot go down without impairing the ability of the company to operate, such as legacy systems and the data network. It is therefore valuable to measure the time required for suppliers to respond to these types of problems. Unfortunately, it is an imprecise measurement. A computer log will not tell a company when a supplier starts work on a problem. Instead, the company must rely on either its own personnel or the supplier to calculate the total response time. Using its own employees is not easy, since they will not see if the supplier is fixing the problem on-line. A better approach is to rely on the supplier, who can track the time from when it became aware of the problem to when it had someone working on problem resolution.

- *Mission-critical problem average time to fix.* A supplier may be very good at responding to a call to fix a computer systems problem, but how good is it at actually fixing the problem? This calls for measurement of the total time to fix the problem, starting with the time when work commenced and ending when the system once again became operational. As noted under the previous bulleted point, this is a very difficult item for the company's staff to measure, so it must rely on information collected by the supplier, which it can then use to derive an average fix time that is based on the total number of problems fixed during the month.

- *Percentage of mission-critical system downtime.* The most critical company systems are those that would stop the company from running if they were to go down for even a few minutes. Examples of these are airline, hotel, and car reservation systems. This is a primary area for uptime measurement, as opposed to measuring the uptime of all company systems, for it matters the most if mission-critical systems are down. The information needed to derive this measurement is most easily obtained from a computer log that tracks the exact times when the computer system is not available to users. The most common measurement is to summarize all instances of downtime during a month, divide this total by the total amount of time in the month, and derive a percentage of mission-critical system downtime per month.

- *Average length of downtime.* It may not be adequate information to know that a computer system was down 100 times in the previous month if the total amount of time that the computer was down was only 100 seconds—one second per system failure, which may not represent a problem for the company. On the other hand, the computer system may have only been down once in the previous month, but it was for the entire month. Therefore, it is important to determine the average length of downtime as well as how many times the system went down. When taken together, a more realistic picture emerges of a supplier's ability to keep a system operational. The average length of downtime is calculated by obtaining the computer log that notes the times of operation, and calculating from it the total time period during a month when the system is down. Then divide this number by the total number of instances when the system was down during the month to derive the average length of downtime.

- *Mean time between failures.* Another way to measure system downtime is to track the average interval of uptime between system failures. This is useful for determining if systems are failing constantly, which can severely disrupt a company's work flow. This information can be gleaned from computer logs detailing the dates and times when the system is down and when it once again becomes functional. An analyst can measure the time intervals between these system failures and divide by the total number of failures in a month to determine the mean time between failures.

- *Downtime percentage during regular working hours.* A company may not care if a supplier frequently takes down the computer system during non-business hours. If this is the case, however, it is important to define "business hours," since a single data center may be providing computer services to a company's facilities in multiple time zones. Also, a company may have multiple shifts of workers who must have on-line access to the data center. Given these restrictions, a company may find that its business hours are of much longer duration that it thinks. To calculate the uptime percentage during regular business hours, first determine what the duration of regular business hours may be. Then go to the computer log for each month and measure all instances of downtime during regular business hours. Then divide this amount by the total time taken by regular business hours during the month to derive the uptime percentage during regular business hours.

- *Network downtime.* All of the previous downtime measurements relate to the downtime for critical system applications. It is also important to consider that the mission-critical applications may be operational 100% of the time, but that the internal company network that distributes this information may be down, which does not allow anyone to access the information. The network is sometimes administered by a different supplier, so it is necessary to assign blame for company employees not being able to access key systems—is it the data center operator or the network operator? To track network downtime, there should be an activity log on the file server that distributes information through the network. This log can be reviewed each month to derive the percentage of downtime, the average length of downtime, downtime during regular working hours, and the mean time between failures.

- *Cost as a percentage of revenue.* The most general cost measurement is the total cost of all computer services as a percentage of total company revenues. This gives upper management a very general idea of the reasonableness of current expenditures based on the same measurement for previous years. There are also benchmark measurements available in some industries for the proportional cost of computer services versus revenues, which also gives management a means for comparing the company's expenditures to those of other companies in the same industry. This is easily calculated by summarizing all computer services costs for the month and dividing them by monthly revenues; these figures can also be annualized.

- *Cost per line of programming.* In the applications-development area, the company is usually charged by the supplier based on hours of work put into the programming by its staff. This does not tie the supplier to any clearly measurable work, however. A better approach is to add up the number of lines of program code that have been created since the last billing, and divide that into the total cost of the application programming since the last billing to derive the cost per line of program code. Other similar measures to consider are the cost per milestone or cost per completed program; however, these are more variable, and are therefore of less use in measuring the productivity of the supplier's programming staff.

- *Cost per network connection.* A common costing method for a voice and data network supplier is to charge a set fee for each network connection installed. This information can be tracked over time to see if the price the supplier is charging is changing over time or varying from the contract rate. This information is easily obtained from supplier billings; if the network supplier only issues a single line item for services provided, the company should work with the supplier to change the billing format into a more detailed layout that includes the cost per network connection installed.

- *Cost per help desk response.* Many help desk suppliers charge for their services based on a minimum monthly fee plus a rate per minute of time spent helping the company's employees (with the per-minute rate sometimes being subtracted from the monthly base fee). The company should track the cost per help desk response, since it tells the company what the supplier's rate per minute is, as well as the average time taken to attend to each employee's problem. The actual rate per minute can be gleaned from the supplier's billing statement, and should be compared to the contract rate as well as tracked over time to see if it changes. The average duration of calls can be determined from the supplier's billing, assuming that the billing is detailed enough, and is useful for seeing how rapidly the supplier can resolve employee issues—long average call durations are indicative of inefficient help desk staffs (though there will be very hard problems that will require long help desk calls, these should average out over a large number of service calls, so that the average call duration should not vary that much from period to period).

- *Days variance from programming milestones.* One of the key measurements for the applications-development function is tracking how close the supplier comes to previously agreed-upon programming milestones. These milestones must be mutually agreed upon with the supplier in advance, or else missing them will not have much impact on the supplier. Of particular concern is when a supplier misses successive milestones, which indicates either a lack of resources or minimal management skill. To measure this variance, extract the milestone dates from signed project workpapers and compare them to the actual dates when milestones were achieved, which should also be contained in the project workpapers.

- *Number of program bugs found subsequent to program release.* A company may want to see how good an applications-development programmer is at testing its programs for errors before releasing them to the company for general use. This can be done by either collecting comments from company employees about programming bugs or by testing the software itself to see what it can find. Since duplicate testing is not cost effective, it is generally best to rely on comments received from employees. However, this measurement must be used with caution, for the definition of a program bug is subject to some discussion—what is considered a "bug" may in fact be a program specification that the company never gave to the supplier, who therefore did not include it in the program specifications; this is not a bug, but a lack of system analysis work.

- *Average years experience of supplier personnel.* A company may be concerned that a supplier is putting its most junior staff on company work. This is a particular concern for those computer services functions that require significant expertise, such as applications development. The company can measure this item by requesting information from the supplier about each staff person assigned to company-related projects. The company can then derive the average years of experience from this information. The company can use several measurements, depending on what it feels is more important. Examples are total years of experience, total years of experience in the industry, or total years of experience with the specific application currently being used (such as experience specifically programming in the C+ language).

• *Average number of complaints by employees.* Though it is a very subjective measurement, it can be useful to track the total number of complaints received from employees regarding suppliers. There may be a basis for action if the level of complaints suddenly rises, though it may be over some very small problem that employees find irksome, but which is not of great operational importance. Complaints may be of more value, not because of the total number received, but because of the nature of each one—a single complaint may reveal the presence of a serious problem. This measurement can be tracked by keeping a written file of all complaints received, which should be summarized at least once a month and reviewed more frequently to see if a really major problem is arising that must be fixed at once.

This section covered a variety of ways to track the performance of a company's computer services suppliers. There was a heavy emphasis on the measurement of system downtime, since this is so critical to the operations of most companies. In addition, there were several measurements for determining the cost of a supplier's services—given the high cost of technical support, this is a mandatory measurement area. There were also a number of measurements for tracking the speed of problem resolution—again, given the critical nature of computer systems to a company's operations, rapid fixes are important, and therefore should be measured. There were also some miscellaneous measurements that may be used to flesh out the mix of measurements used, such as the average number of employee complaints, years experience of supplier staff, and the number of bugs found subsequent to program release. A judicious mix of some of the measurements presented in this section should give a company a good idea of how its computer services suppliers are performing.

5.6 MANAGING THE OUTSOURCED FUNCTION

The computer services function is especially difficult to manage when it has been outsourced. This is because, for all but the smallest companies, the outsourcing fees are extremely large, and poor management of suppliers can result in costs that are excessive enough to wipe out all company profits. Also, this function involves many different areas of technological expertise; one manager alone is usually not competent enough in all of these areas to do an adequate job of managing all of them. This section notes how to overcome these problems with proper management.

A computer services coordinator should be appointed as soon as a company decides to outsource this function. The coordinator is in charge of the selection of suppliers, negotiating contracts with them, handing over control of the various functions, and managing the suppliers on an ongoing basis. There are two differences between the computer services coordinator position and the coordinators used for other functional areas. One is that the computer services function involves such a wide range of technological expertise that it is mandatory, for all but the smallest companies, that the coordinator be provided with a support staff, each of whom specializes in one functional area and advises the coordinator on how to manage that area. This staff should include experts in the following areas: voice and data networking, data center operations, application development, and the help desk. An organization chart that reflects the support needed by the computer services coordinator is shown in Figure 5.4. There may be a need for several people in some of these areas, such as application development, where there is so much work being performed by the supplier that one person cannot maintain proper oversight of all activities. The second difference is that many companies do not outsource all computer services functions, so that the coordinator must adopt the dual role of managing suppliers and managing some in-house functions as well. Consequently, the computer

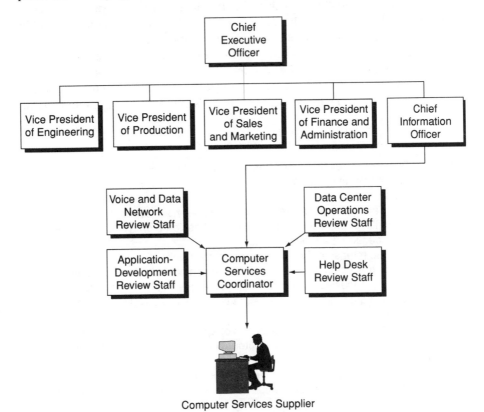

Computer Services Supplier

Figure 5.4   Organization Chart for Outsourcing the Computer Services Function

services coordinator is more likely to be the former department head in charge of this function than is the case with other functional coordinators—management of the in-house functions is considered so important that the existing manager is frequently appointed to the coordinator role. Thus, the computer services coordinator must be given proper personnel support to adequately manage the function, which may include the management of some in-house functions.

The computer services coordinator will have the same responsibilities as the vice president of any functional area. These should include negotiating and authorizing any agreements or changes to agreements with suppliers, approving new supplier projects or changes to those projects, and managing a budget. The coordinator must also monitor service levels and resolve issues as soon as they arise. These items and more are noted in Figure 5.5, which contains a more complete description of the computer services coordinator's job.

If the coordinator must manage a set of in-house functions as well as a group of suppliers, it is useful to differentiate between the costs of these two areas. This may require some changes to the chart of accounts to allow proper tracking of all costs, as well as changes to the budget to reflect the changes. If there are a number of suppliers, the coordinator may want to track costs separately for each one, which may require a further differentiation of costs within the chart of accounts. Since changes to the account code structure and budget are not taken lightly, the coordinator should consult with the corporate controller over this issue at as early a date as possible.

In a distributed environment where each functional area of a company has its own computing facilities, the computer services coordinator may have no control over these other systems. This situation was possibly caused by those functions being fed up with poor service from the in-house computer services function, resulting in the

Figure 5.5 The Computer Services Coordinator's Job Description

---

Employee Title: Computer Services Outsourcing Coordinator
Reports to: Chief Executive Officer
Responsibilities:

- Sign off on all agreements with the computer services supplier.
- Review the list of programming priorities and assign them to suppliers for development based on a ranking system.
- Authorize the release of funds for payment to suppliers.
- Compare actual costs charged to costs listed in contracts to determine the causes of variances; follow up on these variances with the supplier.
- Verify that programming milestones are being reached and work with the supplier to correct any problems.
- Authorize changes to the specifications of application-development projects.
- Measure service levels for all computer services areas and resolve any problems.
- Manage the transfer of functions from the company to suppliers.
- Manage any tasks within the computer services function that have been kept in-house.

procurement of their own systems. Any intrusion by the functional coordinator seeking to turn these separate systems over to a supplier will probably be greeted with the corporate equivalent of nuclear warfare—the various department heads have gone to some trouble to take control over the computer services provided to their departments, and they will not look warmly on any attempt by the coordinator to take those systems away from them. Though top management could order these departments to hand over their computer systems to the coordinator for outsourcing, this will not create an environment of trust for the coordinator. Thus, it is better to leave these separate computer systems alone and wait for the rumor of good supplier service to spread through the company before making periodic polite requests to have the systems turned over to suppliers. This is not the most practical solution, but it recognizes the reality of the political climate within most companies.

In summary, any outsourced computer services function will need the management help of not only a coordinator with all the authorities and responsibilities of a vice president, but also a support staff that is well versed in the functions and technologies used by suppliers. The coordinator may have the unusual role of managing some in-house computer services functions as well as possibly more than one supplier, since many companies choose not to outsource all of this function. Also, many departments have built up their own computing resources, and it is unwise for the coordinator to attempt to outsource these areas as well, due to the high level of political opposition that will likely be encountered. In short, the coordinator position is a demanding one that requires lots of staff support and political savvy—choose this manager carefully!

5.7   POTENTIAL CUSTOMER SERVICE ISSUES

Outsourcing the computer services function can have a major impact on customer service. The function has customers both within and outside of the company, and both groups can be impacted if computer services do not function properly. This section explores the various problems that can impact both types of customer service, and how those problems can be avoided.

First, the computer services function has internal customers. These customers are company employees who rely on the output of the computer services function to properly perform their jobs. If internal customers are not properly serviced, this can also have an impact on the level of service given to a company's external customers. Internal customers can be impacted if they do not receive computer reports in a timely manner, if data is not input within a reasonable time period, if the computer-processing functions they rely on (such as being able to search the warehouse on-line for a part) are not available, or if the information they receive is not accurate. Company management will first hear about these problems through complaints from internal customers. If the problems are not dealt with promptly (usually through supplier penalties until the problems are fixed), the next sign of internal customer dissatisfaction is the installation of additional computer systems within the company to service the needs of each functional area. Functional managers purchase, install, and run these systems on their own because they cannot get the level of service they need from the supplier. Though this solution clearly circumvents the entire outsourcing solution, the real resolution to the problem is not to take away these extraneous computer systems, but rather to fix the problems with the supplier and then persuade the managers of the other functional areas to try the outsourced computer services function once again. If improperly managed, the outsourced computer services function can impact many internal customers, who can react through complaints or by setting up their own computer systems; this can be corrected by working with or imposing penalties on the supplier.

Second, the computer services function has external customers. These are a company's paying customers. A computer services supplier can impact a company's relations with these customers in a variety of ways. One is if, by providing poor service, (such as minimal computer uptime), the customer cannot be provided with the product it is accustomed to receiving. For example, a malfunctioning airline reservation system will not allow customers to book flights with an airline. Alternatively, a malfunctioning computerized order-entry system will not allow a customer to place an order, while a nonfunctioning warehousing system will not allow a company to pull products from stock to send them to a customer. In short, poor performance by a computer services supplier can potentially interfere with all aspects of service to a customer. This may lead to reduced sales, which can drastically lower company profits. The best way to avoid this problem is to rigorously and continuously measure the supplier's performance and penalize any substandard behavior, while also rewarding above-average work. Only by this close management can a company avoid continuing customer service problems.

In summary, a computer services supplier who provides low levels of service can cause complaints from internal customers, which sometimes leads to the establishment of competing computing installations within the company, or lead to reduced sales to affected external customers. Continual measurement and management of computer services suppliers can keep these problems from occurring.

5.8   GETTING OUT OF THE OUTSOURCING ARRANGEMENT

Your computer services provider has consistently fallen below all service guidelines, the computer downtime exceeds the uptime, and applications-development work has fallen far behind all milestone dates. This supplier has got to go. What special considerations should a company keep in mind when getting rid of a computer services supplier?

If the company has sold its data center to a supplier, it must negotiate terms for the return of the computer equipment. This consideration should have been covered in the original outsourcing agreement with the supplier, but, if it was not, the supplier will want a return of some of the money it originally paid for the equipment. An equitable settlement is to reduce the amount paid back by a reasonable level of depreciation on the equipment. The market value of computer equipment drops very rapidly, so the depreciation deduction may be quite large. Buying back computer equipment is a concern when a supplier is dropped.

If the company wants to shift the computer services function to a different supplier, there should be a clause in the original contract stipulating that the supplier will cooperate in shifting the work to the new supplier. If this contract language is not present, the company may try to sweeten the loss of business for the original supplier by paying it a premium to assist in transitioning the work to the new supplier. The original supplier may be so angry at the turn of events that it simply stops working with the company in any capacity. In this kind of case, the company must be prepared with a disaster-recovery plan to shift its computer operations at once to a new computing facility, and to use backup copies of its programs and data files to resurrect its operations at that facility. If the company has not taken the precaution of retaining backup copies of all applications programs and software and the supplier is being obstreperous, the company may have to resort to a legal solution to have the missing files returned. A company should integrate clauses into the original contract that specify what the supplier must do if the company chooses to end the relationship; if the contract does not contain these clauses, the company faces a series of less palatable alternatives for moving its computer services business elsewhere.

When software is turned over to a supplier, the licenses to that software are usually given to the supplier, so that it can integrate the company's applications with those of other clients, and strike cheaper licensing deals with the software providers. These licenses must be returned once the outsourcing deal is concluded; otherwise, the company must purchase the software all over again from the supplier. If the return of licenses is not noted in the original contract, the company can resort to the more expensive alternative of paying a bonus to the supplier for the license. If nothing else works, the software provider can be drawn into the battle to force the supplier to relinquish the license(s). Suppliers do not like to give up this kind of business, because they then have a smaller number of users per software license, for which software providers charge a higher per-user price (even though the total price may drop). Thus, several alternatives are available for taking software licenses away from computer services suppliers.

A large number of company employees may have been moved to a supplier as part of an outsourcing deal. If the company wants to bring its computer services function back in-house, or just move it to another supplier, it may want to make job offers to those former employees who now work for the supplier. If so, the original contract should state that the company is allowed to make job offers to those employees. If this was not included in the contract, then the company can either hire a search firm and give it the company's list of employees who were transferred to the supplier, or give the same task to its internal human resources department. The search firm or internal staff can then ferret out the new addresses of those employees and communicate to them that the company wishes to hire them back.

If a company does not want to hire back those employees who were originally transferred to the supplier, the supplier may have to terminate them. If so, it may pay them termination pay, the cost of which it will want to share with the company. This can be a reasonable request, especially if the employees were only recently transferred to the supplier, but is much less valid after a number of years have passed. Therefore, if this item was not already covered in the original contract, the company could agree to share in making termination payments, but on a declining scale based on the amount of time that has passed since the employees were shifted to the supplier.

A company's concerns related to ending a computer services outsourcing arrangement will vary considerably based on which element of the function was given to the supplier. For example, terminating the outsourcing of a data center is a major item, since it involves the transfer of software, hardware, and staff. It is also a serious matter to end an applications-development arrangement, since all software code that has so far been written, along with all accompanying notes, memos, and flowcharts, must be transferred back to the company, with the attendant loss of development time. This is also the case for the help desk application, since there may be a considerable database of information about resolving various software bugs that the supplier has built up, and may not be willing to relinquish. However, other outsourced tasks are easier to terminate, such as voice and data networking, which can usually be moved to a different supplier with little trouble. Likewise, the repair and upkeep of desktop computing equipment is usually not difficult to switch to an in-house staff or to a different supplier, though the desktop hardware and software inventory must be taken by whomever takes over the function (a major endeavor if a company has thousands of desktop computers). In short, the risk of ending an outsourcing relationship varies greatly by the type of computer services function that is being moved either in-house or to a different supplier.

This section discussed a variety of issues to consider before terminating an outsourcing arrangement. Of particular importance was the continual reference in this section to making sure that termination-related clauses are included in the original contract with the supplier. If they are not, the company will have a much more difficult time getting out of an outsourcing deal. Therefore, the reader should peruse the section earlier in this chapter that dealt with contract-related issues, for all of the contract-termination issues noted in that section should be included in a computer services outsourcing contract. If a company has already signed a contract without those clauses, it should consider renegotiating the contract to ensure that those clauses are included.

5.9 SUMMARY

This chapter dealt with one of the company functions that is most frequently outsourced: computer services. This area now requires so much technical skill and so many financial resources that many companies, even multibillion-dollar ones, cannot keep abreast of the latest technological developments and must farm out many aspects of this work to suppliers. There may be many suppliers for one company, for there are a number of important specialties within the realm of computer services, such as applications development, help desk, network management, desktop computing services, legacy systems maintenance, and data center management. Making the transitions of these various tasks to several suppliers and then managing their activities can be a daunting task, and so these items in particular are noted in some detail in this chapter. Other topics included the disadvantages of outsourcing computer services, what should be included in the contract with the supplier, and how to measure and control the activities of the various suppliers. For this most important of all outsourcing areas, this chapter provides a good overview of the topics that are of concern to today's managers; however, for a more detailed coverage of this function, some of the books noted in Appendix A that only cover computer services outsourcing should be consulted.

CHAPTER SIX

Outsourcing the
Customer Service Function

One of the newest and fastest-growing services in the outsourcing arena is customer service. With this service, a company allows all inbound customer calls to be routed to a supplier-owned call center that answers customer questions, routes field-service personnel to customer locations for repairs, enters service or product orders from customers, and courteously tries to persuade customers not to return products or cancel services. Examples of these services abound. For example, who has not contacted a call center to cancel a credit card, only to be routed to someone who gives many persuasive reasons why not to do so?

Customer service suppliers are rapidly growing in size and financial power, with considerable consolidation occurring. The largest publicly owned customer service company is SITEL, based in Omaha, Nebraska. It has 65 call centers in 11 countries, and employs 17,000 people. One customer is Allstate, for whom it operates a 24-hour call center that provides answers to billing inquiries and coverage questions, assisted by a direct connection to Allstate's Advantis network. Other large suppliers are Denver-based Teletech Holdings, which specializes in handling inbound calls for such Fortune 500 companies as AT&T, Apple Computer, Novell and United Parcel Service, and ALLTEL Information Services, which has a similar arrangement with National Commerce Bancorporation.

What is so special about a customer service supplier? A good supplier has the management ability to quickly create a call center and recruit sufficient people to staff it, frequently in as little as a few months. For example, SITEL assisted with a credit card launch for General Motors by constructing a call center and hiring and training 2,200 people to staff it—all in just 65 days! This takes a large burden off a company that wants to respond to company calls while also managing its core competencies. A customer service supplier usually has much better technological expertise as well. This can extend to blended call handling (taking inbound calls while also making outbound calls, as in a field service function), interactive voice response (sorting customer calls by having them press numbers on the keypad), highly customizable client reporting, and callback verification to ensure that orders are correct. These are functions that a company that is new to the function will not know how to install or manage. In short, a customer service supplier has the management skill, experience, and technical expertise to set up and run an inbound call center far better than most companies.

There are two sides to the customer service supplier. One is its inbound call function, as previously described. Its other, and more well-known, function is outbound telemarketing sales calls. Since that function is not customer service, it is more appropriately discussed in the sales and marketing chapter.

This chapter discusses the advantages and disadvantages of using a customer service supplier, as well as the contractual issues that a company should know about prior to signing a contract with a supplier. The chapter also notes a number of transition issues to consider when moving an in-house call center to a supplier, as well as how to control, measure, and manage a supplier. The chapter ends with coverage of several customer service issues and how to terminate a relationship with a customer service supplier.

6.1   ADVANTAGES AND DISADVANTAGES

The number of large companies that are taking advantage of the services of customer service suppliers has increased dramatically over the past few years. Why the sudden interest? There are several key factors that make the outsourcing decision an easy one for many companies. This section discusses those advantages, as well as a few disadvantages that, though not critical, should be considered as part of the outsourcing decision.

An important reason for using a customer service supplier is that the company is dealing directly with the customer through this function, and must present the best possible face to the customer—and this is the primary area of expertise for the supplier. A good customer service supplier has long experience in taking calls and answering customer queries in a courteous and considerate manner. A company may eventually learn how to do this if it sets up its own inbound call center, but it would take time to ascend the learning curve, and the company may alienate customers in the meantime. Hiring a quality customer service supplier gives a company a professional image with its customers.

One of the major advantages of outsourcing customer service is that the best suppliers, such as SITEL, have great experience in rapidly installing call centers. This includes acquiring and training new staff, locating new facilities, installing phone and computer terminals, and building any required links to the company's computer system—and all in record time. It is unlikely that a company without this experience could install a call center on such short notice or do so with a minimum of installation problems that would result in extra costs and time. Thus, a company with a time-critical need for a new call center should contact a customer service supplier.

One of the biggest management problems involved with a call center is personnel issues. This is because the customer service function is not considered by employees to be a critical job function to list on a resume, so companies routinely hire sub-par employees and are plagued with poor attendance and high turnover, which leads to problems with having to constantly recruit new employees and train them. A company can avoid this major management headache by giving the task to a supplier. The best suppliers have finely tuned recruiting skills that they use to select just the right kinds of people, pay and benefit levels calculated to retain their existing staffs, and ongoing training programs designed to maintain the quality of their staffs. In short, suppliers can handle call center personnel better than most companies.

Some customer service suppliers specialize in specific industries. Among the more common areas for suppliers are credit cards, insurance, and magazine subscriptions. A supplier who specializes in one of these areas has an in-depth knowledge of how to treat customers through special employee training and through scripting that is targeted at those industries. This results in higher customer satisfaction and even higher retention rates—in those cases where customers are calling to cancel products or services, it is the job of the call center personnel to keep them from doing so. It is in the interests of a company to hire a supplier that specializes in its industry in order to draw upon its special knowledge of the field.

In addition to the more common customer service functions, a company can also turn over its field service dispatch function to a supplier (usually the same one who handles all other inbound calls). This has the advantage of allowing field service calls to be taken as long as the call center is open, which is usually well beyond the company's normal operating hours. In addition, a supplier can usually utilize blended call handling for greater efficiency; this is when a call center employee calls out to arrange for field service while waiting for any inbound calls to arrive. The only disadvantage is that this service is somewhat more expensive than answering a simple customer query, since the call center employee makes an additional call or computer entry to schedule field service.

When a company has its own call center, this is entirely a fixed cost—the company must pay the salaries of all employees irrespective of call volume. A company can convert this fixed cost to a variable one by switching to a supplier who will only be paid based on the volume of inbound calls. This conversion to fixed costs lowers a company's break-even point, since there are fewer fixed costs to cover, which makes it somewhat easier to earn a profit on lower sales volume. The only downside is that a typical supplier contract includes a minimum fee per month, so there is a fixed cost—but less than would be the case if a company did not outsource this function. In short, the size of the fixed cost involved in customer service is reduced through outsourcing.

If a company uses a customer service supplier, it will require a minimum of staff to monitor the supplier's activities, as compared to other functional areas. This is because a good supplier can generate a vast array of reports that show the supplier's performance, such as the average customer time on hold, average length of call, types of problems reported by customers, inbound sales volume, and the volume of calls at various times of the day and week. Though the company should use its internal audit staff to review the accuracy of these reports, there is not much need for anyone but a functional coordinator to deal with the supplier on an ongoing basis. The in-house staff cost of using a customer service supplier is low.

When a company uses the services of a customer service supplier, it no longer needs to invest in a call center—the supplier incurs this expense. If the company's inbound call volume is large, this might otherwise require a significant investment in office space, cubicles, phones, computers, and wiring. However, the supplier must recoup its costs in this area, so the company will be charged a premium by the supplier to cover the supplier's capital costs. This expense may be spread over a long time interval, so the financial impact on the company is not as profound as when the company incurs this expense on its own.

Another advantage of shifting to a customer service supplier is that the company can release the office space previously used by the in-house call center for other purposes. Since this space usually already includes cubicles that are pre-wired for computer terminals and phones, the space can be readily converted to office space. The only problem is that cubicles used by a call center tend to be very small, so the cubicles may require reconfiguration to create larger cubicles, which also means that the computer and phone wiring may have to be reconfigured to match the new cubicle spaces.

If a company is uncomfortable with the concept of fully outsourcing the entire customer service function, or if it is able to adequately handle most inbound call volume already, it may still make sense to give all overflow call volume to a supplier. This is most practical when a company experiences sharp changes in the inbound call volume, which its existing staff cannot handle during peak periods. Since customers must wait on hold during such times and the company may not want to add excess staff to its call center to cover these extra calls, it makes sense to simply reroute overflow calls to a supplier for more prompt handling. This gives customers better service while avoiding the fixed costs of additional staff for the company. Using a supplier for overflow calls is an excellent reason to undertake inbound call outsourcing.

The most significant disadvantage of using a supplier is that the supplier must charge a profit in order to get a return on its capital, and also must incur sales and marketing costs that a company would not spend if it had an in-house customer service function. These costs must be passed on to the customer, so the price of using a customer service supplier is somewhat higher than the cost of keeping the function in-house. It is up to company management to determine if the many advantages of using a supplier are outweighed by its prices.

Another disadvantage of outsourcing the customer service function is that the supplier may need access to the company's database. This happens, for example, when the supplier is answering customer queries on the status of orders, and the supplier must access the company's shipment database to answer the question. This presents the danger of having supplier employees gain unauthorized access to other parts of the company's database, as well as making incorrect changes in that portion of the database that they *are* authorized to access. These problems can be overcome by allowing read-only access to the database, as well as by constructing a special interface for the supplier that does not present any other menu options than those for which the supplier is allowed access. Database security may be an issue if customer service is outsourced, but there are several ways of providing that access that mitigate the risk of database damage.

This section covered the advantages and disadvantages of using a customer service supplier for inbound calls. The more important advantages include access to a supplier's expertise in dealing with inbound calls, fast call center construction, and staff recruiting and management. A company can also avoid significant capital spending and fixed costs by shifting the cost of the call center to a supplier. Offsetting these advantages are the higher cost of using a supplier and possibly taking the security risk of allowing the supplier's call center personnel some level of access to the company's computer database.

6.2   CONTRACT-SPECIFIC ISSUES

This section covers any special contractual issues that may be of concern when outsourcing the customer service function. Most other functional areas concentrate on pricing in the contract, but this one has an added set of contractual objectives: providing customer service through call center availability and avoiding keeping callers on hold. Since the company is dealing directly with customers through this function, the customer service aspects of the contract tend to take precedence over pricing issues.

When a company decides to outsource the customer service function, it may have a specific target date in mind for when the function must be made operational by the supplier. For example, this is a problem for a software supplier who is about to release a new software package, and who must have a call center available as of the release date to answer questions about the new software. In these cases, the contract should include a bonus payment if the target date is met, and penalties if it is not. The penalty should not be a single lump sum. Instead, it should be a cumulative amount that increases for every day beyond the target date that the call center is still not operational. A penalty and bonus clause should be included in the contract if the supplier must have an operational call center as of a specific date.

When a supplier is rushing to create a call center and assemble a staff to man it, one of the key determinants in completing the project is assistance from the company in creating linkages between the computers in the call center to the relevant database information located in the company's computer system. This requires considerable and active cooperation from the company's computer services staff. Without this help, the supplier cannot meet its target completion date. Therefore, the supplier may rightfully insist that any completion requirements and associated penalties or bonuses must be contingent on full cooperation by the company's computer services department.

The company must also specify in the contract the availability of the call center. One of the elements of availability is the business hours of the call center. The length of open hours will be a function of the time zones served as well as the types of product problems encountered by customers. For example, if customers are worldwide, the call center must be open around the clock, but if the time zones served are just in the United States, two shifts will probably be sufficient. Also, if the types of calls are for repairs on sewing machines, the subject is not critical enough to warrant having the call center open all day and night; but if customers are calling in about flight reservations or insurance claims on home damage, the call center should be open at all times. Finally, availability is impacted by system downtime, which can be caused by hardware breakdowns in the computer or phone systems, or by power shortages. All three of these availability issues should be addressed in the contract, which should specify the times when the call center will be accepting calls as well as the percentage of allowable system downtime during business hours.

Even if a customer finds that a call center is open for business, there may be no available staff person to talk to, resulting in a long wait on hold. This problem is a function of the number of people staffing the call center, and also a function of the volume of calls, which can vary dramatically through the day and week. This issue can be addressed in the contract, which requires a specific average wait time for customers. Since the average can mask a small percentage of callers who must wait far longer than the average, it is also possible to include in the contract a maximum percentage of callers who are allowed to exceed a specific wait time. The contract should state that the supplier must take whatever action is necessary to maintain caller wait times at a specific level, which allows the supplier to address the issue by a variety of means—adding staff, altering the script, speeding up access time on computer terminals, or providing better training. The contract should specify an average allowable customer wait time.

One of the key elements of the contract is pricing. The supplier usually charges a fee per call received, plus a minimum price per month, irrespective of the number of calls received. Another variation is to charge for the amount of time on the phone with customers (since the length of calls can vary dramatically when customers are calling in, as compared to outbound telemarketing calls, which tend to have very predictable call lengths). The supplier may also have made a large investment in creating a call center for the company, and will require a minimum contract length or a termination payment to ensure that this investment is recovered. All of these factors are negotiable. The key pricing issue to focus on is the price per call. If the company anticipates a very large inbound call volume that will continue for a long time period, it can negotiate a very low price per call, which will still be attractive to the supplier, since it can earn large profits from taking a few cents profit from each of thousands of calls. There are many pricing variations to consider for the contract, but most of the money the customer will pay is for the price per call, so this should be the focal point of negotiations.

If the company decides to terminate the contract with its customer services supplier, the company will need help from the supplier in moving the function either back to the company or to a new supplier. The supplier, having just been terminated, may be less than willing to do this. To avoid the problem in advance, the contract should require the supplier to render all possible assistance during the conversion effort. Also, since the supplier may try to charge unusually high prices for this work, the initial contract should specify the hourly rates to be charged for this work. Thus, the possibility of termination should be covered in the contract by requiring conversion assistance by the supplier at pre-set rates.

This section covered the usual pricing concerns that are common to outsourcing all functional areas, but also included several customer service items, which were call center availability and keeping callers from being put on hold for an inordinate length of time. Other issues included bonus and penalty provisions for bringing a new call center on-line as of a target date, and conversion assistance by the supplier in case of termination.

6.3   TRANSITION ISSUES

This section addresses the transition issues that arise when moving the customer service function to a supplier. This transition is unique among most functional areas in that, depending on the call volume involved, there is a strong likelihood that a call center may be constructed, along with an entirely new staff, to meet the company's needs. Since this must be done from scratch, there is often a large amount of management time involved, and variations in completion dates are likely due to the large number of potential pitfalls that may be encountered. Thus, depending on volume, this can be one of the more challenging transitions, though the bulk of the transition work will be handled by the supplier. The transition steps are as follows:

1. *Select customer service coordinator.* A functional coordinator is necessary to coordinate the selection of a supplier, as well as final contract negotiations, the transition to the supplier, and ongoing management of the function. Without this position, the entire process will be slower and may result in higher costs due to lack of attention to the details of the contractual agreement.

2. *Develop supplier-selection criteria.* The functional coordinator should derive a set of selection criteria for picking a supplier. These criteria should be as quantitative as possible, and include such items as the supplier's record in setting up call centers, the degree of supplier knowledge of the company's industry, experience with the volume of calls the company is anticipating, and technological expertise in linking to the company's database.

3. *Select supplier.* The previously noted selection criteria should be completed for each candidate supplier so that there is a good basis of comparison. Then the coordinator can use the completed criteria to compare suppliers and make an informed choice. The best way to use the criteria is to assign an importance weighting to each potential supplier's score on each item, and then multiply the scores by the weighting factors. The supplier with the highest

score should be selected. If other factors are also used to select a supplier, then the criteria weighting system should at least be used to eliminate those suppliers from contention who have the poorest scores.

4. *Finalize contract.* Once the supplier has been picked, the supplier will need a due diligence period in which to investigate all of the company's needs in detail so that it will be able to negotiate the contract on a knowledgeable basis. It is best to give the supplier all necessary project details prior to signing a contract, since the supplier might otherwise agree to terms that are unrealistic based on actual requirements, resulting in a lengthy renegotiation of the contract at a later date.

5. *Set up facility.* If the company anticipates a very large volume of incoming calls, the supplier will probably not have enough excess capacity available to handle it. Instead, the supplier must construct or rent a facility, install cubicles, and add computer terminals and telephone connections. This can require a considerable amount of time, depending on the availability of work crews with the technical skill to install and test phone and computer wiring and phone and computer terminals. The existence of sufficient rental space in the facility target location is also a factor.

6. *Test and install computer linkages.* For a customer service operation where customers are calling in to ask questions, the supplier will not always know what to answer unless it has access to the company's database. For example, a customer may inquire about the due date on a delivery. The person answering the phone must have access to the company's shipping records to know the answer. Another example is taking orders from customers; this can be done on paper, but it is much easier to enter orders directly into the company's order entry database. In these cases, the company and supplier must work together to install high-volume phone lines between the company's data center and the new call center, as well as install a sufficient number of terminals for the supplier's employees. This can be a lengthy process, so it should be started as early in the process as possible.

7. *Develop script.* Incoming calls from customers will probably cover a wide range of topics, which the supplier's staff must be prepared to answer. Given the large number of potential topics, it is difficult to script all possible responses. The usual alternative is for the company and supplier to work together to develop scripts for the most common customer issues, and then route the more difficult calls to a smaller team of more highly trained professionals who are better equipped to answer those questions.

8. *Develop training plan.* Once the scripts are completed, they form the foundation of a training program that all new hires must attend. The training program must include simulated calls with management monitoring, so that employees gain considerable exposure to realistic situations with immediate management feedback.

9. *Transfer staff.* The company may have an in-house staff that had previously taken on the tasks now being moved to the supplier. If the supplier needs these personnel, it will hire them. If so, the company and supplier should work together to talk to each employee being transferred. The discussion should include filling out all paperwork to terminate the employee at the company and sign him or her up for payroll and any benefits at the supplier. Each employee deserves as much time as possible for explanations covering the details of the transfer.

10. *Hire new staff.* The supplier must hire new employees to staff the new calling facility. Depending on the number of incoming calls anticipated, this may be a very large number of people. For example, a recent national rollout of a credit card required the hiring of 2,200 employees. Extra time may be required to find these people if the region where the calls are to be fielded has a very low unemployment rate.

11. *Conduct training.* The supplier must conduct in-depth training for all personnel who will be answering the phones. The company may need to have representatives present to answer questions, especially if the service center has a computer linkage to the company's database. Company personnel will have a much better knowledge of how to use this database than anyone else, so their presence to provide occasional training on the more difficult computer access issues will make the training proceed more smoothly. The supplier should also set up a call-monitoring program in which supervisors monitor real phone calls handled by the supplier staff and provide additional and ongoing training based on the results of that monitoring.

12. *Final QA Test.* Before allowing the phone facility to go on-line, the supplier's quality-assurance group should simulate a number of calls, using different customer problems, and monitor all of the calls as they are received to ensure that previous testing was sufficient to handle all possible situations. The functional coordinator should be present for this test or review the results of it, so that he can request additional training if some responses are inadequate. The coordinator should also be involved in designing the simulations, since the coordinator has more experience in the industry, and can spot missing or faulty simulations that the supplier's quality-assurance team might miss.

The above transition steps are noted in Figure 6.1. This section covered the primary transition steps involved in moving the customer service function to a supplier. If there is a small amount of call volume that a supplier can handle with its existing staff, and the computer linkages are minimal, this can be an easy transition. However, if the call volume is large or the number of possible customer problems is significant, the management skill of the supplier becomes a key factor in the success of the transition, since there are new facilities to acquire, new employees to hire, and a customer response program to create. Depending on the circumstances, this can be a challenging transition.

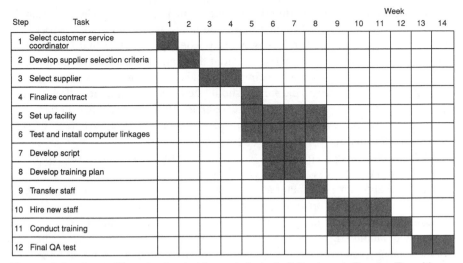

Figure 6.1 Gantt Chart for the Implementation of all Customer Service Transition Issues

6.4 CREATING CONTROL POINTS

This section covers the possible control points that a functional coordinator can use to ensure that the customer service supplier's actions are consistent with the contract and the company's customer service objectives. The controls include supplier reports, comparisons of prices to the contract, and automated database usage measurements.

The primary control point when dealing with a customer service supplier is the supplier's activity report. The report can be generated as frequently as the functional coordinator wants, and can include a vast array of information, such as the dollar volume of inbound customer orders, inbound calls per hour, average length of call, time on hold, retention rates for customers calling to cancel service or products, customer problems based on general problem categories, field service calls dispatched, and system downtime. This information is more than adequate for the functional coordinator to determine every possible aspect of supplier performance. The one catch to this control is that the reports are generated by the supplier, who is being judged based on the results shown on the reports. Since this is a conflict of interest, the functional coordinator must use the services of the company's internal audit staff to verify the accuracy of the underlying detail that rolls up into the supplier's reports. The coordinator can recommend audit objectives for the internal audit team, which will then create its own audit programs, review the supplier's reported information, and report its findings back to the functional coordinator, who can then correct any problems detected by working with the supplier to resolve them. The coordinator can also plot the results of the supplier's reports on a trend line to see if there are problems occurring over a long time period that would not be evident by reviewing a single status report. An example of such a trend line is shown in Figure 6.2, where it is evident that customers call in less frequently when they realize that they will be put on hold for a long time; this is a pattern that can result when a supplier cuts back on the number of staff answering the phone, resulting in long waiting periods. Any clear and unfavorable trends should be brought to the attention of supplier management for discussion and corrective action. Thus, the supplier's activity report, when reviewed for accuracy, is the primary control tool for the functional coordinator.

While the audit team is reviewing the accuracy of the supplier's reports, there are a few other items it can examine that create more controls over the supplier. One is a review of the supplier's computer system log to determine how frequently the computer systems were shut down during regular business hours. An excessive amount of downtime on a continuing basis reduces the supplier's ability to service customers, and should trigger a conversation between the functional coordinator and supplier management to have this problem fixed, as well as a follow-up review by the audit team at a later date.

The functional coordinator should compare the supplier's billing statement to the original contract every month. This review should include a comparison of the prices charged to the prices listed in the contract, with an emphasis on the key pricing

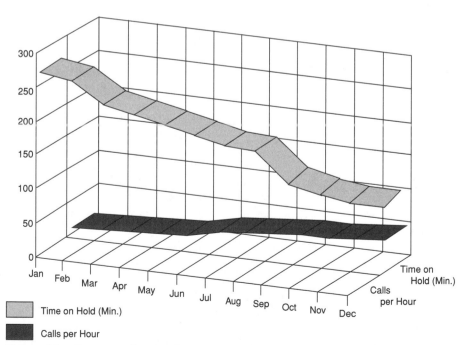

Figure 6.2 Customer Service Trend Line Analysis

points, which are usually the cost per call and the minimum base price per month. The reviewer should also look for the dates on which prices are set to change, based on inflation escalators or some similar reason. It is helpful to extract the key pricing points from the contract for the purposes of this review, since this allows the reviewer to spend less time digging through the contract, looking for the clauses containing pricing information. A periodic comparison of billed prices to contract prices gives some control over supplier costs.

Another control is over the supplier's access to the company's database. The supplier may need this information in order to answer queries about order status from customers, or it may need to enter orders directly into the company's order entry database. The computer services function will want to exercise tight control over this item, since the supplier may have access to sensitive information, or even alter information. There are several controls that address this problem. One is to give the supplier read-only access, which keeps supplier employees from modifying any data. Another option is to create a special screen for supplier personnel to read that excludes any confidential information. Another option is to periodically transfer a portion of the company's database to a computer located at the supplier's call center that has been screened for confidential information. This approach is also useful if the supplier is allowed to modify information, since the computer services staff can review the database as it is periodically downloaded back to the company to see what changes have been made. A final control option is to have supplier personnel make all data updates to a special holding file that the computer services staff reviews before allowing it to be merged with the company's database. Any or all of these options can be used to avoid problems with confidential information being released or data being incorrectly modified.

If the supplier is given on-line access to the company's database, this also gives the company an opportunity to audit the activity of the supplier in using that database. For example, the company's computer services staff can install controls over the database that monitor the supplier's usage volume and error rates in inputting data to the database (especially through the order entry function). This information can then be reported back to the functional coordinator by the computer services staff, who can follow up on problems with the supplier if necessary. Permitting the supplier to directly access the company's database allows the company to measure the supplier's use of that database.

In summary, the primary control over a customer service supplier is the reports generated by the supplier. Since the supplier is reporting on its own activity, this is a conflict of interest, so the company should periodically send in an audit team to review the accuracy of those reports. The functional coordinator can also compare the supplier's prices to the prices noted in the original contract to verify that prices are correct. There are also a variety of options available for controlling access to the company's database by the supplier, which includes several automated performance measurements. These help the functional coordinator to maintain control over the supplier.

6.5   MEASURING THE OUTSOURCED FUNCTION

This section covers the primary performance measurements that the functional coordinator should track on a continuing basis. These cover the revenue and cost per call, as well as the supplier's ability to retain sales to customers who are calling in to cancel the company's product or service. The measures also note the supplier's ability to correctly take an order from a customer as well as to keep its systems operational. Finally, if the company has an in-house call center and only uses the supplier for overflow calls, there is a measurement for tracking the percentage of overflow calls. A combination of these measurements will give the functional coordinator a good idea of the performance of a customer service supplier.

- *Cost per call received.* The primary cost billed to a company by a customer service supplier is the cost per call received. This rate is normally specified in the contract, and a monthly task for the functional coordinator is to compare the billed cost to the contractual rate to ensure that the supplier is billing the correct amount. To calculate this measurement, take the total cost billed to the company in one month and divide this amount by the number of calls received by the supplier, as noted on the supplier's monthly call report.

- *Revenue per call.* If customers call in to order parts or products, the functional coordinator will want to know the average revenue per inbound call. This number can be increased with proper scripting, since call center personnel can recommend add-on parts, services, or warranties to customers. Thus, a quality supplier can increase a company's revenues even on inbound calls. To calculate this measurement, summarize the revenues entered into the system by the supplier from inbound calls, and divide this amount by the number of calls received by the supplier, as noted on the supplier's monthly call report.

- *Retention rate.* Customers frequently call a company to cancel parts or service orders. This is particularly common for magazine subscriptions and credit cards. A good call center employee can reduce the number of these cancellations by persuading customers to continue with the product or service. This is a function not only of the sales skills of the call center employee, but also of the script used when talking to these customers. A good supplier can recover a large amount of revenue for a company in this area. To calculate this measurement, summarize the number of calls made into the call center to cancel a sale, then divide this amount into the number of callers who were persuaded not to cancel.

- *Total cost per month.* There may be a mix of prices charged to the company by the supplier, such as a price per call received, a minimum base price per month, extra fees for activity reports, and charges for time spent on the phone with customers. To calculate this measurement, use the total cost shown on the supplier's monthly summary billing. Track this on a trend line to spot any long-term variances.

- *Percentage of system downtime.* If the supplier's computer or phone systems are not operational, then customers cannot contact anyone to place orders, issue complaints, or have product questions answered, which leads to customer dissatisfaction and lost sales. It is therefore important that the functional coordinator track the percentage of system downtime and work with the supplier to fix any recurring problems. To calculate this measurement, take this information from the supplier's downtime report, or poll customers to determine an approximate downtime percentage.

- *Percentage of changes on callback.* A poorly trained supplier staff may have trouble properly recording information from a customer. This is a particular concern if the customer is placing an order and the call center employee takes down the wrong information, resulting in the wrong item being mailed to the wrong address. To keep this from happening, an independent callback supplier can call customers on a test basis to verify information taken down during the inbound call from the customer, and report to the functional coordinator on the amount of incorrect information recorded during the first call. To calculate this measurement, determine the percentage of changes made to orders placed during calls to the original supplier, as reported by the callback supplier.

- *Percentage of overflow calls.* Some companies have their own in-house call centers, and only use suppliers to take extra calls that the in-house staff cannot handle during periods of high-volume inbound calls. If the percentage of overflow calls going to the supplier is consistently high, the company has proof that it should increase the size of its in-house staff. However, to make this decision, management must measure the percentage of overflow calls. To calculate this measurement, take the total number of overflow calls received by the supplier and divide this by the total number of calls fielded by the in-house customer service staff.

This section covered the primary measurements used to track the performance of a customer service supplier. The measurements included the cost and revenue per call, customer retention rates, and supplier errors and system downtime. Using these measurements gives a functional coordinator a good idea of the performance level of the customer service supplier.

6.6   MANAGING THE OUTSOURCED FUNCTION

This section discusses the type of management structure needed to oversee the outsourced customer service function, which primarily involves the functional coordinator position.

There needs to be a lead person who directs the supplier selection team, negotiates with candidate suppliers, oversees the transition of the customer service function to the supplier, and monitors the supplier's performance. This can be a full-time functional coordinator position, depending on the size of the outsourced function. If the company also has an outbound (telemarketing) supplier, the same coordinator will probably be used for this supplier as well. The position usually does not require a senior management person, so it reports to the vice president of sales and marketing, rather than being that position. The coordinator sometimes collects information from the supplier regarding customer complaints about products, so there may also be a dotted line reporting relationship with the vice presidents of engineering and production, so that they can use this information to fix product problems. These reporting relationships are shown in Figure 6.3. There may be no support staff for this position, since a quality supplier will generate enough activity reports to give the coordinator sufficient management information without anyone else to gather the information. However, the functional coordinator may work closely with the company's internal auditing team to go to the supplier call center and compare its management reports to supporting detail records to en-

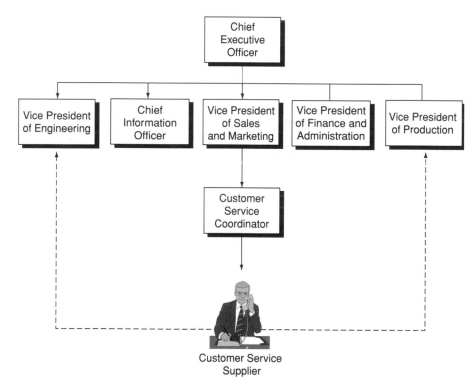

Figure 6.3   Organization Chart for Outsourcing the Customer Service Function

sure that the reports are accurate. Thus, the functional coordinator tends to be a mid-level manager with minimal staff.

The customer service coordinator does not need an excess of skills in any particular area. Instead, the person should have experience in the industry and in dealing with customers, as well as a strong familiarity with the company's product offerings, so that he or she will spot problems in proposed scripts presented by the supplier for dealing with customers, as well as product-specific items not addressed by the supplier's training program. This means that the coordinator can come from the sales, customer service, engineering, or marketing departments. Of more importance than technical skills are people skills; the coordinator must be able to present product problems to the company's production and engineering personnel without implying that anyone is at fault for the problems—the intention is to fix problems, not affix blame. The coordinator must also be able to work with the supplier to improve customer service measurements, such as convincing the supplier to add staff or phone lines so that customers have easier access. The coordinator must also meet regularly with the supplier's quality-assurance personnel to review problems revealed through call monitoring, and to discuss training and script changes that will fix those problems. It is also important to persuade the company's computer services manager to allow the supplier access to that portion of the company's database that is needed to answer customer queries. A summary-level functional coordinator job description is shown in Figure 6.4. Thus, people skills and product knowledge are more important for the functional coordinator than other technical skills.

In summary, the management of a customer service supplier involves a functional coordinator. This person rarely has a significant support staff and is not a high-level manager. The position requires good product knowledge and excellent people skills, since interaction occurs not only with the supplier but also with the production and engineering departments.

Figure 6.4   The Customer Service Coordinator's Job Description

Employee Title: Customer Service Outsourcing Coordinator
Reports to: Vice President of Sales and Marketing
Responsibilities:
- Sign off on all agreements with the customer service supplier.
- Authorize the release of funds for payment to the supplier.
- Review the results of the supplier's call-monitoring program.
- Compare actual costs charged to costs listed in contracts to determine the causes of variances; follow up on these variances with the supplier.
- Measure service levels based on supplier reports and resolve any problems.
- Supervise giving the supplier's call center computer access to relevant portions of the company's database.
- Manage the transfer of functions from the company to the supplier.
- Advise the internal audit team regarding supplier control points to investigate.
- Approve proposed scripts for use by the supplier's staff.

6.7   POTENTIAL CUSTOMER SERVICE ISSUES

Since this chapter covers the customer service function, it seems reasonable that there is a potential for lots of customer service issues! These include not being able to get through to the call center, not getting a response to an answer, having poor supplier training or scripting, and having the computer system nonoperational. All of these points are discussed below.

The first problem a customer may have with a call center is either getting a busy signal when calling or sitting on hold for an inordinate period of time. Either problem is poor customer service. The first item—receiving a busy signal—can be solved by having the supplier add to the number of incoming phone lines at the call center. This is a difficult item to include in a contract, since no one knows in advance how many phone lines are needed. However, the functional coordinator can work with the supplier's management to decide when extra lines should be added based on phone reports showing the number of inbound calls that were met with a busy signal. The second problem, being on hold too long, is caused by not having enough staff available to answer calls. This is a common problem for understaffed government agencies, such as the Internal Revenue Service, but does not have to be the case for a supplier. The functional coordinator can review reports from the supplier to determine how long the average person is on hold, and work with the supplier to add staff to reduce this amount. Unfortunately, there are "hot" periods during the week when call volume will swamp the available staff, and wait times will lengthen. The coordinator's best approach to this is to either keep the average call length down to a target amount, or work on only subjecting a target percentage of customers to an inordinate wait period. Both of these goals can be reviewed with phone reports and modified by changing staff levels. In short, customers can get access to the supplier with more phone lines, and can be on hold for less time if there is more staff at the call center.

A customer cannot receive the correct answer to a problem if the person receiving the call is not properly trained to answer questions. There are three solutions to this problem. One is to provide additional training to new call center personnel and refresher training to existing staff. Another approach is to use a small team of experts who can answer even the most difficult customer questions. If the person receiving a call cannot answer the customer's question, the customer is passed along to one of the experts for resolution. Yet another solution is to have a team of quality-assurance personnel monitor calls being received to see what problems are not being dealt with correctly by the call center employees. This tells the quality assurance people what kind of additional training is needed to correct the problems they discovered during the monitoring. Thus, customers can receive better answers to their problems by giving call center employees more training, adding a core group of experts to the call center, and monitoring inbound phone calls for quality-assurance purposes.

Some inbound calls are for a set purpose that can be answered with a scripted response, such as for a customer who wants to place an order. This can be a bad experience for the customer if the script is faulty, resulting in the call center employee not entering the order properly. This is solved through adequate script testing in advance, before the call center goes on-line, and also by using the quality-assurance personnel to monitor calls once the call center is opened to verify that the script is adequate to serve the needs of customers.

It is also not very useful if customers succeed in contacting the call center, only to find that the supplier's computer system is down, so that the staff cannot research customer queries, forcing customers to call back at a later time. There are three reasons for this problem, all of which can be solved with extra equipment. The first reason is that there is a power failure at the call center. This can be solved by adding an uninterruptible power supply (UPS) and an alternate power source to the call center's computer. The second reason is the same thing, but for the *company's* computer—the call center's computers may be linked to the company's database, so if the company's computer is not available, the call center will not be functional. The solution is the same: Add a UPS and alternate power source to the company's computer. An alternate solution is to periodically transfer the database used by the call center from the company's computer to a local computer at the call center, thereby eliminating the on-line linkage to the company's computer. The third reason is that the call center's central computer may have hardware problems, requiring downtime to fix. This can be solved by using a fault-tolerant computer, of the type produced by Tandem Corporation. These computers have redundant systems, so if one part fails, a similar part elsewhere in the computer will take over. These computers are used heavily for bank ATM systems and airline reservations, where systems cannot go down even for a short time. Thus, system downtime can be reduced by installing alternate power sources and fault-tolerant computers.

To summarize, the primary customer service problems for this function are not being able to get phone access to a call center and not getting adequate service when the connection is made. These problems can be solved by installing an adequate number of phone lines and hiring enough staff to answer the phones, ensuring that the computer systems are fully operational during business hours, having adequate scripting and training, and using experts to answer the most difficult customer questions.

6.8   GETTING OUT OF
THE OUTSOURCING ARRANGEMENT

This section discusses the problems with terminating an agreement with a customer service supplier. This is a particularly difficult arrangement to get out of if the supplier has built a call center for the company, which is quite common for companies with large inbound call volumes. In these situations, the supplier can have several possible billing arrangements with the company that allow it to earn back its investment in the call center. These arrangements can include a termination payment or a minimum payment per month for a minimum number of months or years. If a company chooses to terminate the contract prior to its minimum term, the company can expect to make a termination payment to the supplier to cover at least some portion of the supplier's investment, and possibly also a profit percentage on lost revenues.

An additional problem with terminating a customer service supplier is that the phone number that customers use to reach the call center will be disconnected, which leaves customers no avenue for talking to the company. The best approach to resolving this problem is to reroute the phone number to the company's in-house customer support function or to a new supplier. In either case, the phone line should not be allowed to become inactive even for a single day, since this might cause customer dissatisfaction.

If the call center being terminated is handling a large volume of inbound calls, the company must be prepared to take on these calls with either a large, fully staffed in-house call center or a call center serviced by a different supplier. In either case, it takes time to develop this capability, so the company must plan well in advance for how it will bring a new call center on-line prior to terminating the agreement with the existing supplier. The conversion to the new call center will probably require all of the transition steps for the original transition to the first supplier. Advance planning to create call center capacity is mandatory when shutting down service from a large supplier call center.

In short, there are several problems to consider before terminating a customer service supplier: termination payments, switching phone numbers, and creating the call center capacity elsewhere to handle inbound customer phone calls once the supplier has been terminated.

6.9   SUMMARY

Telemarketing companies have greatly expanded the scope of their services over the past decade. Starting with a base service of outbound calls (contacting people for sales calls), they have now expanded into inbound calls (responding to customer queries or taking customer orders). The telemarketing service is covered in the sales and marketing chapter, while the second service—inbound calls—was discussed in this chapter. The inbound customer call can be about product questions, general complaints, part or product orders, or field-service requests. All of these calls can now be handled by a telemarketing company. The key points made in this chapter are as follows:

- The primary advantage of this approach is that the supplier has experience in rapidly setting up the call centers and training the staff needed to accept customer calls, which is not a primary area of expertise for most companies.

- The key contractual issues are pricing and ensuring that the call center is open for a sufficient number of hours and has enough staff to rapidly handle all inbound calls.

- The transition to the supplier is mostly handled by the supplier, but the company must be sure to assist with installing any connections to the company's computer database as expeditiously as possible.

- Control over the supplier comes from the large array of activity reports that a competent supplier should be able to issue to the company, coupled with audits of those reports to ensure their accuracy.

- Measurements can cover system downtime, cost or revenue per call, the overflow call percentage, and retention rates.

- The company's functional coordinator tends to be a mid-level manager with good product knowledge and people skills.

- Customer service concerns are that customers cannot get through to the call center, and that they cannot receive an answer to their queries once they have gotten through.

- Termination of a customer service supplier requires advance planning to ensure that inbound calls are switched to either an in-house service or a different supplier.

In short, for a company with a significant volume of inbound customer calls, using a supplier to manage a call center provides top-notch customer service while keeping the company's investment in money and management time to a minimum.

CHAPTER SEVEN

Outsourcing the Engineering Function

The engineering function is usually viewed by management as the last function to be outsourced. The engineers' knowledge of the company's products is considered to be so crucial to the survival of the company that moving the engineers to an engineering supplier is considered far too risky—the engineers may resent the switch and quit, the company's product engineering information may find its way through the supplier to competitors, or the supplier will then hold a "knowledge club" over the head of the company, and can charge any price for its services.

There are no engineering companies at a national level that provide a total set of engineering services to companies, though there are many regional engineering firms that provide these services. However, there are a number of specialty engineering design firms that provide services to companies anywhere in the country. These companies focus on the exterior design of a product. They include RKS Design, Ideo, ECCo Design, Stone & Co., Designhaus, Botzen Design, and Kroll Associates.

There are a number of circumstances where it is reasonable to consider outsourcing all or a part of the engineering function to an engineering supplier. These circumstances include poor internal management of the engineering function, having large swings in the number of engineering projects, stripping away noncrucial engineering projects, or when the supplier's engineering staff is better than the internal staff. In these cases, the company has a valid reason for changing to an outsourced solution. This chapter discusses the advantages and disadvantages of making such a change, contractual issues related to engineering, transition problems that may arise, and control points to install to ensure that the outsourced engineering function will operate correctly. In addition, appropriate measurements are described, management issues discussed, potential customer service problems noted, and, finally, several points are laid out related to getting out of an engineering outsourcing arrangement. This chapter should give the reader sufficient information to make a "go / no go" decision for outsourcing the engineering function, as well as information on how to manage the transition and ongoing issues thereafter.

7.1   ADVANTAGES AND DISADVANTAGES

There are a variety of advantages and disadvantages to outsourcing various portions of the engineering function. These issues should be carefully considered by company management before any decision to outsource is reached. Though the obvious issue is that the company is transferring a potentially significant knowledge base to a supplier, there are other issues to be considered as well. This section details all of the arguments both in favor of and against the decision to outsource the engineering function, and also presents some halfway solutions.

The first issue to consider is that the typical engineering department is composed of two sets of people: engineers and drafting personnel. The company's true knowledge base lies in the engineers and not in the drafting personnel, whose job it is to translate the engineer's efforts onto various types of drawings. If the company feels that knowledge of its products is too valuable to outsource, it may prefer to retain its engineering staff and outsource the drafting component of the department. However, the engineers may want to work as physically close as possible to the drafting personnel, which usually results in more efficient and accurate drawing work. If this is a major concern for the engineers, it may be a factor in selecting a drafting supplier who is geographically quite close to the engineering staff, or who may be willing to manage a group of drafters at the company's location. Thus, the company has a choice of outsourcing all or a portion of the engineering department, and of how far away any split-off sections should be.

There are a variety of reasons for not outsourcing the engineering function of the engineering department. One is that the company may lose a valuable knowledge base that is critical to the construction of its new products. This is of particular concern if the company's key competitive advantage is in the design of its new products (as opposed to other advantages, such as having a top-notch distribution network); in some cases, the speed of new product design may also be a competitive advantage. This advantage is usually centered in a core group of very experienced and knowledgeable engineers who represent such a competitive advantage for the company that it would be a great loss to move them to an engineering supplier. At its worst, this problem can be exacerbated in the hands of an unscrupulous supplier—by waiting until it has obtained all of a company's engineers, it then holds a "knowledge club" over the company, which can no longer create its own products without recreating its engineering staff at great expense, and who must therefore accede to any demands made by the supplier for extra reimbursement.

Another problem with outsourcing the engineering function is that the company may lose its ability to protect its new product designs with patents. This problem is highly dependent on the exact wording of the company's agreement with an engineering supplier; it could specify that the supplier retains the patent (since its staff came up with the product), that the company owns the patent (since it paid for the work), or that either one owns the patent but that all resulting profits are split between the two companies. Unless this issue is specified in the outsourcing agreement, the company may find that the supplier owns the rights to the products it is designing for the company.

The company may also find that, by supporting the engineering work of a supplier, its engineering expertise in the company's industry becomes so great that the supplier is able to offer the same engineering services to the company's competitors, who are then able to compete more closely because they are, in effect, sharing in the knowledge that the company helped the supplier to build. This type of problem can be avoided by adding a non-compete clause to the company's contract with the supplier, and may also be of no concern if there are no competitors in the supplier's geographical area. However, transferring knowledge to competitors through the engineering supplier is always a danger to be considered.

The final disadvantage of using an engineering supplier is that the knowledge obtained by the supplier from the company may be transferred to competitors through other means than having the supplier design similar products for them. For example, the supplier may be bought in whole or in part by a competitor, who thereby receives all engineering information and (more importantly) the engineers who are knowledgeable in the design of new products in the company's industry. This information can also be transferred by a direct sale of the information to a competitor, or by the hiring of key engineering staff by a competitor (which is quite likely if the supplier is no longer interested in providing services in that industry, and therefore decides to release the engineering staff for employment elsewhere). The company can cover itself by contractually requiring the transfer of all information back to itself at the conclusion of each project or in the event of the sale of the supplier, and it can require that a confidentiality agreement be signed at the beginning of the outsourcing arrangement. In addition, the company can require that the supplier notify it when certain engineering personnel are to be laid off, which gives the company a chance to extend a job offer to those people before a competitor has a chance to make them an offer. Nonetheless, the loss of key engineering information or staff to competitors can be a concern significant enough to stop any move to outsource the engineering function.

While there are a variety of reasons why a company should never outsource its engineering functions, there are also several good reasons in favor of doing so. One is that engineering is one of the most difficult functions to manage; if done improperly, the company may find itself investing enormous amounts of resources in the design of new products, resulting in very expensive design work that is being completed far later than expected. If the company can find a supplier with better engineering management, it may be worthwhile to transfer its entire engineering staff to that supplier just to take advantage of its better management, since it could result in lower engineering costs and the quicker completion of designs.

Another advantage is that the supplier may have a higher-quality engineering staff than the company. This may give the company a decided advantage in designing higher-quality products faster than it may be able to do with its in-house staff. This is a particular problem for those companies with relatively new engineering departments, which may be staffed with engineers having a very small number of years experience, and which have not yet learned to work together to efficiently create new products. The only disadvantage of this approach is that any resulting outsourcing of the function may result in the firing of the entire in-house engineering staff rather than moving them to the supplier, since the supplier has no need for junior-level engineers.

Outsourcing the engineering function is also of use for a smaller company that cannot fully utilize its in-house staff on enough projects to keep it busy all of the time. In this case, the company must sustain a significant fixed cost even when there is a slowdown in business. By outsourcing this cost, the company can convert a fixed cost to a variable cost that must only be incurred if new engineering projects come up. This argument can also be used by companies with highly variable swings in the volume of its engineering work—it can maintain a small core of engineers who can handle all of the work that the company attracts during its slowest periods, and then outsource all extra work that comes in when the company's sales exceed the minimum level. This ensures that the largest possible portion of the company's engineering expense is converted to a variable cost that will go away when the volume of business drops. By outsourcing all or a portion of its engineering work, a company can convert the cost to a variable one or keep its fixed personnel costs at a minimum.

A final advantage to outsourcing the engineering function is when the engineering work being performed is of a noncompetitive nature. For example, many companies design their own buildings and production layouts in-house, above and beyond the more common engineering work on new-product development. If company management has a concern about outsourcing the engineering function because crucial competitive information will be moved outside of the company, then it should consider retaining the new-product development engineering staff and outsourcing the engineers who are occupied with other tasks that are not so important. By outsourcing engineering work that is not related to new-product development, the company can focus its engineering resources on only the most strategically important issues, and let someone else handle less competitively important tasks.

So far we have discussed the advantages and disadvantages of outsourcing the engineers in the engineering department, showing that there are situations when a company's management will be fully justified in retaining the engineering function, while there may be opportunities in certain cases for outsourcing a portion or all of the engineering task as well. There is another group within the engineering function that must be considered as well, one that may outnumber the engineers: the drafting group. These people convert the conceptual drawings of the engineers into more detailed drawings. This group is not as skilled as the engineers, but must still be capable of creating detailed electrical, air conditioning, and mechanical drawings. Many junior engineers start work as drafting employees and then work their way up into engineering positions. Some drafting personnel are skilled enough that they are considered to be just as valuable as full-fledged engineers. Nonetheless, this is a lesser skill position with a lesser knowledge base, and, consequently, there are different advantages and disadvantages to outsourcing the drafting function. These issues are discussed in the following paragraphs.

One problem with outsourcing the drafting function is that there is some risk that the completed drawings will find their way into the hands of competitors—this despite the presence of a confidentiality agreement, since drawings can be sufficiently modified to make it unclear as to the source of the information, rendering the confidentiality agreement meaningless in the hands of a less-than-ethical person. Drawings are especially easy to transfer when they can be removed from the premises on a diskette or even sent by electronic mail from the supplier's location to a competitor. However, this same problem can occur if the company has a disgruntled employee, so the danger of spreading confidential documents to competitors is not necessarily heightened by outsourcing the drafting function.

Another problem is that it is more efficient to have the drafting staff located as close as possible to the engineering staff, since these two groups must work closely together, with the engineers continually giving guidance and revising drawings that are in process. One way around this problem is to have the supplier's drafting staff relocate to the company's offices so that they are near the company's engineers, or outsource both the engineering and drafting functions to the same supplier, so that both functions are kept together. It is also possible for engineers to electronically access drawings by modem and review them over the telephone with drafters, who can see the engineers' updates marked on their electronic drawings. A less perfect alternative is video conferencing, which allows the engineers and drafters to see each other on television screens alongside images of their drawings, but the drawing images may not be clear enough for the engineers to properly review. Physical proximity of the engineers to the drafting staff is important and may be a good reason for not outsourcing the drafting function, but there are electronic alternatives that allow engineers to still review drawings regularly.

These disadvantages can be offset by several issues that make outsourcing the drafting function a viable option. One is that the company may have an inefficient in-house drafting function, which may be caused by lack of experience or poor management of the function. If there is a supplier with a more experienced staff or better drafting management, the company may experience an immediate improvement in the speed of completion and quality of its drawings by transferring the drafting work to that supplier. The only disadvantage of this approach is that the supplier may not want to hire the company's in-house drafting staff, who must then be laid off.

Another reason for outsourcing the drafting function is that it is not a critical company function. Unlike engineering, which requires a much higher degree of knowledge, the drafting function falls into a high-end clerical category—the drafter translates the engineer's concepts to paper, but does not add a considerable amount of value to the end product. Thus, by retaining the key engineering staff but moving the drafting staff to a supplier, a company can retain its crucial engineering knowledge base while avoiding the expense of managing an associated group that essentially has only clerical skills.

An option that allows some of the drafting function to be moved off-site is that there are nonessential drafting tasks that are not related to the creation of a company's next line of products, and which therefore do not require as much drafting skill, management by on-site engineers, or proximity to the company. These tasks are prime targets for outsourcing. Examples of such tasks are design work on production or administration facilities. There may even be suppliers available who specialize in the design of such building or machinery layouts, and which clearly have more skill in this area than the company's staff.

In summary, there are a large number of reasons why a company will not outsource any part of its engineering function, with the primary reason being that engineering is considered to be a mission-critical knowledge base. However, there are several good reasons why some companies should consider outsourcing this function—if the in-house staff lacks experience, management of the function is poor, some portions of it are engaged in less critical activities, or because there is an urgent need for large amounts of additional engineering skill. In these cases, company management may be fully justified in moving the engineering function to a supplier.

7.2   CONTRACT-SPECIFIC ISSUES

There are several contract-related issues that are unique to outsourcing the engineering function that must be settled before a company agrees to move the engineering function to a supplier. Without including these issues in the contract, the company is at risk in such areas as losing critical information to competitors, not being able to retrieve staff if the outsourcing agreement falls through, and losing patents developed by the supplier with the company's funding. This section explores these and other issues.

If there is one function that requires a confidentiality agreement, it is the one with an engineering supplier. There is considerable risk that a supplier will take on a company's engineering work, create a store of information regarding its products, and then use that information to solicit business from other companies within the same industry. The supplier is motivated to do this because it acquires industry expertise by hiring the company's engineering staff or building expertise over time by having its in-house staff work on the company's projects, and wants to use this expertise to expand the scope of its business. The company can avoid this problem by including in the contract a provision that entitles the company to pursue damages if the supplier is found to have transferred any company-specific knowledge to a competitor. It is very difficult to prove if information has been transferred, since drawings may be extensively modified, so an even better clause is to require the supplier to do business with no one else in the industry, which is a much easier activity to prove in court. The problem with this second option is that the supplier's ability to sell its services elsewhere in the industry will be curtailed if it agrees to this clause, and so there will be great resistance to it. A possible midway point of agreement here is to prohibit the supplier from doing business with any competitors for a specified number of months or years following completion of work with the company. This variation may be more palatable to the company, since engineering work in most industries is obsolete after a relatively short period of time, which makes the loss of this information to a competitor of less importance if a small amount of time has passed. These non-compete agreements are easier to include in the contract if the volume of engineering work to be transferred to the supplier is quite large, since the supplier has a large profit incentive. If the company has only a small amount of business to give to the supplier, then forcing it to not do business elsewhere within the industry is not likely. A confidentiality agreement is a core part of the engineering outsourcing agreement; however, due to some difficulty in enforcing it, a better approach is to add a non-compete clause to the agreement, which may be a difficult clause to get the supplier to agree to.

There should also be a clause in the contract related to the transfer of assets from the company to the supplier. This is much less of an issue than for other functions, such as computer systems, where the total cost of assets transferred is quite large. The only assets to be transferred for the engineering and drafting functions are any computer-aided design (CAD) computers and the CAD software that runs on them. The company will no longer have a need for them, and the supplier will need to purchase computers for any transferred staff, so the transfer of these assets may be included in the contract. However, the licenses for some of the better CAD software may be restricted to the use of the company, with no option to transfer the software to another company. This problem should be reviewed with the software supplier prior to including any software-transfer clause in the contract with the engineering supplier. Also, the supplier may have standardized on a different kind of software, and will not want to purchase the company's software. The supplier also may not want to purchase the computers or software if no staff is being transferred to the supplier—in this case, it will have no need for the equipment. Finally, the company may want to include a clause in the contract that specifies the prices at which it will buy back all computers and software if the agreement with the supplier is terminated. However, computers decline in value so rapidly that the buy-back agreement should include a sliding scale that allows the company to buy back the equipment for prices that rapidly go down over the next few years. Given that computers are essentially worthless after a few years, the clause should also specify that the company is under no obligation to buy back the equipment after a specific number of years, certainly no more than three years. Since the company may want to purchase newer and more powerful computers after a few years, it will be even less enthusiastic about buying back old computers if the outsourcing agreement is terminated. In short, the company may want to sell its engineering computer hardware and software if it outsources this function, but the supplier may not want it if it already has enough equipment or uses another kind of software; also, the company may not want to buy back the equipment and software if the agreement fails, since it will become obsolete very rapidly.

There are several contract issues related to the engineers and drafting personnel who are to be transferred to the supplier when the outsourcing agreement is finalized. One issue is that these people may not find the supplier to their liking, and will leave. If the company has a desire to retain some engineering presence within its own walls, it can insert a clause into the contract that requires the supplier to notify the company of any such departures as soon as they occur, so that it has a chance to hire back the former employees. However, there are not many employees who will want to go back to a company that has already let them go once! Another personnel-related clause is that the supplier may not try to hire away any remaining engineering staff that the company retains (and vice versa). The company is likely to retain its most experienced staff to act as coordinators, and this is exactly the staff that the supplier can use the most, so this is a real concern. An effective clause to prevent this problem is to have the supplier pay the company some large penalty, such as six months of the employee's pay, if such an employee is hired. This may not be a large concern, since the supplier may not want to jeopardize its relationship with the company by hiring away key staff, especially if the outsourcing contract is a large one. A final employee-related issue is that the supplier may want the company to make severance payments to any employees that were transferred to the supplier in the event that the contract with the supplier is canceled. This is a reasonable request if the supplier is not in a position to move the staff to other outsourcing projects. The severance-payment amount should drop over time, however, as the company does not want to be in the position of having to make large severance payments for its former staff who were transferred to the supplier 10 years before. A reasonable severance-payment agreement would use the following scale, which reduces the portion of the severance paid by the company over four years:

Year	Percent Paid by Company	Percent of Pay Paid to Staff
1	100%	20%
2	75%	20%
3	50%	20%
4	25%	20%
Subsequent	0%	20%

If the company agrees to pay for severance, it is important to include in the contract the formula for calculating severance payments. Since engineering personnel have, on average, high pay rates, this severance amount can be substantial if it is based on some percentage of their base pay. The above example assumes that each engineer will receive 20% of annual base pay. Another common formula is one week of pay for every one year of service, which should include the combined number of service years with both the company and the supplier. Thus, the contract should include clauses that cover hiring employees back from the supplier, preventing the supplier from hiring away any remaining engineering staff, and severance-payment requirements in case the contract is canceled.

Another important legal issue is the rights of the company and the supplier to any patents that are developed as a result of the supplier's engineering work for the company. The supplier's view of this situation is that it should be entitled to all patent rights, since its staff came up with the idea for the patent. The company's view of the situation is that it should at least have some share in the benefits of the patent, since it paid the supplier to come up with the idea. The two entities should decide on this issue and insert appropriate language into the initial contract to cover this eventuality, even if there does not initially seem to be any likelihood of products or techniques being invented that can be patented—this keeps the two parties from squabbling later on if a patent *does* result from the work being done by the supplier for the company. One possible clause is to give one party all rights to any future patents, in exchange for greater benefits to the other party, such as a change in the fee structure. Another option is to give one party the right to apply for any patents, but with both parties taking some portion of any resulting profits; if this approach is used, it is generally best to include additional wording regarding any future splits of development costs (which can greatly exceed the initial cost to invent the product or process). It might also be convenient to include a termination date for any profit-splitting agreements; otherwise, the company doing the profit-sharing calculations may end up continuing to make the calculations for many years after the bulk of the cash flow resulting from a patent has stopped. It is useful to anticipate any conflicts arising out of one party's filing for a patent based on the work of the engineering supplier that is being funded by the company.

There are several contract-specific issues in the engineering area that do not arise or are less important when other company functions are outsourced. One is the need for confidentiality agreements, since engineering information is frequently considered to be core company information. Another issue is the transfer back and forth of engineering computers and software between the company and its supplier, because of problems with the transferability of software licenses and the rapid decline in value of software equipment. Yet another concern is "stealing" of engineering staff from the company by the supplier, as well as issues surrounding who makes severance payments to engineering staff if the company shuts down its outsourcing agreement with the supplier. Finally, the two parties must decide in advance who will receive the benefits from any patents that originate from work done by the supplier for the company. For all of these reasons, a company should pay particular attention to the creation of the engineering outsourcing contract between the company and its supplier.

7.3   TRANSITION ISSUES

There are an unusually large number of steps involved in the engineering transition process that moves a company's engineering function to a supplier. This is because there are really two functions—engineering and drafting—that must be moved, as well as because transferring staff is a key issue—engineers are usually moved to the supplier rather than laid off, so they must be treated especially carefully during this transition phase. In addition, there are almost always ongoing projects that must be moved to the supplier when they are only partly completed, which requires good managerial skill to achieve. For these reasons and more, the transition of the engineering function to a supplier is especially important.

The first step in the transition process is selecting the in-house engineering coordinator. This is a step that many companies leave for much later in the process, but that means that there is no designated company representative who is completely responsible for completing the early stages of the transition process. The coordinator should be a very senior engineer who has considerable engineering and management experience. If there is any choice between having more engineering skill or more management skill, the company should select the person with more management skill. This is because the coordinator's role involves a great deal of oversight of and contact with the supplier. Once selected, the coordinator must be given complete authority and responsibility for completing the contract negotiations with the supplier as well as all subsequent transition steps. By keeping these steps away from a committee—which would surely slow down the decision-making process—the company will complete the outsourcing process much more quickly.

The next step is to create a skills database for each engineering and drafting employee. Since the outsourcing decision is still being kept secret, this information can be gleaned from employees' human resources records as well as from discussions with a few selected engineering managers. It is important to have this information completed in advance, since it can take some time to complete, and is a step that would otherwise hold up completion of the outsourcing process once the decision has been announced to the staff—and any slowdown in the process once the staff has been informed gives the staff extra time to become worried, search for work elsewhere, and leave before being hired by the supplier.

Once there has been a preliminary selection of a supplier, the supplier must sign a confidentiality agreement. This is because the next step is for the supplier to review the company's engineering operations to verify that its initial bid was accurate—after this phase, which is called the "due diligence" phase, the two organizations will finalize the contract. During the process of reviewing the company's engineering operations, it is likely that the supplier will obtain a good idea of the company's strengths and weaknesses, such as the quality of the staff, the lateness of problems with various current projects, and the nature of those projects. This type of information may be useful to competitors if the supplier were to transfer it to them, so the confidentiality agreement must be signed prior to giving the supplier access to any inside information. The confidentiality agreement is sometimes necessary when suppliers are being used to outsource other company functions, but the engineering function is the one area where it is mandatory—this is usually an area where much critical, competitive information resides, and losing it through a supplier could have a serious impact on the company's market share and profitability.

Once these steps have been taken, it is time for the prospective supplier to go through the due diligence phase to ensure that the information the company has given it, and which it used to submit its bid, is correct. The key part of this due diligence phase is determining the quality of the engineering staff. This is of major importance, since the supplier will probably want to use a significant proportion of the existing staff to continue working under its employment. One way to ascertain the quality of the engineering staff is to review their resumes and a database of their skills; information that was prepared in a previous step. More information can be gleaned from discussions with the company's engineering management, which is likely to have insights into the work habits and knowledge of each engineer. However, the supplier will eventually have to interview each engineer, and this means that the company must, at this point, reveal to the staff that outsourcing is being considered. The major part of the due diligence phase is reviewing the background and skills of the existing engineering staff.

The initial contact with the engineering staff is extremely important. The company's management must bear in mind that the core competency of the engineering department is its staff, not its patents, software, or hardware. If anything is said during that first meeting to worry the engineering staff, they will take new jobs elsewhere very quickly, which can seriously impact the company's—and the supplier's—ability to continue the engineering function. It is important that the engineering staff be told everything: the status of negotiations, expectations for hiring staff into the supplier's company, and a timeline for activities that must be completed before the outsourcing agreement is finalized. It would be useful for the presenters of this information to role-play the situation in advance, with someone asking all of the most uncomfortable and difficult questions, so that the presenting team is satisfied that it can reasonably answer all questions. If there are any questions that cannot be answered yet for lack of information—such as the severance-payment formula to be used—it may be worthwhile to obtain that information before the meeting so that employees will receive the most complete package of information possible at that time. This is particularly difficult for the company's managers who take part in the employee meeting, since they are not likely to have gone through this painful process before. This meeting is a normal part of business for the supplier, and so its representative at the meeting is likely to be prepared for most questions already. After the meeting is over, the presenters should make themselves available to all engineers for additional questions for as long as it takes to answer every question. By taking these steps, the company and the supplier can give the engineering staff as complete a set of information as possible, which helps to retain the staff during the transition phase.

In-depth communication with the engineering staff is particularly important once the outsourcing decision has been made. This is because engineers are generally able to switch jobs with comparative ease, and will be tempted to jump ship and move to some other organization if they suspect that their pay, benefits, or working conditions will degrade as a result of the transfer to the engineering supplier. The only way for them to gain some assurance about the supplier is to have supplier management regularly come in and discuss the progress of the outsourcing situation. It would be very beneficial if the supplier's engineering manager—who will be managing all business with the company—can talk to the staff, since they will want to get some idea of the management methods and style of their new supervisor. Any questions by the engineering staff should be answered as honestly and clearly as possible, since they will be comparing what they are told to what actually happens, and some loss of staff is likely if they perceive any difference between the two.

The next transition step is to transfer to the supplier all project status information, so that the supplier can rapidly continue with existing projects with a minimum amount of downtime. At a high level, the supplier needs to have a schedule of all projects currently under development, which should include hours expended versus budgeted hours, as well as milestones already achieved and the due dates for all remaining milestones for each project. This information not only gives the supplier a good idea of the status of each existing project, but also some idea of the expectations of company management—this is the schedule that the company's management expected to achieve prior to the outsourcing agreement, and management will likely expect the supplier to achieve it as well. The company's new outsourcing coordinator must be deeply involved in this phase, since this will be the coordinator's job: overseeing the completion of projects by the supplier. The supplier should therefore staff the project sufficiently to meet the expectations of this initial project schedule. At a lower level, the supplier should discuss the engineering project schedule with the engineering staff to spot any unrealistic milestones that are coming up. If anyone knows of any problems with the schedule, it is likely to be the existing engineering staff, so these discussions should take place as soon as possible so that the supplier will gain a realistic view of the schedule that it has been given. The best way to get some idea of the scope of existing work is for the supplier to review the existing engineering project schedule with the engineering staff.

Once the supplier has reviewed the staff and its qualifications, as well as the current project schedule, it should work with the company to finalize the contract. The final contract should include the following items that are specific to the engineering function:

- *Time to begin.* The supplier will need time to marshal its internal resources (such as engineering and drafting staff, as well as management) so that it can complete the company's current schedule of engineering projects. This time-to-begin clause should also include the time to obtain workstations, work space, and software licenses for the engineers and draftsmen. The time needed by the supplier before it can take over the engineering function should be built into the contract.

- *Agree to complete current projects.* The contract should have an attachment that lists the company's current short-term schedule of engineering projects. The supplier should agree in the contract to complete this work within the specified time frame, with various penalties occurring if these deadlines are not met. This clause prevents the company from having any short-term problems with project completions.

- *Employment contracts.* Some of the top engineers must be retained to work on company functions. This clause should not only stipulate that these people will be offered guaranteed positions with the supplier, but also that they will be used only on company projects for some prearranged time period, and not moved off to some other client of the supplier.

The above contract clauses are noted here instead of in the previous section on contract-specific issues because they are contract changes that typically occur at the last minute, after the supplier has gone through the due diligence phase. It is only at this point that either party to the contract will be sure of the time needed for the supplier to take over the function, which projects must be completed and the timeline needed to do so, and which staff will be hired by the supplier.

The next step is to announce the finalized contract to the staff. Once again, the company and the supplier must go to great lengths to ensure that the entire engineering and drafting staff have been fully informed of the parts of the contract that relate to them—who is going to the supplier, who is being retained by the company, and who is being given guaranteed employment contracts. The supplier must be up front with those of the staff who will be transferred to the supplier, but who will then be transferred to some other location to service the needs of a different client. New pay rates will also be an issue for anyone being moved to the supplier, while severance packages will be of the greatest concern to those leaving the company. Since most of the information being disseminated at this point is confidential to each member of the engineering staff, it is usually best to have a brief meeting with the full staff to go over a few general points, and then meet with each member of the department individually to go over their situations. It may still be necessary after those steps are completed to meet with the full department one more time to see if there are any remaining issues to be discussed. It is important during this step to thoroughly cover those parts of the completed contract that impact each member of the engineering department.

Once the contract has been signed, the company must transfer a large amount of information to the supplier to ensure a smooth transition. This information should include employee files as well as nearly everything related to each current or upcoming engineering project: bills of material, drawings, meeting minutes, specifications, memos, and Gantt charts. The company should put a considerable amount of time into ensuring that this information is properly organized and reviewed with the supplier to ensure that the supplier files it away in an organized manner. This helps to ensure that the supplier will not lose any information, and that it will have ready access to the correct information, which will make it operate more efficiently on the company's projects once the transfer has been completed. Doing this extra work for the supplier is in the company's best interests, since the supplier will come up to speed more rapidly. An additional point is that the company should make copies of all documents sent to the supplier. This information may be needed in case the relationship with the supplier falls apart, requiring the company to rapidly restart its engineering operations. Organizing and promptly sending all engineering information to the supplier helps to ensure a smooth transition, while retaining a copy of this information keeps the company from being unable to complete projects in process if the supplier cannot complete the work.

The staff must then be transferred to the supplier. Physically, this can be a very simple process if the department is being kept on-site by the supplier—in fact, there will be no difference. The staff will simply show up for work and be managed by the supplier's managers. However, this is rarely the case. The engineers and drafting personnel are usually moved to the supplier's location. The company should be as helpful in this process as possible, partially to make the transfer for its former staff as easy as possible, and partially because it wants its former staff to be up and running on its projects as soon as possible. For both reasons, the company should assist in moving the personnel to their new quarters, which may include paying for moving them and any of their equipment that is going to the supplier. In terms of human resources paperwork such as medical and tax documents, the company and the supplier should work together, so that each employee can go to one session with representatives from both organizations and be terminated from one organization and enrolled into the other. The supplier may also want to arrange a tour of its facilities for those engineers who are being moved there, which may include an informal meeting with the supplier's staff, so that the engineers will become more comfortable with the idea of making the transition. The emphasis on this transfer is to make the move as painless as possible for the engineering staff—they are valuable, and this process must go smoothly to ensure that no one will want to quit and go elsewhere.

Finally, the company must find other uses for the office space previously occupied by the engineering staff. If part of the outsourcing agreement is to have the engineering staff stay on in its current location, this is not an issue. However, if the engineering staff is being laid off or moved to the supplier's location, the company will have excess space to dispose of. This space is frequently office space that is in the same building as the offices of other administrative or production functions, which makes it difficult to sell or sublease the space to other companies. The best option, unless the vacated space is sufficiently stand-alone to warrant subleasing or sale of the building, frequently is to leave the space empty until some other unrelated function has enough of a surge in business to warrant adding staff and moving it into this space. If there is valuable office equipment or furniture in the vacated engineering space, the company can either put it in storage until other parts of the company need it (an option that occupies storage space and ties up working capital) or sell it to an office equipment broker. In short, the company may be forced to retain the office space used by the engineering staff subsequent to outsourcing, but may be able to dispose of the engineers' office furniture and equipment.

The transition of the engineering function from the company to the supplier must be handled carefully, primarily because the extremely valuable and irreplaceable members of the engineering department may be motivated to leave if the transition is not fully explained to them at all steps of the process, and is not handled in an employee-sensitive manner. Thus, the most important steps in the process involve announcing the possibility of outsourcing to the staff, and, later, announcing a finalized agreement, which should include one-on-one interviews with the engineers to go over each person's situation under the new outsourcing arrangement. If the engineering staff is not handled properly, engineers may leave rather than work for the supplier. Other transition steps, which are noted in Figure 7.1, include designating a coordinator early in the process, having the supplier sign a confidentiality agreement, going

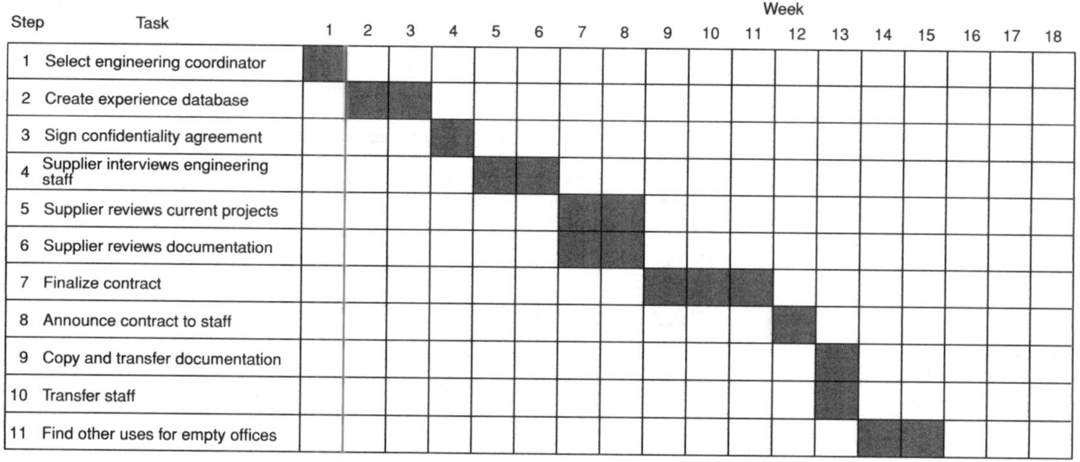

Step	Task	1	2	3	4	5	6	7	8	9	10	11	12	13	14	15	16	17	18
1	Select engineering coordinator	█																	
2	Create experience database			█															
3	Sign confidentiality agreement				█														
4	Supplier interviews engineering staff					█													
5	Supplier reviews current projects							█											
6	Supplier reviews documentation								█										
7	Finalize contract									█	█								
8	Announce contract to staff												█						
9	Copy and transfer documentation													█					
10	Transfer staff													█					
11	Find other uses for empty offices															█			

Week

Figure 7.1 Gantt Chart for the Implementation of all Engineering Transition Issues

over all current and upcoming projects with the supplier, and ensuring that all project-related information is completely organized before being transferred to the supplier. These steps must be handled as completely and professionally as possible to ensure a smooth transition of the engineering function to the supplier.

7.4   CREATING CONTROL POINTS

It is essential to maintain tight control over the engineering function for several reasons. One is that it is easy for the supplier to expend too many hours on company-related work, resulting in very expensive billings to the company—after all, engineering rates per hour are very high. Another reason is that the supplier may end up producing drawings of the wrong products unless the company retains tight control over the specifications that the supplier is using to create new products. A final reason is that the timing of the work being completed by the supplier may stray from the budget unless it is closely reviewed by the company at regular intervals. For all of these reasons—cost, results, and time—it is mandatory that the company set up a strong set of controls to monitor the outsourced engineering function. This section describes those controls.

One of the most important ways to control an engineering project is not by direct oversight, but by ensuring that the supplier has enough information about the project to complete it properly. If the supplier has enough information, there is less chance that anything will go wrong with the project, which therefore requires less oversight by the engineering coordinator. One way to give more information to the supplier is for the coordinator to write and distribute the minutes from all meetings involving engineering designs, budgets, or milestones. These minutes should be in sufficient detail for all parties to be accurately informed about any changes resulting from the meeting. The supplier's team should also have a chance to revise the minutes if they think they contain inaccuracies. Both the coordinator and the supplier can then store these minutes in a project file, which becomes a valuable database of information about each project. An example of such project minutes is shown in Figure 7.2. The minutes should include the date of the meeting (since subsequent meeting minutes may supersede these), who attended, what items were agreed upon, and what is still to be done.

One of the meeting attendees in the example memo was a project librarian. Having the supplier use an engineering librarian to store information about each project is a useful, though indirect, way to maintain control over a project, since the supplier is assured of having ready access to all information about the project. This leads to fewer problems from having insufficient information, which means that the coordinator will have fewer control problems with the supplier.

Providing project minutes to the supplier is a passive form of control. A more active control is the use of change order tracking. This method requires the company to formally write down and present to the supplier any changes to a design that the supplier is working on for the company. The supplier then formally logs in the change

Figure 7.2   Project Minutes

Arbuthnot Computer Company
Date: June 20, 19XX
To: Jeff Hicks, Supplier Project Manager
         David Rogers, Supplier Assistant Lead
         Martha Romble, Project Librarian

From: Alice Smythe, Company Engineering Coordinator
Project Meeting Date: June 19, 19XX
Attendees: Smythe, Hicks, Rogers, Romble, Davis, Von Stuble

Items Agreed Upon:
1. Change case cover to black matte finish.
2. Change case cover composition to aluminum.
3. Move company logo on case cover to upper right corner.
4. Flip board slots over sideways for "slimline" look.
5. Move fan to back left corner.
6. Integrate sound card into mother board.
7. Change mother board completion date to June 7, 20XX.

Items Still to be Agreed Upon:
1. Reduce number of board slots to three from five.
2. Integrate modem into mother board.
3. Increase speed of modem.
4. Add four additional RAM plug-in slots.
5. Bring forward project completion date to November 30, 20XX.

---

order request, determines the impact on its schedule of the change, and writes back to the company regarding the impact the change will have on the fees and project deadlines. The company's engineering coordinator and the supplier's project manager then meet to formally negotiate and agree upon the changed fees and project deadlines. Once agreement has been reached, a formal change order is completed, signed by both parties, and used to change the project schedule. This process may seem slow (it is), but it allows both parties to retain good control over the course of the project. A supplier would probably go out of business without change control, since it would be snowed under by a flurry of changes by the company, who would have no incentive *not* to make as many changes as possible. Only with proper change order control can both parties be fully aware of the impact of changes on the cost and timeline of an engineering project.

Another good control is frequent review meetings with the supplier. These meetings should be attended by the engineering coordinator on behalf of the company, and by the supplier's project manager and anyone who is working on the specific project being discussed. The purpose of these meetings is to review in detail the ongoing progress on each project. The topics should include a review of any completed drawings, upcoming milestones, costs versus the budget, and changes to specifications. The intent here is to ensure that the engineering team does not go too far off course before being corrected by the engineering coordinator. The cost of redoing work that has not been monitored is very high, since hourly engineering costs are among the highest supplier hourly costs of all functions. For example, a typical small engineering task force would include an engineer and two drafting personnel. If they work a 40-hour week and have chargeable rates of $125 and $70 per hour, respectively, this adds up to $10,600 of work that would have to be redone if they were to stray off course for only one week! Thus, tight control through frequent project meetings is mandatory.

Another form of control is through the presence of milestones, due dates, and penalty clauses. The supplier cannot be expected to complete a project on time if the company does not even negotiate a deadline for the project—something that happens surprisingly frequently. A properly controlled project should include a Gantt chart that contains all upcoming project milestones and deadlines; this should be accompanied by a penalty schedule that lists how much the supplier will either pay to the company if it completes its work late, how much it will be unable to bill the customer if its work is late, or what kind of a bonus it will receive if its work is completed early. Most engineering suppliers will not agree to penalty payments, but it is possible to force a supplier to absorb extra costs by adopting a fixed-fee arrangement for each separate contract, under which the supplier receives a fixed amount of money, with alterations to this amount only being made through formal, signed change orders. The worst form of control is to pay a straight hourly rate to the supplier with no limitation. This gives the supplier an incentive to stretch out the project as long as possible in order to collect the largest amount of money for the project.

Another control point is for the coordinator to have a staff person regularly compare the work being completed by the supplier to the work specified in the original contract for each project. This review will frequently reveal that the supplier is charging the company extra for items that are listed in the original contract as being performed at no additional cost. To do this, the coordinator must have a complete file of all contracts, meeting minutes, supplier billings, and other correspondence, so that a comparison of all available information can be used. This comparison should not be done at the end of the project, but rather after each billing is received from the supplier. This allows the company to spot billing irregularities immediately and have them corrected, rather than be billed too much throughout the life of the project and then have to negotiate with the supplier after all work is completed for the return of excess payments. Frequent reviews of supplier billings to contract terms will probably uncover extra billings for items that should be part of the baseline work to be completed by the supplier.

Once a project is complete, the engineering coordinator should have a staff person conduct a completed project review to verify that all work has actually been completed. This is the point where the company wants to be sure that every detail has been completed before the supplier disbands the project team that created the engineering drawings and disperses them to other teams for other projects. This review should verify that all drawings have appropriate management sign-offs (which may include approvals by other managers, such as manufacturing personnel who must use these drawings to produce the product), that all drawings have been completed, and that all terms of the original contract and subsequent change orders have been met. This is a fairly mechanical process; the engineering coordinator can systematize it by creating a checklist of standard items that should be reviewed at the completion of all projects. For example, the checklist for reviewing the completion of drawings could look like the one in Figure 7.3.

One of the problems with controlling the engineering function is that it is very difficult to bring in the company's internal audit group to conduct a review. This is because engineering is a very specialized function that is not easily measured. The only things that an internal audit group could look at would be the existence of basic management items that give some indication that the engineering coordinator and the supplier's project manager are doing their jobs. This review of project management could include a review of the project file to verify that there have been project-review meetings (perhaps compared to the coordinator's schedule to verify that all scheduled meeting dates have minutes on file) and that official meeting minutes were kept. This review could also include a review of how many days it took to distribute the minutes, based on the date on the meeting minutes; this is important, since quickly distributing revisions to the engineering team results in a cost savings if they would otherwise be spending their time working under incorrect specification assumptions. The distribution list for the meeting minutes can also be cross-checked against the team member list as well as a list of all other managers who should see this information to verify that all team members have been copied. Finally, the audit team can verify the number of days the project is running behind, and check the meeting minutes to see if there have been specific discussions about how the project can be brought back within its time budget. (This same approach can be used for the cost budget.) This review can also check the team's progress over time to see if it is falling further and further behind schedule. A sample audit program is shown in Fig-

Figure 7.3   Checklist for Final Review of Engineering Drawings

Drawing No.	Refers to Higher-Level Drawing?	Refers to Subsidiary Drawing?	Coordinator Sign-Off?	Mfg Sign-Off?	Confidentiality Notice?	Attached Bill of Materials?
14-0672	Yes	Yes	Yes	Yes	Yes	No
14-5133	Yes	N/A	Yes	Yes	No	No
14-3152	Yes	N/A	Yes	Yes	Yes	No
14-8821	Yes	Yes	No	No	Yes	Yes
14-7190	Yes	N/A	No	No	Yes	Yes
14-0031	Yes	N/A	Yes	Yes	Yes	No
14-0585	No	N/A	Yes	Yes	Yes	No
14-9032	Yes	No	Yes	Yes	Yes	No
14-9401	Yes	Yes	Yes	Yes	Yes	No

ure 7.4 that contains these steps. By taking these steps, the internal audit group can form an opinion about the supplier's level of control over its project team.

This section noted several controls that allow the company's engineering coordinator to maintain control over the engineering function, even when it is being run off-site by a supplier. These controls include periodic reviews of change orders, fre-

Figure 7.4   Sample Engineering Audit Program

Objective: Verify that the engineering function is being properly managed.
Audit Program: The following steps:
  1. Verify that all scheduled meetings have written minutes on file.
  2. Calculate the number of days to distribute minutes.
  3. Verify that all team members are on the distribution list.
  4. Determine if the project is behind schedule.
  5. Verify that the meeting minutes include a discussion of how to bring the project in line with the time budget.
  6. Determine if the project's cost is exceeding the budget.
  7. Verify that the meeting minutes include a discussion of how to bring the project in line with the cost budget.
Sample Size: Ten projects.
Test Detail: As follows:

Project	Minutes on File?	Days to Distribute Minutes	Everyone on Minutes Distribute List?	Project Behind Schedule?	Discussed Ways to Get Back on Schedule?	Cost Exceeding Budget?	Discussed Ways to Get Back on Schedule?
99-001	Yes	0	Yes	Yes	Yes	Yes	Yes
99-002	Yes	5	No	No	No	No	No
99-003	Yes	1	Yes	Yes	Yes	Yes	Yes
99-004	Yes	1	Yes	Yes	Yes	Yes	Yes
99-005	Yes	4	No	No	No	No	No
99-006	Yes	1	Yes	Yes	Yes	Yes	Yes
99-007	Yes	2	Yes	Yes	Yes	Yes	Yes
99-008	Yes	1	Yes	Yes	Yes	Yes	Yes
99-009	No	N/A	N/A	No	N/A	No	N/A

Results: Project 99-009 had just begun and therefore had no meeting minutes or time or cost overruns. Projects 99-002 and 99-005 have difficulty issuing meeting minutes within a regular time frame, do not issue minutes to the full list of personnel who should receive them, are behind schedule in terms of both time and cost, and have not discussed these problems as part of the meeting minutes.
Recommendations: Projects 99-002 and 99-005 are clearly having management problems. The engineering coordinator should discuss with the supplier the need to supplement or replace the management of these two projects. Also, schedule another audit of these two projects for one month from now; if problems continue, the engineering coordinator should insist that the managers of both projects be replaced.

quent drawing and specification reviews, regular dissemination of meeting minutes, imposing penalties for being late at various milestones, and conducting operational audits. When all of these controls are used, the coordinator will have a good idea of the day-to-day progress of the various projects being completed for the company by the supplier, resulting in a reduced chance of the supplier creating incorrect products, completing product designs too late, or going over budget on their designs.

7.5   MEASURING THE OUTSOURCED FUNCTION

Measuring the performance of the engineering department when it is located in-house, much less at a supplier, is one of the most difficult measurement tasks a corporation faces, because the results of the department are highly qualitative—producing an innovative, unique product is not something easily subject to measurement. It is very difficult to measure how much better the company's new product is than competing products. However, there are ways to measure the performance of the engineering function based on relative costs, project budget, initial error rates, experience, and the cycle time needed to fix product problems. There are problems associated with most of these measurements that the reader must be aware of before taking these measurements as gospel, but when reviewed as a group, all of these measurements can give management a clear picture of the performance of its engineering function. The following measurement descriptions include how to calculate a measurement, why it is useful, and what problems are associated with using it. The measurements are as follows:

- *Cost per drawing.* This measure is sometimes used to get a general idea of the productivity of the drafting staff. The measure is calculated by adding up the total number of drawings completed and signed off on by engineering management during the period, and dividing this number into the total cost incurred by the drafting function during the period. However, this can be a very misleading measurement for several reasons. One is that the time needed to complete a quality drawing can vary greatly between drawings, with perhaps an hour required for a simple mechanical drawing of one minor part and a week needed for a full side view of a general assembly drawing. Another problem is that the supplier's management will try to mix the drawings completed in each reporting period so that the target cost per drawing is achieved, with an emphasis on the easier drawings to ensure that the measurement goal is met. This means that the more difficult drawings will be left for last, even if those drawings are needed sooner. In short, using the cost-per-drawing measurement can result in disfunctional behavior that will skew the performance of the engineering supplier.

- *Cost by milestone.* The company can also work with the supplier to create a cumulative budgeted cost at each milestone in an engineering project. This cost can be used to compare to actual cumulative costs incurred at each milestone. This is a useful measurement from the perspective of keeping some control over ongoing costs, but does not address the problem of how long it takes for the supplier to reach each milestone—in today's competitive environment, it is at least as important to complete an engineering project on time as it is to do so within the budgeted cost.

- *Cost as a percentage of revenue.* It is not possible after the first year or two of having outsourced the engineering function to compare the current outsourcing cost to the company's previous engineering cost, because the company's volume of engineering work will probably have changed significantly, either up or down. Therefore, the company must find a different way to see if the total cost of the outsourced engineering function is still reasonable. One approach is to compare the total engineering cost (including the cost of the engineering coordinator and any attached staff) to the company's total revenues. However, this measurement assumes that there is a direct relationship between the company's engineering costs and the level of sales, which is not always true in the short run. For example, the company could spend a large amount of money to develop a product for which there is no market; years may be required to develop the market, so revenues will not increase even though the engineering expense has already been incurred. Another problem is that engineering costs may be expended on a product that fails in the marketplace—this not a case of having revenues lag the engineering expense, but rather of having no revenue increase at all. On the other hand, comparing the engineering expense to revenues over the long term is a more successful approach, since an ongoing engineering effort over many years typically does lead to an increase in revenues.

- *Days variance from milestone budgets.* One of a coordinator's best performance-tracking measurements is the number of days variance from various project milestones. This measurement is constructed by working out a project timeline and milestones in concert with the supplier, and then tracking the number of days variance from those milestones. The coordinator can use the measurement to calculate the most likely completion date for the entire project, since early variances from milestones are likely to carry forward to the end of the project. For example, if the variance from the completed conceptual drawings milestone is 10 days, the supplier will have considerable difficulty in erasing this variance on subsequent milestones, since it must complete the following milestones in a total of 10 days less than the budgeted dates. The coordinator can therefore use the cumulative number of days variance from the budgeted milestone dates to predict the actual completion date of the project. In addition, this is an excellent measure for ascertaining the level of supplier management. If the number of days variance continues to increase for all milestones, the supplier is clearly unable to manage the project. If the number of days variance does not increase after an initial jump due to missing one milestone, it is an indicator that the supplier has brought the project under control. If the number of days variance drops, the supplier appears to have strong management that is working to overcome the initial variance from an early milestone. All three types of trends in this measurement are noted in Figure 7.5.

• *Percentage of drawings that have passed review.* The company can get a good idea of the amount of work remaining on a drafting project if it knows in ad-

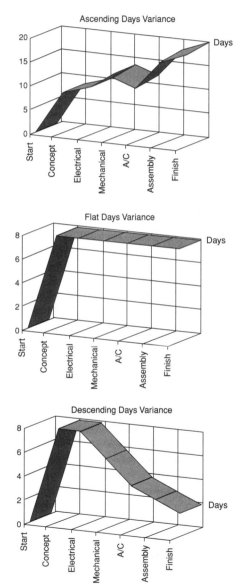

Figure 7.5   Number of Days Variance from Milestone Budgets

vance how many drawings are required for the entire project and then tracks the percentage of completed drawings that have passed the review process. This is a very good way to track the performance of the supplier, since the coordinator must review each drawing and agree that it is complete before it is added to this performance measurement. This gives the supplier less of a chance to manipulate the performance measurement. Unfortunately, it is still possible for the supplier to do so, since the easiest drawings can still be completed first, which may give a skewed view of how far along the project has progressed. In addition, it is possible (if not likely) that the project may require additional drawings as the design work progresses, which changes the baseline on which the percentages are being calculated.

- *Percentage of customer complaints / warranty claims.* The company can indirectly measure the quality of the engineering work performed by the supplier by determining the percentage of complaints about the product created by the supplier and seeing if this percentage is inordinately higher or lower than the company's historical experience with these types of products. The percentage is determined by accumulating either the total number of customer complaints or warranty claims received about the product and then dividing this number by the total number of units sold. This measurement can give the company some idea of the supplier's ability to design a product that is durable and useful, but the company should keep in mind that bad results in this area may have nothing to do with the supplier, for several reasons. First, the in-house engineering coordinator should have signed off on all drawings prior to having the production department begin production, so the responsibility for customer complaints can fall on the coordinator. Another reason is that the complaints may be related to poor manufacturing processes, which should have nothing to do with the supplier. Finally, the complaints may be related to the product concept, which was created by the company's research group, and which may have ordered the engineering supplier to design the product to its specifications, which were faulty. In short, there may be some validity to assigning responsibility for customer complaints to the engineering supplier, but the fault can also (rightfully) be placed elsewhere.

- *Percent of customer complaints / warranty claims after fixes.* This is a more realistic way to ascertain the quality of the supplier's work than measuring initial complaints or warranty claims, since problems causing initial claims may be the responsibility of other departments. However, the responsibility for fixing design flaws that are uncovered by customers lies primarily on the engineering function (with the production and materials departments having some responsibility as well, depending on the problem). If the level of complaints or warranty claims drops off after the product is modified by the engineering supplier, this is a sign that the supplier is doing a good job.

- *Average years experience of supplier personnel.* It is common for a supplier to present a very experienced team to the company (or at least show their resumes in the proposal) and then substitute a weaker team after the proposal has been accepted. To see if this is happening, the coordinator can track the average years experience of the supplier's team. This measurement can be for the total number of years experience since leaving college, but this will not factor in the most critical experience, which is the total number of years of engineering experience. Another related type of measurement is the number of years with a particular job title (such as "manager"). Though any of these measurements are of some use in getting an idea of the supplier team's general skill level, there are some problems with this approach. One is that some people can be vastly experienced but still have poor engineering ability. Another is that any measurement related to job title assumes that the person with a high-ranking title deserves the position. Since many supplier's are motivated to promote people to higher ranks as early as possible in order to bill them to the company at higher rates, this is not necessarily a correct assumption. If this measurement is to be used, the most valid one is the average number of years of engineering experience, since it focuses the most tightly on the key knowledge area that will impact the quality of work performed for the company.

- *Number of errors found during peer review.* The work of a single member of the supplier's engineering team is in its rawest form at the time when other people in the group review that person's drawings in what is known as a peer review. A large number of mistakes are typically found at this time, and therefore this can be a good way to determine the skill level of each person on the supplier's team. The problem with this approach is that the company's engineering coordinator does not usually attend peer reviews—this function is at a lower level that is almost always completed before the coordinator sees any drawings. One way to get around this problem is to have a subordinate of the coordinator attend peer reviews. Since everyone will know that the subordinate is attending the reviews only to make recommendations to the coordinator concerning who should be removed from the supplier's team, this will not be a popular person!

The previous measurement descriptions show that there are a large number of measurements that are available for the tracking of the performance of a company's engineering supplier. A single measurement is not sufficient for the oversight purposes of the engineering coordinator, however. Rather, it takes a cluster of measurements to determine if engineering work is being done on time, at the correct cost, and with a minimal number of errors. The coordinator may require an internal staff that is focused on tracking, summarizing, and presenting these measurements to the coordinator. Some of the measurements, such as errors uncovered during peer review, require substantial amounts of staff time to track, whereas others, such as the cost as a percentage of revenue, require very little time. Due to the wide range of efforts needed to track engineering measurements, the amount of resources available to the coordinator for this function may determine which measurements are used. When a mix of the above measurements are closely followed and acted upon by the engineering coordinator, the company should be able to spot problems in the engineering process and act to fix them before they become major issues.

7.6   MANAGING THE OUTSOURCED FUNCTION

It is more important than for any other function that the engineering function be properly managed, both by the supplier and by the company. This is because the engineering function yields information that is critical to the company's success in the marketplace, and because it provides information to downstream operations such as manufacturing—if the information reaching these other departments is incorrect, then the operations of those departments will suffer. In this section, we review the need for a strong engineering coordinator and support staff, how to manage outsourcing work if only the drafting function is outsourced, how reporting relationships should work, and the role of the coordinator.

The key to managing the outsourced engineering function is a strong engineering coordinator who works for the company, not the supplier. This person may have been the manager of the in-house engineering function, or may be brought in from some other company. The advantage to using an in-house person in this role is that it is helpful for the coordinator to have a firm grasp of the technical issues involved in designing the company's products—knowledge that an outside person may not have. However, the coordinator's key skill is not product knowledge but management expertise. The coordinator must be able to monitor the progress and cost of all engineering projects being managed by the supplier and resolve all issues promptly to ensure that projects are completed properly and on time. This is increasingly important as all industries become more competitive and market windows for the introduction of new products continue to shrink. An additional task is to verify with the company's manufacturing staff that the information being produced by the supplier is sufficient for it to use to create new products. This usually means complete assembly drawings and bills of material, and is most important for custom or semicustom jobs where only a small number of units are being built, which does not give the manufacturing group enough time to work out on its own how the item is to be constructed. Also, the coordinator must be authorized to sign all contracts and contract changes with the supplier, as well as to himself authorize changes to engineering change orders for specific changes to individual projects—this is needed so that the coordinator has an appropriate combination of authority and responsibility to do the coordination job. A typical engineering coordinator's job description is shown in Figure 7.6.

Once the engineering coordinator has been selected, the company must be sure to provide that person with a top-quality staff, which should be comprised of the best engineers the company has on staff at the time of transition to the engineering supplier. Because of the high hourly rates charged by engineering suppliers for their project staff, it is important that a company invest in its own engineering review staff to help the coordinator, so that the progress of each of the supplier's engineering teams

Figure 7.6   The Engineering Coordinator's Job Description

Employee Title: Engineering Outsourcing Coordinator
Reports to: Chief Executive Officer
Responsibilities:
- Sign off on all agreements with the engineering supplier.
- Review the database of current product problems and determine which problems will be fixed and their order of work priority.
- Authorize the release of funds for current product repair problems.
- Track actual costs incurred against budgeted amounts by project and work with the supplier to correct any problems.
- Verify that project milestones are being reached and work with the supplier to correct any problems.
- Verify that work being completed by the supplier is sufficient for the manufacturing department to use to create products.
- Authorize the addition or termination of engineering projects.
- Authorize changes to the specifications of products being designed.
- Authorize changes to the scope of engineering projects.
- Authorize all product design change orders.

is closely monitored, thus reducing the number of hours' work charged to the company that is wasted on incorrect tasks. These engineers must assist the coordinator in regularly reviewing each engineering project to ensure that it is meeting its time and cost goals. If a project is not meeting its goals, these engineers must be of sufficient experience to recommend to the engineering coordinator a course of action to improve the situation. This staff is also needed if the coordinator is not experienced in the intricacies of some aspects of engineering (e.g., electrical, air conditioning, or mechanical design work), and requires some advice on those areas. For the larger and more intricate engineering projects, this is likely to be the case. The number of engineering staff given to the coordinator will be based on the number and size of projects undertaken by the supplier for the company. A top-notch engineering support staff is needed by the engineering coordinator to ensure that all engineering projects are properly reviewed.

A separate management issue is how to deal with the outsourcing of just the drafting function. If only the drafting function is outsourced, the company can either assign a drafting coordinator to this effort, have each outsourced drafter report directly to an in-house engineering team, or combine the two options, with a coordinator exercising light control over the drafting function. It is better to have a drafting coordinator available in some capacity, even if the position has little authority, because someone must be tracking the accomplishment of milestones and the level of expenditures, which may not be adequately reviewed by engineering teams who are more concerned with designing a product. With time to market being so critical, it is acceptable to have outsourced drafters work directly with in-house engineering teams, which keeps the drafting coordinator from having to act as intermediary between the two groups and slowing down the process. In short, maintaining control over an outsourced drafting function works best if the drafters work directly with the in-house engineers while a drafting coordinator exists in an overview role, checking on the progress of work and the ongoing cost of the drafting personnel. Any problems uncovered by the drafting coordinator are then channeled back through the director of the in-house engineering department for resolution by that person with the drafting supplier.

In summary, we noted that the engineering coordinator is especially important to the company for keeping close watch over the time and cost budgets of all engineering projects undertaken by the supplier, and that giving a strong support staff to the coordinator is important to ensure that the coordinator is receiving enough detailed information about each project to ensure that sufficient control over each project is being used. Also, several variations on how to manage an outsourced drafting function were presented, with the best option being to have a separate drafting function coordinator who reports to the engineering coordinator. The organization chart with the engineering function included is shown in Figure 7.7.

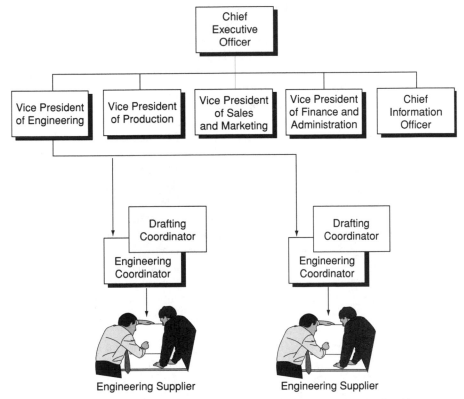

Figure 7.7 Organization Chart for Outsourcing the Engineering and Drafting Functions

7.7   POTENTIAL CUSTOMER SERVICE ISSUES

When a company outsources its engineering function, it must confront several issues related to pass-through services and product fixes, which directly impact customer service. This section discusses those issues.

A company has pass-through services when it represents to a customer that it is directly providing engineering services to that customer, but then subcontracts the services to another company. There are several customer service issues that arise when this occurs. One is that the customer, not knowing the engineering supplier, will be concerned that the engineering services will degrade, and will force the company to terminate the outsourcing arrangement or else take its business elsewhere. To avoid this problem, the company can either hide the outsourcing relationship from the customer or tell the customer in advance that an outsourcing arrangement is being contemplated, and keep the customer regularly apprised of the situation. Since the customer may be unhappy if it ever learns that the function has been outsourced, it is usually better to be clear with the customer about the prospective arrangement before any outsourcing arrangement is finalized. Another problem is how to have the supplier deal with the customer for whom services are being provided. The company can force all communications to flow through the engineering coordinator or a designated subordinate when the coordinator is absent, but this can greatly slow down a project's time to completion, since an extra communications step is being added to the process. It can be a considerable problem if the coordinator is not thoroughly familiar with all of the engineering concepts involved in the project—passing along bad or incorrect information to the supplier will result in many product design problems. A better approach is to have the customer deal directly with the engineering supplier, with the coordinator attending all meetings between the two parties. This keeps the company informed of progress on the customer's project while improving the level of communications between the customer and the engineering supplier. The problem with using this approach, however, is that the customer will want to eliminate the company from the business relationship and deal directly with the supplier. This problem can be avoided either by having the supplier sign a non-compete agreement or by convincing the customer that the company can manage a variety of functions for the customer, and that the company can save the customer the effort of handling such management issues as negotiating and managing engineering contracts with engineering suppliers. In short, a company should inform its customers if some engineering services are subcontracted, and should allow the engineering supplier to work directly with the customer to ensure that communications between the two parties are accurate and complete.

A significant customer service issue for a company is determining which product problems should be redesigned by an engineering supplier, how they should get access to the problem information, and how the supplier should be compensated for those fixes. If these issues are not dealt with correctly, design flaws in existing products may cause customer defections, leading to a loss of market share and profits. Each problem and an accompanying solution is noted in the following examples:

- *How to determine which product flaws to redesign.* The company must have control over which product flaws are fixed. This is because the supplier may incorrectly prioritize the sequence in which flaws are fixed, resulting in serious flaws being ignored while resources are committed to repairing minor design issues. Also, a supplier who is given complete authority to fix all product flaws may use this as an excuse to spend large amounts of time on fixing inconsequential issues that really required no change at all, and can then charge the company for the cost of these fixes. This can be an expensive proposition. A better approach is to have the company's engineering coordinator decide which flaws will be fixed by the supplier, and the order in which the problems will be addressed.

- *How to send product problem information to the supplier.* Once the coordinator has decided which flaws will be fixed, the company must give the supplier complete access to all records related to the product flaw. This information should be collected into a database that includes customer complaints, warranty claims, and product returns. The supplier should then be given on-line access to this database so that it can review additional information about the product flaw as soon as it is collected and added to the database. This is a great improvement over a paper-based listing of complaints, which must be reissued to the entire distribution list whenever additional information is added.

- *How to compensate the supplier for product redesign work.* The cost to fix a product flaw is generally difficult to determine in advance, which means that engineering suppliers are not willing to agree to a fixed-fee contract to complete the fix. It is also quite time consuming for both parties to negotiate a new fixed-fee contract every time a product flaw must be redesigned. A better approach is to set up a time-and-materials blanket purchase order with the engineering supplier and release a specific amount of money against the blanket purchase order for each product fix. The engineering coordinator can then extend additional funds to the supplier from the blanket order based on its actual time-and-materials billings. This approach requires minimal negotiation and allows the engineering coordinator to retain control over the supplier's billings for fixes.

The engineering coordinator may want to have regularly scheduled product problem meetings with the supplier, where the team reviews incoming information about problems with existing or beta-test products, and determines how to deal with them. This is not a bad approach, but if there are long intervals between these meetings, a critical product problem may not be addressed for a long time. It is useful as a safety measure to have a subordinate reporting to the engineering coordinator review the problem database every day, note any critical problems that are arising, and immediately bring this information to the attention of the engineering coordinator, who can then call an emergency meeting with the supplier to have these problems addressed and fixed at once.

In summary, a company may have to deal with the relationship between its customers and the engineering work being done for those customers by its engineering supplier—open communications with all parties, rather than channeling all information through the engineering coordinator, is generally the best option. Also, nearly all products require some design changes subsequent to release. The company should have the engineering coordinator determine which problems should be fixed as well as the priority of the fixes, give the supplier access to an on-line database of all information pertaining to customer problems with the product, and pay the supplier for this work on a time-and-materials basis.

7.8   GETTING OUT OF
THE OUTSOURCING ARRANGEMENT

The engineering function is critical to many companies, and so it is very important that a company be able to get out of its contract with an engineering supplier as rapidly as possible if the relationship is clearly not working out. This section discusses how to ensure through the contract with the supplier that the company can step back from the relationship as quickly as possible.

If the company realizes that the relationship with the engineering supplier is not working, it must have the option to back out immediately. This is not an area where the company should give the supplier an option to take an extra 30 to 90 days to correct deficiencies. Because the engineering function is so critical, the company should insist on a clause that allows it to give written notice that the relationship is immediately terminated; this allows to company to quickly switch the engineering work to a more competent supplier or to bring it in-house. The company should not be required to prove that the supplier's work is not acceptable, since this takes time, is subjective, and may require lengthy arbitration to prove. Instead, the termination should be "at will," with no reason for termination needed. For a key function like engineering, the company must be able to rapidly switch suppliers if its original supplier proves to be incompetent.

If the company decides to terminate its relationship with an engineering supplier, there may be computer hardware or software that it sold to the supplier that must be returned. If the company is required to repurchase this equipment, there should be a clause in the contract that allows the company to buy back the equipment at greatly reduced prices; this is because computer equipment depreciates in value so quickly. A reasonable buy-back clause could state that the company buy the equipment back at the original transfer price for the first year, with the buy-back price dropping by one-third for each subsequent year. The company may not even want to purchase the equipment if it is no longer state of the art. In this case, the company may want to include an option in the contract for the supplier to retain the equipment in exchange for a small penalty payment by the company (or no penalty at all). Another issue related to this equipment is that the company may want to have the licenses for the engineering software transferred back to it from the supplier. If so, there should be a contract clause stating that the supplier will transfer all software storage media and related documentation back to the company in exchange for a fee, and cooperate with it in having the software company switch the software license from the engineering supplier to the customer. The transfer of engineering workstations and software back to the company in the event of a termination of relations should be covered in the contract.

The company may want to shut down the relationship with the supplier because it wants to bring the engineering function back in-house. If this is the case, the company should have a clause in the contract that requires the supplier to give the company access to all engineers who were transferred to the supplier at the start of the outsourcing agreement, so that the company can make job offers to them. This can cause considerable friction with the supplier if such a clause is not included in the contract, because there are likely to be a few outstanding engineers whom the supplier is unwilling to part with.

A final issue is that the supplier will probably insist on having a severance-payment clause added to the contract. This clause requires the company to pay severance to those engineers who will be let go by the supplier if the company terminates the outsourcing agreement with the supplier. This is a reasonable request by the supplier, but it should be modified in several ways. First, the payment should exclude all personnel who can be rerouted to other jobs by the supplier. Second, it should not apply to those engineers who have already been moved to projects being conducted for other companies. Third, this payment should only apply to those engineers who were originally transferred to the supplier from the company (e.g., it does not apply to any personnel later recruited by the supplier from outside of the company). Fourth, and most controversial, the company should insist that the proportion of severance it pays must drop over time; since an outsourcing agreement can theoretically span several decades, it is not reasonable for the company to still be responsible for its former staff many years later. A reasonable rate for dropping the amount of severance payments to be made is 20% per year. The amount of this severance can either be a percentage of the employees' pay or a fixed amount that is specified in the contract. It is in the interests of the company to have a fixed amount per person, since there will then be no risk of paying an excessive amount of severance because some personnel have subsequently been awarded large pay increases.

This section discussed how a company can easily pull back from a relationship with an engineering company. Some of the problems discussed were the transfer of engineering workstations and software, avoiding clauses that give the engineering supplier the chance to correct deficiencies, being able to offer jobs to former employees who now work for the supplier, and paying severance to former employees. By including these issues in the initial contract with the supplier, the company can avoid several significant problems that might arise later if it must back out of the relationship with the supplier.

7.9 SUMMARY

This chapter focused on the factors that company management should address when making the decision to outsource the engineering function; these factors are crucial, for there are many instances where the company should retain the function. However, there are a variety of situations where all or part of the engineering function should be moved to a supplier who can provide better management, create drawings or concepts at lower cost, or provide a higher level of expertise.

This chapter also covered a number of specific contractual, transition, control, and measurement issues that are useful for the company that has decided to outsource the engineering function. In addition, many issues related to managing the engineering supplier, customer service issues, and getting out of the outsourcing arrangement were discussed. Among the most important issues noted were control over and measurement of the supplier, because the engineering function can rapidly incur large cost and time overruns that can significantly impact a company's ability to roll out new products as rapidly as possible and at a low enough cost to make them cost competitive in the marketplace. By addressing the issues noted in this chapter, a company that is contemplating or has already outsourced its engineering function has a good chance of successfully moving its engineering function to a supplier and controlling the resulting work after the move has been made.

CHAPTER EIGHT

Outsourcing the Human Resources Function

Many aspects of the services provided by the human resources function are clerical, and as such can be handed over to suppliers who are better equipped through better technology or economies of scale to administer them. Many human resources services fall into this category, such as medical, life, and workers' compensation insurance. Other services, though not clerical, are better left to specialists, such as recruiting, training, outplacement, and relocation. Some tasks are highly unsuitable for outsourcing, such as succession planning and the design of training classes, since these areas require an in-depth knowledge of the company and its employees. However, those tasks to be kept in-house are few, and this points toward an inevitable reduction in the number of people who will work in a company's human resources department in the years to come.

Who will be left after the outsourcing drive has ended? There will always be a need for some in-house clerical staff to handle the inevitable paperwork associated with the insurance needs of each employee, though this need will go down over time as automation takes over some tasks. There will also be a strong need for human resources managers who are skilled in managing a multitude of human resources suppliers. This calls for a senior management–level person with the negotiating skills to deal with suppliers, the systems knowledge to strive for more automation, and the compassion to hear the problems of employees and work with suppliers on their behalf to resolve those problems. This revised and reduced staff mix is sufficient to run an outsourced human resource function.

There are many suppliers who can attend to every facet of a company's human resources needs. Some are regional suppliers who only provide service to nearby firms, while others are international in scope and can provide services to even those multinational companies with branches in dozens of countries. A few examples of the larger suppliers are as follows:

- *Ernst & Young LLP.* This Big Five accounting and consulting firm specializes in providing human resources services to those company employees who are on international assignments for extended periods. Some of their clients are Mallinckrodt, Inc. (manufacturers of health care products), Lennox International (manufacturers of heating and air conditioning equipment), Oakwood International (brokers in executive apartments), Mattel, Inc. (toy manufacturers), the Quantum Corporation (manufacturers of computer hard drives), and Perot Systems (information systems management and consulting).

- *Learnshare.* This company was founded by Owens Corning, Motorola, General Motors, Deere & Co., Owens-Illinois, 3M, Reynolds Metals, Pilkington, and Aeroquip Vickers to collect customized courses covering function-specific topics that are donated by the founders as well as create new courses, which are distributed over the Internet as well as on CD-ROM.

- *Intellitrain.* Does all of the training for Prudential Bank and Trust Company.

- *TriNet Employer Group.* Covers a wide range of services, from payroll processing to workers' compensation administration and customized benefits plans.

- *ABR Information Services.* Administers benefits programs to more than 10 million company employees, dependents, and retirees.

This chapter covers the basic issues of human resources outsourcing: the advantages and disadvantages, contractual issues, transition problems to be aware of, and ways to control, measure, and manage suppliers. Several important employee-relations issues are also described. Finally, a number of problems with terminating supplier relations are noted, as well as ways to mitigate those problems. By covering these topics, the reader should have a clear understanding of the benefits and problems associated with outsourcing the human resources function, as well as many of the steps needed to go ahead with an outsourcing decision.

8.1   ADVANTAGES AND DISADVANTAGES

This section addresses the advantages and disadvantages of outsourcing the many tasks grouped within the human resources function. The advantages and disadvantages for each task are grouped together, so that the reader can more easily weigh the reasons in favor of and against outsourcing.

One of the major arguments in favor of outsourcing the human resources function is that this is not a strategic area for any company. Though it is important to treat employees as well as possible, this is not an area in which a company should expend a large amount of its management resources. For that reason, as much of the function as possible should be handed over to a set of suppliers who can manage various tasks just as well as an in-house staff, if not better.

The advantage of using an outplacement supplier to handle all laid-off staff is that a supplier has a full-time professional staff that is experienced in providing such services as resume writing and psychological counseling to outgoing employees. These are skills that most companies do not have in-house. Even if they did, they would be fixed costs, whereas they become a variable cost by outsourcing this task, since the company will only be charged a flat fee for each former employee referred to the supplier. However, the downside of using a supplier is that the supplier must make a profit, and so will have an incentive to give the minimum amount of time to each employee who needs its services, whereas an in-house staff might be more inclined to give extra time to each person. This problem can be avoided by specifying in the contract with the supplier the minimum amount of resources that will be made available to each employee who goes to the supplier. Another problem with some suppliers is that they, in turn, outsource some of their functions to other suppliers, which means that former employees must travel to the locations of several suppliers. This problem is readily avoided by prescreening potential suppliers to ensure that they provide all services with their own in-house staffs. In short, suppliers can offer a wider range of services to laid-off employees and at less cost to the company, though they may be inclined to give employees the minimum level of service and make people travel to multiple locations to obtain those services.

The primary advantage of outsourcing the life insurance function is that the company can avoid the risk of large losses that accompanies the self-insurance approach. Also, term insurance for large numbers of employees is extremely inexpensive, and requires minimal paperwork. Finally, many medical insurance suppliers throw in life insurance coverage for free if the company signs onto its medical insurance program, so this can be a no-cost option. There are no significant disadvantages to outsourcing life insurance.

Nearly all companies outsource their medical insurance, and there are good reasons why they do this. One is that self-insurance may save a company a small amount in the short run, but there is the risk that a small number of very large medical claims will bankrupt the self-insurance fund. It is possible to cap the amount of loss in a self-insurance fund with an umbrella policy, but most companies do not want to go through this hassle, and use a supplier instead. Also, there is a significant fixed cost associated with having an in-house staff that evaluates medical claims and pays doctors. Not only is it much easier to pass along this work to a supplier, but this also passes the onus of rejecting medical claims to the supplier, which has the peculiar benefit of improving employee relations within the company. Though medical insurance suppliers are more expensive than in-house insurance alternatives, there is no risk of large losses, and the company can shift most of the administrative burden to the supplier.

Recruiting is commonly outsourced. The main reason for this is that recruiting suppliers are only paid if they present a viable candidate to the company, who is then hired. If the supplier cannot find the right person, the company is under no obligation to pay anything to the supplier. In contrast, an in-house recruiter is a fixed cost who will be paid even if this person cannot find any prospective employees. Even for situations where the company is paying a recruiting supplier for hours worked, it is only paying for those hours that can be specifically justified by the supplier, and not all of the other hours in the week that the supplier works. In contrast, a company pays an in-house recruiter for every hour worked, even if those hours are not spent on recruiting tasks. Another good reason for outsourcing is that suppliers have a strong incentive to find good candidates, since otherwise they will not be paid. Alternatively, an in-house recruiter has no incentive, unless there is a bonus arrangement in addition to base pay for the recruiter. Despite these clear advantages, there are three problems with recruiting suppliers that may give companies a reason not to use them. The first is that a supplier only addresses a company's employment request for a short time; it will review its files of available candidates, send in a few for interviews, and then drop the request rather than spend unprofitable time trying to find another candidate. This problem does not arise if the supplier stands to earn a large amount of money from a successful hire. Another way around this problem is to pay the supplier on an hourly basis, which keeps the supplier looking even after the obvious candidates have been reviewed. The second problem is that recruiting suppliers do not make as much money on recruiting for employees at the low-pay positions (since they are receiving a portion of the person's first-year pay), and therefore do not try too hard to fill these positions. Once again, the solution is to pay recruiters on an hourly basis. Another option is to pay an increased percentage of first-year pay for recruiting these positions. A third solution is to offer a bonus premium payment for recruiting these positions. The final problem is that some companies go to college campuses to recruit employees and want to present a solid image of the company to potential employees during those visits—if this is the case, using an in-house employee who is thoroughly versed in company operations, and who can communicate the "company line" to recruits, is most acceptable. Using recruiting suppliers converts the recruiting cost from a fixed to a variable one, though hourly pay to suppliers may be the best solution to such problems as a short-term focus by suppliers and less attention being paid to recruiting for low-pay positions.

Some companies maintain large internal training staffs. More do not, having found that using training suppliers has several advantages over an in-house staff. One reason is that a company only pays for hours actually spent training, as opposed to paying for all of the hours worked by an in-house staff, whether or not they are conducting any training. Another advantage is that training suppliers create their own courses, and spread the cost of making the classes among the large number of companies who use their services. This is in contrast to making classes in-house, where the company cannot share the cost of the courses with other companies. These two items highlight the major reason for using training suppliers instead of an in-house staff: the cost of a supplier is totally variable, while the in-house cost is totally fixed. However, there are situations where an in-house staff is necessary. The main area is when the company needs to train its employees in very specialized in-house systems that are not available through a supplier. All companies have a few systems like this—for example, hydraulic repairs for truck manufacturers, sewing techniques for tent manufacturers, or welding for bridge builders. In these cases, the company is justified in maintaining a specialized in-house staff, but the functional coordinator can also work with a supplier to develop course materials for these areas, so the in-house expense can be reduced even in these areas. Training is already outsourced by most companies because of the high fixed cost of maintaining an in-house staff, except for cases where courses are so specialized that no suppliers offer the training.

A company can reduce the cost of an in-house relocation staff by switching this work over to a relocation supplier, thereby changing the cost from fixed to variable. The disadvantage of doing this is that the supplier may have strong ties to (or be owned by) specific moving companies that will charge the company above-market rates to move employees, which eliminates any cost savings from switching to the supplier. However, this problem can be avoided by tracking the cost of moves, as noted later on in the measurement section, and also by giving the supplier bonuses if it can beat current market rates, as noted in the next section on contractual issues. Using a relocation supplier converts a company's costs to variable costs, though it is possible that the supplier will pass through high moving fees unless incentives are set up to avoid this problem.

In this section, we reviewed the advantages and disadvantages of outsourcing many of the services that fall under the umbrella of the human resources function. Arguments were presented both in favor of and against the use of suppliers for outsourcing life insurance, medical insurance, recruiting, training, and relocation. On the whole, the arguments in favor of outsourcing human resources functions strongly outweigh the arguments against it. At a minimum, most companies should retain no more than a stripped-down human resources function and farm out a large part of their work to suppliers.

8.2   CONTRACT-SPECIFIC ISSUES

This section covers the contractual issues associated with the various human resources functions. The bulk of the negotiation points cover the costs of services provided. Other items include the location of training classes, trainer selection, life insurance quantities, moving-damage compensation, and outplacement services. This section is intended to give the reader some pointers on what contractual items to look for when finalizing agreements with human resources suppliers, rather than showing actual contract language—exact wording is so different by industry and service provided that it is difficult to show boilerplate text that is usable by most readers.

An important issue when using a training supplier is the ownership of the course materials. If the company is paying the supplier to create a new course, then the company should own the course. All course materials should be copyrighted by the company to verify ownership. Also, if the supplier wants to use the course material elsewhere, the contract can list a variety of options for the supplier, such as a reduced up-front fee for developing the course, copyrighting by the supplier in exchange for unlimited free use of the materials by the company, a royalty payment to the company by the supplier in exchange for using its materials, or some variation on these options. If the company does not include clauses in the contract to cover these eventualities, there may be squabbling between the parties regarding ownership of course materials.

There are several ways to specify in the contract how the company is to pay the supplier for training courses. One option is to set a price schedule, possibly in an appendix to the contract, that itemizes each course by name, and the price to be paid each time it is taught. However, this does not leave room for the addition of any courses. A better approach that allows the contract to expand to cover new courses is one that sets a flat fee per hour of each course taught. This fee should be on a per-person basis if the company is sending employees to a supplier training facility, where the employee may be taught alongside people from other companies. A common variation on this system is for a company to purchase a large quantity of training vouchers from the supplier at a discount, and then hand these out to employees who will present them at classes as payment for the training; this approach allows companies to pay less for training classes, based on the volume of vouchers purchased. Suppliers also like this approach, since companies are paying for training in advance. A second fee should also be specified for training at the company location that is for each hour taught by the instructor—this covers company-only classes where the company can send as many of its own people as its wants to a class. There can also be a separate payment to the supplier for classes taught at the company location, rather than at the supplier's training facility, but only if there is a significant distance between the locations of the supplier and the company, so that it can be proved that the supplier's trainers are going well out of their way, and perhaps incurring excessive travel charges, to teach at the company location. A contract with a trainer can specify a per-employee, per-hour charge if employees go to the supplier's training facility, or a per-hour charge if the supplier sends its trainers to the company, as well as an added fee to cover the cost of transporting trainers to the company facility.

The contract with a training supplier should also cover the cost of having the supplier create training classes. The supplier always prefers to charge an hourly rate for all course creation work, since there is no risk of losing money when a course takes an inordinately long time to create. The company wants a fixed fee per course created, since this keeps the supplier from taking too many hours to create a course and charging an exorbitant fee. One way to combine these two approaches is to allow the supplier an hourly rate, but cap the amount paid with a not-too-exceed fixed fee, so that the company's risk of spending too much on a new course is mitigated. A more difficult variation is to allow an hourly fee, but to give the supplier a bonus if it can complete the course in under a specific number of hours. The problem with this last approach is that the supplier may complete the course materials and earn the bonus, but do so by creating low-quality course materials. Since it is difficult to specify the quality of course materials, this can be a source of contention if the company denies a bonus based on its perception of course materials being of poor quality. Thus, pricing for the creation of course materials can be on a per-hour basis, a fixed fee, a per-hour basis with a fixed-fee cap, or with a bonus if costs are kept below a specific level.

A final contract clause for a training supplier is the right to request or reject specific trainers. This option cannot apply if the company is sending its employees to supplier classes where employees from other companies are also being trained, since this means that the company would have control over the trainers used for other companies, which will not be acceptable to the other companies. However, this a valid point if the company is paying to have the supplier send trainers to the company location. In these cases, the company will want the tightest possible control over the quality of training given to its staff, and should have the right to request specific trainers, or to reject those whom it does not feel are good trainers.

Life insurance is frequently included in a medical insurance package as an added benefit that is given to all company employees for the term of the medical insurance package. This is normally a small amount, such as $10,000 of life insurance per person, or sometimes a sliding scale that is a percentage of each employee's base pay. This life insurance is considered by many suppliers to be a free addition to the insurance package that is included to sweeten the pot and convince the company to contract for the supplier's services. The company rarely sees any separate cost on the supplier's billing statement for the life insurance. Since the life insurance is essentially free to the company, it makes no sense to try to reduce its price, but it makes a great deal of sense to negotiate for as much of it as possible. The most common tactics are to increase the base amount given to each employee or to convert to a percentage of each employee's base pay, which tends to benefit those employees who earn more money (and who are presumably negotiating this contract). Thus, the best negotiating tactic for life insurance is to work on increasing the amount of it that is offered for free as part of a larger medical insurance package.

Medical insurance is not negotiable in any way, except for pricing for the largest companies. Medical insurance suppliers package their insurance in a cookie-cutter format that is used for all of its customers. There are several plans to choose from, but none of the elements of each package are negotiable. Pricing is difficult to alter for smaller companies, since they have no negotiating leverage to use in procuring the lowest possible rates; however, medical insurance suppliers are eager to obtain the business of larger companies with thousands of employees, since one such deal can generate millions of dollars in policy premiums for them. In these cases, it is worthwhile for the company to have annual competitive bidding between suppliers to drive pricing down to the absolute minimum. This advantage is possible for some smaller companies that have banded together to form cooperatives that can obtain better insurance pricing. In short, medical insurance is only negotiable on price, and even then only for the largest companies.

Contracts with moving companies are negotiable on price and compensation amounts for damage. The compensation amount is usually fixed by the supplier's damage insurance policy, but if the company does enough business with the mover, it may behoove the supplier to pay the higher premium for an insurance policy with higher coverage limits. Realistically, however, most suppliers already carry insurance with sufficient coverage for most damage claims. As for pricing, suppliers prefer to give a total amount per move, and then issue a variety of discounts to arrive at a net price to the company. This is not a good way to do business for the company, for it disguises the cost per mile and the cost to load and unload each van. Instead, the company should insist on a fixed fee to load and unload each moving van, plus a cost per mile to transport the van to the new location. This rate structure allows the company to clearly determine its costs and see if it is getting a good deal. If the company's current supplier is not willing to price its moving services in this manner, then it is likely that the supplier is trying to hide high prices behind an unclear pricing structure. In these cases, the company should look for a new moving supplier. Thus, the traditional single-price invoice for moving services should be replaced by an invoice that clearly identifies each cost element associated with each move.

Outplacement services are negotiable on the price per person as well as on the services offered. Pricing is usually a fixed fee per person being laid off by a company. This fee is most negotiable if there are a large number of employees being laid off. (This does not mean that a company should lay off extra employees in order to obtain a better outplacement price!) The services provided can be extensive, including psychological counseling, retraining, interview coaching, resume writing, office space, phones, copiers, and mailing services. The company should negotiate to include as many of these services as possible in the fixed fee per person. The one exception is retraining, which is usually priced on a per-hour basis. For that reason, most companies do not provide retraining—the high variable cost of retraining can easily exceed the cost of all other outplacement services provided. Negotiations with outplacement suppliers should cover the price per person as well as the range of services made available.

An agreement with a recruiting supplier is negotiable on price, exclusivity, and the return of fees. The most important issue is the price charged. If the supplier is being paid on an hourly basis to recruit, then the hourly rate can be forced downwards in exchange for the promise of a certain number of hours of work over the course of a year. If the company and supplier find after the year is over that not all of the hours promised actually occurred, then the agreement can allow for a retroactive change in the hourly rate based on the actual number of hours charged. If the supplier charges a percentage of the first year's income of the person hired (the most common approach), then this rate is also negotiable based on the number of positions the company asks the supplier to locate potential employees for. This percentage is also more negotiable if the company offers to give the supplier a set time period during which it has the exclusive right to search for potential candidates. The company should also insist on a time period of at least 90 days following the hire of any employee located through a search firm, during which the company can insist on a full refund of all fees paid if the employee leaves or is fired. A less desirable variation is that the supplier keeps the money but undertakes to find a new employee for free. Since the supplier will not be paid for this second effort, it will probably not put as much effort into the search as it did the first time around. A company can use volume business and the promise of exclusive work to drive down its recruiting costs, while also securing the promise of returned fees if new employees leave early.

There are many discounts available through a workers' compensation contract, and this is the primary area in which a company should focus its negotiations. As is the case with other human resources areas, a company's primary leverage on pricing is the number of employees it can bring into the coverage of the insurance. If there are many employees, there is an opportunity to include very large discounts that will reduce the price of the workers' compensation insurance.

This section covered a number of areas in human resources contracts that are open to negotiation. The primary negotiation area is pricing, especially if the company has a large number of employees who will be covered by the contract, which means that the potential revenue for the supplier will be large enough to justify some price decreases to obtain the company's business. Other contract areas are also negotiable when dealing with the suppliers of training, outplacement, and moving services.

8.3 TRANSITION ISSUES

This section covers the transition issues to consider when moving a human resources function to a supplier. In some cases where it is common practice to already have the function outsourced with a supplier (such as medical insurance), the steps are noted for moving that service to a new supplier. Also, unlike most of the other chapters, there is no Gantt chart in this section that plots the steps needed to make a transition. This is because there are so many disparate services contained within the human resources function that there is no way to present an integrated Gantt chart that shows all of the functions being transitioned to suppliers—companies prefer to outsource these functions piecemeal, so the Gantt chart would not reflect reality.

The transition for life insurance sometimes requires no paperwork whatsoever—all employees are automatically covered for a standard amount of life insurance. Other suppliers require that each employee sign and forward a form to the supplier. This information is normally acquired by an in-house staff person. It is uncommon to require employees to take medical examinations for small, standardized life insurance policies that apply to all employees. However, employees will certainly be required to take examinations if the company is taking out large policies on them. This is of particular concern, since the person being forced to take the examination is probably a high-level company officer who may not have the time or inclination to do so, and will be sure to let the human resources coordinator know his or her thoughts on the matter. These tasks must be considered before a company switches to a new life insurance provider.

When the company switches to a new medical insurance supplier, every employee using the new medical plan must fill out a sign-up form, and those employees who do not want it will be asked to sign a form stating that they are declining coverage. This is a major task if the company has a large number of employees, and is especially difficult if there are many company locations or employees who travel and cannot easily be reached. The remaining in-house human resources staff usually takes care of this paperwork, and they must be trained in the use of each form before they go over this information with employees. Also, there will be problems during the period when employees stop using their old doctors and switch to new ones, for someone inevitably will go to an old doctor who is not covered by the new plan, and will then be charged in full for the visit. This problem can be avoided either by not switching plans, by trying to use plans that have many of the same doctors, or by sending notices to employees before the changeover date, telling them when they must start using their new suppliers. Finally, the functional coordinator must be sure to throw out all old insurance sign-up forms from the previous supplier to ensure that new employees do not accidentally sign up for the wrong plan. Some insurance companies now offer an insurance policy that covers a company's liability in such cases where companies accidentally do not sign up employees for insurance and the employee then incurs significant medical fees. This is good insurance to obtain if the company has experienced paperwork-processing difficulties. Thus, there is a flood of paperwork processing to be performed when switching to a new medical insurance supplier, with some risk of employees being left uninsured because of the switch.

If the training function is moved to a supplier, the first step is to examine the subjects already being taught through in-house programs, as well as any additional training needs. This list of requirements should be compared to the supplier's course offerings to see what items are not covered by the supplier's curriculum. The company must then determine how any training shortfalls are to be covered. One option is to pay the supplier to develop and teach any of the necessary courses, while another option is to retain a small in-house staff of specialists who only teach those topics that the supplier cannot cover. The functional coordinator should then examine the course materials to be taught to ensure that the company's quality standards are being met, and then have someone sit through and evaluate formal training sessions for all classes to be taught by the supplier, to ensure that the instructors are of sufficient quality. Only then should the supplier be allowed to train company employees.

This section covered several key problems that most companies will encounter when transitioning various human resources services from one supplier to another or from in-house administration to a supplier, with suggested solutions wherever possible. The biggest problem for most human resources transitions is the paperwork, which is a difficult obstacle in some cases, but rarely keeps a transition from occurring.

8.4   CREATING CONTROL POINTS

This section notes the best ways to maintain control over the suppliers of human resources functions, with particular emphasis on the recurring investigation of costs and evaluation forms submitted by employees who have used supplier services.

One of the best human resources control points is a continuing review of costs. This can apply, for example, to the insurance cost per employee, the training cost per hour, or the recruiting charge per hour worked. These costs should be tracked over time on a chart such as the one shown in Figure 8.1, so that a quick glance at the chart is sufficient to tell where costs are increasing too much. An alternative approach is to have a separate line item in the budget for each supplier, showing the actual cost next to the budgeted amount every month. This is not as good as a trend line, for it only shows the current month and the year-to-date amount, from which it is difficult to ascertain a trend.

The second-best human resources control point is the evaluation form. This can be used to evaluate training classes, employee moves, outplacement services, and how employees were treated by medical insurance suppliers. These forms should be scanned immediately upon receipt for the presence of any glaring problems requiring immediate resolution. Then the forms should be entered into a database that summarizes and reports on the results of many of these forms to give management statistical information about the performance of its suppliers. These evaluation results can even be tied to supplier bonuses and penalties, though few companies take such an aggressive approach to the use of evaluation forms.

The final control point is the use of meetings. These can be used to go over with suppliers any problems found using the first two control points. They are also useful for workers' compensation suppliers, because the functional coordinator should go over with the supplier the cause of each workers' compensation claim, how it was resolved, and the types of safeguards that can be installed to ensure that the problem is mitigated in the future. The number of these meetings should be based

Figure 8.1   Human Resources Annual Cost Review Chart

Description	1999	1998	1997	1996	1995
Life insurance cost per person	$120	$118	$112	$109	$110
Medical cost per single	$1,440	$1,370	$1,200	$1,350	1,375
Medical cost per family	$4,160	$4,100	$3,950	$3,800	$3,402
Workers' comp cost per clerical employee	$172	$171	$170	$169	$168
Workers' comp cost per high-risk employee	$540	$580	$600	$590	$580
Training cost per hour	$85	$90	$88	$82	$73
Moving cost per mile	$.27	$.26	$.24	$.20	$.18
Recruiting cost per hour	$75	$70	$70	$70	$65
Recruiting cost as percentage of pay	22%	24%	26%	26%	27%
Outplacement fee per person	$320	$390	$370	$340	$310

on the number of claims the company has. If there are few claims, there is no need for a meeting. Meetings are also useful for controlling recruiters, since the coordinator wants to be sure that the recruiters are conducting searches for the right types of people. The best way to transmit this information is to do so in person, rather than to fax job requirements to the supplier, for there are inevitably going to be questions about the job requirements, and these are best answered in person. This is especially important for positions that are very high level, or for which there is a rush on hiring—the company wants to be sure that no time is wasted in looking for the wrong type of person. Thus, periodic meetings are useful for going over problems found during the cost and evaluation form reviews, and are a control over such human resources areas as workers' compensation insurance and recruiting.

In summary, the best control over outsourced human resources is a continual review of costs, usually plotted along a trend line. A continuing review of employee evaluation forms for the various human resources services is also useful. Finally, periodic review meetings with suppliers are useful to go over problems that were noted in the first two control areas. These methods give the functional coordinator good control over the human resources function.

8.5 MEASURING THE OUTSOURCED FUNCTION

This section covers the performance measurements that can be used to determine how well a supplier is doing its job in the human resources area. These measurements have a strong orientation towards cost per person, because it is difficult to measure the outcome of supplier tasks in any other manner. For example, it is not easy to determine how well an employee was treated while being moved by a relocation supplier, or how well an outplaced person was counseled by an outplacement supplier. Thus, the bulk of the measurements found in this section relate to, for example, the medical, relocation, or recruiting cost per person of a human resources supplier. The following measurements contain a brief description of each measurement, its strengths and weaknesses, and how it is measured. The measurements are as follows:

- *Medical insurance cost per person.* Medical insurance suppliers will offer a company at least two insurance prices: one rate for singles and another rate for families, with possible additional rates based on the number of family members an employee wants to cover. It is not sufficient to measure a supplier's total charge per each type of insurance, for there are two variables to consider that have a profound impact on the company's costs. One is the mix of employees using each type of insurance. For example, it does little good to give a high performance ranking to a supplier because it has a cheap single medical rate, when the bulk of company employees use the family rate, which is priced much higher than the competition. Consequently, the company must estimate, based on historical usage, the number of employees who will use each type of insurance, derive the total cost, and then divide it by the total number of employees to determine the actual cost to the company of medical insurance. However, we have not yet factored in the second variable, which is the amount of the insurance that the company pays for. For example, a supplier may offer a high single rate and a very low family rate. Since the company has a large proportion of employees who always take the family medical rate, this appears to be the most cost-effective way to go. However, the company pays for a very small percentage of the single rate and a high percentage of the family rate. Thus, though it is more cost effective for employees if the company continues to use this supplier, the company will save money if it switches to a supplier that offers lower single rates and higher family rates, due to the company's policy of covering the cost of this insurance. The best way to calculate this measurement is to multiply the single and family insurance rates by the number of employees who are likely to take each type of insurance, subtract the amounts that employees will pay to derive the amount to be paid by the company, summarize this information, and divide it by the total number of employees to determine the medical insurance cost per person.

- *Proportion of rejected medical claims.* One of the few non–cost performance measurements in the human resources area is the proportion of rejected medical claims. This is a good indicator of how much a medical insurance supplier is trying to cut its costs by being excessively strict in denying claims by company employees. It is a good indicator of supplier niggardliness if there are a sufficient number of employees filing claims to give a statistically valid basis for determining that there is something wrong with the supplier. However, if there are only a small number of employees, then even one claim rejection may incorrectly give the company the idea that the supplier is not giving proper service to its employees. This measure is determined by notifying employees that they should appeal all claim rejections to the functional coordinator (which they most assuredly do, since they will otherwise pay the medical costs themselves), who then compiles this information and divides it by the total number of claims submitted, which is usually obtained from the supplier. If the supplier does not have the total number of claims submitted, then the coordinator can have all claims submitted through him, and compile the information in that manner.

- *Life insurance cost per dollar of insurance.* A small amount of life insurance is frequently added to many benefit packages without the company knowing how much this added feature costs. It is frequently necessary to require the supplier to break out this cost on its periodic billings to the company so that the company can calculate the cost per person. The measurement is calculated by multiplying the amount of life insurance offered for each employee by the number of employees covered, and then dividing this amount by the annual cost of the insurance. The resulting amount tends to be a very small fraction.

- *Workers' compensation cost per person.* Workers' compensation bids are usually only listed as totals, not as per-person costs. Instead, workers' compensation providers charge a fixed fee through the year, and then conduct an audit of personnel at the end of the period, and adjust the price of the insurance based on that audit. This means that the company cannot determine the per-person workers' compensation insurance charge from the supplier's billing statement, especially after the multitude of discounts are included in the supplier's bid (as is common). This can be a difficult measurement to derive, because different insurance rates are charged for employees in different work categories. For example, clerical personnel are almost free, whereas people working in high-risk positions (such as metal workers) will be charged an extremely high insurance rate. The best way to determine the workers' compensation cost per person is to throw out all clerical personnel who have minimal workers' compensation insurance charges so as to derive the number of employees with significant insurance risk. Then divide this number into the total annual workers' compensation cost, as adjusted by the year-end audit, to determine the insurance cost per person. The calculation must include the year-end audit adjustment, because many companies underreport their head count to the insurance supplier during the year in order to artificially reduce their insurance costs during the year. Also, removing the clerical head count from the calculation is important, for a large number of personnel with no real impact on the cost of insurance would water down the cost-per-person measurement.

- *Recruiting cost per person.* A recruiter can be paid based on a percentage of the newly recruited person's starting salary. This is the payment scheme most preferred by recruiters, since they can make a large amount of money if they find the right employee. Typical payment percentages range from 20% to 30% of a recruited employee's first-year pay. The proper way to measure recruiters who are compensated in this manner is not by the total amount paid to the recruiter (since this varies with the salary of the employee they recruited), but by the percentage they charge. If they use a sliding percentage scale that changes with the amount of the recruited person's salary (a common approach), then measure the recruiter based on the percentage rate that would apply for the most common salary range that they would be likely to recruit for. Alternatively, a company may pay its recruiters based on an hourly rate, irrespective of the results of an employee search. In these cases, the company can measure the recruiter based on the cost per employee hired. To do so, accumulate the cost of all searches for a specified time period, then divide this amount by the number of employees recruited through this supplier as a result of the search cost. This measure can be flawed due to the long time period sometimes needed to recruit a new employee—the cost of the search may fall into one measurement period, while the person may not be hired until the next measurement period.

- *Outplacement cost per person.* Outplacement companies typically charge a fixed fee for each employee to whom they offer outplacement services, though this fee can vary depending on the type of employee—blue collar, clerical, or management. If the fee is split into these or other categories, it is still a simple matter to extract the per-person fee from the supplier's periodic billing statement and track this information over time to spot any costing trends.

- *Relocation administration cost per person.* Relocation suppliers sometimes have links to moving suppliers or real estate agencies, and offer their services to the company for free in exchange for routing business through those movers or real estate agencies, so that the relocation administration cost is hidden. If there is a billing from the relocation administration supplier, however, this should contain a fixed fee per person relocated, which can be tracked on a trend line to spot any changes.

- *Relocation cost per mile.* It is difficult to determine if a company is receiving a good deal on moving costs, since each employee will have a different volume and weight of materials to move, and will move a different number of miles. The best way to standardize this measurement is to first determine the cost per moving van. For example, if a move costs $2,000 and there are two vans, the cost per van is $1,000. Next, divide the cost per van by the number of miles the goods must be moved to the new location. For example, if the moving distance in the previous example is 1,000 miles, then the cost per mile is $1.00. This measurement approach gives the functional coordinator a rational way to compare the cost of disparate quantities and distances for goods to be shipped for different employees.

- *Training cost per person/hour.* A training supplier can be rated based on the cost per person who attends its classes. This information is easily extracted from the training expense account in the general ledger, and divided by the number of employees who attended classes. Another approach for classes offered on-site, irrespective of the number of employees attending, is the cost per hour. To calculate this measurement, also take the training cost for in-house classes from the general ledger expense account, and divide this cost by the hourly length of the classes offered to derive the training cost per hour.

- *Training evaluation scoring.* The previous measurement for the cost of a class does not tell the functional coordinator if the supplier is doing a good job of presenting the materials, or if the materials are useful to company employees. To determine this information, the company can issue an evaluation form to any employees attending training classes. The evaluation forms should let employees rank the classes on a scale, such as from 1 to 10. They should be asked to evaluate the relevance and quality of the training materials and the trainer, as well as the quality of the supplier's classroom facilities (irrelevant if the classes are conducted at a company location). The measurement can then be compiled by summarizing all of the scores for all employees for each course and dividing by the number of people who submitted evaluation forms.

- *Average number of complaints per move.* A moving company may damage or lose an employee's possessions during a move, may be delayed in arriving for pickup, or may be delayed in dropping off the articles at the new location. Any of these problems may spark a complaint by an employee. The functional coordinator should be the recipient of all employee complaints related to moves. The total number of these complaints can then be divided by the total number of moves to determine the average number of complaints per move. This information can then be compared for different movers, or tracked on a trend line to see which mover is better, or if the performance of the company's preferred mover is changing.

- *Employee turnover percentage.* Employee turnover does not tell a company the exact reason why employees are leaving the company, but it can tell if there is a problem, especially when compared to turnover rates for the same industry. For example, a 50% turnover rate may be very low in the fast food industry, while anything over 5% in the government sector requires immediate action. The measurement is easily calculated by adding up the number of people who left the company during the year and dividing it by the total number of people employed by the company at the beginning of the year.

This section covered the performance measurements that are used to determine the efficiency and effectiveness of the various human resources functions. The primary measurement focus is on the cost per person of each function. There are a few other types of measurements, too, such as employee evaluations of training classes and the average number of relocation complaints. However, in general, this is a cost-driven function, and should be measured as such.

8.6   MANAGING THE OUTSOURCED FUNCTION

This section describes the management issues that must be dealt with when outsourcing all or part of the human resources function. The need for a functional coordinator is noted, as well as a clerical support staff. Also, a functional coordinator's tasks are briefly described. In addition, the necessary job skills of the coordinator are discussed. This section is intended to give the reader a general understanding of how an outsourced human resources function is to be managed, and the type of employee who is needed to do the managing.

The human resources function is considered to be one of the lesser functions in many companies, because it does not directly contribute to a company's strategic purpose. Instead, it is considered to be a function that handles the paperwork related primarily to the payroll and medical insurance needs of employees. This is not an entirely fair portrayal, since companies with a more advanced view of the function also use human resources for improving relations with employees as well as for succession planning. Nonetheless, the majority of companies do not give the human resources function a high priority, which has an impact on the level of person hired into the role of human resources functional coordinator. This person tends to be ranked at a lower level than the functional coordinators of other functional areas. In the smallest companies, there is no coordinator at all—instead, the function falls into the management area of the controller, who assigns the task to a subordinate. However, in most companies, the functional coordinator is separate from the controller, but reports to the same person as the controller, who is normally the vice president of finance and administration. This reporting relationship is shown in Figure 8.2. Thus, the functional coordinator role exists, but is considered a lower-level position than would be the case for the coordinators of other functional areas.

There is a large amount of paperwork associated with the human resources function. This includes sign-ups, change forms, and termination forms for life insurance and medical insurance, accident reporting forms for workers' compensation claims, and training evaluation forms. Some of the more technologically progressive companies have automated some of these forms by having employees fill them out on-line.

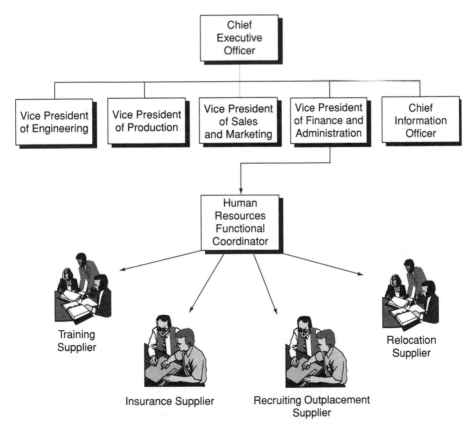

Figure 8.2   Organization Chart for Outsourcing the Human Resources Function

However, the vast majority of companies have not done so. Outsourcing the human resources function only reduces a small portion of this paperwork, so the functional coordinator will still need a clerical support staff to handle the forms.

The functional coordinator will also require some staff support to track supplier performance measurements each month, but this is normally only a small part of one person's job. There will also be a need for some staff to handle employee problems and complaints. Since the human resources function is entirely focused on company employees, the number of employee problems that the department must handle can be inordinately large. This is not something that an off-site supplier can handle, so company management must assume that the in-house staff already in place to handle employee problems will not go away when the human resources function is outsourced. Instead, some portion of the existing staff will act as facilitators in solving employee problems related to any human resources issues. The number of these clerical support positions can be quite large if the company has a large number of employees.

The human resources coordinator's job is similar to that of other functional coordinators because this person must manage all suppliers, measure their performance, and assist in negotiating contracts with them. These tasks are noted in the abbreviated job description shown in Figure 8.3. In addition to these basic requirements, the human resources coordinator must also have excellent people skills, since there is constant interaction with company employees, mostly concerning the resolution of their problems in a number of areas: insurance, training, workplace injuries, or other topics. The coordinator must also be well grounded in labor law and have strong contacts with the company's legal department or outside legal counsel. An entirely different, but very important, skill is an in-depth knowledge of human resources systems, particularly concerning how the flow of paper for each of the various human

Figure 8.3   The Human Resources Coordinator's Job Description

---

Employee Title: Human Resources Outsourcing Coordinator
Reports to: Vice President of Finance and Administration
Responsibilities:
- Sign off on all agreements with human resources suppliers.
- Track actual costs incurred against budgeted amounts by supplier and work with each supplier to correct any problems.
- Measure service levels for all human resources areas and resolve any problems.
- Manage the transfer of functions from the company to suppliers.
- Periodically review the services provided by insurance suppliers to employees.
- Periodically review the performance of outplacement suppliers and recruiters.
- Periodically review the summarized evaluation forms turned in from various supplier-taught classes.
- Continually review the nature of all workers' compensation claims and work on safety programs to reduce the most common or dangerous potential accidents.

resources functions moves through the company and on to its suppliers. If the co-ordinator does not have a solid knowledge of process flows in this most paper-intensive of all functional areas, then there is a strong possibility that the coordinator will not properly manage the function, resulting in inefficiencies and excessive costs. If the human resources coordinator has the required people skills, legal train-ing, and workflow background, then the function is much more likely to operate as smoothly as possible.

8.7 POTENTIAL CUSTOMER SERVICE ISSUES

In this section, we explore the customer service issues of the human resources func-tion. There is only one customer of this function, and it is internal to the company: the employee. The human resources function provides all of the benefits, training, career counseling, and accident-prevention services to the employee, so it is evident that this function can go a long way towards creating a happy work force—or a bel-ligerent one.

The primary area for employee dissatisfaction within the human resources func-tion is medical insurance. Employees can be intensely unhappy over rejected med-ical claims or late payments to doctors, resulting in secondary billings to employees. By tracking employee complaints over these two items, the functional coordinator can determine if there is a problem and follow up with the supplier to correct it. Bad service in this area definitely means that the supplier should be replaced. Another customer service issue related to medical insurance is the company's fault: switching suppliers too frequently, which means that employees must continually fill out new medical insurance forms and select new doctors. The functional coordinator should consider retaining the current medical insurance provider for multiple years if switching suppliers has become a problem for employees.

Blanket life insurance coverage for all employees is of no concern to younger or single employees, but of much greater concern to older employees, those who are married, or those who have medical problems. If the company does not provide any life insurance, these people (especially those with medical problems) may have to procure their own insurance at very high prices. A good way to retain these employ-ees is to provide them with this insurance, which a company can obtain for far less money per person than can an individual.

Some of the more aggressive insurance companies make a habit of challenging all workers' compensation claims. While this practice is intended to drive down a com-pany's workers' compensation costs, there is a fine line between cost reduction and irritating employees who have legitimate medical claims. If it is apparent that the ac-tions of an insurer are continually irritating employees, the coordinator should dis-cuss this issue with the insurer. However, since policies to challenge claims are fre-quently built into the infrastructure of some insurers, making it difficult to change the behavior of the insurer, it is possible if not likely that the functional coordinator will have to replace the insurer.

Poor training instructors or materials will not be a cause for active employee dissatisfaction, but rather of mild annoyance at wasting employee time. This problem can be discovered through employee evaluation forms. The functional coordinator can sometimes correct this problem by asking to have instructors replaced or training materials revised. (This is easy to do if the company is paying for the revision work!) If the supplier cannot meet the company's performance standards, then the functional coordinator should replace the supplier or consider taking the training function back in-house.

A cause of major dissatisfaction is when a relocation supplier damages or loses employee property during a move, especially when the property is valuable. The functional coordinator should track the number of complaints per move to see which relocation supplier consistently causes the least damage, and shift the company's business to that supplier. Also, the coordinator must follow up on damage complaints to verify that employees are being reimbursed for their damage claims in full and as soon as possible. Any continuing problems in this area should be grounds for immediate dismissal of a supplier.

A surprisingly important area is outplacement services, especially if the company is located in a small, tightly knit community. The reason is that word will travel rapidly through the community if the company provides exceptional outplacement services to employees who are being laid off. This is important if the company begins to hire people again, for they will be more likely to apply for jobs if they know the company pays attention to the welfare of its staff. Thus, tracking the quality of outplacement support during exit interviews is good customer support.

In summary, the human resources function provides customer service to a company's employees in many areas: medical insurance, life insurance, workers' compensation insurance, training, relocation, and outplacement. Proper attention to these services results in a happier work force, which has a direct impact on employee turnover.

8.8   GETTING OUT OF
THE OUTSOURCING ARRANGEMENT

This section covers some issues to consider when terminating a human resources supplier. Since there are a number of suppliers who can assist a single human resources department in a variety of tasks, there are several different problems to think about before conducting the termination. This section covers those issues, along with some ways to mitigate the problems.

It is difficult in the long run to abruptly terminate insurance suppliers, because word travels fast in the insurance industry, and prospective suppliers will be less willing to submit bids to the company for its insurance business. An insurance company normally signs a company to a one-year contract to supply life insurance, medical insurance, and/or workers' compensation insurance. The insurance company must expend some time in sales calls as well as in preparing bids. It prefers to incur this sales expense as infrequently as possible, so it is less likely to submit a bid to a company that has acquired a reputation for continually cutting off suppliers before contract terms are up. Thus, it is better to terminate insurance suppliers only at the end of the contract period.

Another problem with terminating insurance suppliers is that, with the exception of workers' compensation, most insurance changes require that employees fill out new insurance forms for the new supplier, and that whomever is left in the human resources department handle this paperwork. While this is a small task if there are not many employees, it is an exceeding large task for a large corporation, and is made especially difficult if the company has multiple locations or large numbers of employees, (such as salespeople) who are constantly on the move and cannot be reached to complete the paperwork. The paperwork issue alone is enough to make a human resources coordinator pause before terminating an agreement with an insurance provider.

A potentially serious problem with switching medical insurance suppliers, and one that very few companies think about, is that it may be impossible to switch suppliers if the company has a high proportion of employees on the current medical plan who have histories of serious illnesses (such as cancer) or who have undergone organ transplants. A large number of such cases will scare off potential new insurance providers, at least until a specific number of years have passed (usually five years) since the last occurrence of these illnesses. Otherwise, a company may find that it cannot find a new supplier to replace the old one.

The remaining problem area for supplier terminations is training. When a company terminates a training supplier, any copyrighted material owned by the supplier that the company was using will no longer be available. Thus, if the company is getting rid of the supplier because of its poor trainers, it may lose some very good training materials at the same time. Some suppliers will allow the company to continue using their training materials in exchange for a fee, but many will be too unhappy over losing the contract with the company to permit the use of materials at any price. This is not a problem if the company has paid the supplier to create customized courses, since the contract usually states that the company copyrights these materials and can keep them when the supplier leaves. Terminating a supplier means that the company will lose the supplier's training materials as well, unless it wants to pay for extra copies or owns the copyright itself.

The remaining human resources areas are not a problem if suppliers are terminated. For example, outsourcing suppliers are paid a fixed fee per person, so once they have been paid to handle the most recent group of laid-off employees, they can be terminated. Likewise, relocation suppliers are paid per employee, and can be terminated once the last employee they have been handling has been moved. Also, if the company is paying recruiters on an hourly basis, it has the right to shut them down at any time, as long as they have been compensated for hours already worked. If recruiters are working on a commission basis, it is standard practice in this very competitive industry to terminate them at any time with no compensation whatsoever if no potential recruits have been found; however, if the company does eventually hire someone who was located by a recruiter who has since been terminated, the recruiter should be paid the previously agreed-upon amount for finding the recruit. Finally, if the company has entered into a long-term contract with any of these suppliers, perhaps in exchange for lower rates, it is frequently enough to give written notice of termination, possibly with a short time period for the supplier to cure any problems before termination is finalized. In short, the termination of several human resources suppliers is easy, and requires minimal notice and no cash outlay by the company.

To summarize, most companies avoid abruptly terminating their insurance suppliers due to the reputation the company can acquire in the marketplace, and also avoid switching them too frequently in order to ship the paperwork hassle for employees. The company must also be aware that it will lose a training supplier's training materials along with its trainers when a training contract is terminated, though purchasing the materials is an option. All other tasks within the human resources area are easy to terminate with minimal notice periods and no cash termination payments.

8.9   SUMMARY

In this chapter we reviewed the many reasons both in favor of and against the use of suppliers to take over the various human resources services. In this area, the numerous advantages of outsourcing clearly outweigh the disadvantages, though it is reasonable to retain a stripped-down in-house staff while farming out most functions to suppliers.

Contractual issues centered on pricing, since most other aspects of human resources contracts are not especially negotiable. Even pricing is inflexible unless the company is so large that suppliers will reduce their rates to obtain the company's business. Some areas in which other contract points are negotiable are training, outplacement, and moving services.

Transition issues center around insurance, where employees must fill out new forms to transfer their medical and life insurance to new suppliers, and the in-house human resources clerical staff must be trained in using the new forms. Another transition area is training, where the company must compare the supplier's course offerings to the company's needs and create additional courses to fill any gaps.

A variety of control points are available for managing human resources suppliers. Monthly cost reviews are the most common, but this function is also uniquely suited to the use of review forms for control purposes, so that the functional coordinator can find out from employees how they think the suppliers are doing.

The voluminous listing of human resources measurements focused on the cost of outsourced services, especially on a per-person basis. Other measurements cover the number of employee complaints per activity. The employee turnover rate is an overall measurement that can be indicative of problems best addressed by the human resources coordinator.

Management of the human resources function is usually by a manager who ranks somewhat lower in the corporate organizational hierarchy than other functional coordinators. This is because the human resources function is frequently considered to be a clerical activity (a viewpoint that ignores the need for employee training and succession planning). The appropriate coordinator should have a good grounding in labor law, supplier management, and human resources systems.

Human resources has one customer, the employee, and problems with this function can make that customer very unhappy. Particular problem spots are rejected medical or workers' compensation claims, missing life insurance, poor training, and damage to possessions during moves. A number of controls can be used to mitigate these problems.

The final section of the chapter covered terminating the relationship with the supplier. Problem areas include gaining a reputation among insurance suppliers for abrupt terminations, not being able to switch insurance carriers due to the health problems of existing staff, and the loss of copyrighted training materials.

This chapter gave the reader an overview of why the human resources function, or at least some portions of it, should be outsourced; which contractual issues to focus on during negotiations; what transition issues are the most important; how to control a supplier and which measurements to use in this effort; the best way to manage suppliers and the type of person needed to do this job; possible customer service issues, and what problems to be aware of when terminating a supplier relationship. This information gives the reader sufficient background information to make a decision to outsource the human resources function.

CHAPTER NINE

Outsourcing the Maintenance and Janitorial Functions

The janitorial function is one of the most commonly outsourced functions, but many companies do not control the outsourced janitorial function very well, nor do they regularly examine the performance of their supplier. This chapter provides many hints that a company can use to extract better janitorial service from its current supplier.

The maintenance function is far less frequently outsourced. It is most commonly outsourced for transportation equipment, which can be easily moved to a supplier's central repair facility, and rarely outsourced for fixed, specialized, in-house equipment. This chapter discusses why some types of equipment are more easily outsourced than others, how to control the supplier's maintenance of that equipment, and what special features to look for when negotiating the initial contract with the supplier. It is of particular importance in this area to arrive at a contract with features that make it worthwhile for both parties to profit, especially when there are very few maintenance suppliers in the area to choose from, and the company must therefore ensure that the supplier is motivated to provide its services.

The chapter also lists a variety of measurements that can be used to track the performance of the janitorial and maintenance suppliers. These measures are unusual in that there are very few financial measures; these are operational in nature, and will require an operationally experienced staff person to compile. There are a large number of implementation issues covered, including transferring the in-house staff to the supplier, training the supplier's staff, transferring maintenance and janitorial records, selling parts and supplies, storing on-site equipment, and the need for a confidentiality agreement.

This chapter gives the reader a good foundation in the advantages and disadvantages associated with outsourcing the janitorial and maintenance functions, as well as in how to implement, measure, and control both functions once they have been transferred to suppliers.

9.1   ADVANTAGES AND DISADVANTAGES

There are a variety of advantages and disadvantages associated with outsourcing the janitorial and maintenance functions, with somewhat more disadvantages in the maintenance area. This section will deal with the janitorial function first and then finish with a discussion of the maintenance function.

The primary disadvantage of outsourcing the janitorial function is that there will still be a need for an in-house person to handle short-notice cleanup problems, such as spills, that cannot wait until the next regularly scheduled visit by the supplier's janitors. Thus, a company may still need an in-house janitor even after the function has been outsourced.

One major advantage associated with outsourcing the janitorial function relates to an accounting problem known as *step costing*. With an in-house janitorial staff, a new janitor must be hired once there is a moderate increase in required services, but that person may not be fully utilized until the facility size has continued to increase for some time. This results in an initial inefficiency that may not be corrected for quite some time, depending on the company facility's growth rate. When this function is outsourced, however, the company only pays an incremental amount for extra square footage that is added to the scope of the janitorial services contract. For example, when the company adds an office, it only pays a small additional fee for cleaning that room, not for the services of an extra full-time janitorial employee. This represents a significant cost savings. Also, in-house janitors who stay with the company for a long time will likely attain pay levels that are well above the norm in the industry; by outsourcing the function, the company can enjoy the reduced cost of the lower-paid employees used by the janitorial supplier. Finally, the company does not have to devote very much of its limited management resources to the janitorial function—or the time of an in-house coordinator who may very well be able to combine this responsibility with a number of other management tasks. In short, there are advantages to outsourcing the janitorial function that save both costs and management time.

There are several disadvantages to outsourcing the maintenance function. The primary disadvantage is that the supplier may have minimal experience in the maintenance of some of the company's more specialized equipment. Since the supplier must either train its own staff or take over the company's maintenance staff (along with their pay scale), there may be no obvious cost savings in this area. The company may even have trouble finding a maintenance supplier who is willing to take on the maintenance work for extremely specialized equipment, since the supplier cannot use this maintenance knowledge as a sales point to repair similar equipment for other companies—no one else has the equipment. There may also be a problem with obtaining a maintenance supplier if all of the equipment to be maintained is of the large, fixed variety that cannot be moved to the supplier's off-site, centralized repair facility. Since the maintenance staff must come to the company, this represents a costly dispersion of the supplier's key maintenance staff away from the efficient central facility. Since the maintenance staff must travel to the company's facility from a point that is likely to be several miles away, this also reduces the response time for repair work that must be completed immediately. A supplier may also be unwilling to stock spare parts for the more specialized types of equipment, since they cannot be used for the supplier's other customers. Finally, if the supplier is operating on a fixed-fee basis, there is an incentive to use the cheapest parts to repair the company's equipment, which may lead to more frequent equipment breakdowns. In short, there are a variety of reasons not to outsource the maintenance function, relating to not only the lack of cost savings but also to the difficulty of finding a maintenance supplier who will perform this kind of work, as well as to the possibility of having more frequent equipment breakdowns and longer repair response times.

Though there are many disadvantages to using a supplier for maintenance work, these problems apply almost entirely to specialized equipment rather than standard equipment. Maintenance suppliers are much more willing to take on new work if it is for common equipment for which their employees already have expertise. Also, if the equipment is very new and is considered by suppliers to be "hot," they will go out of their way to take on the maintenance work and train their staffs in any new maintenance techniques that may be required (quite possibly even paying for the special training themselves). This circumstance arises when suppliers think that the equipment is likely to be used throughout the industry or geographical area, and want to advertise their expertise in it. There is also a better chance of obtaining supplier help if the company has consistently invested in large quantities of standard equipment from the same manufacturer—this greatly reduces the supplier training needed, and makes taking on the work more palatable to the supplier. A classic example of this situation is Southwest Airlines, which owns Boeing 737 airliners and no other type of jet. This greatly reduces the complexity of their maintenance operation.

Another reason for outsourcing maintenance (though a minor one) is that the company will no longer have to obtain insurance coverage for the exceedingly expensive tools that are typically required for most maintenance operations—this is because the supplier will own all the tools. Also, the company can do away with its investment in facilities and replacement parts by liquidating them or selling them to the supplier, which reduces the company's working capital requirements. In addition, the supplier is likely to give more training to its maintenance technicians than the company was previously able to do, because the supplier must provide this training in order to stay competitive, whereas the company has no strategic reason to upgrade the training of its in-house staff. Another reason is that maintenance can take an unusually large amount of management time to competently perform, because it is a specialized function that requires the coddling of a highly trained staff. By moving the management task to a competent supplier, the company can reduce its management needs in this area. Finally, the only way to achieve a significant reduction in maintenance costs is to send any rolling stock to a centralized maintenance facility owned by the supplier. This is only possible for equipment that is easily transported, such as trucks and jets. Suppliers can create significant cost savings by creating a central repair facility where they can concentrate their staffs near new and specialized repair equipment, and bring their customer's equipment to the staff. This is the most common form of maintenance outsourcing, and is the type of maintenance most likely to be implemented, since the cost savings are immediate. In short, the number of advantages to using maintenance outsourcing can offset the disadvantages, especially if the equipment to be maintained can be shifted to the supplier's central maintenance facility for lower-cost servicing.

9.2 IMPLEMENTATION ISSUES

There are a large number of implementation issues to be considered when switching to a supplier for the provision of janitorial and maintenance services. One such problem is who keeps the supplies left over when the functions are outsourced? There will probably be a moderate quantity of janitorial supplies left over at the time of the transition, and there may be a considerably larger quantity of maintenance parts (especially if there are a large variety of machines being maintained). The easiest solution is to sell the supplies to the supplier at the beginning of the contract period. However, if there is a large amount of this material, the supplier may hesitate to incur the expense of acquiring all of the supplies (most common in the case of large numbers of maintenance parts). In these cases, it is most common for the supplier to pick and choose the parts it can use, and leave the remaining parts with the company, which must dispose of the leftover parts in whatever manner it deems appropriate (e.g., sell to the parts suppliers, retain in stock, or throw away). The disposition of existing supplies should be determined at the commencement of the relationship with a new janitorial or maintenance supplier.

Once the company and its new supplier have decided who will own the supplies, there is still the issue of where they will be stored. It makes little sense for janitorial supplies to be stored off-site and brought back to the company when they can more easily be retained at each company facility. Also, the company may be required to retain some of the maintenance parts at its own facility, especially if the equipment cannot be moved off-site due to its size or weight. If the supplier has spent a considerable amount of money on the purchase of parts from the customer, it will be more inclined to require a longer-term maintenance contract as well as a large lump-sum payment to abrogate the contract, since it must cover its financial exposure. In short, the company may be able to reduce its working capital needs by requiring a supplier to purchase some or all of its janitorial and maintenance supplies, but this will be offset by long-term contracts with suppliers and the cost of retaining the parts in storage facilities at the company.

There is a similar issue with the equipment used to conduct ongoing janitorial and maintenance activities. The company is likely to already own much of this equipment itself, and will no longer want to retain it. The supplier may already have some or all of the equipment, and will not want to purchase it from the company. If so, the company may have to sell it through a broker. If the equipment is capitalized, this may mean that the company will incur a loss on the sale of the equipment; the potential expense of this loss should be factored into the outsourcing budget for the first year. If the maintenance supplier decides to use the equipment, it may want to discuss other alternatives than a straight purchase of the equipment—this is because some maintenance equipment, such as lathes or welding machines, is quite expensive, and may represent an excessive expenditure for the supplier to purchase. Even if the supplier does agree to purchase the equipment, it may want to insert a buy-back clause in the contract that requires the company to repurchase the equipment, less a suitable depreciation allowance, following the termination of the service agreement with the company. A better alternative for the supplier is to have the company continue to own the equipment, but to lease it to the supplier. The equipment lease is rarely recorded as a separate document. Instead, the periodic payment to the supplier for maintenance work performed is reduced by the amount of the equipment lease. This arrangement also ties the lease term to the term of the supplier's maintenance contract with the company, which is an appropriate linkage of the terms of two separate transactions. Thus, a company may find that it must sell any equipment it owns related to the janitorial and maintenance functions, but may be able to lease the equipment to the suppliers in exchange for lower total payments to them for services performed.

The company and its maintenance supplier must also decide if the in-house maintenance facilities will be retained or if they will be moved to the supplier's location. If equipment being repaired is vehicles, then the supplier is likely to already have adequate repair facilities at its location, and can easily drive or transport the equipment there. This means that the company's in-house repair facility for transportation equipment will no longer be needed. An alternative use must be found for this space. Since maintenance areas for transportation equipment are not designed for conversion to office space, the company may find that the cost of such a conversion is extremely expensive, which limits its choices to using the space for storage or as a receiving or distribution center. However, if the majority of the equipment being maintained is fixed and cannot be moved to an off-site maintenance center for repair work, the supplier will probably have to take over the company's in-house maintenance facility for its own use. If the supplier takes over this space and equipment, the company will probably want to sell the equipment to the supplier and lease it the space in order to eliminate some assets. However, the supplier will almost certainly not want to pay for the space or the equipment, since this will represent a significant up-front expenditure. The best way to meet the needs of both business partners is to either have the supplier purchase the equipment but be awarded a long-term guaranteed contract that assures long-term compensation for the expense incurred, or have the company retain the assets in exchange for lower maintenance fees and a short-term contract. The supplier usually does not want to invest in the maintenance equipment, especially if the equipment is only useful for repairing very specialized equipment that few other companies own. However, the supplier may agree to purchase the equipment in the interest of acquiring a long-term contract with the company, which carries the side benefit of keeping its maintenance staff highly utilized for a long time period, as well as providing a steady stream of revenue for the duration of the contract. Selling the company's maintenance equipment and renting its facilities to the maintenance supplier involves several options and risks for both parties, which must be carefully considered prior to making a decision.

The company may want to consider having the supplier sign a confidentiality agreement. This is rarely an issue for janitorial suppliers, but it may be a concern for maintenance suppliers, since their staffs will be able to take a detailed look at company equipment that was developed in-house and is considered to be critical to the company's competitive situation in the marketplace. This is of particular concern if the company deems the equipment to be so secret that it has not even patented the designs, thereby keeping the drawings away from public scrutiny at the patent office, but opening up the risk that someone can immediately copy and use the designs elsewhere if they can somehow steal this information. If the equipment being maintained is exceedingly carefully protected from outside eyes, the company's best recourse in terms of maintaining it is to keep the maintenance function in-house rather than run the risk of having representatives from any outside company regularly review the machinery. However, if outsourcing must be done, a confidentiality agreement should be a mandatory part of the arrangement.

When using outside suppliers for these functions, the company must also be prepared to hand over its janitorial and maintenance records. The main benefit of giving janitorial records to a supplier is that the supplier then has a good idea of the company's expectations for the cleanliness of its various areas; the actual janitorial records may vary considerably from the expectations verbally communicated to the supplier, who should compare the records to what it is being told and bring any discrepancies to the attention of the company's janitorial coordinator, who should resolve any differences. For example, the coordinator may inform the supplier that cleaning the executive offices twice a week is sufficient, but the janitorial records reveal that they are being cleaned every day. Since the executives sign the checks paying the supplier, it would be prudent of the supplier to ensure that the level of executive office cleanliness be maintained at its preexisting level, or have something in writing from the janitorial coordinator that says otherwise. The need for handing over maintenance records is much greater, because the maintenance supplier must use this information to develop its own maintenance plans and pricing. For example, if the company's records reveal that a particular truck requires far more than the usual amount of maintenance, perhaps due to overuse or being a poor-quality vehicle, the supplier must schedule additional maintenance up front, rather than putting it on a typical maintenance regimen and having it break down for lack of the level of maintenance that it requires. Also, the supplier's pricing may change based on a review of the company's records, since it will be able to develop a much better idea of the particular maintenance quirks of the equipment and of the changes in labor and materials that will be required to attend to those problems. This gives the company a much more accurate idea of what the supplier's actual charges will be, and also keeps the supplier from entering into any fixed-fee arrangement that may be unfair due to excessive maintenance issues that it would otherwise be unaware of. By giving its historical janitorial and maintenance records to its suppliers, a company will receive better janitorial and maintenance service, as well as more accurate maintenance contract pricing.

Part of the implementation process is determining the base price of the contract with the supplier. The company will find that there is more price competition for the maintenance of transportation equipment, since there are more suppliers in this portion of the maintenance outsourcing field who are competing against each other for the company's business. However, this is not the case for the maintenance of more specialized in-house equipment. In these cases, suppliers cannot take the equipment to their centralized and highly efficient maintenance facilities (as is the case for transportation equipment), which therefore requires them to send their personnel to the company, which is a less-than-efficient use of their time. Also, the equipment tends to be more specialized, so the supplier will have difficulty obtaining personnel who can maintain the equipment. Thus, the company will find few prospective suppliers for the maintenance of its in-house equipment, which creates less price competition and will lead to higher contract prices. In contrast, janitorial services are provided by so many suppliers that the company should be able to drive prices down through competitive bidding of the work. In short, a company will find that suppliers are willing to provide services for very low prices for janitorial services, somewhat higher prices for the maintenance of transportation equipment, and very high prices for the maintenance of specialized in-house equipment.

Prospective maintenance suppliers must also be allowed time to personally examine the equipment to be maintained. This gives the suppliers a better idea of the condition of the equipment and allows them to bid as accurately as possible on the maintenance work. This is in the company's favor, since a maintenance supplier may bid too low without having seen the equipment, and then provide shoddy maintenance service, since this is the only way to avoid losing money on the contract. By giving suppliers every opportunity to collect accurate information about the equipment to be maintained prior to signing a contract, the company is more likely to receive a fair and accurate bid from the supplier.

The pricing proposals received from maintenance contractors may even include variable-rate pricing depending on the age or usage of the equipment. For example, the maintenance on a truck may be charged at 2 cents per mile until the truck reaches 50,000 miles, at which point the rate changes to 2.5 cents. This tiered rate structure is used to cover the supplier's additional costs to replace larger numbers of parts as the equipment receives more use. A more common alternative is to tightly define what is involved in maintenance work (e.g., oil changes, wiper changes, or fuel filter replacement), with every other activity by default falling outside of the standard maintenance agreement. These additional items will then be charged to the company as an extra (and usually expensive) fee. It is the task of the company's legal team both to increase the scope of the items defined as standard maintenance work and to reduce the price of the work that falls outside of this area—otherwise, the cost of the contract could be excessive.

It is quite possible that the company will not be able to find one maintenance supplier that can fulfill all of the company's maintenance needs, probably due to the great variety of its equipment or its geographical dispersion. If so, it may be necessary to award the work to multiple maintenance suppliers who are, as a group, better able to service the equipment. If this happens, the company must make some provision for notifying suppliers if it moves equipment between the territories of its various suppliers, which includes transferring maintenance records from one supplier to another to go along with the equipment. This also makes the task of the maintenance coordinator more difficult, and may call for more than one coordinator, depending on the number of suppliers used and the number of locations where the equipment is located. Using several suppliers increases the level of outsourcing complexity, but is likely to result in better maintenance of the company's equipment.

One of the most important implementation issues is the transition plan, which gradually transfers the responsibility for janitorial and maintenance services from the in-house staff to the staff of the supplier. The key transition issues are as follows:

- *Training the supplier's staff.* There may need to be a breaking-in period while the new staff receives training from the equipment manufacturer, from the company's management, or from the company's staff, who are being retained long enough to transfer their skills to the supplier's personnel. Training by the equipment manufacturer may require off-site training at the manufacturer's location or travel by the manufacturer's training staff to the company location; in either case, the company and its supplier must determine in advance who is going to pay for this training and all related travel costs. The worst of these options is usually retaining the company's staff strictly for training purposes—since they are subsequently being laid off, they may therefore not do the best training job due to resentment.

- *Transferring staff to the supplier.* The company may do well to retain the skills of the in-house maintenance staff by transferring them to the supplier who is taking over the function. This provision should be included in the contract with the supplier. Moving staff to the supplier is of particular importance if the staff is especially knowledgeable in the maintenance of specialized company equipment, and less necessary in the janitorial area, where there are few necessary skills to be retained.

- *Dealing with user complaints.* Users will inevitably have problems during this transition period. Complaints will be caused by missing or inadequate services that will gradually be fixed as the new supplier learns more about the company's needs. The best way to handle these complaints is through improved communications. Be sure to tell all users prior to the conversion period that a new supplier is taking over, that there will inevitably be some problems, and to please bear with the company during this transition period. Also, once complaints are received, the in-house service coordinator must be sure to address the problems immediately; otherwise, the company's employees may develop a permanent disregard for the new supplier before it has really had a chance to prove itself.

Clearly, there are many steps to complete before the implementation process can be considered complete. The sample Gantt chart shown in Figure 9.1 shows the implementation steps to be completed, the sequence in which they must occur, and the duration of each step. Actual implementations may vary considerably from this sample, since some steps may have to be added or subtracted, and the term of the implementation may vary drastically, depending on the complexity of the changeover to the supplier.

9.3   CREATING CONTROL POINTS

One of the best ways to retain control over the janitorial and maintenance functions is to periodically conduct an operational audit. This audit involves directly examining the facilities and equipment to verify that they are being maintained, comparing janitorial and maintenance records to the facilities and equipment to verify that all recorded tasks are actually being performed, and then comparing prices billed against the contractually agreed-upon rates as well as tracking the trend of cost changes. The resulting audit report should go to the coordinators for the janitorial and maintenance functions, who will find it to be a valuable tool for correcting any problems uncovered. The report should also go to the corporate audit committee, which thereby obtains an independent review of the performance of these two outsourced functions.

The sample audit report in Figure 9.2(a) gives an overview of what is being tested in the janitorial function, followed by specific audit instructions and a summary of the findings from the audit. This sample is detailed enough to be used as is by a company's internal auditing department, especially since the janitorial function is so generic that few companies will have alternative janitorial functions than those outlined here. The primary issue with auditing the janitorial function is when to conduct the review; the audit team should do this right after a scheduled visit by the janitorial staff to ensure that it is covering areas that should have just been cleaned. If the janitorial staff is cleaning portions of the facility on a rolling basis, the audit team should have a copy of the janitorial group's work schedule, so that it can follow behind the janitors to review recently cleaned portions of the company's facility.

The sample audit report may seem overlong, but this is the primary means for a company's in-house janitorial and maintenance coordinators to determine the quality of work being performed by their respective suppliers. Unlike other outsourced functions, such as engineering, there is no obvious deliverable that can be personally reviewed and approved by the coordinator; instead, there are a large number of small cleaning or maintenance actions that must be reviewed to give the coordinator a proper view of how well these functions are being handled. Also, since the audit

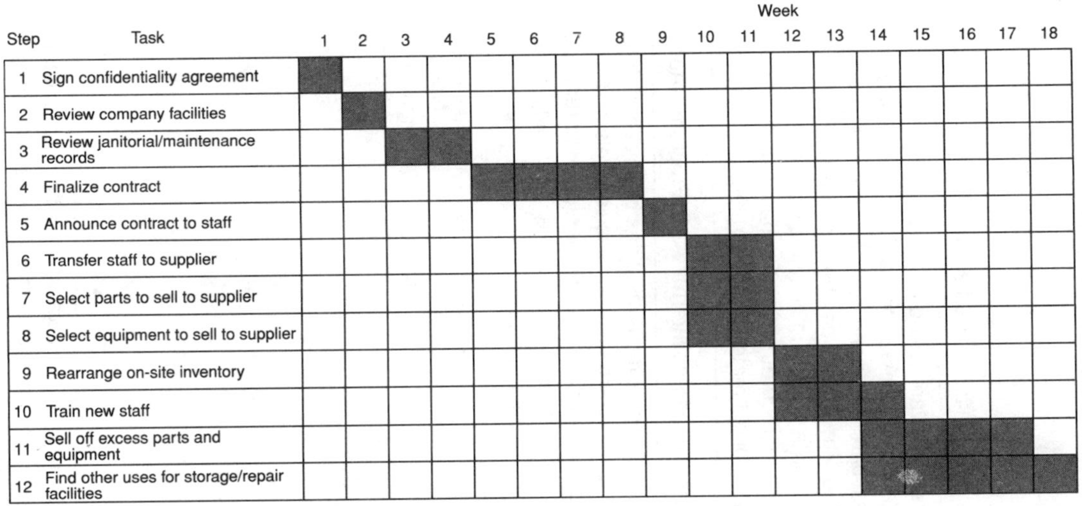

Figure 9.1 Gantt Chart for Implementing a Conversion of the Janitorial and Maintenance Functions

steps required to examine the janitorial and maintenance functions are quite different, the audit programs for *both* functions are listed in some detail. Thus, the best way to derive an objective view of the quality of the supplier's work in these areas is the operational audit, which is reproduced here in such length and level of detail. Figure 9.2(a) shows an overview of the janitorial internal audit program, which is shown in detail in Figure 9.2(b), and concludes with a findings section in Figure 9.2(c).

Figure 9.2(a)   Sample Janitorial Internal Audit Program—Overview

1. Verify that adequate vacuuming has been completed.
2. Verify that adequate floor waxing has been completed.
3. Verify that adequate waste removal has been completed.
4. Verify that adequate dusting has been completed.
5. Verify that adequate bathroom cleaning has been completed.
6. Verify that janitorial records are being maintained.
7. Verify that prices billed match contract rates.

Figure 9.2(b)   Sample Janitorial Internal Audit Program—Audit Instructions

Objective: Verify that adequate vacuuming has been completed.
Audit Program: Test selected areas for excessive levels of dirt, obvious particles that were not picked up during vacuuming, and particles still remaining on the floor in out-of-the-way locations, indicating inadequate vacuuming coverage.
Sample Size: Ten areas around the company.
Test Detail: As follows:

Area Reviewed	Adequate Vacuuming	Needs Improvement	Vacuuming Not Done
Accounting Offices		✔	
Corridors—Front Office		✔	
Corridors—Production			✔
Executive Offices	✔		
Marketing Offices	✔		
Materials-Management Offices			✔
Production Offices			✔
Purchasing Offices			✔
Reception Area	✔		
Sales Offices	✔		

Objective: Verify that adequate floor waxing has been completed.
Audit Program: Test all linoleum or ceramic surfaces in selected areas to determine if wax has been applied (use touch test); conduct visual test to see if enough buffing has been added to eliminate all wax swirls from view.
Sample Size: Ten areas around the company.
Test Detail: As follows:

Area Reviewed	Full Floor Coverage?	Buffing Completed?	Full Area Coverage?
Accounting Offices	Yes	Yes	Yes
Corridors—Front Office	Yes	Yes	Yes
Corridors—Production	No	No	No
Executive Offices	N/A	N/A	N/A
Marketing Offices	Yes	Yes	Yes
Materials-Management Offices	No	No	No
Production Offices	No	No	No
Purchasing Offices	No	No	No
Reception Area	N/A	N/A	N/A
Sales Offices	Yes	Yes	Yes

Objective: Verify that adequate waste removal has been completed.
Audit Program: Test all sample areas to determine if wastebaskets have been emptied. Also, see if other trash in the form of any items too large to fit in a wastebasket and clearly marked as "trash" has been removed. Finally, verify that all materials left in recycled materials containers have been removed.
Sample Size: Ten areas around the company.
Test Detail: As follows:

Area Reviewed	Wastebaskets Emptied?	Extra Trash Removed?	Recycle Items Removed?
Accounting Offices	Yes	Yes	Yes
Corridors—Front Office	N/A	N/A	N/A
Corridors—Production	N/A	N/A	N/A
Executive Offices	No	No	Yes
Marketing Offices	No	No	Yes
Materials-Management Offices	Yes	Yes	Yes
Production Offices	Yes	Yes	Yes
Purchasing Offices	Yes	Yes	Yes
Reception Area	Yes	Yes	Yes
Sales Offices	No	No	Yes

Objective: Verify that adequate dusting has been completed.
Audit Program: Test all sample areas to verify that bookshelves, desks, and credenzas have been dusted. Wipe selected areas with a white cloth to verify that these surfaces are clean—a darkened cloth indicates that no dusting was conducted.
Sample Size: Ten areas around the company.
Test Detail: As follows:

Area Reviewed	Bookshelves Dusted?	Desks Dusted?	Credenzas Dusted?
Accounting Offices	Yes	Yes	Yes
Corridors—Front Office	N/A	N/A	N/A
Corridors—Production	N/A	N/A	N/A
Executive Offices	Yes	Yes	Yes

Figure 9.2(b) Continued

Area Reviewed	Bookshelves Dusted?	Desks Dusted?	Credenzas Dusted?
Marketing Offices	Yes	Yes	Yes
Materials-Management Offices	No	No	No
Production Offices	No	No	No
Purchasing Offices	Yes	Yes	Yes
Reception Area	Yes	Yes	Yes
Sales Offices	Yes	Yes	Yes

Objective: Verify that adequate bathroom cleaning has been completed.
Audit Program: Test all sample areas to verify that bathrooms have been cleaned. Look for particles or stains on the floor, in sinks, or in toilets; verify that paper towels have not run out; and ensure that there is at least one backup roll of toilet paper in each stall.
Sample Size: Ten areas around the company.
Test Detail: As follows:

Area Reviewed	Floor Cleaned?	Sinks Cleaned?	Paper Towels?	Toilets Cleaned?	Toilet Paper?
Executive Bathroom—Female	Yes	Yes	Yes	Yes	Yes
Executive Bathroom—Male	Yes	Yes	Yes	Yes	Yes
Front Office Bathroom—Female	No	No	No	No	No
Front Office Bathroom—Male	Yes	Yes	Yes	Yes	Yes
Manufacturing Bathroom—Female	Yes	Yes	Yes	Yes	Yes
Manufacturing Bathroom—Male	Yes	Yes	Yes	Yes	Yes
Reception Bathroom—Female	No	No	No	No	No
Reception Bathroom—Male	Yes	Yes	Yes	Yes	Yes

Objective: Verify that janitorial records are being maintained.
Audit Program: After verifying that any of the previous activities in this audit program have been completed, trace the activities back to the janitorial records to determine if those activities were originally scheduled, that the schedule was updated to reflect the completion of the activity, and that a supervisor signed off on the activity once it was completed. The auditor should also trace activities forward from the janitorial records to verify that these activities were completed.
Sample Size: Ten areas around the company.
Test Detail: As follows:

Area Reviewed	Services Scheduled?	Records Updated?	Supervisor Review?
Accounting Offices	Yes	Yes	Yes
Corridors—Front Office	Yes	No	Yes
Corridors—Production	Yes	Yes	Yes
Executive Offices	Yes	No	Yes
Marketing Offices	Yes	Yes	No
Materials-Management Offices	Yes	Yes	No
Production Offices	Yes	Yes	No

Area Reviewed	Services Scheduled?	Records Updated?	Supervisor Review?
Purchasing Offices	Yes	No	No
Reception Area	Yes	Yes	Yes
Sales Offices	Yes	Yes	Yes

Objective: Verify that prices billed match contract rates.

Audit Program: Review the supplier's bills for the last three months to determine if a bill was sent to the company, if the charges on the bill match the activities actually conducted, and that the rates charged match the rates noted on the company's contract with the supplier. If the bill does not break out individual activities and costs per activity, this should be treated as an exception.

Sample Size: Select the bills from the most recent three months.

Test Detail: As follows:

Description	Billing Exists?	Billing for All Areas Cleaned?	Billing Rates Match Contract?
March Billing	No	N/A	N/A
April Billing	Yes	Yes	Yes
May Billing	Yes	Yes	No

Figure 9.2(c)   Sample Janitorial Internal Audit Program—Findings

1. Verify that adequate vacuuming has been completed.
   - Findings: The primary problem is the vacuuming of the production area, which was missed entirely. Not all portions of the accounting and front corridor areas were vacuumed.
   - Recommendations: Station additional vacuums in the production area so that they do not have to be transported from the front office area. Require more supervisory follow-up of vacuuming by the supplier's management.
2. Verify that adequate floor waxing has been completed.
   - Findings: Floor waxing is adequate in all areas except production, where it was completely missed. The level of expertise appears to be sufficient.
   - Recommendations: Station wax-buffing equipment in the production area so that this equipment does not have to be transported from the front office storage area. Focus on having additional supervisory reviews of the areas being waxed to ensure that no areas are missed.
3. Verify that adequate waste removal has been completed.
   - Findings: Trash is not being removed from the executive, sales, and marketing offices. Recycled materials are being removed from all locations.
   - Recommendations: Have the supplier's management review all wastebasket locations with its staff to ensure that all trash is removed in the future. Verify that the supplier's supervisors are following up on this point.
4. Verify that adequate dusting has been completed.
   - Findings: The production offices are not being dusted.
   - Recommendations: Have the supplier's supervisors review all dusting locations with the supplier staff to ensure that all areas are dusted. Since

Figure 9.2(c)   Continued

the manufacturing area has heavy dust accumulation, it is likely that any problems in this area will be promptly reported back to the auditor by employees in that area, so the time to follow-up can be lengthened.

5. Verify that adequate bathroom cleaning has been completed.
   - Findings: The women's bathrooms were not cleaned.
   - Recommendations: If the supplier has a policy of only having female employees clean women's bathrooms, verify that it has enough female staff to perform this function. If there is no such policy, continue to review these locations and bring clean-up problems to the attention of the supplier's management.

6. Verify that janitorial records are being maintained.
   - Findings: Though there are schedules kept for all activities, there are persistent problems with updating those records. Also, supervisors are not approving all work.
   - Recommendations: The primary problem is not updating records. If schedules are not being updated after the supplier has been notified of this problem, the issue may have to be presented to higher levels of supplier management.

7. Verify that prices billed match contract rates.
   - Findings: The earliest billing in the sample could not be found. The most recent billing contained prices that did not match those shown in the contract.
   - Recommendations: The earliest billing appears to have been merged into the billing for the next month; notify the supplier that monthly billings are preferred so that the company can recognize its expenses in a timely manner. As for the incorrect billing rate, only the rate listed in the contract should be paid. A letter to the supplier should explain why there is a difference between the amount billed and the amount paid.

The sample audit report in Figure 9.3(a) gives an overview of what is being tested in the maintenance function (showing different audit steps primarily for transportation equipment), followed by specific audit instructions [Figure 9.3(b)] and a summary [Figure 9.3(c)] of the findings from the audit. This sample should *not* be used as a model for a company's internal audit instructions, since each company's maintenance functions will vary widely depending on the types of equipment owned. A key issue for the audit team is when the auditing work should be performed. The best time is immediately after the latest time period (for in-house equipment) or largest amount of mileage (for transportation equipment) when maintenance should have been performed, thereby ensuring that the maintenance teams have no excuse for not having completed periodic maintenance activities. For example, if maintenance is supposed to be performed on the company's automobile fleet every 15,000 miles, with a maximum allowable variance of 2,000 miles, the audit team should schedule a review of any automobiles that have just exceeded 17,000 miles since their last scheduled maintenance.

Figure 9.3(a)   Sample Maintenance Internal Audit Program—Overview

---

1. Verify that vehicle cleanliness has been achieved.
2. Verify that various oil changes have been completed.
3. Verify that the wiper fluid container has been filled.
4. Verify that all filters have been changed.
5. Verify that the tire pressure is at the recommended level.
6. Verify that ball bearings have been replaced.
7. Verify that brake pads have been replaced.
8. Verify that engine belts have been replaced.
9. Verify that maintenance records are being maintained.
10. Verify that prices billed match contract rates.

Figure 9.3(b)   Sample Maintenance Internal Audit Program—Audit Instructions

---

Objective: Verify that vehicle cleanliness has been achieved.
Audit Program: Verify that both the inside and outside of the front and side windows have been cleaned; they are assumed to be clean if there are no visible smudges on either side of the glass. If the floor mats in front of all seats are free of dirt, they are assumed to be clean. If the vehicle body is free of dirt, it is assumed to have been washed.
Sample Size: Six vehicles selected using stratified sampling; at least two vehicles must have more than 60,000 miles.
Test Detail: As follows:

Unit Description	Windows Cleaned?	Floor Mats Vacuumed?	Body Washed?
Truck Number 1137	Yes	Yes	Yes
Truck Number 1009	No	No	No
Truck Number 1249	Yes	Yes	Yes
Truck Number 1931	Yes	Yes	Yes
Truck Number 2704	Yes	Yes	Yes
Truck Number 0082	No	No	No

Objective: Verify that various oil changes have been completed.
Audit Program: Examine the dipstick for the engine oil and remove a sample of oil from the differential and transmission casings by removing the oil plug from each area. Compare the color of the oil to a color chart that shows the usage of the oil for various color ranges; this tells the auditor how recently the oil has been changed.
Sample Size: Six vehicles selected using stratified sampling; at least two vehicles must have more than 60,000 miles.
Test Detail: As follows:

Unit Description	Fresh Engine Oil?	Fresh Differential Oil?	Fresh Transmission Oil?
Truck Number 1137	Yes	No	Yes
Truck Number 1009	No	Yes	No
Truck Number 1249	Yes	No	Yes
Truck Number 1931	No	Yes	No

Figure 9.3(b)   Continued

Unit Description	Fresh Engine Oil?	Fresh Differential Oil?	Fresh Transmission Oil?
Truck Number 2704	Yes	No	No
Truck Number 0082	No	No	Yes

Objective: Verify that the wiper fluid container has been filled.

Audit Program: Examine the fluid reservoir. The reservoir is considered to be filled if the fluid level is within two inches of the top of the container.

Sample Size: Six vehicles selected using stratified sampling; at least two vehicles must have more than 60,000 miles.

Test Detail: As follows:

Unit Description	Wiper Fluid Filled?
Truck Number 1137	✔
Truck Number 1009	
Truck Number 1249	✔
Truck Number 1931	✔
Truck Number 2704	✔
Truck Number 0082	

Objective: Verify that the air filter has been changed.

Audit Program: Remove the air filter from the air filter housing and compare the color of the filter element to a color chart. If the color is darker than the minimum color level, the air filter is considered to be too covered with particulates to be useful, and should be replaced.

Sample Size: Six vehicles selected using stratified sampling; at least two vehicles must have more than 60,000 miles.

Test Detail: As follows:

Unit Description	Air Filter Changed?
Truck Number 1137	✔
Truck Number 1009	✔
Truck Number 1249	
Truck Number 1931	
Truck Number 2704	✔
Truck Number 0082	✔

Objective: Verify that the tire pressure is at the recommended level.

Audit Program: Take the tire pressure of each vehicle and compare it to the recommended tire pressure that is posted on the inside door panel of each vehicle. The actual tire pressure is considered to be within specifications if all tires are within three pounds of pressure of the recommended level.

Sample Size: Six vehicles selected using stratified sampling; at least two vehicles must have more than 60,000 miles.

Test Detail: As follows:

Unit Description	Actual Tire Pressure	Recommended Tire Pressure	Within Three Pounds of Recommended?
Truck Number 1137	42	32	
Truck Number 1009	38	32	✔
Truck Number 1249	18	32	
Truck Number 1931	24	30	
Truck Number 2704	19	30	
Truck Number 0082	20	34	

Objective: Verify that ball bearings have been replaced.

Audit Program: For those vehicles that are not yet scheduled to have their bearings replaced in accordance with the manufacturer's instructions, just check the bearings for signs of excessive wear. For those vehicles that should have had their bearings replaced, examine the bearings to ensure that the bearings show no signs of wear— if they show no such signs, they will be considered to have been replaced.

Sample Size: Six vehicles selected using stratified sampling; at least two vehicles must have more than 60,000 miles.

Test Detail: As follows:

Unit Description	Bearings Need Replacement?	Bearings Been Replaced?
Truck Number 1137	Yes	No
Truck Number 1009	No	N/A
Truck Number 1249	Yes	Yes
Truck Number 1931	No	N/A
Truck Number 2704	Yes	No
Truck Number 0082	Yes	No

Objective: Verify that brake pads have been replaced.

Audit Program: For those vehicles that have passed the manufacturer's recommended mileage goal for replacing brake pads, verify that new brake pads have been installed. For those vehicles with lesser amounts of mileage, verify that there is sufficient brake pad material left to safely stop the vehicle.

Sample Size: Six vehicles selected using stratified sampling; at least two vehicles must have more than 60,000 miles.

Test Detail: As follows:

Unit Description	Mileage Goal for Replacement?	Actual Vehicle Mileage	Brake Pads Been Replaced?
Truck Number 1137	60,000	62,000	No
Truck Number 1009	65,000	78,000	Yes
Truck Number 1249	80,000	81,000	Yes
Truck Number 1931	45,000	32,000	No
Truck Number 2704	45,000	38,000	No
Truck Number 0082	60,000	23,000	No

Objective: Verify that engine belts have been replaced.

Audit Program: Verify that a complete set of new engine belts has been installed in those vehicles for which the manufacturer's recommended belt-replacement mileage

Figure 9.3(b) Continued

has been exceeded. Also, test the belts on vehicles with lesser amounts of mileage to see if the belts are frayed, pitted, or have excessive amounts of flex.
Sample Size: Six vehicles selected using stratified sampling; at least two vehicles must have more than 60,000 miles.
Test Detail: As follows:

Unit Description	Mileage Goal for Replacement?	Actual Vehicle Mileage	Engine Belts Been Replaced?
Truck Number 1137	90,000	62,000	No
Truck Number 1009	95,000	78,000	No
Truck Number 1249	85,000	81,000	Yes
Truck Number 1931	100,000	32,000	No
Truck Number 2704	100,000	38,000	No
Truck Number 0082	90,000	23,000	No

Objective: Verify that maintenance records are being maintained.
Audit Program: After verifying that any of the above activities were completed, trace those activities back to the maintenance records to verify that the activity was originally scheduled in the maintenance plan, that the completed activity was noted in the maintenance log, and that a supervisor signed off on the activity, signifying that the supervisor reviewed the work.
Sample Size: Six vehicles selected using stratified sampling; at least two vehicles must have more than 60,000 miles.
Test Detail: As follows:

Unit Description	Services Scheduled?	Records Updated?	Supervisor Review?
Truck Number 1137	Yes	Yes	Yes
Truck Number 1009	No	No	No
Truck Number 1249	No	No	No
Truck Number 1931	No	No	No
Truck Number 2704	Yes	Yes	Yes
Truck Number 0082	Yes	Yes	Yes

Objective: Verify that prices billed match contract rates.
Audit Program: Review the supplier's billings to the company for the last three months to determine if bills were received, that charges on the billings are only for actual activities, and that the activity rates charged on the billings match the prices listed on the company's contract with the supplier. It is important that enough detail be listed on the billings for the auditor to determine this information—if it is not, this should be noted as an exception, with the supplier henceforth being required to supply billing information at a level of detail sufficient for this audit step to be completed.
Sample Size: Select the bills from the most recent three months.
Test Detail: As follows:

Description	Billing Exists?	Billing for All Functions?	Billing Rates Match Contract?
September Billing	No	N/A	N/A
October Billing	Yes	Yes	No
November Billing	Yes	Yes	Yes

Figure 9.3(c)   Sample Maintenance Internal Audit Program—Findings

1. Verify that vehicle cleanliness has been achieved.
   - Findings: Trucks 1009 and 0082 were not cleaned.
   - Recommendations: Bring this deficiency to the attention of the supplier's manager and put them on the audit sample for the next review to ensure that the cleaning has been performed.
2. Verify that various oil changes have been completed.
   - Findings: A number of vehicles have not had recent oil changes in all areas—engine, transmission, and differential oil. There is a clear lack of maintenance in this area.
   - Recommendations: Due to the wide-ranging level of neglect in this area, the supplier's manager should be notified immediately, and a follow-up audit should be conducted as soon as possible to verify that this service area has been fixed.
3. Verify that the wiper fluid container has been filled.
   - Findings: The fluid levels in vehicles 1009 and 0082 were low.
   - Recommendations: This is a minor service area. Just notify the supplier's manager of the deficiency and pay increased attention to the issue if subsequent audits reveal that this is a continuing problem.
4. Verify that all filters have been changed.
   - Findings: The air filters in vehicles 1249 and 1931 should be changed.
   - Recommendations: This is a relatively minor service area. Notify the supplier's manager of the problem and only take additional action if this is revealed to be a continuing problem by subsequent audits.
5. Verify that the tire pressure is at the recommended level.
   - Findings: So many tires are outside of the recommended range that it is clear that this function is not being attended to at all.
   - Recommendations: This issue should be brought to the attention of the supplier's manager immediately, and an extra follow-up audit should be scheduled to verify that service in this area has been improved.
6. Verify that ball bearings have been replaced.
   - Findings: Only one vehicle in the sample shows any signs of having had its bearings replaced, even though several trucks were in need of this maintenance.
   - Recommendations: This is a moderately important service issue that is not being attended to with the frequency that its importance demands. Bring the issue to the attention of the supplier's manager, and be sure to examine this

Figure 9.3(c)   Continued

issue again during the next scheduled audit. If it is still a problem at that time, it should then be treated as a major problem that requires immediate action.

7. Verify that brake pads have been replaced.
   * Findings: The mileage on truck number 1137 indicates that the brake pads should have been replaced, but inspection reveals that they have not. However, the recommended replacement mileage had only just come up for this vehicle, and further review shows that all other vehicles in the sample that have passed their recommended pad-replacement mileage have had their brake pads replaced.
   * Recommendations: No action necessary.
8. Verify that engine belts have been replaced.
   * Findings: None of the vehicles tested had yet reached the mileage levels where belt replacement was recommended by the manufacturer. One vehicle, number 1249, had a new set of belts installed even though the recommended mileage level had not yet been reached.
   * Recommendations: Since there were no problems and there was even some proactive maintenance work in this area, there is no need to take additional action.
9. Verify that maintenance records are being maintained.
   * Findings: Service had been properly scheduled, completed, and reviewed for three vehicles. However, there was no service scheduled for three other vehicles, two of which were sufficiently well used in terms of their amount of mileage to require continuing maintenance work. Since other steps of this audit show that work has been completed on those vehicles, it is apparent that either those records have not been maintained or that they are missing from the supplier's manager's files.
   * Recommendations: The first step is to request that the supplier's manager conduct a search for the ostensibly missing maintenance records, which should be reviewed by the audit team if they are recovered. If the records cannot be found, this should be noted as a serious failing requiring immediate correction by the supplier.
10. Verify that prices billed match contract rates.
   * Findings: No billing was received for the month of September, though this amount was included in the October billing. The October billing was charged at rates that did not match the agreed-upon rates shown in the contract with the supplier.
   * Recommendations: The October billing has already been paid, which includes an incorrect unit cost. The November billing should be paid in full, but a credit should be included in the payment that covers the excess amount paid in the previous month. A letter should accompany the payment that explains why the credit was included in the payment.

9.4   MEASURING THE OUTSOURCED FUNCTION

The outsourcing coordinators for the janitorial and maintenance functions will need a variety of performance measurements to see if their suppliers are performing properly. The following measurements should be tracked on a trend line so that the coordinators can see if any adverse trends are developing, and take action to correct them:

JANITORIAL

- *Cost per square foot.* The janitorial services coordinator needs to know how much a supplier is costing the company on a continuing basis. Rather than relying on a lump-sum figure, the coordinator should use a cost per square foot, which allows better comparison of bids for the work, of costs between different regions, and especially of the cost for the existing supplier to add janitorial services to an additional area for the company. The coordinator can rely on the cost per square foot to see if the supplier's estimated price to provide services to new company facilities is reasonable, and negotiate the price further if it is not. The measurement is easily calculated by determining the company's total square footage subject to janitorial services and dividing this amount into the monthly billing by the supplier for services performed.

- *Cost per person.* The primary problem with the previous performance measurement is that it does not track what kind of office space is being cleaned. For example, the cost to clean office space is quite different than the cost to clean factory space. Therefore, it is reasonable to track janitorial costs per white collar or blue collar person instead. The measure is calculated by determining the company's total square footage used by each of these two categories of workers and dividing these amounts into the monthly billing by the supplier, which will also need to be split by the supplier into different costs for each area cleaned.

- *Cost per office.* Some people (especially members of unions) object to placing people in different categories, practice used in the preceding performance measurement. A more politically sensitive way to track the same information is to track the cost of janitorial services for office space and production space. The measure should yield approximately the same information as the janitorial cost per person. It is calculated by determining the company's total square feet of office space and production space and dividing these amounts into the monthly billing by the supplier, which will also need to be split by the supplier into different costs for each area cleaned.

- *Average number of complaints per employee.* One of the primary factors that the janitorial services coordinator must consider is the company's opinion of the supplier. If they are highly dissatisfied with the performance of the supplier, this should be a key factor in the periodic decision to change suppliers. For this measure, it is not good enough to track a grand total of complaints received; the company's head count may change so fast that a sudden surge of complaints may simply be caused by the arrival of many new employees and have nothing to do with the performance of the supplier. A better measurement is to tally the complaints received by the end of each month and divide this by the total number of employees (a figure easily obtained from the payroll or human resources department), which results in the average number of complaints received per employee.

- *Proportion of missed cleaning points.* Employees do not always voice their dissatisfaction with the level of janitorial services, so the services coordinator may want a more objective performance measurement. A more reliable one is to review all cleaning areas on a spot-check basis and note the number of cleaning points that are missed (these can be waste baskets not emptied, windows not cleaned, carpets not vacuumed, or desks not dusted). The number of cleaning points missed can then be compared to the total number of cleaning points examined to determine the proportion of missed cleaning points. If enough cleaning points are checked as part of this review, the resulting proportion should be statistically valid.

MAINTENANCE

- *Mean time between failures.* One of the primary reasons for outsourcing the maintenance function is to ensure that production or transportation equipment will not fail. If the outsourcing coordinator finds that equipment is failing at an excessive rate, this should be the primary reason for changing suppliers. The best way to track this issue is to measure the mean time between failures, which shows the average duration, usually measured in days, between occurrences of maintenance problems that are sufficient to stop the use of equipment. The measure is best tracked by having the outsourcing coordinator or a subordinate track the times when equipment failures occur for each piece of equipment, and create an average at the end of each month based on the results for all equipment—or, if the equipment types vary considerably and have quite different failure rates, this information can be divided into subclusters of equipment.

- *Proportion of preventive maintenance conducted on schedule.* A maintenance supplier can reduce its costs by skimping on preventive maintenance. This type of maintenance is the type that prevents equipment breakdowns from occurring, but cutting back services in this area is something that may not be noticed by the coordinator, and may not result in an increase in equipment failure rates for quite some time. To monitor this potential problem, the outsourcing coordinator should have a copy of the supplier's preventive maintenance schedule, and should audit actual maintenance against this schedule to see if any maintenance is not being performed. The measurement is calculated monthly by auditing a fixed number of preventive maintenance steps on the dates when they are supposed to be completed and recording all actual maintenance activities observed as being successfully completed. The number of successful maintenance activities is then divided by the total number of activities audited to arrive at the proportion of preventive maintenance activities conducted on schedule.

- *Average time required to initiate repairs.* The outsourcing coordinator needs to know how soon maintenance is initiated by the supplier following a report of equipment failure. This gives the coordinator a good idea of the supplier's response speed, availability of resources, and commitment to the company. This item is best measured by having the coordinator measure the time period between the first report of equipment failure and the arrival at the equipment of the supplier's maintenance staff. This can be done on a spot-check basis rather than continually, since a sample will still yield an accurate average time required to initiate repairs.

- *Average time required to complete repairs.* Even if the coordinator finds that the supplier can bring staff to broken equipment quickly, there is still the issue of whether or not the supplier can actually *fix* the equipment. The coordinator can measure this item by taking a sample of repair jobs, recording the time when repairs were initiated and completed, and interviewing the equipment operator to verify that the equipment is indeed functional once again. This repair time duration can be averaged over several repair jobs to arrive each month at an average time required to complete repairs.

- *Average time to failure after servicing.* Once the supplier repairs a piece of equipment, it is important to determine how long the repair work lasts before there is another problem. This measure is useful for determining the quality of the repair work—particularly the quality of the repair parts being used by the supplier. Cheap replacement parts will have to be replaced more frequently, and this measurement will at least hint at the existence of this problem. However, the maintenance coordinator must be careful to determine if any reduction in the average time to failure is caused by the same repair problem over and over again, or if the equipment is suffering from different complaints each time, which may have nothing to do with the quality of the repair work. Also, very old equipment may skew the measurement, since the equipment may be increasingly prone to failure irrespective of the quality of the repair work being performed.

- *Average number of complaints per employee.* Other performance measurements are sufficient for determining how well the supplier is conducting the maintenance function, but it is also important to see how well the supplier's staff is behaving in its relations with the company's staff. Even if the maintenance function is being performed flawlessly, the supplier may have to go if there are significant personnel issues that cause friction with the company's employees. This measure can be determined by adding up the number of complaints in a reporting period and dividing it by the total number of company employees. However, this is also a subjective measurement—a very small number of vociferous complaints may carry more weight than a large number of mild complaints, and should at least trigger an investigation of the personnel problem(s) involved.

- *Average maintenance cost per piece of equipment.* Maintenance fees are typically paid to the supplier in a lump sum at the end of each month, and do not give the maintenance coordinator a good idea of how much it costs to maintain

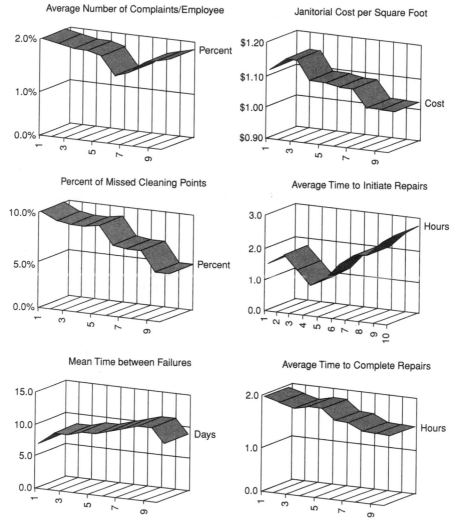

Figure 9.4   Selected Trend Lines for the Janitorial and Maintenance Functions

each piece of equipment. Thus, it is useful to divide the total monthly cost by the total number of pieces of equipment being maintained to determine the average maintenance cost per unit. This measurement can be tracked over time to determine any trends in the average cost. However, the measurement is least useful if there is a large variety of equipment being maintained, since the addition of excessively hard- or easy-to-maintain equipment to the mix will significantly skew the average maintenance cost per unit.

The above list of measurements makes it look as though the janitorial and maintenance coordinators spend all of their time collecting performance information about their suppliers. Though they can perform this function, it is also possible to have the internal auditing department or someone in a clerical position collect and report on these performance measures on a continuing basis. The internal auditing staff will probably resist this measurement task, since the chore is too clerical for them to handle regularly—they would be more interested in occasionally verifying the accuracy of the measurement calculations. This means that the task is most likely to fall upon someone in a clerical position.

It is important that these measurements be tracked along a trend line so that the service coordinators can immediately spot any changes that are continuing through multiple periods. Trend lines can be tracked manually on graph paper or on an electronic spreadsheet. Samples of several trend lines for some of the above graphics are shown in the charts in Figure 9.4.

9.5 MANAGING THE OUTSOURCED FUNCTION

The maintenance and janitorial functions are frequently managed by different departments within the corporation. The maintenance function, whether it be for transportation equipment or equipment located in a factory, almost always falls within the supervisory area of the vice president of production. However, janitorial services can be supervised either by production or, more frequently, by the vice president of finance and administration. Janitorial services are logically more a part of the administration function, since this covers the entire company facility, whereas the production function only covers the production area within the company facility. Thus, outsourcing maintenance and janitorial functions will likely require an in-house coordinator for each of the two functions. The positions of these outsourcing coordinators within the corporate organizational hierarchy are shown in Figure 9.5.

The outsourcing coordinator for the janitorial function may find that this is not a full-time position in a smaller company, whereas there may even be a small in-house support staff for the coordinator if the company is a large one. The coordinator should have the job description shown in Figure 9.6.

The supplier may suggest that it provide the phone number of its janitorial services manager to all of the client company's staff, which allows them to directly call the supplier with problems. However, the client company should keep this function

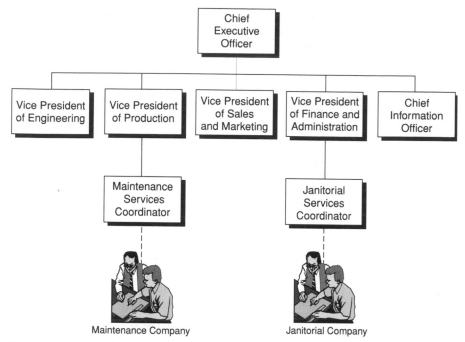

Figure 9.5   Organizational Chart for Outsourcing the Maintenance and Janitorial Functions

in-house, since it allows the client to collect information about janitorial problems, follow up on how well they are being corrected, and use this information to evaluate the performance of the supplier. If the supplier provides this service instead, the client company has no way of judging the performance of the supplier (which may lead to retaining the supplier even if its performance is subpar).

Figure 9.6   Janitorial Services Outsourcing Coordinator's Job Description

---

Employee Title: Janitorial Services Outsourcing Coordinator
Reports to: Vice President of Finance and Administration
Responsibilities:
   • Collect problem information from all employees and pass it along to the supplier.
   • Follow up on the resolution of problems brought forward by employees.
   • Track performance measurements for the supplier.
   • Authorize payments to the supplier.
   • Coordinate in-house janitorial work on an emergency basis.
   • Coordinate pricing negotiations with the supplier.
   • Track actual costs incurred against budgeted amounts and alter costs as needed to match the budget.
   • Authorize changes to the level of janitorial services.

Figure 9.7   Maintenance Outsourcing Coordinator's Job Description

Employee Title: Maintenance Outsourcing Coordinator
Reports to: Vice President of Production
Responsibilities:
  • Collect problem information from production and materials-management employees and pass it along to the supplier.
  • Follow up on the resolution of problems brought forward by employees.
  • Track performance measurements for the supplier.
  • Authorize payments to the supplier.
  • Coordinate pricing negotiations with the supplier.
  • Track actual costs incurred against budgeted amounts and alter costs as needed to match the budget.
  • Authorize changes to the level of maintenance.

The outsourcing coordinator for the maintenance function is more likely to have a full-time position devoted to just the coordination role, especially if there is not only in-house equipment being maintained but also transportation equipment. The maintenance outsourcing coordinator should have the job description shown in Figure 9.7.

One of the key items in the job description of the maintenance outsourcing coordinator is altering the level of maintenance. If preventive maintenance is used, the company will be making larger expenditures up front for maintenance work, since there will be more maintenance conducted in advance of any actual maintenance problems. However, if the coordinator attempts to cut back on this level of service in favor of maintenance of equipment that has already failed, the company will find that its total costs have increased, since the cost of having production or transportation equipment not functional may interfere with the company's ability to produce or deliver goods, which will reduce sales and therefore profits. Thus, a shortsighted coordinator in the maintenance coordinator role can cut costs within his area yet end up costing the company as a whole more money.

Both of the coordinators are responsible for negotiating annual contracts with their suppliers. However, since they are both probably more skilled in janitorial and maintenance tasks than in negotiating service contracts, it is likely that the purchasing department should be brought in to assist at this stage. The purchasing staff can survey comparable companies in the marketplace to determine a reasonable price for the services being provided, assist in the actual negotiations, and review the resulting contract for problems. Once the annual contract is finalized, the purchasing staff can withdraw from the management of the janitorial and maintenance functions until the following year's negotiations are due to arise.

9.6   POTENTIAL CUSTOMER SERVICE ISSUES

In this case, the customer is internal: the company's employees who may be impacted by problems with the janitorial or maintenance functions. The primary customer service issue for both functions is that the supplier's staffs are usually located off-site and are therefore not available to handle problems that require immediate resolution, such as a liquid spill in a high-traffic area or a machine breakdown that halts all production. In both cases, the company can enter into an immediate-service agreement with the supplier whereby, for an extra fee, the supplier agrees to have someone on-site within a specific time period, or even keep someone on-site at all times to deal with such emergencies. The alternative to a rush-service agreement is for the company to retain a small number of its own staff for this purpose; thus, when a function is outsourced, the company agrees to retain just enough personnel to handle immediate issues, and only outsources those functions that can be performed with longer lead times. Either keeping staff on hand or ensuring that they can be rapidly brought in will alleviate customer service issues related to both the janitorial and maintenance functions.

9.7   GETTING OUT OF THE OUTSOURCING ARRANGEMENT

The decision to terminate an outsourcing arrangement is much easier if this issue is considered when the initial contract with the supplier is written, since these terms will provide guidelines for the amounts of notice and penalties to be paid (if any) to void the agreement.

The terms of the janitorial contract are much easier to write than those of the maintenance contract, since the janitorial function is much less critical to company operations. Typical terms are for termination upon 30 days written notice by either party, with no penalties paid. Since there are so many janitorial firms vying for a company's business, the company should not be forced into a position of signing a more restrictive contract—even terms allowing the supplier time to cure any complaints by the company are unnecessary. Simply provide written termination notice to the current janitorial supplier, and move on to the next supplier.

The issue is more complicated for the maintenance supplier, since it may have purchased the company's maintenance parts as well as possibly its entire maintenance facility, plus it may have incurred the expense of training its staff in the intricacies of maintaining some of the company's more specialized equipment. The supplier will rightfully want compensation for these up-front expenses. The best way to deal with the reimbursement of these costs in the contract is to set up a sliding scale that gradually reduces the company's liability for paying back the supplier in case services are terminated. For example, the following terms could be used:

- If services are terminated within 1 year, 100% of the up-front costs must be reimbursed.

- If services are terminated within 2 years, 80% of the up-front costs must be reimbursed.

- If services are terminated within 3 years, 60% of the up-front costs must be reimbursed.

- If services are terminated within 4 years, 40% of the up-front costs must be reimbursed.

- If services are terminated within 5 years, 20% of the up-front costs must be reimbursed.

Though shrinking the period of time over which reimbursement is required may appear to be an obvious negotiating point, keep in mind that, if this happens, the supplier will be forced to increase its monthly fees to the company to recoup its up-front expenses more rapidly.

The company should verify that there is a complete listing of expenses to be reimbursed, in case of an eventual split with the supplier. An example of such a list is as follows:

- The cost of parts sold by the company to the supplier, less the cost of the amount used in the interim.

- The cost of equipment sold by the company to the supplier, less depreciation at a rate of _____ % per year.

- The cost of training the supplier's staff in the maintenance of the company's equipment (with a cap of $ _____).

- The cost of severance for all employees to be laid off as a result of the termination of the supplier's contract with the company (with a cap of $ _____ per person).

It is likely that the decision to sever relations with a supplier will not occur precisely on the day when the amount of up-front costs to be reimbursed drops by some set percentage. Thus, it is prudent for the company to build into the contract a provision that reduces the amount of the termination penalty to be paid based on the number of days or months that have gone by since the last contract date when the amount to be paid was established. For example, if the percentage of costs to be paid back to the supplier dropped to 80% of the total as of January 1, the amount will drop again to 60% as of the following January 1, and it is now February 1, the company should insist on paying the 80% less $1/12^{th}$ of the additional 20% reduction that will occur during that year, which results in a final payment of 78.33%. Since this clause is not favorable to the supplier, do not expect to find it in a contract originating with the supplier.

In summary, it is usually quite easy to get out of a janitorial contract with only a minimal written notice period required. However, due to the up-front capital costs involved, getting out of a maintenance contract may very well require the payment of a termination penalty; the company should spend a great deal of time negotiating the terms of this termination penalty, since it can be a large sum.

9.8   SUMMARY

Both the janitorial and maintenance functions are well worth the effort of outsourcing for a variety of reasons. They are not strategic functions, a supplier can almost always do them just as well as any in-house staff, and the company may be able to sell its janitorial and maintenance supplies and equipment to the supplier, which may put some working capital back into the company's coffers. However, these functions must be adequately controlled by in-house service coordinators. The primary vehicle for this control is a continuing, in-depth operational audit that rapidly reveals any problems and allows the service coordinator to follow up with the supplier's management in a proactive manner, rather than passively sitting and waiting for user complaints to arise. There are also a large number of performance measurements that the service coordinators can use to track the efficiency and effectiveness of the suppliers in both areas. If the outsourced functions are carefully monitored and problems are quickly corrected, a company can obtain significant benefits from outsourcing the janitorial and maintenance functions while enjoying just as high a level of service as was previously the case when these functions were handled by in-house employees.

CHAPTER TEN

Outsourcing the Manufacturing Function

One of the chief functions in most companies is manufacturing. It uses the largest amount of capital, personnel, and management time of all functional areas, with exceptions in only a small number of industries. An increasing number of companies are outsourcing this function to suppliers with more manufacturing prowess, leaving them to pursue the further improvement of their core competencies, which may lie in other areas. A sterling example of such an arrangement is the PC manufacturer Monorail Inc., based in Marietta, Georgia. This leading producer of small personal computers outsources all of its manufacturing to Kansas City–based Phelps Technologies, which assembles and ships all of its computers. As the number of qualified suppliers increases and companies become more comfortable with the idea of outsourcing such a critical function, there will be an increasing number of similar outsourcing deals in this area.

There are several ways to outsource the manufacturing function. One option is to outsource the manufacture of components, which a company then assembles in its own facility. Many companies, such as all of the automobile manufacturers, already do business this way. Another option is to have a supplier only assemble the final product. This is becoming increasingly common among personal computer companies, who have third-party distributors assemble and ship computers based on the exact requirements of customers. This option allows a company to avoid having to assemble to stock, which eliminates the risk of having obsolete inventory. A variation on this approach, and still an uncommon one, is for the supplier to take on all manufacturing or sourcing of parts, as well as the final assembly stage. This option means that a company gives up virtually all direct management of the manufacturing process. However, as suppliers become more expert in their tasks, this will become a more viable option for many companies. It is also possible for a company to sell its production facilities to a supplier, who then manufactures products for the company at those locations under a long-term contract. It is also possible under any of the

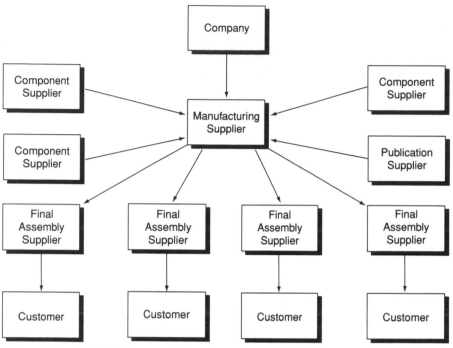

Figure 10.1   Totally Outsourced Manufacturing

above options to have the supplier drop-ship products directly to the company's customers, thereby eliminating any need for the company to manage the distribution of its products. Finally, nearly all completed products include some kind of printed materials—warranty cards, instructions, and guarantees. A company can outsource the printing of these materials to an outside printer, who can either send complete print runs back to the company for distribution to various manufacturing areas, or drop ship them directly to those locations. Figure 10.1 shows an amalgamation of all of the above outsourcing approaches for a company that has outsourced its component manufacturing, assembly, printing, and distribution functions. With so many manufacturing options, it is no surprise that so many companies are exploring the outsourcing of their production requirements.

10.1   ADVANTAGES AND DISADVANTAGES

This section describes the advantages and disadvantages of outsourcing the manufacturing function. Disadvantages immediately follow the advantages noted for each point, so the reader has all the information needed to arrive at a decision on each item. The points cover three functional areas within the overall topic of manufacturing: the publishing of materials for inclusion in finished-product packages, the assembly of components into finished products, and the manufacture of complete products or components.

One of the primary advantages of outsourcing all three manufacturing areas is that the suppliers have special skills in this area, and can manufacture products more cheaply and with better quality than the company. This advantage may be due to long experience in the field, more capital investments, proprietary technology, or top-quality management or staff. It may be possible for a company to match this level of expertise, but only at the price of diverting management time and funds away from the company's primary strategic area, which may be somewhere entirely different, such as marketing or engineering. For example, a software company's job is to develop software, not to manufacture the software packages that are distributed to its customers. It may be able to eventually create a top-notch manufacturing facility to handle this function, but why bother if someone else can do the job right now? In such a case, the function should be handed over to a supplier, leaving the software firm to concentrate its efforts on developing more software. A good reason for adopting outsourcing is that suppliers can do it better, leaving companies to work on core competencies.

One disadvantage of giving your production work to a supplier is that it may be such a good supplier that it is inundated with work. Whether the supplier intends to or not, this can easily lead to a capacity problem in which the company's production work is delayed or simply not done. This is a particular problem if the company's orders are only a small fraction of the supplier's total backlog. In such cases, the supplier normally gives the best service to the company giving it the most business, with other companies having a lower priority on the supplier's production schedule. This problem can be mitigated by maintaining constant communications with the supplier to make the company's needs known. Another approach is to pay a premium for work performed, so the supplier will have an incentive to produce the company's products in front of the manufacturing needs of its other customers. A third way to avoid this problem is to use a small supplier; the company's proportion of a smaller supplier's orders will be larger, and so the company will have a better chance to keep its work at a high-priority level on the supplier's production schedule. In short, a serious disadvantage is the delays caused by sharing the supplier's production capacity with other companies, but there are several mitigating factors.

If a company cannot convince a top-notch supplier to take its business, it will need to drop down a notch to a lesser supplier who may not be able to manufacture products with the same quality or do so on time. If the supplier does a poor enough job, the company will not be able to get good products to its customers on time, resulting in lost sales and market share. If the supplier's performance is bad enough, it could even put the company out of business! This problem can be avoided by taking lots of time in advance to thoroughly review the operations of a prospective supplier, and by using process engineering teams to continually review the operations of suppliers once the company has contracted with them to take over its production work. Also, keeping close tabs on customer complaints will quickly highlight any production problems. If the company cannot find a supplier who meets its production criteria, then it absolutely should not outsource the function. This is far too important an area to give to a supplier who cannot do the work.

An important advantage of using a supplier for manufacturing is that a company does not have to invest large quantities of capital in manufacturing facilities. This can be a vast sum in some industries, such as computer chip manufacturing, where facility investments can run into billions of dollars. By giving this function to a supplier, a company can greatly reduce its need for funds, which reduces its need to water down its equity by selling shares to investors. Also, the company's return on investments will increase, since it will have a smaller investment in assets. In addition, the company avoids any continuing fixed costs for utilities, depreciation, personnel, or maintenance that go along with production facilities, which lowers its break-even point to a level where it can still turn a profit even at relatively low sales and margin levels. However, there is a downside to all of this good news. First, suppliers must incur the capital cost that the company is foregoing, so supplier prices are likely to be higher than the variable prices that the company would incur if it were manufacturing products itself—suppliers must include some capital charge in their product prices, or they would not be able to get a return on their capital investments. Also, if there are few suppliers available, suppliers can raise prices in the short term with impunity, for a company without its own production facility has no option but to pay the supplier's prices while frantically looking for other suppliers or building its own facilities. If there is only one supplier, a canny competitor can even buy the supplier, thereby wiping out a company's production capacity and possibly putting it out of business. Thus, there are good capital-based reasons for outsourcing the manufacturing function, but there can be serious risks, especially if there are only a small number of suppliers available.

Outsourcing the manufacturing function gives a start-up company immediate access to a large amount of production capacity that it would not otherwise be able to develop in-house without a considerable investment of time and money. For many start-up companies, the biggest problem is time—they are trying to bring new products to market within a narrow time frame, and may not be able to do so if they do not have the necessary manufacturing facilities. Some suppliers have the additional capability of distributing products as well as manufacturing them, so start-up companies can outsource two functions through one supplier, thereby off-loading additional tasks from the management team. However, there are two disadvantages to this approach. One is that some suppliers may be wary of the credit rating of new companies, and may not want their business, or will insist on very short credit terms, if not advance payments, before agreeing to enter into a production agreement. Another problem is that the best suppliers do not have much excess capacity, since many companies want their services. This does little for a start-up company that needs to reserve large quantities of production capacity to meet high demand for its products. This problem can be avoided by having several suppliers who, when combined, have sufficient excess capacity for the company's needs. Outsourcing manufacturing is a useful option for start-up companies who want to bring new products to market as rapidly as possible, though suppliers may not have enough capacity for their needs.

It is also possible for a supplier to purchase a company's entire manufacturing facility in exchange for a guarantee from the company that the supplier will provide the company with all of its product needs for a fixed time period and at a fixed price. This is an especially useful approach for companies who are in financial distress and need the cash that would be obtained by selling facilities. This also releases cash for companies who are in good financial condition but want to use their resources for other purposes, such as buying other companies, buying back stock, or improving the reported return on investments. The downside of this approach is that the supplier will want guaranteed prices and quantities for products sold to the company so that it is assured of a return on its investment. This can be a problem if the market for the product becomes smaller or price competition becomes a factor. In this case, the company will not want as much product and may incur a loss to buy it from the supplier at the previously agreed-upon price. Thus, this arrangement is good in the short term for companies who need the cash, but runs a risk of using cash in the long run to satisfy the resulting purchasing contract with the supplier.

A more common approach than the previously described option of having the supplier buy the company's entire production facility is for the supplier to buy the company's production equipment. This is a more satisfactory arrangement for the supplier, since it can buy only the equipment it needs and then move the equipment to its own facility, which allows the supplier to concentrate production facilities at the minimum number of locations. While this still allows a company to bring in some cash in the short run, it has the disadvantage of leaving the company with an incomplete production facility, which is not operable and must therefore be liquidated. The facility in which the equipment is housed must also be liquidated. Also, since the supplier will have cherry picked the equipment and probably taken the most valuable items, the remaining equipment will probably not have a high resale value, so the company may incur a substantial loss when these items are liquidated. Thus, transferring selected production equipment to a supplier is not as attractive an option to a company as moving an entire facility to a supplier.

An increasingly common variation on manufacturing outsourcing is having distributors assemble the final product at a variety of locations. There are a number of advantages to this approach. One is that, by sending components to distributors instead of completed products that may have a large number of variations, a company can produce a smaller range of products while still offering a large number of production variations to the final customer (since distributors can make changes to the products at the distribution points). This requires much less inventory, which represents a reduction in working capital. Also, with fewer finished goods in stock, a company has a far smaller chance of having to write off obsolete inventory. In addition, the company can eliminate its final assembly staff by having distributors do this work. Finally, the company can move its products closer to customers for more rapid delivery times by stocking inventory at the distributors' locations. However, there are several points opposing these advantages. One is that distributors may do a poor job of assembling products, leading to customer complaints and a poor reputation in the marketplace. Another problem is that distributors may charge exorbitant prices to assemble the products. To mitigate these problems, a company can send process engineers to the assembly locations to monitor the assembly quality, while high-priced distributors should be replaced. Outsourcing the final assembly of products to distribution points gives a company several cost advantages, though there is a risk of lower product quality.

The printing of instruction manuals for products presents a special set of advantages and disadvantages for a company. One advantage is that a printing supplier has the production capacity to produce a very large amount of printed material in a very short time, since a good supplier has large-capacity presses that can create far more material than the limited printing equipment that most companies own. However, most printing suppliers must keep these large presses running at maximum capacity in order to turn a profit, so their capacity may be booked solid for some weeks or months in advance, which can reduce a company's flexibility in producing new printed materials on short notice. Also, printing suppliers have such long setup times for print jobs that they offer very low prices for large print jobs. For those company products for which large quantities of printed materials are needed, this can represent a significant cost saving for the company. Another advantage is that printing suppliers generally have far more versatile printing equipment than the desktop publishing systems that most companies use. This equipment can handle a wide variety of colors and paper weights, which allows a company to include an exceptional variety of materials with its products. One issue with using a supplier, however, is that they must charge a significant premium for short print runs, since they must spread a high setup charge over a small number of documents. Thus, there are apparent advantages to using a printing supplier for larger document quantities or those requiring special paper weights or colors.

A company runs the risk of retaining the services of a supplier who engages in illegal business practices. For example, several well-known companies have recently gained adverse publicity for outsourcing their manufacturing activities to suppliers who employ illegal immigrants or children, or who pay rates far below the legal minimum. If this information becomes public knowledge, a company can be the subject of consumer boycotts even if it had no knowledge of the supplier's illegal practices. The best way to avoid this problem is to periodically audit supplier activities with the specific audit objective of finding any illegal activities. However, suppliers who are doing something illegal will take steps to hide it, so even a detailed audit may miss such activity. Using an illegal supplier remains a valid risk for a company seeking to outsource its manufacturing function.

In short, there are many good reasons to outsource the manufacturing function. These include giving the function to a supplier who can do the work better, avoiding the capital investment of building a production facility, gaining cash by selling existing production facilities, and gaining rapid access to extra production capacity. Opposed to these points are a loss of control over when products will be produced, the quantities produced, and their quality.

10.2 CONTRACT-SPECIFIC ISSUES

This section covers the contractual issues for outsourcing the manufacturing function. The primary areas of concern to the company are per-unit and fixed prices charged by the supplier, as well as performance criteria, which are the quality and on-time delivery of products. The company is less concerned with how the supplier produces the product, since that is a manufacturing input that drives the profitability of the supplier, not the company. Other areas that the contract should address are the right of the company to periodically review supplier processes, terms for termination, legal reasons for termination, and the need for copyrights on published materials.

Many companies insist on contract terms that reduce the amounts charged by suppliers every year, continuing into the foreseeable future. Prices are usually reduced by a fixed percentage each year in exchange for a higher volume of business from the company, as well as engineering assistance from the company in achieving the cost-saving targets. If this pricing structure is used, the contract should clearly specify the percentage reduction in costs each year. A common problem is whether the reduction is from the previous year's price or from the baseline price that existed at the beginning of the contract. Precise formulas of price reductions are necessary if the company and supplier agree to continual price cuts.

The company must realize that the price per unit charged by the supplier is very likely to be higher than the company's own variable cost if it were to produce the product itself. This is because the supplier must build in a charge to cover its profit and sales costs, and especially the cost of the fixed assets used in its production facility. Since the company is not spending money on fixed assets, it must be prepared to pay extra to a supplier who is undertaking this cost. Thus, price negotiations should allow the supplier a fair price increase for its extra costs over the variable product cost.

Most companies will agree to per-unit prices that vary based on the volume of products purchased from the supplier. For example, the per-unit price is $150 if the annual volume is between 50,000 and 75,000 units, but then drops to $135 if the volume exceeds 75,000 units. The trouble with this pricing formula is determining what price to start with at the beginning of the year, and how to adjust pricing at the end of the year based on actual volumes. The initial price should be based on the expected production volume for the upcoming year, though using the actual volume from the previous year is also acceptable. The company should not artificially drive the per-unit cost down by basing the price it charges on an unrealistically high production volume that it knows it will not need—this may keep prices low through the year, but the company may be hit by a crippling extra payment at the end of the year, based on actual quantities produced. The year-end adjustment for actual volumes produced should allow for the use of a designated third party to calculate the actual volume produced, in case there is a dispute between the two parties. Also, the volume calculation should be clearly specified in the contract. The volume produced can be subject to considerable interpretation, since it can apply to the number produced or the number shipped to the company, while the number of rejected or returned products can be deducted from the total quantity produced. Given the number of variables in this calculation, it is best to precisely define the formula and include it in the contract.

The contract will probably include initial fees charged to the company for the acquisition of product molds and equipment, or the retooling of existing equipment. These costs are necessary for the supplier to set up its operations to manufacture products for the company, and the company should be prepared to pay for them. However, a supplier may attempt to add a profit onto the cost of this equipment; for example, a supplier may purchase a mold for $100,000 and then tack on a 10% profit of $10,000, when it only required a few hours of purchasing time to acquire the mold. Though the company should pay the supplier something extra for setup charges and the cost of acquiring the equipment, a high profit percentage is not reasonable in this instance.

The company should be prepared in advance to terminate the relationship with a manufacturing supplier. This avoids any arguments at the time of termination regarding the return of or payment for assets. Contract clauses in this area should cover the return of all molds purchased by the company and sent to the supplier for production purposes. If the supplier originally bought the molds, the company should compensate the supplier for them, less a reasonable amount of depreciation. This also applies to any equipment or facilities purchased from the company by the supplier. Also, the supplier will probably have some work in process at the time of termination. If so, the company should either allow the supplier to convert this into finished goods, or should compensate the supplier for all raw materials and works-in-process, with these materials then being shipped by the supplier to the company. By making these arrangements in advance, there will be less trouble at the time of termination regarding the payments needed to settle accounts between the two parties.

The contract should always allow the company to unconditionally back out of the arrangement if it finds problems during any production test runs or during normal production. The measurements used to come to this conclusion must be clearly stated, along with the measurement levels that are considered to be substandard. If the supplier wants a time period in which to correct problems, the company should keep this period as short as possible. The reason for this clause is that the company can be ruined if its supplier manufactures shoddy products, so it must be able to rapidly terminate production if this appears to be the case.

If the company has an outside publisher print all instruction materials added to product packages prior to shipment, it is useful to have those materials copyrighted. This is not a contractual issue and does not need to be referenced in the contract, but the printer must be prevented from passing along the materials to some other company for copying and inclusion with similar products. This is not a significant problem, since most competing products are sufficiently different to require completely rewritten manuals, but it is best from a competitive standpoint not to give other companies an easy way to create their published materials by copying.

Some suppliers can be very security conscious, and will not allow visitors into their facilities. This is a problem if the company wants to send in engineers to help suppliers cut their costs so that some of those cost reductions can be passed along to the company. To avoid any problems with this issue, the contract should clearly state that the company has a right to frequently send in engineering teams, and possibly even keep people on-site permanently, in order to assist the supplier with its product quality and manufacturing processes. The more secretive suppliers will require that all visitors sign a confidentiality agreement, which should not be a problem for the company. If the company finds that a supplier is unwilling to allow company engineers into its facilities, it is a sign that the manufacturing systems may be substandard, and the company should look elsewhere for another manufacturing partner. Allowing continual company access to supplier facilities is a necessary part of any manufacturing contract.

The contract should also note the content and timing of information that will be regularly transferred between the company and supplier. This information should include shipment information to the company that it needs to bill its customers, as well as billings from the supplier to the company for products produced. The contract should not include procedural issues such as the method of communication of this information, since it tends to change over time, progressing from paper-based communications to electronic formats such as e-mail or electronic data interchange.

Another contractual issue is who does the billing to customers. Some suppliers will not only drop ship products to a company's customers, but will even bill the customers on behalf of the company. This is not a common approach, for the company must still enter the invoices into its own accounts receivable database for both collection and financial-reporting purposes. Since this data entry must be done even if the supplier is doing the billing, it is normally easier to have the supplier send shipment information to the company as frequently as possible and have the company do the billing. If the contract calls for billing by the supplier, it should also specify the rapid transfer of billing information to the company so that it can keep its accounts receivable records up-to-date. In short, if the supplier does the billing, the billing information must be sent to the company as soon as possible.

Finally, the contract must include quality parameters that the company expects the supplier to meet. These parameters should be very specific, such as one dead-on-arrival (DOA) product per million, or no more than one warranty claim per hundred thousand products within one year of their shipment. An appendix is an appropriate place for the detailed explanations of these parameters. The contract should also include the bonuses or penalties that will arise if actual experience varies from the specified parameters. Only by having tightly defined parameters can a company successfully impose penalties or pay bonuses based on supplier performance.

This section covered the essentials of the most important contract clauses needed when dealing with manufacturing suppliers. These clauses should include varying price levels based on volume, future price decreases, termination terms, up-front fixed fees, copyrights, facility access, and target quality parameters. If these issues are addressed, the company can expect fewer subsequent problems with suppliers.

10.3 TRANSITION ISSUES

The transition process for the manufacturing function is at least as difficult as the transition for computer services. It requires the seamless integration of a number of interlocked steps, and can bankrupt a company if the transition effort fails. This section describes the multitude of steps required to successfully transition a manufacturing process from a company to its supplier. However, the time frame noted for the completion of the steps is highly variable, and can extend to more than a year, depending on the complexity of the manufacturing process involved.

The following transition steps assume the simplest possible installation. There is no assumption that the company will require a complex production system as soon as the outsourcing relationship is established. Instead, it is assumed that the company will want the simplest possible production system so that there will be fewer chances for failure during the initial transition process. If the company successfully completes a simple transfer of the production function, then it can later upgrade the function to include electronic data interchange, drop shipments straight to customer locations, and on-site customer billings. The simplest transition process is the most successful process.

The most basic transition steps for moving a manufacturing operation to a supplier are as follows:

1. *Select manufacturing coordinator.* The functional coordinator should be in charge of the entire transition process, since this is the person who will be responsible for the resulting operation. The selection process should be a careful one, for a good coordinator can make this important transition go very smoothly.

2. *Construct review agenda.* The functional coordinator should create a set of items to review when examining prospective suppliers. This list should include such measurements as the percentage of work shipped on time (as shown on the production schedule), quality based on a variety of factors (depending on the type of product), the presence of an ISO 9001 certification, the location of the supplier, and the qualifications of the supplier's manufacturing management, such as the average number of years in the business. Answers can be either free form or on a rating scale; the important point is to use the same agenda for all suppliers reviewed, so that there is some common basis for comparison.

3. *Evaluate supplier sites.* The functional coordinator should select a team of process engineers who will come along to all supplier sites. The company should do a thorough job of reviewing as many qualified suppliers as possible, for it is crucial that the company pick the right supplier—the wrong one can bankrupt the company if it cannot produce to specifications. The same team should review all of the sites, so that they all have the same basis of experience on which to make a selection. These visits should be supplemented

by calls or visits to a number of the references given by each supplier. The references should all be asked the same questions for comparison purposes, with questions centering around the quality of products manufactured and the ability of each supplier to deliver on time. If there are problems with all of the suppliers but some problems appear to be resolvable, the functional coordinator should meet with those suppliers to tell them about their deficiencies. Then the company can schedule a follow-up review later on to see if the problems have been fixed.

4. *Select supplier.* The final supplier selection will probably involve some politics, such as the "gut feeling" of the most senior person on the selection committee. A better approach, however, is to assign a weighting to each review factor noted in the agenda and multiply the average score for each agenda item by that weighting. Then the highest-scoring supplier is awarded the work. At a minimum, this scoring system should be used to drop the lowest-scoring suppliers from contention, which will keep a company from making a serious mistake in hiring a poor supplier.

5. *Sign confidentiality agreement.* There may be some trade secrets involved in the production process or the product specifications (such as the formula for Coca-Cola) that the supplier is handing over to the new supplier. If so, the company will want to protect these secrets. The supplier should sign a confidentiality agreement to cover the company's interests. The agreement should specify that the company can terminate the outsourcing arrangement immediately if there is evidence that the agreement was violated, and that the company can sue the supplier for its expected losses caused by the loss of secrecy. If the supplier refuses to sign this agreement, then the company should not finalize its outsourcing contract with the supplier.

6. *Deliver production specifications.* The company should prepare a detailed engineering package that covers exact product specifications, assembly drawings and work instructions, and shipping dimensions and weight. The company should also give the supplier its expected delivery schedule. The supplier needs this information to see if it is capable of producing the company's product, and what equipment, personnel, and facilities it must acquire to initiate production at the levels projected by the company. The supplier may not receive all of the information it needs, so there should also be a formal meeting or at least an exchange of letters in which the supplier asks for more information and the company agrees to a date by which that information will be provided.

7. *Finalize the contract.* Once the supplier has reviewed the product specifications and production requirements, it is in a much better position to knowledgeably negotiate a contract with the company. This is also in the best interests of the company, since it does not want to continually renegotiate the contract with the supplier based on the supplier initially being misinformed about key aspects of the outsourcing agreement.

8. *Transfer equipment and molds.* The company should then transfer any equipment and molds to the supplier that are specified in the contract as being needed by the supplier. However, if the company wants to reserve some in-house capacity in case the supplier does not work out, it may be better to retain these materials and have new equipment and molds sent to the supplier. This equipment should be accompanied by company personnel who are expert in its use, so that the materials can be integrated into the supplier's production lines as rapidly as possible.

9. *Transfer staff.* There may be some production personnel who are being transferred to the supplier as part of the outsourcing agreement. These are usually at the supervisory or maintenance levels rather than direct labor, since the supplier can draw on the local population for direct labor, but needs the expert assistance of the supervisory and maintenance personnel to assure that the transition runs smoothly and continues to operate in that manner. Representatives from the company and supplier should jointly meet with all transferred staff to fill out all paperwork needed to move them to the supplier's benefits package and payroll system.

10. *Create measurement systems.* The company should install measurement systems at the supplier's production facility before any products are manufactured. This allows the company to obtain immediate input on the first production runs regarding scrap, labor costs, production time, and product quality. If measurements were to be installed later, the company might certify the supplier for full-scale production without realizing that the supplier may not be producing in an efficient and effective manner.

11. *Test run production facility.* The company should require a small-scale production run to see if the supplier is capable of manufacturing the product. It is not yet appropriate for the supplier to undertake full-scale production, for there may be problems that will ruin many products before the problems are spotted and fixed. The results of this limited test run should be carefully reviewed to ensure that all standards have been met before authorizing a full-scale production run.

12. *Test manual information transfer from production facility.* The company must also be assured that the supplier can consistently inform it of how much production has been completed, where it has been shipped, and what charges have been made to the company for that production. Following the test run of the production facility is a good time to do this, for the supplier can fill in the company's standard reporting forms with information from the test run. At the lowest levels of information transfer, either the postal service or faxes are used—more complicated electronic data transfers are covered in a later step, after the initial production problems are resolved.

13. *Full production run with testing points installed.* When all of the problems found during the test run have been resolved, it is time to complete a full pro-

duction run. This will frequently reveal other problems that could not be found during the test run. These problems usually relate to volume, such as running equipment at full production speed, increased equipment-maintenance requirements, and training for the larger numbers of direct labor personnel involved in the process. It is best to run this test for one product line at a time rather than for all possible products and product configurations, so that problems can be more easily isolated in smaller production areas and fixed. These problems must be resolved before proceeding to the final steps.

14. *Test run assembly facility.* The previous tests involved the manufacture of products, as opposed to the final assembly of products from premade components. This step is only needed if the company is using one or more final assembly points, which are usually being fed component parts from a manufacturing facility. This step is sometimes added after the transition to the manufacturing supplier has been completed. The assembly test run is a tightly monitored assembly test for the assembly of a small number of products. The company should verify that the supplier segregates all inventory in a separate warehouse area so that the company's components are not mixed with those of other companies.

15. *Test manual information transfer from assembly facility.* As was the case for the production facility, it is important to train the assembly supplier in the use of the company's reporting forms and the methods for transferring the forms to the company. This step includes training, along with any retraining if it appears to be necessary.

16. *Full assembly run with testing points installed.* Once the problems uncovered during the assembly pilot test have been fixed, the assembly supplier can perform a full assembly run with close monitoring by the company's team of process engineers. Training issues are the most common problem found when a full assembly run is completed. The run should be reiterated until the training and other problems are resolved.

17. *Test distribution back to company.* Once the production and assembly operations have been tested, the company must verify that the suppliers know how to ship the completed products back to the company. This involves testing their ability to properly package and ship the completed products. This process should be closely monitored by the process team so that any problems can be spotted and fixed immediately.

18. *Test electronic information transfer.* This step is usually addressed well after all other transition steps have been completed, since it is not an essential part of a "bare bones" manufacturing transition. Electronic information transfers are a better way to exchange information. This step can be completed on two levels of difficulty. The easier level is to manually enter transactions in a computer at one location and have the other party manually extract them from a computer at the other location. This is easy to do and to test, but does

not introduce any great efficiencies into the process. The higher level of difficulty is to have a programming team create computer interfaces for both the supplier and company that allow for automated information transfers. For example, an entry into the supplier's computerized shipping log will automatically generate an electronic transaction that is sent by its computer to the company's computer, which automatically translates this message into a format readable by the company's accounting and manufacturing computer system, which receives and acts upon this information. Extensive programming and testing using dummy information is needed to complete this higher level of electronic information transfer, with a proper installation taking months to complete. Obviously, given the amount of work required, this level of electronic data transfer is only achieved by those companies and suppliers who intend to work together for many years.

19. *Test drop shipping distribution.* Once the company is sure that its suppliers can reliably send completed products to the company warehouse for distribution by the company, it is time to allow them to distribute straight to the company's customers, which reduces the time it takes for products to reach the customer. This test should include a very limited test shipment to fake customer locations (such as the homes of company officers) to ensure that any problems are not seen by real customers. Test items should include the transfer of shipment information on customers from the company to the supplier, the appropriateness of packaging, the type of shipping service used, the timeliness of shipment, and the transfer of this new shipping information to the company for billing purposes. Having the supplier bill the company's customers is not a step that many companies take during the initial transition, because there are too many potential problems, including interfacing the supplier's billing system with that of the company, or extending a terminal connected to the company's computer system to the supplier location for use in billing customers. For the initial transition, it is best to avoid this extra level of complexity by sending notice of shipment to the company, which uses it to bill customers with its regular accounting system. Greater billing complexity can come later, if desired. Full-scale shipments should only be allowed once all of these problem areas have been fixed. Problems in this area will be spotted by customers, so it is important to get this step right before shipping anything to them.

20. *Create feedback mechanisms.* After all other steps are completed, the process team must arrange to have the performance calculations made by the supplier and forwarded to the company for review. This gives the company a feedback mechanism for constantly determining the quality and delivery performance of the supplier. The company should also create and implement an audit schedule for reviewing the accuracy of the measurements forwarded by the supplier.

21. *Dispose of excess space.* Once the supplier has taken over production, the company will have excess production space to dispose of. This may be con-

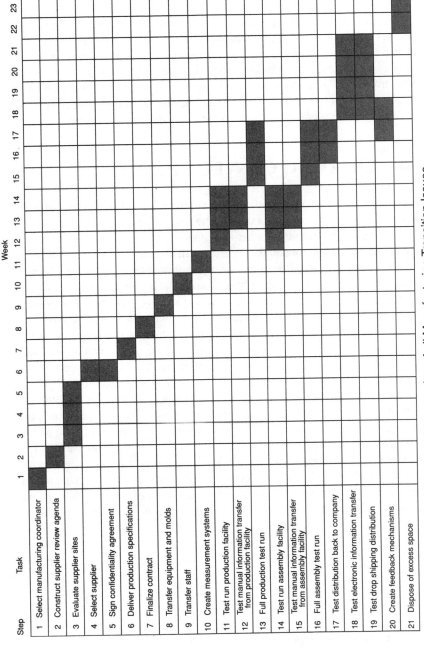

Figure 10.2 Gantt Chart for the Implementation of all Manufacturing Transition Issues

verted to office space, used for storage, sold, or leased. The most common fate for such space is sale or lease, since there is usually so much of it that the company cannot readily find a use for it.

This section covered the many steps needed to successfully transition the production process to a supplier. Not all of the steps are needed, since some companies will never use electronic data transfer, final assembly by a supplier, or drop shipments. Nonetheless, there are many steps to complete in this transition process for even the simplest transfer of production, and company management must assume a long transition period, possibly much longer than the one shown in Figure 10.2, before it can expect a supplier to successfully take over its manufacturing function.

10.4   CREATING CONTROL POINTS

The primary control over a manufacturing supplier is the frequent use of audits by process engineers. This section explores the use of process engineers, as well as other methods for controlling supplier activities.

The principle method for controlling a manufacturing supplier is to send in a team of process engineers. Why? Because the primary problems that arise with a manufacturing supplier are product quality and late delivery, and these are two areas in which process engineers are trained to spot and resolve problems. For example, an engineer can compare a production schedule to actual production records to see if a supplier is not producing according to its own schedule, or if it is altering the schedule to manufacture products for other customers. An engineer can review materials management records to see if a supplier is having trouble receiving the correct components from its suppliers in time for it to assemble them into finished products in accordance with the production schedule. An engineer can also review the production process to see if there are problems with the production flow, personnel, or manufacturing equipment that are keeping production from being completed on time. In the quality-control area, an engineer can sample components as well as finished goods to see if they meet the company's quality standards. An engineer can also review a supplier's statistical process control charts, which reveal when a production process is varying from the production standard. For all of these reasons and more, a company should regularly dispatch teams of process engineers to its manufacturing suppliers in order to maintain control.

A lesser control is the use of financial auditors instead of engineering auditors. These people can review the supplier's billing and shipping records to verify that the supplier has correctly billed the company for the actual amount of products manufactured. This is an appropriate use for a financial auditor instead of an engineer, since the financial auditor has more experience with this type of information. However, the financial auditor should be limited to this task; the engineer should review all other manufacturing areas, as previously noted.

Another control point is to track the cost of each product sold to the company by the supplier. When plotted on a trend line, any changes in price from one billing to the next will be immediately apparent to management. This is a task that can be completed at the company's location, since there is no need to send an audit team to the supplier to collect this information—all necessary data can be extracted from the supplier's billing statement. An example of such a trend line comparison is shown in Figure 10.3.

The company should also create and maintain a customer complaint tracking and response system. This is a very useful control, for it tells the company when customers are discovering problems with the manufacturing process that result in poor products. To have a properly functioning complaint system, all incoming complaints should be funneled to one employee (possibly the functional coordinator), who responds to complaints, summarizes them to discover trends, goes over problems with the supplier, and follows up to make sure that problems were fixed. If there are a large number of complaints, this information can be stored in a database to which the supplier is given read-only access. This allows the supplier to find out about new complaints as soon as they are received, but doesn't give it the opportunity to delete or change the text of complaints that appear to be critical of the supplier. A good complaint tracking and follow-up system is a powerful tool for exercising control over a manufacturing supplier.

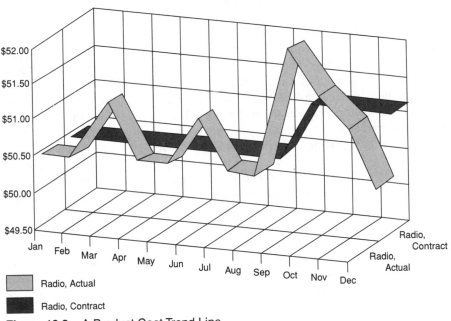

Figure 10.3 A Product Cost Trend Line

A more passive control method is to require a supplier to be ISO certified. A manufacturing supplier should be certified under the ISO 9001 standard. All this means is that an independent review company must verify that the supplier has procedures that cover the supplier's main transactional areas, such as for receiving, shipping, and quality control, and then verify that the supplier is indeed following those procedures. Though an ISO 9001 certification is no guarantee that a supplier is capable of shipping quality products on time, it at least indicates that the supplier has spent some time in setting up procedures and enforcing their use. Requiring a supplier to complete the ISO 9001 certification process gives a company some assurance that the supplier has the proper manufacturing procedures in place, and is following them.

This section covered the reasons for using process engineers as a first-line control over suppliers, as well as the need for financial auditors, complaint tracking systems, and independent verification of ISO 9001 status to give more complete control over the manufacturing function.

10.5 MEASURING THE OUTSOURCED FUNCTION

The measurements used to track the performance of a manufacturing supplier vary from those used for other functional areas in that there are two levels of measurement: one level concerned mostly with price and delivery times and a second level that is more detailed. The first level of measurements are used for those companies that have arm's-length relationships with their suppliers—they only care about getting products at the agreed-upon prices and on time. This level covers most companies. The second level of measurements are used by those companies who are committed to in-depth relationships with their suppliers, sending in engineers to help them improve their operations and save money. These companies need to know far more about their suppliers so that they can help to save costs, and then share in those costs savings through reduced product prices. Accordingly, the following list of measurements is split into two pieces: those measurements used by most companies to evaluate suppliers and those measurements used to gain a detailed understanding of supplier operations. The first set of measurements including descriptions and how they are measured are as follows:

- *Percentage of time shipped within promised date.* One of the primary ways to judge a supplier is on its ability to ship products to the company on the date requested. Some companies who operate on just-in-time principles even request deliveries within a one-hour time frame on a specific day. Any variation from this date—either too late or too early—is considered bad shipment performance. This measurement can be impossible to track if the supplier ships products straight to customers instead of to the company. In these cases, the company can send an audit team to the supplier to examine the shipment dates in its shipping log, or it can order products to be shipped to company addresses and track the dates when products arrive at those locations. To track this measurement, add up the number of complete orders received from the supplier on the correct date (as noted in the receiving log) and divide it by the total number of shipments that should have been received. This measurement is normally reported on for one month's worth of shipments. For the purposes of this shipment, partial shipments are assumed to have not been received, and either early or late shipments are dealt with in the same manner. Some computer systems can automate this calculation if the receipt date on the purchase order is stored in the same computer database as the information that would normally be recorded in a receiving log.

- *Percentage variance from contract prices.* Another major measurement is the price variance of the actual unit prices billed to the company from the rate noted in the contract. This measure should be tracked closely and acted upon rapidly if there is any variance from the contractual rate (unless it is too low). This can be a useless measurement if there are many variations on the product configuration, all with different prices. In such cases, the only way to determine if the supplier is pricing products correctly is to compare the invoiced price to the contract price for each product, usually on an audit basis. To compute this measurement, take the unit price from the supplier's invoice and divide it by the unit price listed on the contract.

- *Percentage of customer returns.* It is of great concern to the company if the supplier is manufacturing products of such a low standard that customers are returning them. An excessively high return rate may be hiding an even higher level of customer dissatisfaction, because not all customers will return defective products—they will just throw them away (depending on the price) and not deal with the company again. However, some products have historically high return rates, so the company must consider the historical return rates for various products before blaming suppliers for the trouble. Also, this is a difficult measurement to use if the company has several suppliers making identical products—it may be impossible to determine which supplier produced the product. The best way around this problem is to have each supplier affix an identifying number to the product that clearly shows where the product was manufactured. To calculate this measurement, divide the total number of units received by the total number shipped. The calculation period should cover several months at a minimum, since there is usually a lag between the purchase and return dates.

- *Percentage of products shipped DOA.* The company cannot let any products get to customers in a nonoperable condition (i.e., "Dead on Arrival"), since this leads to a rapid decline in customer satisfaction, accompanied by much bad publicity. The number of DOA units is easy to track, for it is forcefully brought to the company's attention by irate customers. This number should be divided by the total number of units shipped to determine the percentage of products shipped DOA.

- *Percentage of accurate picking for assembled products.* Many products require assembly by the customer, usually because the company is trying to ship products in the smallest possible package in order to save on packaging materials and shipping costs. In these cases, it is very important that the customer receives a complete set of components. If not, the company must waste time and money shipping extra parts to customers, and will also develop a reputation for poor-quality products. This measurement is best calculated on a spot basis, perhaps by an audit team. To do so, break down a sample of ready-to-ship products and compare the actual number of parts to the bill of materials. If any parts are missing, count the product as incorrect. Divide the total number of incorrect products by the total number sampled to arrive at the percentage of accurate picking for assembled products.

- *Production backlog.* A company that buys from a supplier needs to know the extent of that supplier's backlog, in order to get a better idea of whether or not its products will be manufactured on time. There are several variations on how to acquire this information. One is to obtain from the supplier the total dollar amount of its backlog, as well as the amount of production it is capable of handling in one month. Then reduce the amount of the total backlog by the amount that the company obtained from the supplier in order to arrive at the total dollar amount of orders from other customers of the supplier. Then divide the amount of the supplier's production per month into the reduced backlog figure. This yields the total backlog assigned to other customers. If this number rises over time, it is likely that the amount of space assigned to the company on the supplier's production schedule will drop, since the supplier must now build more products for other customers with the same production capacity. This is a most inexact measure, for the company may have enough leverage with the supplier, either through jawboning, extra payments, or the size of its orders, to always command a premium position on the supplier's production schedule, irrespective of the size or number of orders received from other customers.

The second set of measurements covers more detailed topics that are of assistance to a company that is actively trying to improve the performance if its manufacturing suppliers. Conversely, these measurements would not be used by a company that has no interest in having very close, supportive relations with its suppliers. Also, if a company uses a number of suppliers for component manufacturing, it may not have enough time or personnel to either track the following measurements or use them; in such cases, the number of suppliers may force a reduction in the number of performance measurements, which would probably limit a company to the other measurements that have already been described. Many of these measurements would also be used to track the performance of a company's internal manufacturing operations. The measurements are as follows:

- *Scrap as percentage of material cost.* A company that wants its supplier to reduce its costs should determine the scrap percentage as soon as it can send a team into the supplier's plant. The reason is that the size of the scrap percentage is a strong indicator of other underlying problems, such as poor management, poor cost controls, ineffective manufacturing processes, and improperly maintained equipment. This can be a difficult figure to determine, for many companies do a poor job of tracking this information. The easiest calculation method is to take the scrap figure recorded in the general ledger and divide it by the total material expense cost for the same time period. However, if there is no such account, the company must derive this information from inexact methods. One approach is to go to the warehouse or production manager and find out where the scrap items are stored. Then have an appraiser estimate their value. Then determine how long the scrap has been on-site, and divide the appraiser's number by the total material cost during that time period.

- *Component defect rate.* The supplier will not be able to ship products on schedule if the components it uses to construct finished products are filled with defects. It will also require extra labor to conduct especially tight inspections of those parts that have a history of defects. To track this information, the company must find the supplier's records of defective components. The easiest place to find this information is some kind of log for returned parts, which is occasionally included in the receiving log. Once this information is found, compare the receipt dates when all defective orders were received to the same dates in the receiving log. Then divide the total number of defective orders received during a month to the total number of orders received during the same month to derive the component defect rate. This can be an exceptionally hard measurement to calculate, for the supplier may maintain minimal information about component returns or the dates on which these items were received.

- *Material cost.* The largest component of most manufactured goods is materials, not labor. Paying close attention to the elements of materials cost is a good way to reduce a supplier's overall costs. The easiest way to track this item is to review the invoices for parts that make up the finished product and derive the product cost from them. This requires a bill of materials, so that the reviewer knows what parts to include in the costing analysis. Once the information is compiled, it should be listed on a trend chart so that a reviewer can quickly spot any sudden changes in costs. If a bill of materials is not available, this can be a very difficult measurement to track.

- *Labor volume variance.* When reviewing labor costs, there are two measurements that must be checked. One, the labor volume variance, shows any changes in the cost of labor due to variances from the expected production level. The second, the labor cost variance, is discussed below. When reviewing what may appear to be an excess amount of labor expense, this measurement is necessary for identifying that portion of the expense that was a necessary part of production that was above the budgeted level. To calculate this measurement, collect from labor routings the total budgeted labor hours per unit. Then multiply this amount by the total number of units produced to arrive at the total number of budgeted hours for the actual production volume. Then compare this number of hours to the total number of hours actually used to complete the job—this yields the labor variance, expressed in hours. To translate this into dollars, multiply the labor variance by the budgeted cost per hour.

- *Labor cost variance.* The second part of a labor cost review is to determine the labor cost variance. This measurement points out how high or low the actual labor cost per hour is from the expected amount. This information is used to track down excessively high labor costs (frequently due to overtime) that cut into supplier margins. To calculate this measurement, first find the total manufacturing labor cost for the period, subtract from it the budgeted labor cost, and then subtract the labor volume variance (as previously calculated). This leaves the labor cost variance. Another calculation method is to subtract the budgeted labor cost per hour from the actual cost per hour to determine the per-unit variance, and then multiply this amount by the total number of units produced.

- *Bill of material accuracy.* One of the major drivers of an efficient production system, whether it be materials resources planning, just-in-time, or some other system, is the bill of materials. A supplier must have a highly accurate bill of materials in order to procure parts for production and to produce on time. Without a bill of material, there is a great deal of waste, both in terms of extra purchasing time to procure parts at the last minute and in terms of wasted production capacity, since work will stop until the correct parts are found and brought to the production area. To calculate this measurement, have a team of engineers review the bill of materials. Mark any missing or excessive component quantities as errors, and then divide this number by the total number of components in the bill to determine the total percentage of incorrect items in the bill. The inverse of this percentage is the bill of material accuracy percentage.

- *Inventory accuracy.* A supplier will have trouble shipping products to the company if it cannot locate the components in its inventory that are needed to build final products. Also, an inaccurate inventory, by definition, has parts that cannot be located, and which must therefore be written off. Any write-offs will impact a supplier's earnings, which will reduce its agreeableness in consenting to further price cuts for products sold to the company. Thus, it is very important to track the accuracy of a supplier's inventory. To calculate this measurement, print out a listing of the inventory and compare a random sample from the printout to the actual inventory. If an item quantity or location code is incorrect, this is an error. Also take a sample of items from the actual inventory and trace them back to the inventory report. If the same information is missing or incorrect, this is also an error. Then divide the total number of correct sample items by the total number of items sampled to arrive at the inventory accuracy percentage.

- *Capital investment.* It is in the interests of the company to keep the capital investments of its suppliers at as low a level as possible while still producing products with acceptable levels of quality and cost. The lower the capital investment, the higher the return on investment that the supplier will experience, which makes the supplier more amenable to allowing price cuts on sales of products to the company. The company can use this measurement to track down large capital investments at the supplier and work to reduce them. To calculate this measurement, have an analyst and a process engineer compare the supplier's fixed asset records to the equipment located on the production line that is manufacturing products for the company. The total of this list of equipment is the capital investment. In addition, it may be useful to divide the total capital investment by the total number of units produced in a year; this yields the capital cost per unit produced, which the process engineering team can review for reasonableness.

This section covered two sets of performance measurements: one set that should be used by every company that outsources its manufacturing function and a second set that is used only by those companies that want to take a detailed look at how their suppliers operate, in order to assist them in reducing their costs. The second set of measurements are rarely used by companies, but may find wider acceptance as companies realize that one of the best ways to reduce costs is to work closely with their manufacturing suppliers.

10.6 MANAGING THE OUTSOURCED FUNCTION

The manufacturing function is one of the most important ones within a company, and must be properly managed to ensure that the company does not fail because of it. This requires the presence of a top-level functional coordinator. This section discusses the powers and qualifications of the coordinator, as well as the type of staff needed for support.

The manufacturing functional coordinator must have full authority to negotiate and sign contracts with suppliers, as well as to pay them. These two powers are necessary to make suppliers listen to the coordinator. If someone else has these powers, the coordinator may be ignored in favor of the other person. The coordinator must also closely monitor a variety of performance measurements and follow up with suppliers if selected measures fall below the company's expectations of supplier performance. The coordinator must also monitor the need for additional capacity, arrange with suppliers for manufacturing differing quantities based on demand, and supervise tests of new facilities to ensure that products are being completed in accordance with company standards. In addition, the coordinator must supervise a staff of process engineers who assist in monitoring, measuring, and recommending improvements at supplier locations. Also, the coordinator must act as an intermediary between the engineering department and the manufacturing supplier to ensure that the product designs completed by the engineering staff are sufficient for the supplier to use in constructing new products. Finally, the coordinator must carefully review all incoming customer complaints to see if there are valid problems with the manufacturing process that are causing the complaints, and then review them with the supplier to resolve the problems. This job description is shown in Figure 10.4. Given the large number of weighty tasks confronted by the manufacturing coordinator, it is clear that the coordinator must have great experience in the manufacturing field, with particular specialization in systems measurement, negotiation, and supervision. This position is frequently at the vice president level or reports directly to that position (as shown in Figure 10.5). Of all the functional areas, the level of responsibility required for the manufacturing coordinator calls for a coordinator of the highest quality.

It is critical that the manufacturing supplier be properly supported by a fully qualified staff of process engineers. In order to fully manage a supplier—including making periodic measurements, investigating customer complaints, doing capacity planning, negotiating contracts, doing pilot testing, and performing other tasks—it is impossible for all but the smallest companies to have a coordinator handle the entire outsourcing task by himself or herself. An experienced team of process engineers can take care of most of these tasks and only call in the coordinator when they are confronted by problems that must be handled at a higher level. This allows the coordinator to take the results of the engineers' inspections to the supplier as well as negotiate better performance or pricing, which is the most appropriate use of the coor-

Figure 10.4 Manufacturing Outsourcing Coordinator's Job Description

Employee Title: Manufacturing Outsourcing Coordinator
Reports to: Chief Executive Officer
Responsibilities:
- Sign off on all agreements with manufacturing suppliers.
- Authorize the release of funds to suppliers.
- Track actual unit costs incurred against contractual amounts and work with the supplier to correct any problems.
- Verify that work being completed by the engineering department or supplier is sufficient for the manufacturing supplier to use to create products.
- Monitor the progress of pilot tests to manufacture new products.
- Monitor supplier quality and delivery performance measurements, and discuss problems with suppliers as they arise.
- Supervise a staff of process engineers and assign them to various supplier audits.
- Monitor the need for more production capacity and work with suppliers to meet this need.
- Review customer complaints and fix problems found by customers.

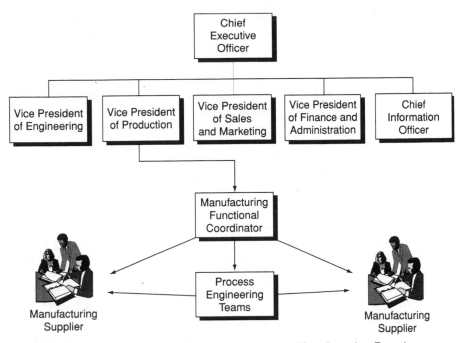

Figure 10.5 Organization Chart for Outsourcing the Manufacturing Function

dinator's time. In short, a functional coordinator must have a support team of process engineers to properly manage a manufacturing supplier.

This section covered the responsibilities and qualifications of a functional coordinator for the manufacturing function. This information was also noted in an organization flowchart as well as a sample job description. In addition, the need for an experienced back-up team of process engineers was described.

10.7 POTENTIAL CUSTOMER SERVICE ISSUES

The quality of a company's customer service can be destroyed by a bad manufacturing supplier. Poor performance in the areas of product quality, completeness of parts in kits, and delivery times are at the root of this poor service. This section discusses each problem area and how to fix it.

Many products are sold in kit form to customers, who perform the final assembly. If even one part of a kit is missing, the affected customer must either create or separately purchase the missing part on his or her own (resulting in the company never knowing about the problem) or he or she must call the company to ask for a replacement part. The least of a company's problems in this situation is that it must incur the cost of taking the customer's call, finding the correct part, and shipping it for free to the customer. The real cost is that the customer will be much less likely to buy from the company again, and this problem may spread to other companies as word of incomplete kits spreads, either through the media or more informally. It is not sufficient to rely on customer complaints to find evidence of this problem, since customers may fix the problem on their own and never contact the company. A better approach is to take apart a sample of completed kits and compare the contents to the bill of materials. If the number of kits with missing parts exceeds the error percentage previously noted in the agreement with the supplier, the company should either impose penalties or give written notice of termination of the outsourcing agreement, subject to a short period in which the supplier is allowed to correct the problem. Only by auditing kits and imposing stiff penalties on suppliers can a company be assured of shipping complete kits to customers.

Product quality is another customer service concern. If the supplier is manufacturing products of shoddy quality, customers will not buy them again. Besides the obviously rapid decline in sales, this will harm the company's reputation for quality, since it is the company's name that is appearing on the product, not the supplier's. Also, because there is no evidence on the product that the supplier manufactured it, it is possible for the supplier to continually turn out poor products for a succession of customers without ever being called to task—the company whose name is on the product will be blamed instead, so the supplier can stay in business as long as it can continue to find a stream of companies that are willing to let it manufacture products for them. The best way to keep this problem from occurring is to have a process engineering team periodically review the supplier's operations. This review can include a check of the supplier's statistical process control charts to see if parts are being manufactured within accepted tolerance levels, a functional test of completed products to see if they work properly, and a review of the scrap and receiving records to see if the quality of incoming components is acceptable. If quality is a continuing problem, this process review team should be permanently stationed at the supplier's manufacturing location. Any problems found by the process team should be reviewed with the supplier's management at a formal review meeting in which the minutes include a description of the problem, a decision regarding how the problem is to be fixed, and a date by which the problem is to be resolved. The functional coordinator can be called in to remonstrate with the supplier if progress is not achieved. Only by close on-site inspection of supplier activities will a company be assured that product quality problems are being addressed.

The final customer service problem is late shipments. This can apply to the supplier if it is either making late drop shipments straight to customers, or if it is shipping late to the company, thus delaying the company's repacking for shipment on to customers. In either case, the supplier is at fault. There are many reasons for late shipments, such as missing components, scrapped parts, labor strikes, producing for some other customer of the supplier, and weather that closes down all transportation. With so many reasons for late shipments, it can take a long time to root them out and resolve them. The most proactive approach for a company that has this problem is the same one used for poor product quality: Send in the process engineering teams.

They must first compare actual production records to the production schedule over a period of time to see if there is a continuing problem with not meeting the requirements of the schedule, and then work their way down through the multitude of reasons for each problem, meeting with supplier management to discuss each problem as it is found. A significant point here is that this is a problem that can be spotted before a company hires a supplier to manufacture its products. During the due diligence phase prior to signing a contract, a process team should compare the supplier's actual shipment records to its production records to see if it has a continuing problem with achieving its scheduled delivery dates. If the problem appears to be a deep one, the company should find a different supplier, rather than be faced with a major and ongoing shipment problem. Thus, late shipment trouble can have many underlying reasons that require the services of an on-site engineering team to resolve.

One way to identify problems with kits, quality, and late delivery is to pay close attention to customer complaints. However, many companies have no formal mechanism for routing incoming complaints to the right person, acting on them, or following up with customers to see if their problems have been rectified. The first thing to do is to make sure that customer complaints are not routed to the manufacturing supplier, as the supplier will sometimes squash these complaints, since they make the supplier look bad. Instead, they should all be routed to the functional coordinator and logged into a database that summarizes them by type of problem. An audit team should periodically review this database to ensure that each complaint was answered, that the problem was reviewed with the supplier, and that action was taken to ensure that the problem will not occur again. Only by bringing complaints into the open and ensuring that action is taken will the number of complaints drop.

In this section, we looked at the primary customer service problems of inadequate product quality (of which incomplete product kits is a subset) and late deliveries. In all cases, a company's best approach is to send in an engineering team to investigate the problem and find solutions. Also, there must be a formal mechanism for collecting customer complaints, resolving them, and ensuring that all complaints are answered. Only by taking these steps will a company improve the quality and delivery performance of its manufacturing supplier.

10.8   GETTING OUT OF THE OUTSOURCING ARRANGEMENT

This section covers the problems that arise when a company wants to terminate an outsourcing arrangement with its manufacturing supplier. There are major problems with terminating this kind of relationship, but they can be avoided with careful planning. This section addresses those planning issues.

The biggest problem when shutting down a manufacturing supplier is shifting the company's production business to a new supplier. This is difficult if the company cannot find a good replacement supplier, for it must build its own production facility, for which it may have neither the money nor the time. If this is the only course of action, then the company must stick with the supplier, whatever its problems may be, until the company-owned facility is built and tested. If other suppliers are available, the company must still retain the existing supplier until the new supplier has proven through test runs that it can manufacture the company's products within the company's cost, time, volume, and quality parameters. This testing process may take a considerable amount of time, so it is imperative that the company keep up good relations with the current supplier until it is ready to make the switch. Thus, a manufacturing supplier can be dropped, but a company may have to wait a long time from when the decision is made to drop the supplier until it is practically possible to do so.

Many suppliers have either purchased or been given special machinery or molds to use in producing the company's products. These must be returned when the outsourcing agreement is terminated. If the supplier is unhappy about stopping the agreement, this may be a difficult proposition. The company's best approach for obtaining the release of these items is to include a clause in the original contract that requires their return if the agreement is terminated. If there is no such clause, the company may have to resort to legal action, buy them back, or have new equipment or molds made. The best way to have equipment returned is to require this in the original contract.

When a manufacturing agreement is terminated, there are almost always a number of raw materials or work-in-process items that are somewhere in the production pipeline. What should be done with this inventory? The most common approach is for the company to purchase any remaining inventory from the supplier, who ships it to the company. If the supplier has more raw materials coming to it from suppliers, the contract should state that the supplier will do its best to stop the delivery of those items, so that the company will not have to pay for them. The contract can even state that it will not purchase any inventory that was delivered to the supplier after the date when notice of termination was given to the supplier. As for the price of the inventory, the supplier is fully justified in at least charging for its cost, which it can prove to the company by producing the invoices from its suppliers that detail the cost. In addition, it is common to charge the company a handling fee or a small profit to compensate the supplier for the work needed to deliver the inventory to the company. This markup percentage should be noted in the original outsourcing contract. The original contract should cover the disposition and pricing of any remaining inventory at the time of termination.

If the supplier has purchased equipment or a production facility from the company, the company should have the option to buy this equipment back from the supplier, less a charge for depreciation on the equipment. The supplier may require that fixed assets will be sold back to the company, since it may have no need for the equipment once it is no longer manufacturing parts for the company. An interesting twist to this problem is that the company may not want the equipment; buying back a facility and then expecting to immediately bring it up to full production speed is not a realistic expectation, unless a company has no other option for having its goods produced. A better approach is to have a new supplier or facility already set to produce products when the old supplier is terminated.

If the supplier made a major capital investment in order to manufacture products for the company, the supplier may want compensation for this investment. There are several options available. One is for the company to purchase any equipment or facilities that the supplier constructed in order to build products for the company. This is very common if the equipment needed to manufacture the company's products is so specialized that there is no other use for the equipment. If so, the payment should only be for the depreciated value of the equipment and facilities or a lump-sum termination payment in partial compensation. However, if this payment is not listed in the original contract, the company is under no obligation to pay anything for the supplier's capital investments. The supplier may, in fact, have other customers who can take up the excess capacity of the new facilities with their own production orders, assuming that the equipment can be converted to other uses, so the supplier may not incur a loss on its investment. If the company agrees to a buy-back provision in the contract under which it purchases the supplier's capital investment, it is mandatory that every capital item be listed in an appendix to the agreement, along with costs and depreciation schedules. Only by formally listing this information in the agreement can the company avoid having protracted arguments with the supplier, probably involving litigation, over the correct price the company must pay the supplier for its equipment and facilities. Thus, buying out a supplier's capital investment may be necessary in some cases; if so, the purchase details should be noted in the original outsourcing contract.

If a company is terminating a production agreement with the printer who supplies materials for inclusion with the company's products, the termination is quite simple. The supplier uses the same production equipment for all of its customers, so there is no need for the company to buy any of the supplier's equipment. The only issue is that the supplier may have printed materials on hand that it has not yet shipped to the company. If so, the company is required to purchase the amount of these stocks that matches the maximum number of printed materials that the company has authorized the supplier to produce under the terms of its last purchase order. Any printed materials that exceed this amount were never authorized by the company, and so it is under no obligation to purchase them. Also, if the company is terminating the agreement because of defects in the printed materials, it should consider refusing to pay for any remaining printed materials on the grounds that they are likely to be defective as well. Thus, terminating a production agreement with a printing supplier only involves the purchase of any remaining inventory that the company had authorized.

If a company has an agreement with a distributor to perform final assembly work on its products, this is a relatively easy agreement to terminate. Final assembly usually requires a minimal capital investment, so the company will not be required to buy any equipment from the supplier. However, the supplier will almost certainly have a quantity of components and finished goods on hand. The company should buy back all of this inventory at cost plus a transaction fee or profit percentage. The exact pricing method to be used should be addressed in the initial outsourcing contract, so that there are no grounds for argument over this issue at the time of termination. One remaining problem is that the supplier may have built or leased a facility in which to perform the assembly work; the contract may stipulate that the company pay a termination fee that allows the supplier to convert this space to other uses, or to terminate the lease. However, in this case, the company is only obligated to make a payment if the contract stipulates that a payment is required. In short, terminating an assembly contract only requires the company to buy back any inventory that is on the supplier's premises.

This section dealt with the issues surrounding the termination of manufacturing suppliers. The chief issues are buying back inventory as well as equipment or facilities. Inventory repurchases are necessary in nearly all cases, whereas the company can resort to depreciation deductions or alternative termination payments to avoid having to buy back equipment or facilities at full price. The main point is that all details of termination payments must be noted in the initial outsourcing contract in order to avoid arguments over the exact amount of payments to be made at the time of termination.

10.9   SUMMARY

This chapter covered the outsourcing of manufacturing, one of the most important functions for a company. The advantages of this approach include reduced capital requirements, access to more production capacity, many final assembly locations, and access to technological expertise. However, these advantages must be weighed against the risk of using a less than top-notch supplier who may not produce with high quality or deliver on time.

Contractual issues to address with a manufacturing supplier include continuous reductions in the per-unit price in exchange for a long-term contract, different prices based on different volumes of products purchased, termination terms such as the repurchase of inventory and equipment from the supplier, product quality parameters, and access rights for the company's process engineers.

The transition from the company to a supplier is especially critical for the manufacturing function, since any interruption in the flow of products to the marketplace can severely damage company profits. Some of the key issues include a thorough review of all prospective supplier candidates, pilot testing new production, adequate initial testing, and a feedback mechanism for rapidly correcting problems. Only if all of these points are properly addressed will a company have a successful transition to a supplier.

Manufacturing controls center around a team of process engineers who regularly review supplier performance and report back to the functional coordinator about any issues needing improvement. Other controls include financial auditors to investigate pricing problems, plotting of product costs on a time line, ISO 9001 certification, and a customer complaint tracking and response system. A mix of these controls gives a company good control over a manufacturing supplier.

Manufacturing measurements focus on the quality of products as well as their billed cost and timeliness of delivery. Other measurements of lesser usefulness are the percentage of customer returns, production backlog, several direct labor variances, the bill of material accuracy, and the supplier's capital investment. The number of measurements used varies with the company's level of intrusiveness in the activities of the supplier.

Managing a manufacturing supplier requires an experienced and highly knowledgeable functional coordinator, possibly at the vice president level, who is assisted by a strong team of process engineers who continually monitor the supplier's activities. An active coordinator is needed to ensure that the supplier delivers quality products on time.

Customer service can be a major problem in the manufacturing area. A company should use on-site audits by process engineers as well as customer complaints to spot problems, and then use bonuses, penalties, and frequent meetings with supplier management to fix all customer service issues. Continuing problems in this area are solid grounds for the termination of a supplier.

Getting out of an outsourcing arrangement with a manufacturing supplier is much more difficult than is the case for other functional areas. The reasons for this include the downtime while production is shifted either in-house or to a new supplier, retrieving molds and equipment, purchases of raw materials and work-in-process from the terminated supplier, and termination payments to cover investments by the supplier. The amount of trouble involved in a termination is so significant that it is almost always better to work through problems with the existing supplier.

Though the manufacturing function is more complex and risky to outsource than many other functional areas, outsourcing it has so many benefits that it is worthwhile to at least investigate the option.

CHAPTER ELEVEN

Outsourcing the Materials-Management Function

The materials-management function is in charge of bringing materials to and from a company's manufacturing facilities, storing finished products, and delivering these products to customers. This important task includes the transport and storage functions, as well as auditing freight billings and freight brokering. All of these tasks can be outsourced. Another related task is fleet maintenance, but that is covered in the maintenance chapter of this book.

Some of the largest companies have already outsourced their materials-management functions. For example, UPS has a five-year, $1-billion deal to provide logistics-management services to JCPenny Company, while TNT Contract Logistics, Inc., has a five-year, $100-million deal to provide logistics-management services to the Timken Company. Miami-based Ryder Dedicated Logistics offers not only trucking services but also freight brokering and logistics-management consulting services. It recently signed a five-year, $280-million deal with the Whirlpool Corporation to operate an inbound material-logistics system. FedEx runs all of National Semiconductor's storage, sorting, and shipping activities out of a distribution center in Singapore. These large companies are giving their materials-management functions to suppliers for several reasons, the most important being that they can cut their working capital and fixed asset requirements and that they can eliminate the substantial fixed costs of this function, converting it to mostly variable costs. Given the substantial advantages of outsourcing this function, it seems sure that this is a major growth area for suppliers.

This chapter covers the advantages and disadvantages of using materials-management suppliers, several contractual issues to keep in mind when settling contract details with suppliers, and a series of transitional issues to consider when shifting the functions from in-house locations to suppliers. Several ways to maintain control over suppliers are also noted, which can be supplemented by a series of measurements that cover the performance of each supplier. Several points regarding managing the materials-management suppliers are also noted, as well as a small number of customer service issues. Finally, the pitfalls associated with terminating supplier contracts are covered, as well as how to mitigate those problems. In short, this chapter is intended to give the reader a thorough understanding of why the materials-management function should be outsourced, how to do it and manage it, and, if necessary, how to pull away from a supplier.

11.1   ADVANTAGES AND DISADVANTAGES

This section covers the advantages and disadvantages of using suppliers to handle a company's freight, warehousing, freight brokerage, and freight-auditing functions. The advantages and disadvantages of using a supplier are clustered together for each function so that the reader can more readily form an opinion regarding the need to outsource each function.

Many companies have too small a volume of shipments, or shipments that are too sporadic, to keep their own truck fleets fully utilized. If shipments do not fill a truck, then a company must incur the full cost of the shipment if it uses its own trucks, but only part of the cost if it uses a trucking supplier, who can merge the partial shipment with shipments from other companies. These advantages cover nearly all smaller businesses, except those that maintain many distribution points and want to have tight control over the rapid replenishment of those locations. In addition, many larger businesses only want to concentrate on their core functions, and do not want to be involved in the trucking business. The hundreds of thousands of businesses that fall into these categories are prime targets for trucking suppliers. However, shifting one's trucking business to a supplier brings up a major problem, which is that the supplier may not be able to deliver products to the company-designated locations as rapidly as could the company's own trucks. This is because the supplier must juggle the shipment demands of many customers, whereas the company's entire trucking capacity is devoted to its own needs. One of the best trucking companies, Ryder Integrated Logistics, avoids this problem by directly accessing the production schedules of its largest customers to see when they will need trucking support, and will schedule an appropriate amount of trucking capacity based on this information. Using a trucking supplier avoids the need for an in-house fleet, but deliveries may not be as fast as an in-house fleet could produce.

There is a surprising amount of paperwork associated with maintaining a trucking fleet, which can lead to very substantial government fines if the paperwork is not completely filled out and correctly filed. For example, there is a fine for every day that a driver with a commercial driver's license (CDL) does not complete a mileage log. There are also requirements for reporting all accidents, as well as keeping a complete maintenance file on each truck owned by the company. By switching to a trucking supplier, all of these paperwork problems can be avoided.

Another advantage of using trucking suppliers is that this greatly reduces a company's fixed asset investment. If a company finds that the expense of purchasing and maintaining an in-house fleet of trucks is absorbing most of its available capital, the solution is to liquidate the fleet, along with any maintenance facilities and equipment, and start using a trucking supplier. One option when doing this is to sell the fleet to the supplier, who can use it to service the company's needs. No matter how the fleet is disposed of, a company will end up with a substantial amount of cash that it can use for a variety of needs: paying off debt, buying back stock, funding expansion, or buying other companies. Getting rid of an in-house fleet can be a considerable source of cash.

Moving part of a company's business to a trucking supplier allows the company to ship the bulk of its product with its own trucks while evaluating the performance of various trucking suppliers. When it finds a trucking supplier that meets its performance standards, it can then shift more business to that supplier. This allows a company to more carefully pick a trucking supplier than could a company who shifted all of its business to a supplier right away, without any evaluation period. A second reason for a partial shift to a supplier is that a company can keep just enough of its own trucks on hand to cover a minimum sales level. Suppliers can then be brought in to handle any excess of business beyond the minimum level of business activity. This method allows a company to retain sufficient control over deliveries of the bulk of its business, while not having to invest in additional trucks to cover sporadic increases in the level of business activity.

An advantage of using both trucking and warehousing suppliers is that a company can convert a large amount of fixed costs to variable costs, which reduces a company's break-even point, making it less likely to succumb to a drop in business. The substantial fixed costs in this area include warehouse facilities, storage racks, forklifts, tractors, trailers, and maintenance facilities. For even a small distribution system, these costs usually are well into the millions of dollars. By eliminating these assets, a company can also achieve a substantial improvement in its return-on-assets measurement. One problem with this scenario is that the amount of fixed costs only drops when the company actually sells off its facilities and equipment—otherwise, the company is paying to maintain it, while still incurring depreciation expenses, and at the same time paying a supplier to perform the trucking and warehousing services. Therefore, as long as assets can be rapidly disposed of, a company can cut into its break-even point by switching its warehousing and trucking functions to suppliers.

Some suppliers are combining the warehousing and transportation elements of the materials-management function in order to present extra value to their customers. For example, an overnight delivery service can store all of a company's goods in one warehouse and then ship from that location to anywhere in the world using overnight mail. This earns the supplier storage fees as well as transportation charges, while allowing the company to keep a minimal amount of inventory concentrated in one location, which reduces the company's working capital costs. However, if a company's customers are not compensating it for its overnight mail deliveries, the cost of the overnight delivery service may exceed the savings from only having one warehouse.

In short, a company can save money on inventory costs by shipping overnight from one warehouse location, but these savings may be offset by the increased transportation cost.

Many companies use a warehouse supplier if they do not have enough inventory to justify building their own storage facility. Another case is when companies build up seasonal inventories, such as those that build for the Christmas season; these companies have a short-term storage requirement, and outsource their storage needs to solve the problem. These companies are prime users of warehousing suppliers. Other companies that have a continuing need for storage space and who have enough storage needs to justify building their own warehouse will sometimes outsource to a supplier, because they do not have the capital required to build their own facilities. Valid reasons for outsourcing include partial inventories, seasonal storage requirements, and a lack of capital.

Using a warehousing supplier is especially useful if a company wants to use a large number of distribution points as final assembly areas. This is one of the newest concepts in distribution management: that of building the smallest number of components to stock and storing these components at a wide range of distribution locations, which are then assembled according to customer specifications at those locations. This results in thousands of possible product variations being shipped with a minimum of inventory. This system requires extra locations for final assembly, and a company may not want to either invest in or manage these final assembly locations. The logical alternative is to hire suppliers who not only maintain the warehouses but who are also capable of assembling the finished products at those warehouses. This allows a company to reduce its investment in inventory while getting finished products to customers sooner, and with no additional investment. The one downside to this approach is that the company is relying on suppliers to assemble products with its name on them, and if the suppliers do a poor assembly job, customers will blame the company, not the suppliers. However, this problem can be mitigated by periodically sending industrial engineers to the supplier locations to observe and correct each supplier's assembly operations.

One problem with using lots of supplier-owned distribution points is that the company has finished-goods inventory and work-in-process spread through many locations, which is difficult and expensive for an external auditor to review during the year-end auditing process. It may be possible to avoid any audit review of these locations if the company maintains inventory quantities at those locations that are considered by the auditors to be insignificant. At a minimum, the auditor may be persuaded to only audit those locations with the largest inventory volumes, thereby cutting back on the expense of sending internal teams to the other locations to accompany the auditors. Additional auditing costs are a consideration when setting up multiple supplier-owned distribution points.

Most materials-management departments do not have the staff available with the experience to audit freight billings with an eye to claiming rebates on freight overcharges. This creates an opportunity for freight audit suppliers, who review a selection of the company's freight bills and collect additional discounts from the freight companies if they spot any discounts that were not applied to billings, or rates that were incorrectly applied. Freight auditors claim a percentage of all savings found as payment, so there is no fixed cost for the materials-management function if this kind of supplier is used—freight auditors are only paid if they produce. Ryder Integrated Logistics takes the freight auditing concept one step further by having freight haulers send their billings straight to Ryder for audit prior to initial payment, so there is no need for after-the-fact negotiations with the freight haulers for reimbursement— Ryder just takes any fee reductions out of the initial payment to the supplier. The only downside to using freight auditors is that they charge a high percentage of all savings as their fee, but seeing that the company would not achieve any savings at all without them, it is better to pay the fee and still collect extra money in freight refunds. Freight auditors give a company demonstrably significant savings on its freight expense while charging a high percentage of all savings found.

Many companies use freight brokers to handle their more oversized or exotic transportation problems, while other companies use them for virtually all of their transportation needs. A freight broker is a specialized discipline in which the broker selects freight carriers, secures insurance for the cargo, monitors the performance of the freight carriers, arranges for storage at any points where inventory is transferred to new modes of transport (such as air or sea terminals), pays duties, and completes all customs documents. They also have branches or corresponding brokers in other countries who handle arriving shipments for them. A good broker is worth every penny it charges to move a company's goods to the designated location. One advantage of using a freight broker is that a company can use the broker's expertise in getting unwieldy or unusual cargoes to foreign destinations that the company would have great difficulty shipping to on its own. Expertise is a major advantage. Second, the broker does a large amount of business with various transportation companies, and can secure excellent pricing on shipments, with some of the savings being passed along to the company. However, the freight broker handles all of the paperwork for a shipment, which means that it pays all of the bills and then recasts the billings for payment by the company—it is easy to include an exceptionally large fee in this recast billing, resulting in the company not knowing the size of the fee it is being charged. Also, a bad broker can destroy a cargo by several means: missing a key date for transport on an oceangoing vessel, not having correct documentation for customs officers, or mislaying paperwork for the transport of cargo out of a midpoint storage facility. These problems can be mitigated by investigating a prospective broker's references and by checking for lawsuits that have been filed against it. Thus, a good broker is a valuable asset to a company, while a bad one can reroute or freeze a company's shipments.

This section covered the advantages and disadvantages of outsourcing the various elements of the materials-management function. Outsourcing trucking is a good idea for those companies seeking to reduce their fixed asset investments, and who ship in small volumes or in less than full-truckload quantities. Freight audit outsourcing is useful for nearly all companies, while freight brokerage services are used by all but the largest companies, which maintain their own in-house brokerage staffs. Warehousing services are useful for those companies that need many distribution or final assembly locations or who want to reduce their investments in warehousing facilities. In short, there are many circumstances in which materials-management outsourcing is appropriate.

11.2 CONTRACT-SPECIFIC ISSUES

This section covers several contractual issues to be aware of when entering into outsourcing arrangements with materials-management suppliers. The principle contract issues in this area are related to pricing and insurance.

A warehouse supplier may try to lock a company into a low rate per square foot in exchange for reserving a minimum amount of storage space for a predefined time period. This is rarely a good idea, for inventory needs may vary dramatically over a short time, and a company should not be locked into minimum storage fees for years when it may have long since eliminated all of its inventory needs. This is of particular concern in today's just-in-time manufacturing environment, where companies are concentrating on cutting back on their inventory stocks. If a company decides that the rate offered is too good to refuse and elects to go ahead with a minimum storage fee, it should at least consider reserving only a minimum amount of square footage, just enough to cover its smallest level of storage needs for the term of the contract; this will limit the company's long-term liability to pay the minimum fee.

A warehouse has very few variable costs. If it is chock-full of inventory or empty, its owners must pay about the same level of expenses. This presents a pricing opportunity for a company willing to negotiate sharply. In business environments where a warehouse is relatively empty, a company can negotiate the storage fees down to very low levels. A warehouse will accept such deals because there are few variable costs, and it is just trying to scrape together enough cash to cover its fixed costs. However, do not expect a warehouse to accept such a deal on a long-term basis, for it will only accept such terms as long as the economy remains soft. Thus, cheap warehouse rates are usually possible only for short-term contracts.

A warehouse must also have insurance that covers the value of any inventory stored on its premises. This is a requirement of most insurance companies who provide primary loss coverage on company inventory. They want this requirement so that they can reimburse the company for any losses, and then go to the warehouse supplier's insurance company and ask for reimbursement to cover their costs.

If a company is willing to outsource to a trucking supplier, this may mean that it is willing to eliminate its own truck fleet. If so, part of the outsourcing deal with a trucking supplier should be that the supplier will either purchase or lease the tractors and trailers from the company, with the right to sell them back at a depreciated rate if the company decides to terminate the outsourcing contract. The price of the fleet will be highly dependent on its condition, so the supplier should have the contractual right to conduct a full maintenance check on all trucks to be transferred to it prior to the two parties settling on a purchase price for the equipment.

A trucking supplier may be willing to give a company exceptionally low pricing in exchange for the exclusive right to haul its freight. This has the advantage of reducing the company's costs, but there is a danger that the company may have trouble breaking out of the agreement if the supplier turns out to be a poor performer in other areas, such as timely delivery and damage to transported goods. An alternative that takes these extra issues into account is to have a clause in the contract that gives the company the option of shifting all of its business exclusively to a single trucking supplier, but only after a suitable time period has passed in which the company can evaluate the supplier's performance in all areas. This variation gives the company the chance to save extra money on freight costs while initially giving it the option to use other freight suppliers.

The company should also require that its trucking suppliers have sufficient insurance to cover the destruction of a full truckload of the most expensive materials that the company could possibly transport in one truck. Some trucking suppliers only provide a minimum level of coverage, so be sure to check on this item before signing a contract with a trucking supplier.

If a company decides to shift all of its freight business to one trucking supplier or freight broker, it should contractually require the supplier to establish and use a computer linkage to the company's production and distribution planning software, so that it will know when trucks are needed to haul away completed production. This ensures that the company will have fewer problems with its distribution system, since the supplier can anticipate when truck capacity will be needed, and can schedule for it in advance.

There are several pricing issues to cover in a contract with a trucking supplier. One is the price to transport a full load. This rate should be included in the contract as a rate per mile. The contract should also include a price per cubic foot of cargo hauled, which is necessary for partial loads. This cost should also be noted on a cost-per-mile basis. These two prices are sufficient for most contracts, but a company can also add a cost to load or unload a truck, as well as special rates, such as the cost to double-team a truck so that it can drive nonstop, or the cost to use special types of trailers, such as air-ride or refrigerator trailers. These extra prices should be included in the contract for those companies that feel they have a need for the extra services.

Freight auditors are concerned with only one item on the contract, which is the percentage they take of all freight rebates found. A company can negotiate this percentage down in exchange for an exclusive deal to give all freight audit work to one supplier. Suppliers typically are in favor of this reduced-rate deal in exchange for exclusivity, because sometimes a competing supplier is given all of the large freight invoices, with another supplier getting the leftover smaller billings, from which an auditor only receives paltry earnings in exchange for much more review work. In short, freight auditors want the right to all of the biggest freight invoices, and may accept a lower percentage rate in exchange for this right.

Freight brokering has many component parts, any one of which can be outsourced to a freight broker. Most brokers want to handle a company's entire distribution process from beginning to end, but the company can insist on just outsourcing a portion of it. If so, the contract should note the pricing that applies to each piece of the distribution system that is handed to the freight broker. For example, there may be separate pricing structures for bond negotiation, duty drawback negotiation, and hazardous materials certification. If the company anticipates keeping some of the administration of its distribution system under its control, the contract with a freight broker must include a finer level of pricing detail than would normally be the case.

A freight broker prefers to pay all bills from subcontractors on behalf of a company and then issue a single billing to the company for all of the services it has provided, which includes the billings that it has already paid. The problem with this approach is that the broker marks up all of these billings, so that the company cannot tell how much it is paying the freight broker for its services—this fee is mixed in with everything else. If a company has enough distribution volume, it may be able to convince a freight broker to list its fee separately on the final billing. Brokers do not like to do this, but a company that can promise a broker lots of business should be able to force the change. Another related contractual issue is to require the broker to open its accounting books to periodic audits of the company's internal audit team, who will compare actual subcontractor invoices to the amounts noted on the broker's billings to the company to ensure that no unauthorized markups are being made. A contract with a freight broker should require the broker to show its fee separately on billings, and allow an audit team to investigate the pricing it passes through to the company.

This section covered a number of contractual issues to consider before signing contracts with freight auditors, freight brokers, trucking suppliers, and warehousing suppliers. The primary issue is pricing, but there are other topics to consider, such as exclusive business deals, audits, and insurance.

11.3 TRANSITION ISSUES

This section covers the primary transition steps to follow when moving the materials-management function to a supplier. The rest of this chapter has assumed that there are four suppliers involved—one each for freight auditing, freight brokering, warehousing, and trucking. This section, however, assumes a specific sequence of events for off-loading all four activities, and the best way to show this sequence is to assume that all four tasks are being given to just one supplier who offers all four services. Since freight auditing is a minor task and easy to transfer, it is not noted as a separate transition step. The specific transition tasks, in sequence, are as follows:

1. *Select materials-management coordinator.* The first step in the transition process is to appoint a functional coordinator who can manage the rest of the process for the company. This transition is a long and detailed process, and requires the attention of a full-time manager for all but the smallest companies. Without someone in this position, the transition process will likely take longer to complete, have more mistakes, and cost more money.

2. *Develop supplier selection criteria.* A materials-management supplier should not be selected based on a personal relationship or through a good sales presentation. Selection should be based on an objective set of criteria, which the selection committee should use to create a numerical ranking of all candidate suppliers. The criteria should be quantitative, thereby avoiding any "touchy-feely" rankings. Examples of good selection criteria are warehouse proximity to the company, on-time delivery record, driver training record, driver accident record, preauditing capability for freight billings, proven record in moving shipments through customs in specific countries, and proven ability to assemble products into final configurations at distribution points. The contents of this list will vary based on each company's requirements, but some sort of list should be compiled in order to form a basis for selection.

3. *Compare supplier pricing to industry rates.* Besides delivery performance, a selection team ranks supplier pricing very high on its performance criteria list. After all, selecting a supplier who costs significantly more than the in-house staff is a decision that will not go over well with company management. The pricing comparison should first establish benchmark average pricing for the industry, as well as low and high pricing ranges. This information can either be obtained from a survey or a benchmarking company. The selection team should then create an average set of materials-management transactions, weighted more heavily for those transactions that will be used most frequently, and come up with a total price based on the pricing tables for each of the candidate suppliers. The resulting summary prices should be compared to the benchmark rates to see how well each supplier fares in relation not only to its competitors but to the average market rates. If the entire group of candidates has exceptionally high pricing, the selection team should consider broadening the number of suppliers under consideration to see what kind of service can be obtained at lower price levels.

4. *Inspect supplier warehouses.* An inspection of supplier warehouses should always be part of the selection process. The selection team should investigate the adequacy of fire-suppression systems, safety features, and insurance coverage. Supplier assurances are not sufficient in this area; only an on-site inspection is sufficient to be sure that these important criteria are being met.

5. *Inspect supplier commercial driver's license (CDL) records.* It is important to know if a possible trucking supplier has drivers with poor accident records. This information is available through the supplier's commercial driver's license activity reports, which must be kept on file by the supplier and should be reviewed by the selection team. Poor driver performance can impact the delivery of a company's goods, and is a sign of either poor driver hiring practices or inadequate driver training.

6. *Inspect supplier delivery records.* One of the primary criteria for hiring a trucking supplier or freight broker is its ability to get materials to the appro-

priate place at the right time. The selection team can get a good idea of a prospective supplier's ability to do this by going to one of its reference companies and comparing the actual ship dates in that company's distribution database to the dates when it was ready for shipment, to see how long it takes for the supplier to take delivery. The selection team can also review the supplier's shipping records to see how long it takes to transport a selection of deliveries. When this information is compared for the different candidate suppliers, there will typically be significant differences among the candidates.

7. *Check supplier references.* A short on-site review of a supplier's operations will not always yield a clear picture of a supplier's performance. Another way to get this information is through reference checks. The selection team should use a standard questionnaire for talks with all references, so that there is a good basis for comparison between all of the references. Also, the references supplied will be the supplier's best customers, and are bound to give sterling references; however, the company wants to find out about the supplier customers that were *not* put on the reference list, and who therefore may have had less pleasant experiences with the supplier. To get the names of these customers, the selection team can look through trade magazines for clues and can ask the references if they are aware of any other customers of the supplier. These additional references can provide far more relevant information than the original references.

8. *Select supplier.* Based on its review of supplier facilities, equipment, performance records, and references, the company can now make an informed decision to select a supplier. However, this should not be a qualitative decision. Instead, the selection team should assign weighting to each of its selection criteria and score each supplier candidate on each of those criteria. The supplier with the highest score should be given the company's business. If there are other reasons for selecting a supplier who does not have the highest score, the selection team should at least use the mathematical scoring approach to eliminate the worst suppliers from the selection process.

9. *Finalize the contract.* Once the supplier has been selected, the supplier must be given time to conduct a thorough review of the company's materials-management systems. This gives it enough information to determine the company's actual requirements, which may vary from the ones the supplier was told about when it was first brought into the selection process. Once the supplier has this information, it is in a much better position to negotiate a final contract with the company, one that is based on realistic knowledge and expectations by both parties.

10. *Test and install computer linkages.* A more sophisticated company may have computer linkages to its own warehouses and internal freight-brokerage departments that link these functions to the company's manufacturing requirements planning and distribution resource planning databases, allowing them

to plan in advance for shipments and warehouse capacity needs. This same information should be made available to the supplier by creating, installing, and maintaining terminal access to the same information. This can be a lengthy process to install and debug such a system (depending on the use of customized interfaces), so it is best to begin work on these computer linkages as soon as the contract is finalized.

11. *Verify that insurance covers inventory move.* Many insurance policies only cover the transport of a maximum dollar value of inventory being moved at one time. During the move to a new warehouse, this amount will be vastly exceeded, so there may be some risk that damage incurred while in transit will not be covered by the company's insurance policy. This potential problem should be investigated in advance and special insurance coverage purchased to ensure coverage of any shortfall noted in the company's primary insurance policy.

12. *Prepare inventory for shipment.* A company may have very fragile inventory items, such as glassware or electronic components, that require special packaging prior to transport to a new warehouse facility. If so, all of this inventory must be properly packaged prior to the scheduled transfer date. In addition, each item must be properly identified, possibly with a bar-coded label, to ensure that it is stored in the correct location once it has been unloaded at the new location. This may require advance planning by a company team that prepositions inventory in exact bin locations at the new warehouse, and then labels the new location code on each inventory item prior to shipment so that it can be taken directly to the correct location and stored as soon as it is unloaded from the trailer.

13. *Move inventory to supplier warehouses.* Once the warehousing contract has been signed, the company must arrange to transfer its inventory to a supplier warehouse. This requires advance planning, since the company must arrange for a sufficient number of trucks to be on hand for the move and enough staff to load the trucks. It must also coordinate with the computer services department, which must transfer the warehouse location codes for all of the moved inventory to the new warehouse location. This keeps any inventory from being lost in the database, which could cause disruptions in those activities (such as a materials requirements planning system) that must know where the inventory is located.

14. *Inspect moved inventory.* Once inventory has been moved, there will probably be some damage, no matter how carefully the inventory may have been transported. If so, the company should find out the extent of the damage immediately so that it can replace those items before the company needs them and finds that they are not usable. Damage may not be immediately apparent when inventory is stored in shipping crates, so the inspection team should look for evidence of damage, such as broken crates, damaged packaging,

damaged pallets, or leaks on or beneath the packaging. Any items showing such problems should be opened and checked for damage.

15. *Transfer staff.* The supplier may be taking on some of the company's staff. This can include warehouse personnel, internal freight-brokerage clerks, freight auditors, and members of the company's trucking fleet and truck-maintenance staffs. The transfer should be conducted with an emphasis on making it as painless as possible for the staff being moved. Accordingly, there should be a single meeting with each employee in which representatives from the company and supplier mutually go over all payroll and human resources forms with each employee and answer any questions. In addition, the representatives should make themselves available for further questions by employees on several occasions.

16. *Conduct shipper delivery test.* A company with a large transport network will not take the risk of dumping the entire thing on a newly selected supplier. Instead, it is wiser to conduct a test of the supplier's ability by transferring to it one small piece of the company's materials-management system—perhaps responsibility for a specific distribution route or for the distribution of a specific product—before handing over the rest of the company's distribution network. This test should include frequent measurements of the supplier's performance, plus feedback of these measurements to the supplier and many meetings to go over and resolve problems.

17. *Transfer all shipments to supplier.* Once the supplier has proved that it can provide quality trucking service based on the shipper delivery test, the company can transfer its remaining business to the supplier. If the company's distribution system is large, however, it may be more prudent to use a gradual transfer, slowly moving new routes to the supplier, until the company is assured that the supplier is adequately handling all of the company's transport needs.

18. *Dispose of excess assets.* There may be a large number of warehouses, tractors, and trailers left over when a complete transition has been made. Much of the warehouse space probably cannot be converted to other uses, since there may a great deal of it, so it must be sold. The trucking fleet also has no other uses, and probably must be disposed of. If the facilities or trucks are in poor condition, the amount realized from sale may be small, even less than book value, resulting in a one-time loss to the company.

The above list detailed the transition process to follow when transferring the materials-management function to an integrated supplier of all materials-management functions. There is a heavy emphasis during the transition on selecting the right supplier, which calls for reviewing the safety, storage, maintenance, and delivery records of all prospective suppliers. The transition once the selection has been made is a careful one, involving extra planning before moving any inventory and only a

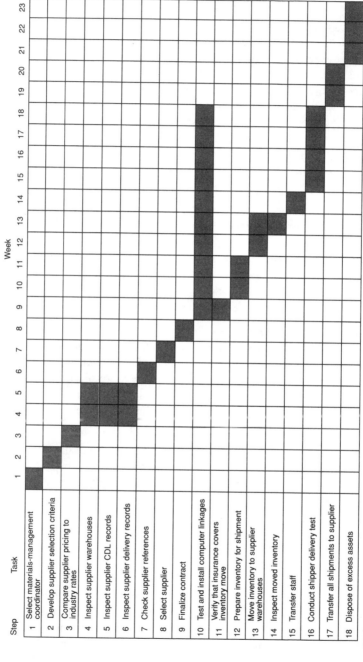

Figure 11.1 Gantt Chart for the Implementation of All Materials Management Transition Issues

gradual transfer of the trucking business to ensure that there are no disruptions within the company's distribution system. These steps are noted in Figure 11.1. The timing of the transition shown in Figure 11.1 can vary greatly depending on the size and complexity of a company's materials-management function.

11.4   CREATING CONTROL POINTS

This section covers the controls that are available for ensuring that a company's freight auditing, freight brokering, warehousing, and trucking suppliers are doing their jobs correctly.

Once a company has been using freight auditors for a sufficient period of time, it knows roughly what percentage of freight expenses will be reclaimed from trucking suppliers based on the efforts of these suppliers. If this percentage suddenly drops, it is a prime indicator that the supplier is not doing its job, frequently because it has a new, less-trained staff person reviewing the company's freight billings. If this percentage drop occurs, the functional coordinator should immediately contact the supplier to see if there has been a staffing change, and request that more experienced supplier staff be put on the company's billing reviews. The best control over a freight auditor is examining changes in the percentage of freight expenses recovered.

A key control over a freight broker is a close examination of the time it takes for the broker to move a company's shipments through customs. In some countries, a delay can clearly be the fault of the government, but a series of delays at customs for shipments managed by the same broker is a clear indication of incorrect paperwork being used to move those shipments through customs. The delay will continue as long as it takes for the broker to reissue new forms to the local customs representatives. The best way to spot this problem is to track the date on which a shipment arrived in customs (information easily obtained from the shipping supplier) and the date when the shipment left customs (which is contained in the completed customs documentation, and must be requested from the broker). If there is a significant difference between the two dates, the functional coordinator should discuss the issue with the supplier to see what happened. The interval when a shipment stays in customs is an indicator of the efficiency of the freight broker.

Another control over a freight broker is a careful and continuing comparison of freight costs charged by the broker to the market rates. This review can either be conducted internally or by a third party that specializes in freight audits. In either case, any significant departures from the market rates are indicative of overpricing by the broker or of a lack of investigation of alternative freight pricing by the broker. Major variances should be brought to the attention of the supplier by the functional coordinator.

There are several controls that a company should use when it has a warehousing supplier. One is to periodically review the supplier's insurance policy to ensure that it covers all company-owned inventory stored in its facilities. The inventory is probably already covered by the company's own insurance policy, but this secondary coverage gives the company's insurance company a means of collecting on any losses from another insurance company, which keeps its insurance costs down. The company should also arrange to have a safety review of the warehouse, with particular attention paid to the adequacy of any fire-suppression systems. These systems must be sufficient to protect the company's inventory. Another control is to investigate any complaints about damage to delivered products to see if the damage was caused when the inventory was stored in the warehouse. A continuing problem with inventory damage is clear grounds for the dismissal of the supplier. A final control over warehousing is to audit the warehouse billing each month to verify that the correct amounts were billed. This audit should include a review of the actual square footage used to verify that this was the amount of space for which the company was charged. Also, the price per square foot should be compared to the contractual rate to ensure that the supplier is charging the correct rate. Any variances in any of these controls should be brought to the attention of the functional coordinator, who can have them fixed by the supplier.

The primary controls over trucking suppliers are for damaged goods, on-time delivery, and pricing. Damaged goods can be easily tracked if inventory is inbound to a company, since the receiving staff will spot the damage and report it to the functional coordinator. Outbound freight damage is more difficult to spot, since the company must rely on the recipient to report any damage. On-time delivery is easy to determine for inbound freight, since the receiving staff (or receiving software) can compare the due date to the actual receipt date to spot any variances; for many companies that use just-in-time systems, early deliveries are considered to be just as bad as late deliveries, since they must be stored until needed. Once again, late deliveries on outbound shipments will primarily come to a company's attention through customer complaints, though an audit of trucker shipment logs, while time intensive, will also reveal this information. Finally, an audit team can compare freight billings to contractual rates, or have a freight auditor compare billings to published rates, to ensure that the company is being billed for the correct freight expenses. A variety of controls are available to maintain control over a trucking supplier.

This section covered the primary controls needed to monitor the performance of materials-management suppliers. These controls include trend lines, customs delay tracking, freight rate audits, customer complaints, and receiving complaints. A mix of these controls provides effective control over the materials-management function.

11.5 MEASURING THE OUTSOURCED FUNCTION

This section covers some of the more common measurements that are available for tracking the performance of materials-management suppliers. They are sorted by type of supplier: freight auditors, freight brokers, truckers, and warehouses. The freight broker measurement assumes that all freight brokerage work performed is for international shipments. There are also a pair of general measurements at the end of the list that cover the entire functional area. Each measurement description includes how to calculate the measurement, and notes any shortcoming to be aware of when using it. The measurements are as follows:

FREIGHT AUDITORS

- *Cost per dollar collected.* Freight bill auditors typically charge a flat percentage of the dollar value of all freight billings recovered from trucking suppliers. This rate may vary with the volume of billings recovered, but is typically a simple flat rate. This calculation is easy to obtain from the freight auditor's billing statement or contract with the company.

- *Recovery rate per dollar of bills reviewed.* It is important to measure the efficiency of a freight auditor, for some auditors are capable of recovering far more from trucking suppliers than others, which greatly reduces a company's freight costs. A company should put as much business as possible in the hands of the best freight auditors, and this is the measurement needed to determine who is the best. To calculate this measurement, determine the total dollar amount of freight billings given to a supplier and divide this into the total dollar amount that the freight auditor has recovered from trucking suppliers. The amount of freight billings given to the freight auditor must be of sufficient size to be a statistically valid sample; a total cluster of billings of less than $100,000 might yield inordinately high or low recovery rates.

FREIGHT BROKERS

- *Cost per mile.* A freight broker handles a number of aspects of transportation for a company's international shipments, such as arranging for ocean, truck, and air transport; temporary warehousing; duties; and customs paperwork. The freight broker can make large profits on all of these transactions by passing along a single lump-sum fee to the company, in which is buried the broker's large transaction fee. It is difficult to get a freight broker to issue a detailed billing statement to see where the various components of a company's international freight costs lie. Instead, it is easiest to take the total expense shown on the freight broker's billing statement and divide it by the cubic volume of the shipment to determine the cost per cubic foot. Then divide this amount by the total miles traveled to determine the cost per mile per cubic foot. This measurement will vary greatly by destination and mode of transport, but can be averaged to give the company a measure of a freight broker's pricing performance. It can also be tracked separately for each shipping destination to see if any individual shipments are being priced by the freight broker at higher rates than the prices of previous shipments.

- *Insurance cost per dollar shipped.* A freight broker will typically obtain insurance for each shipment made out of a country, whereas shipments within a country are usually covered by a company's annual insurance policy. To see if the rates obtained by a broker for international shipments are reasonable, determine the total cost of a shipment, break out the insurance cost from the freight billing, and divide this insurance cost by the total cost of the shipment. This rate will vary wildly depending on where the shipment is going (some countries and methods of transport being more risky than others), but can be averaged out over many shipments to spot trends in insurance costs.

TRUCKERS

- *Cost to load/unload truck.* Companies typically use their own labor to load and unload trucks that arrive at their own warehouses. Truckers not only do not participate in this process, they may also be restricted from it due to the requirements of their insurance policy, since moving cargo onto or off of a truck carries the risk of damaging the cargo. However, truckers must move the cargo if trucks are going to a trucker-owned warehousing facility for movement to another truck for transportation elsewhere. In these cases, some truckers simply waive the cost of loading and unloading the truck. If the supplier does charge for this service, the company should track the cost and compare it to market rates to see if the supplier is charging an inordinate amount for this service.

- *Full-load cost per mile.* Trucking suppliers prefer to charge base rates for full-load hauls, plus or minus a bewildering variety of special fees and discount rates. This billing structure effectively disguises the cost per mile that a load is hauled, which is the underlying measurement that the functional coordinator should use to judge the prices of a trucking supplier. One way to avoid this problem is to force the supplier to recast its billings in a cost-per-mile format. However, it takes a large company—with lots of business to give a supplier—to force this change. An easier approach is to accept supplier billings as is and divide the total cost by the number of miles traveled, which is easily obtained from a variety of distance rating guides. This calculation yields the full-load cost per mile, which is valuable for determining how competitive the pricing may be for various trucking suppliers.

- *Partial-load cost per mile.* Many companies only have enough inventory to fill a portion of a trailer, and so the above calculation for full-load costing is not of much use. Instead, the trucking supplier will charge the company based on the cubic volume of space taken up in the trailer by the company's shipments. To determine this partial-load cost, take the freight cost from the supplier billing and divide it by the cubic volume shipped to determine the cost per cubic foot shipped. Then divide this figure by the number of miles traveled, which yields the cost per mile per cubic foot shipped. A company will find that this rate varies enormously, for freight companies charge rates for partial loads that do not necessarily have any bearing on the distance traveled.

- *Trailer rental rate per month.* It is very common for a company to rent trailers from a trucking supplier for use as semipermanent storage facilities. For example, a company may have highly seasonal sales, such as the Christmas season, yet produce year-round for that sales period, resulting in large finished-goods inventory levels just before the prime sales season. Since it is expensive to own warehouse facilities that can contain the maximum amount of inventory, it is financially wiser for a company to own a small warehouse facility and supplement this space with rented trailer space that can be conveniently parked near the warehouse, effectively expanding the warehouse during the peak part of the inventory buildup. Trailer rates are per unit, per day, and can be reduced if the company rents large numbers of trailers. To calculate this measurement, extract the price per trailer from the supplier's billing statement. This rate can be tracked over a trend line to spot any variances.

WAREHOUSES

- *Cost per square foot.* Warehouses can charge a company for storage in a variety of ways that are only limited by the imagination of the warehouse operators. The typical method is to charge for square feet of space taken up by the company's inventory, but this rate can be accompanied by charges for moving the inventory within the warehouse, charges for cubic feet of space occupied (such as a fee per storage rack used), or even charges for a minimum amount of space, irrespective of the actual amount of inventory being stored. It is hard to present measurements for every variation on warehousing fees, so this section contains the basic one: the cost per square foot. The easiest way to calculate this measurement is to take it directly from the supplier's billing statements. If the statement does not contain this level of detail, an audit team can calculate the actual warehouse space used and divide this amount into the monthly fee to determine the cost per square foot.

GENERAL

- *Working capital employed.* The materials-management function can take up a startlingly large amount of working capital because of the large amount of inventory of all kinds—raw, work in process, and finished—that is used throughout a company's production and distribution functions. When these functions are outsourced, the amount of working capital not only shrinks, it almost disappears. The only reason to have any working capital employed at all in a fully outsourced environment is if the company retains stocks of finished goods for later sale, rather than only building to specific customer orders. This is one of the easiest measures to calculate. Just take the inventory figure from the balance sheet at the end of the month and track it on a trend line to monitor changes.

- *Fixed assets employed.* A large company can employ a very large amount of fixed assets in its materials-management function. Examples of fixed assets are trucks, planes, barges, and railroads purchased by a company to transport its own goods; warehouses in which to store the inventory; and forklifts to move the inventory within the storage facilities. When this function is outsourced, all of these fixed assets go away. To calculate this measurement, assign a department code to each fixed asset in the fixed asset ledger and sort the ledger by that department code to extract all assets belonging to the materials-management function. Then track this number on a trend line to monitor changes.

This section covered the measurements that can be used to track the performance of the various materials-management suppliers. It is evident that there are solid qualitative measurements available for tracking all suppliers in this area.

11.6 MANAGING THE OUTSOURCED FUNCTION

This section covers the management of the materials-management function. As usual, a functional coordinator is needed to administer the function, but the mix of skills and responsibilities differs somewhat from those needed for other functional areas.

The materials-management function is an important one, so the functional coordinator should report straight to the vice president of production. With this direct access, the coordinator has a better chance of involving top management if supplier problems are encountered that the coordinator cannot solve alone.

The functional coordinator may have to manage the activities of multiple suppliers, for only a few suppliers currently offer services that blanket the entire range of materials-management activities. Unless a company is using one of those multiservice suppliers, the coordinator will have to coordinate the activities of freight brokers, freight auditors, trucking suppliers, and warehouses. This multitude of tasks is shown in Figure 11.2. However, not all companies outsource every possible materials-management activity at once—it tends to be a more cautious advance from one task to the next. Consequently, the coordinator's real job is to direct the activities of both outside suppliers *and* inside staff.

Given the complexity of managing both inside functions and suppliers, the functional coordinator position is clearly one that requires extensive analyst support. For larger companies with hundreds or thousands of shipments in transit as well as possibly dozens of storage locations, the coordinator will need a support staff that will vary in size based on the scale of the transport and storage systems involved. This staff must not only monitor the performance of suppliers, it must also track the movement of materials through the company's supply and distribution systems. Suppliers can do this for a company, but a failure by the supplier could be fatal to the company, since a problem with inbound transport could stop the company's production, while outbound problems could stop the shipment of finished products to cus-

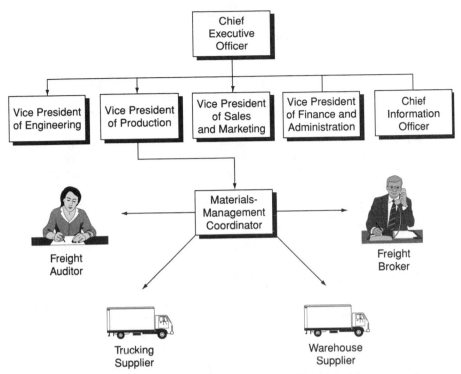

Figure 11.2 Organization Chart for Outsourcing the Materials Management
Function

tomers. Thus, given the critical nature of the supply and distribution systems, the coordinator's support staff should be actively engaged in monitoring the progress of
materials to and from the company.

The functional coordinator requires a unique set of skills. These include a general
knowledge of distribution resource planning (DRP); rates for transport by truck, rail,
ship, and airplane; as well as duties, customs paperwork, and packaging requirements. This is a discipline that is increasingly being impacted by information systems, so the coordinator should also have some knowledge of electronic data interchange (EDI), onboard computers, routing and scheduling systems, load utilization,
and dock scheduling. In addition, the coordinator must be able to manage a staff of
analysts, and possibly some in-house materials-management functions, as well as
possess the negotiation skills to settle contractual issues with suppliers. Clearly, this
is not a position for an employee trained in general management skills, but rather
one who has years of experience in the field as well as in-depth management expertise. A brief job description for this position is shown in Figure 11.3.

This section covered the management issues associated with outsourcing the
materials-management function. The key issue is the functional coordinator, who
must have exceptional knowledge of the function as well as strong management

Figure 11.3   The Materials Management Coordinator's Job Description

Employee Title: Materials-Management Outsourcing Coordinator
Reports to: Vice President of Production
Responsibilities:

- Sign off on all agreements with the materials-management suppliers.
- Authorize the release of funds for payment to suppliers.
- Monitor the flow of materials through the company's inbound and outbound transportation systems.
- Compare actual costs charged to costs listed in contracts to determine the causes of variances; follow up on these variances with each supplier.
- Measure service levels for all materials-management areas and resolve any problems.
- Supervise the extension of access to the company's distribution database to relevant suppliers.
- Manage the transfer of functions from the company to suppliers.
- Work with suppliers to upgrade the company's materials-management systems.
- Manage any tasks within the materials-management function that have been kept in-house.
- Manage the staff of analysts who monitor suppliers and the flow of materials.

skills and a support team of analysts. Only with this staffing combination can a company hope to adequately manage an outsourced materials-management function.

11.7   POTENTIAL CUSTOMER SERVICE ISSUES

There are two customer service problems associated with outsourcing the materials-management function: One is that the supplier cannot get the product to the customer on time or in the proper condition, and the other problem is that, if the supplier is performing the final assembly of the product, the assembly is poorly done, resulting in a final product of poor quality. This section covers why these problems occur and how to fix them.

The underlying cause of the first problem is surprisingly hard to determine. A product can be damaged at a warehouse (which is the fault of the warehouse supplier) or during transit to the customer (which is the fault of the trucking supplier), or it may have been damaged back at the company's production facility, in which case it was damaged by that functional group. The solution to this problem is not an easy one. The company must use an audit team to localize the problem. This means that the audit team must first review a large sample of products as they leave the production facility to see if the damage is occurring there, and then do the same at the warehouse. If products are not damaged in these locations, that leaves the trucking supplier as the culprit. An alternative approach is to review the types of damage claims coming from customers. If the damage is actually caused by poor assembly methods, the fault clearly lies with the production facility, whereas damage caused by dropping is more likely to be a transport issue. Once the source of the problem has been found, the supplier causing the problem should be given sufficient time to cure the problem. If this reprieve is not sufficient, then drop the supplier. Finding the cause of damaged products usually requires an audit team, and may result in the termination of the offending supplier.

If a product is reaching a customer too late, this is a much easier problem to resolve. Once again, appoint an audit team to track down the problem. Then obtain from the complaining customer the date on which the product arrived. Compare this to the date on which the customer expected the product to arrive in order to determine the number of days late. Then go back through the delivery process to the warehouse from which the product was shipped to find the date of shipment. If the date of shipment gave sufficient time for the product to arrive on the customer's expected date, then the problem was with the trucker, who took too long to deliver the product. However, if the warehouse did not receive the product in time to ship it, then it was not produced in time, which is the fault of the production facility. For a detailed discussion of problems with production, see the manufacturing chapter (Chapter 10). The problem may even lie further back than the production process, for component manufacturers may not be getting their products to the production facility in time for it to meet its production schedule. In this case, component suppliers are at fault and should be given a specific time period in which to cure their delivery problems—if they cannot cure the problem in that time, they should be terminated. Another possibility is that a freight broker may be at fault, since this person is in a position to misdirect a shipment or stall it in customs with incorrect documentation. An alternative to firing suppliers is to install terminals at all supplier locations in the distribution chain that are linked to the company's distribution schedule. This allows everyone to look at the most recent updates to the schedule and see if anything is late in being delivered. This method reduces problems in the distribution chain by spreading up-to-date information along it. There are many players in the distribution system, and each one can delay delivery to the final customer; possible cures are finding new suppliers and giving suppliers better delivery information.

The second problem is poor assembly of final product configurations at distribution points. When this happens, it is not always clear who is at fault, since there may be many suppliers assembling products at different distribution points, and the final product could have come from any of them. However, the source of information about bad complaints—the customer—is the solution to the problem. The customer will tell a company about bad products, and the customer can read off an identifying number from the product that identifies the final assembly point. Another approach is to have the customer tell the company the name of the distribution point, as listed on the return address. However, this is not such a good approach, since the customer may have thrown away the shipping materials by the time it realized that the product did not function properly. Once a company has identified an assembly problem, the best approach is to send in a process engineering team to track down the cause of the assembly problem and fix it. This allows a company to avoid terminating a supplier in most cases.

This section discussed how to track down the causes of late deliveries and damaged products, as well as how to deal with the problem once it has been located. Better information systems and process engineering teams can fix these problems some of the time, but a company may sometimes have to terminate a supplier and look elsewhere for better performance.

11.8 GETTING OUT OF THE OUTSOURCING ARRANGEMENT

This section covers how a company can terminate its outsourcing relationships with the various suppliers of materials-management services. Some—such as freight auditing—are quite easy to terminate, while others—such as warehousing—require considerable advance planning. The termination problems for each functional area are covered here, as are suggested solutions.

It is very simple to end a relationship with a freight-auditing supplier, since there is no long-term contract or transfer of staff or assets involved. The easiest approach is to let the freight-auditing supplier finish reviewing its current batch of freight billings, and then simply not assign them further audit work. It should not even be necessary to give them formal written notice of termination.

Freight brokers tend to work on a shipment-by-shipment basis, without any long-term contract. Once again, there is rarely any transfer of staff or assets involved, so the company simply stops sending shipment deals to the broker. No notice of termination is required.

It is more difficult to get out of an outsourcing deal with a warehousing supplier. The major reason is that the company must find an alternate location for its inventory. This requires time to line up alternate facilities as well as to find trucks and work crews to transport the inventory to the new locations. Other suppliers may also have to be notified so that they discontinue shipping to the warehouses of the supplier being terminated. Also, the supplier is unlikely to allow any movement of inventory out of its facility until the company pays all outstanding invoices. An additional problem stemming from the contract is that some companies sign long-term deals with warehousing suppliers based on unusually low storage rates in exchange for minimum payments that must be made to the supplier, even if the company is not using as much storage space as it is entitled to under the terms of the agreement. These deals can be difficult to get out of, and sometimes require a termination payment. Thus, ending a warehousing relationship is more difficult, due to contractual problems and the effort required to move the inventory.

It is relatively easy to get out of an outsourcing deal with a trucking supplier. If the company does not have a formal outsourcing agreement, it is a simple matter of not assigning further business to the trucker after its last shipment was completed. However, if the company has signed a long-term exclusive agreement with a trucking supplier, the company will likely have to give written notice of termination to the supplier, as well as wait a designated time (such as 90 days) for the supplier to attempt to cure any problems noted by the company in its termination notice. Also, an exclusive contract at low prices is based on the supplier's expectation that the company will give it such a large volume of business that it can offer lower prices; if the contract is terminated, this volume will not appear, so there may be a termination payment that adjusts the freight costs upwards for those services already billed at the low rates. The biggest potential problem is if a company has sold its trucking fleet to a supplier as part of the initial outsourcing deal. If the deal is terminated, the supplier may want to sell the equipment back to the company or, conversely, the company may want to buy it back. This option should be covered in the original contract, including a depreciation calculation for determining the prices at which the tractors and trailers will be returned. Thus, depending on the terms of the original outsourcing contract, it may be more difficult to withdraw from a trucking outsourcing deal.

Some companies have extended their computer systems to their warehouse and trucking suppliers. This gives them direct access to the company distribution planning software, which they can use to schedule shipments and deliveries. This is a very efficient way to handle the distribution function, but becomes a problem when suppliers are terminated, for the company must transfer the computer access to new suppliers, train them in its use, and monitor their activity to ensure that they are using it properly. While not technically difficult, this is not an overnight proposition—it takes time to train new personnel and make sure that they are using the software appropriately. Thus, a company must schedule sufficient time prior to a termination to bring new suppliers up to speed on the use of its information systems.

This section noted the ease of termination for the freight-brokering and freight-audit functions, as well as the range of problems that may be encountered when terminating a warehousing supplier. Trucking suppliers are a particular problem if they have purchased a company's trucking fleet and want to return it at the time of termination. It is also important to extend access to a company's distribution-management database to new suppliers prior to terminating old suppliers. This section highlighted the most common problems encountered when terminating materials-management suppliers and suggested solutions to those problems.

11.9 SUMMARY

This chapter covered the outsourcing of the materials-management function. This encompasses several functions: freight auditing, freight brokering, trucking, and warehousing. The chapter assumes that each function is handled by a different supplier, but this is not necessarily the case—some suppliers are now offering a complete, integrated materials-management service. The advantages and disadvantages of outsourcing were noted, with particular benefits accruing from the reduction in fixed assets and the gain in materials-management expertise, while problems could develop if a supplier proves to be less capable than expected. Contractual issues centered around pricing and how it could be improved based on transaction volumes and exclusivity agreements. Transitional issues include moving inventory to supplier warehouses and checking the performance records of trucking suppliers. A mix of controls are available, such as costing and complaint trend lines, delay tracking, and freight rate audits. Measurements are almost entirely concerned with the cost of services provided, while the return on assets is also strongly impacted when the fixed assets used for in-house transportation and storage are eliminated. The function requires a functional coordinator to not only manage suppliers, but to manage any parts of the function that have been retained as in-house departments. The potential danger of outsourcing materials management is that customer service may suffer, since products may be delivered late or be damaged when they are delivered. Finally, terminating a trucking supplier is a problem if the company has already eliminated its in-house fleet, while planning is needed before terminating a warehousing supplier, since the company's inventory must be moved from the supplier's warehouses. In short, the materials-management function is slowly being consolidated and improved by outsourcers who offer convenient, cost-effective service to companies. The benefits of using them strongly outweigh the negatives.

CHAPTER TWELVE

Outsourcing the Sales and Marketing Functions

Many companies already outsource portions of their sales and marketing functions. This trend is likely to expand as new areas of specialization arise within the area. Outsourcing has been common for many years in the areas of public relations, advertising, distribution, and outside sales, and two of the newer areas that are increasingly being outsourced are telemarketing and direct mail. The public relations and advertising areas have been outsourced for so long because these suppliers have been able to prove for a long time that their expertise is better than what most companies can create within their ranks. Telemarketing and direct mail suppliers are now proving that they also have more expertise in their fields than most companies, though their expertise is not founded on creative talent, as is the case with public relations and advertising suppliers, but rather on management skill and technical expertise that allows them to expertly manage difficult services in a cost-effective manner. The rise of these two new service areas allows a company to outsource a large part of its sales and marketing function.

This chapter discusses the advantages and disadvantages of outsourcing the sales and marketing function, as well as the key contractual issues to be aware of when negotiating contracts with suppliers. It also covers the transition steps to follow when shifting a function to a supplier, as well as how to control, measure, and manage the supplier once the transition has been completed. It finishes by noting several potential customer service issues and how to prevent them, as well as noting several points to consider when contemplating the termination of a supplier's outsourcing contract. This chapter is intended to give the reader an overview of the key issues to consider when outsourcing the sales and marketing function.

12.1 ADVANTAGES AND DISADVANTAGES

This section describes the advantages and disadvantages of outsourcing the various sales and marketing functions to suppliers. Advantages and disadvantages for each function are grouped together in order to give the reader easy access to both sides of the outsourcing decision.

There are two advantages to outsourcing the advertising function. One is that a company can do away with the fixed cost of having an in-house staff by replacing it with the variable cost of a supplier. By reducing the amount of fixed costs, a company can reduce its break-even point. The other advantage is that a large advertising agency can call upon a large pool of creative talent to design the company's advertising campaign, which may result in a higher-quality advertising product than would otherwise be the case if the function were left in-house. These advantages are offset by the higher cost of an advertising supplier, whose fees are normally substantially higher than those of an in-house staff.

As was the case with advertising, a company can reduce some of its fixed costs by shifting its public relations work to a supplier, who only charges for the time spent working on the company's behalf. A public relations agency also has better media contacts than most in-house staffs, and is usually quite responsive to a company's short-term publicity needs. Offsetting these advantages is the supplier's lack of knowledge of the company's industry and product line, which may appear in any publicity releases issued by the supplier. A company can avoid this problem by reviewing all publicity documents before they are released, as well as by training the supplier with management interviews and facility tours.

There are several good reasons for using a telemarketing supplier, which is why this field of outsourcing has increased so rapidly in the last decade. The most important advantage is that a supplier is far better than most companies at setting up and managing a call center. Creating a call center and staffing it with, in many cases, thousands of new employees is a task that would bog down the management of most companies, but which a reputable supplier has long experience in handling. By giving this function to a supplier, a company can focus its limited management resources in other, more productive areas. Also, a company can avoid the capital cost of building a call center, thus releasing funds for other uses. In addition, a telemarketing supplier has greater experience than most companies in writing the scripts used to solicit sales. These enhanced scripts can lead to more sales per call. Also, a global telemarketer has employees who can make calls in more than one language, which gives a company the ability to sell in parts of the world or in ethnic communities that it has not previously accessed. The final advantage is that, unlike inbound customer service calls, there is less need to give call center employees access to a company's database to answer company queries—a practice that presents a computer security risk. Instead, the company will have to give access to nothing more than its order-entry system for outbound call centers. Offsetting these strong advantages are several disadvantages. One is the higher variable cost per call of the supplier, whose prices are high because it must pass through to the company its profit margin and the capital cost of its call centers. Another problem is that the company does not have direct control over the people making the calls, so it is possible that customers will be turned off by these callers. This last problem is controllable by ensuring that the supplier has an active call-monitoring program that reviews caller conversations with the company's customers and immediately corrects any problems. In short, the expertise of a telemarketing supplier as well as the lower capital and fixed costs resulting from outsourcing telemarketing must be weighed against the higher variable fees and reduced amount of direct control over the calls being made.

There are several solid advantages to using a distribution supplier. One is that the company no longer has to invest in its own inventory, service facilities, or sales staff in the distributor's area, which allows it to concentrate its funds elsewhere. Also, the company vastly reduces its need to focus management attention on sales in the distributor's region, allowing it to work on other problems and opportunities. The distributor also very likely already has a solid base of customers to whom it can sell the company's product line, which eliminates the company's need to establish customer contacts in the distributor's territory. This also means that the company can achieve higher sales levels more quickly, since it does not have to spend time building up its customer base. Finally, the decision to outsource to a distributor does not have to be a permanent one—a company can always terminate the relationship at a later date, when sales levels have risen to the point where the company feels it can make more money by selling direct. Several crucial disadvantages must be considered before proceeding with the outsourcing decision, however. One is that a distributor may sell several competing lines of products, so the company may not sell as much through the distributor as it might by selling its own products exclusively. This problem can be avoided by insisting that its distributors carry no competing products from other companies. Another problem is that a distributor sells those products that give it the highest margins. If a company does not offer a distributor a sufficiently large discount, it may carry the product line but not go out of its way to sell it, resulting in poor sales. Finally, a company gives up some of its profits by giving discounts to distributors. In short, a distributor can provide an immediate customer base as well as sales and service facilities at zero cost to a company, though at the cost of competing with the distributor's other products and giving up some profits through discounts offered to the distributor.

There are solid advantages to outsourcing the sales force, but a significant disadvantage as well. One advantage is that a company pays no base salary to an outside salesperson—that person must subsist on nothing but commissions, with the exception of occasional market-development funds. This means that a company can cut into its fixed sales costs by converting them to variable costs that are not incurred unless the salesperson sells product. Another advantage is that an outside salesperson is most useful in faraway regions or ones with low sales volume that a company cannot afford to pay a full-time employee to occupy. Finally, an outside salesperson is most useful in other countries, where someone must speak the local language and know the customs, but where the company cannot afford the expense of maintaining its own staff. The problem with outsourcing the sales staff, however, is that the commission paid to these people is usually much higher than the amount paid to an in-house staff. This is because the in-house staff is normally paid a small base salary as well, and also receives reimbursement for its travel and entertainment expenses. The commissions for outside salespeople may be so high that they exceed the cost that a company would have expended on an in-house sales staff, and may even cut seriously into the company's product margins, resulting in fewer profits. Consequently, the reduced fixed cost and increased geographical range of using an outside sales staff must be balanced against the size of the commissions paid.

This section described the advantages and disadvantages of outsourcing all of the sales and marketing functions. Outsourcing tends to reduce fixed costs and capital investments, while also giving a company immediate access to high-grade advertising, public relations, mailing, and telemarketing services, as well as a customer base through distributors. These powerful advantages are counterbalanced by the increased variable cost of using supplier services, as well as by the reduced loyalty of the salespeople and distributors, who may be selling the products of other companies, too.

12.2   CONTRACT-SPECIFIC ISSUES

This section covers contractual issues to keep in mind when finalizing agreements with sales and marketing suppliers.

It is common for public relations suppliers, and sometimes advertising suppliers as well, to operate on a retainer basis. This means that the company must pay a fee in advance for work to be performed by the supplier. This may be acceptable at the start of a relationship, when the supplier is uncertain of the company's ability to pay its bills, but it is unacceptable once the outsourcing relationship has been underway for some time, and the company has proven its creditworthiness to the supplier. It is an especially galling requirement for large companies who already have a proven financial record. Thus, it is reasonable for a company to allow no more than an initial retainer payment to a supplier, with the supplier reverting to normal credit terms once the initial retainer has been drawn down. The only exception is companies with a poor credit record.

A public relations company is normally paid by the hour. This hourly rate should be included in the contract. Since there may be several hourly rates for different job levels within the public relations company, the contract should specify an hourly rate for each one. The supplier can get around this restriction by shifting all work to its most expensive people or by promoting those of its employees working on the company's account to a higher pay level. This problem can be avoided outside of the contract by having the functional coordinator for sales and marketing regularly meet with the supplier to go over the mix of staff levels that are assigned to the company's account, which may result in changes to the mix. The contract with a public relations supplier should include hourly rates for each staff position at the supplier.

It is common for an advertising supplier to be paid not on an hourly basis, but as a percentage of the advertising work that it supervises. For example, it may charge 10% of the expense of all television advertising that it supervises. It can either collect subcontractor bills itself, pay them, and forward an inflated invoice to the company, or it can just send its own fee to the company as a separate billing. This arrangement pushes an advertising supplier in the direction of television advertising, since these ads are more expensive, resulting in larger fees for the supplier to charge the company. There are several ways to get around this problem, all of which can be included in the contract. The first is to stipulate a percentage distribution of funds among various types of advertising media. Another is to reduce the supplier's billing percentage on the more expensive types of advertising. Either change will keep the supplier from directing the company's money into the most expensive types of advertising. These contract modifications will keep advertising expenses within budget and will not inflate payments to the supplier.

An outside salesperson should be paid on a commission basis only. It is dangerous to also pay for the salesperson's travel expenses, for these can be abused. At most, a travel and entertainment allowance should only be paid when a salesperson is starting out, in order that he or she has sufficient resources to develop a sales territory. Even in this limited situation, it is best to include in the contract a provision to have the allowance deducted from future commission payments. A good salesperson will be more than willing to work for nothing more than a commission, as long as the commission is large enough. The size of the commission is the key subject of negotiation. It is invariably larger than what is paid to an inside salesperson, since that individual is usually also paid a base salary and reimbursed for travel and entertainment costs. Since the outside salesperson has none of this extra compensation, the commission must be large enough to offset these payments. The exact amount of the commission is normally the same for all outside salespeople, with override payments for sales regions in which sales are particularly difficult to secure. Thus, the key contractual issue for an outside salesperson is the size of the commission percentage as well as any extra payments.

A company has a number of commission payment options if it terminates the contract with an outside salesperson. One possibility is to pay all remaining commissions at the time of termination, even though the company would not otherwise be obligated to do so until sales were finalized. Another option is to immediately pay the salesperson a final payment that is less than the full amount, the reasoning being that the salesperson might not otherwise be paid for a long time (especially if the company's sales cycle was long) and that the company wants to cover itself in case any sales later result in bad debts. A final option is to wait until sales are completed on all open sales made by the terminated salesperson and make the final commission payment at that time. One of these options may appeal to a company more than others, based on the customary commission structure in the industry and the length of the company's sales cycle—if the cycle is very short, there is no need to delay payments. Several commission payment plans are possible in the event of termination; whichever plan a company adopts should be itemized in the sales contract.

A distributor expects to be given a territory. This can be as large as several states or as small as a few blocks in a city. The expectation is reasonable if the distributor has done a good job of developing sales and increasing revenues. If not, the company should not continue to give the distributor its own territory. This can be noted in the distributor contract by specifying a territory, but noting that the territory boundaries will be reviewed periodically by the company and adjusted based on the performance of the distributor. What that performance may be tends to be left vague in most distributor agreements, which gives the company room to terminate the distributor and either take over sales in the region or give them to someone else. Giving a distributor an exclusive territory is fine, but the contract must give the company the option to take it away.

A distributor expects to be given a discount on product sales. A company normally has a standard discount rate that applies to sales to all of its distributors. There are federal laws that prevent a company from showing favor to a particular distributor through unusually high discounts, so a flat, across-the-board discount rate is typical. However, it is quite legal to give additional discounts for volume purchases. Rather than have the contract include the exact baseline discount rate and additional discounts based on volume, it should state that the distributor will be subject to the company's standard schedule of distributor discount rates. This provision allows the company to change its discount schedule at will, without having to renegotiate the contracts with all of its distributors every time it wants to change the percentages. Thus, the contract should refer to the company's standard distributor discount schedule.

A company should be allowed reasonable grounds for terminating a distributor. To do this, the contract should note that the contract is immediately voided if the distributor files for bankruptcy protection. In addition, the contract can state that the company has the option to terminate the distributorship agreement if the supplier has a poor payment history. In order to avoid wrangling in court over what this means, the contract should state the exact number of days overdue for an average of all invoices, and the minimum time period over which this condition must exist in order to give the company grounds for termination. The reasons for distributor termination should be clearly stated in the contract.

In case of termination, a distributor will want to return to the company all of its inventory and be paid back at the original purchase price. The company does not have to allow this return of inventory since, in most cases, it sold the inventory to the distributor with no right of return. If the original sale was actually on consignment or with an unlimited right of return, then the company must take back the inventory, though this is an unusual circumstance. On the other hand, the company may want the inventory back to restock its own shelves. If so, the contract should include a provision that allows the company to pick from the distributor's stocks those items that it wants to repurchase. Also, the repurchase should be subject to a restocking fee. In addition, the company can specify that the distributor will be paid back at the current distributor cost for each part (less the restocking fee); this avoids any arguments about paying back at the original price paid—as the sale may have been years before, this would require large amounts of research to discover. The contract should note any rights of inventory return in case of termination, as well as restocking fees and prices to be paid.

A company may want to get its telemarketing program on-line in a hurry. This is usually the case if the company is linking the telemarketing to advertising programs that are rolling out on the same date. If so, it can include a provision in the contract that pays the telemarketing supplier a bonus based on the number of days by which it can beat a target date to have a call center operational. This provision can also be extended to penalties that go into effect if the call center is operational too late. The contract should note the target date on which to be operational, as well as the daily bonus or penalty.

A telemarketing company has several fee structures, all of which should be specified in the contract. One option is to charge the company a flat fee for each call made. This is usually linked to a minimum fee per month, which reduces the supplier's risk in case it has built a call center and hired staff for it, and then has a minimal number of calls to make. Another option is to pay the supplier a percentage of all sales brought in through telemarketing sales. This option is preferable for those companies that have little spare cash to pay telemarketers, though the percentage of sales the supplier keeps is normally more than the company would pay the supplier on a per-call basis. The supplier may also require a termination fee if the company ends the contract before a minimum amount of time has passed. This fee is justified if the supplier has invested in building a call center for the company, and must recoup its investment. The monthly fee structure and any termination fees should be included in the contract with a telemarketing supplier.

An issue that arises with both telemarketing and direct mail suppliers is the return of mailing lists if the contract is terminated. This is less of a problem with a telemarketing supplier, unless the company has given the supplier its only copy of its contact list and is not able to reconstruct it without great expense. The main problem is when a direct mail supplier keeps the mailing list for all contacts to whom mail has not yet been sent. This is a problem because a company normally buys its mailing lists from marketers of contact lists. These lists are frequently supplied in label format, with the stipulation that the labels not be copied—they can be used just once, and then the company must purchase a replacement contact list. Therefore, it is important for a company to avoid the expense of buying a new mailing list by retrieving its old one from the supplier.

When a direct mail company is terminated, it will probably have in its possession the master "camera ready" copies of the company's direct mail pieces. Since the company may want to use these master copies again for other mailings, the contract should specify that the supplier is required to hand over all master copies at the time of termination. It is not acceptable if the supplier adds a clause stating that it will only hand over these materials after all bills have been paid, since the supplier could inflate the final billing to the extent that the company is essentially paying a ransom to obtain the master copies. In short, a direct mail contract must state that master copies be returned at the time of termination.

This section covered the key contractual issues to keep in mind when outsourcing the various sales and marketing functions. As always, pricing is an issue—hourly rates, minimum rates, commissions, percentages of expenditures, penalties, bonuses, and retainer fees are all negotiable items in this functional area. In addition, a company must be aware of several contract termination issues, such as termination payments to telemarketing suppliers, retrieving mailing master copies from direct mail suppliers, recovering mailing lists from telemarketing and direct mail suppliers, and dealing with returned inventory from distributors. Particular attention to the methods of supplier compensation will prevent later trouble with sales and marketing suppliers.

12.3   TRANSITION ISSUES

This section covers the transition of the sales and marketing functions to suppliers. Since there are many suppliers covered in this section, it is not possible to include a Gantt chart for the transition, as was the case in other chapters where only a single supplier was taking on the company's work. The transition steps for distributors and telemarketers include the selection of the supplier, though this is not really part of the transition process—the reason for its inclusion is to highlight the importance of selecting the right supplier in these two areas. When reviewed together, this section is unusual in that, because they are so different, there are very few transition steps that are common to the transitions for all of the functional areas. The transition process for a distributor bears little resemblance to the transition for a direct mail supplier.

The transition to a public relations supplier is relatively straightforward. The transition hinges on educating the supplier in the company's previous public relations work and in giving it a good knowledge of the company's industry and products. One of the easiest ways to transfer this knowledge is to transfer the company's in-house public relations staff, which already knows the company, to the supplier. Another approach is to have representatives from the public relations supplier meet a selection of company managers who can give the supplier a good overview of the company's operations. This can include tours of a selection of company facilities. This background gives the supplier a better foundation of knowledge to draw upon when dealing with the media on behalf of the company.

There are several steps a company should go through when transitioning some of its business to a distributor. The steps are as follows:

1. *Select supplier.* The company should select a distributor based on several factors, such as its reputation in the marketplace, ability to generate sales, financial standing, and service capabilities.

2. *Assign territory.* Some industries do not make a practice of assigning territories to distributors. However, if a company does intend to assign a territory, it must keep in mind the impact of this new territory on sales in surrounding territories that have been assigned to other suppliers. Other suppliers in neighboring territories should be contacted as a courtesy so that they will know who is being given the distributorship. This also gives the other suppliers a chance to protest the size of the distributorship being granted. The size is dependent not only on the presence of nearby territories, but also on the ability of the new distributor to service the entire territory being granted. If the distributor is small, it may be better for customers if the company splits the territory into smaller pieces that can go to several distributors, thereby giving customers better service.

3. *Provide training.* A distributor must know something about the key sales points of a company's product line, as well as how they are to be serviced. A company can address this problem by either sending a training team to the distributor or by having distributor employees come to the company. It is frequently better to have the distributor send its people to the company if the size of the product line makes it difficult to bring it to the distributor location for a training session.

4. *Monitor performance.* A company should maintain tight control over its distributors once they have begun selling the company's product. This control focuses on revenues earned by the distributor. The time required to ramp up to the sales level of an established distributor will vary by industry, and a company should make allowances for low sales during this period. Later on, however, the company should respond to reduced sales with immediate inquiries regarding a distributor's efforts to sell its products.

The transition for an outside salesperson is much easier than is the case for a distributor. First, there is less need to carefully select the salesperson, since it is easier to replace a salesperson than it is a distributor. Second, there may be no territory to assign to each salesperson, and if there is one, it is frequently smaller than one that is issued to a distributor (since the distributor may have many salespeople who can service a larger territory). Third, there is minimal training to be concerned about with a salesperson, since the salesperson is not expected to service the product, as a distributor would. Instead, the salesperson can come to the company location to receive enough elementary training to be able to sell the product. Thus, the transition to an outside salesperson is much easier than the transition to a distributor.

There are several well-defined steps that a company must go through when transferring its telemarketing function to a supplier. They are as follows:

1. *Select supplier.* A company can select a telemarketing supplier based on a variety of criteria, such as price, call-monitoring capability, experience in the company's industry, or ability to create and staff a call center very quickly. It is up to the company to pick a supplier based on which of these (or other) criteria are most important.

2. *Determine setup time.* The new supplier must meet with the functional coordinator and go over the size of the call list that the company proposes using, as well as the time period over which the company expects to have the calls completed. This tells the supplier what kind of call center and employee capacity it needs to handle the company's requirements. The supplier should then calculate the time it needs to set up a call center to meet the company's requirements. The company and supplier may debate the requirements for a short time, which allows the supplier to modify its assumptions and change its setup times.

3. *Transfer staff.* If the company has been running its own call center, it may want to shut it down and transfer the staff over to the supplier. If so, representatives

from the supplier and company should work together to meet with the employees to be transferred. These meetings should cover any issues the employees wish to talk about and also sign up the employee for the supplier's payroll and benefit systems. Each employee should be given as much time as necessary for all questions to be answered.

4. *Set up scripting and related training programs.* Based on its experience in the industry, the supplier will create a call script that each employee of the call center will use to contact customers. This script is then linked to a training program that teaches employees how to handle variations in customer responses.

5. *Set up and approve capture format.* If the supplier is taking orders or other information over the phone, it must have some computer or paper-based format to capture this information. The exact layout is frequently of concern to the supplier—since it wants the most efficient use of its employees' time—and by the company, since it wants the information recorded in a format that will be accepted by its computer systems.

6. *Approve script.* The supplier sends the proposed script to the functional coordinator, who may alter it based on knowledge of the company's customers, its products, or the industry. The coordinator does not approve the supplier's training program, since this is derived from the script, which *is* approved by the coordinator.

7. *Obtain call list.* A company does not always call customers from its own call list. If it wants new customers, it purchases a call list from a call list broker. The supplier can take care of this purchase on the company's behalf.

8. *Conduct test calls.* Despite all parties' best efforts, it is possible that the scripting is not adequate. The best way to find out is to conduct a test with a small number of calls to customers. These calls should be closely monitored by management to see what problems arise. Another option is to try several test scripts and go with the one that has the best customer response rates. The supplier and functional coordinator should jointly alter the script as necessary after this test has been completed.

9. *Fully implement the call program.* Once all testing is complete, the call center can go ahead with full-scale calling. This presents its own problems, such as ensuring that there is sufficient call monitoring by management to discover any training problems with staff that result in low customer response rates or irate customers. These problems are fixed by the following step.

10. *Conduct continuing quality assurance.* One of the primary tasks of supplier management is to conduct an ongoing quality-assurance program that centers on monitoring outgoing calls and correcting any problems discovered during the monitoring.

11. *Conduct feedback sessions.* The supplier should issue periodic activity reports to the functional coordinator regarding a number of issues (see the con-

trol section of this chapter for a complete listing); the primary issue is any change in the response rate from customers. If this drops, the coordinator should meet with supplier management to determine how the problem can be corrected, with typical solutions being a new call list or a change in the script.

The transition to a direct mail supplier covers some of the same points as those previously shown for a telemarketing supplier, though there are far fewer steps. The steps are as follows:

1. *Design mail piece.* Many direct mail companies are not involved in the design of a mail piece—they just mail it for the company. However, on the assumption that the supplier performs this function, it is the first step in the transition process, and generally requires several reviews by the functional coordinator before a final design is approved.

2. *Obtain mailing list.* The company decides on the type of mailing list it wants, and either the company or the supplier then obtains it. Mailing lists are commonly sold by a mailing list distributor who acts as a broker for a third party. A company pays a price per name, with a minimum base price. The names can be supplied as labels that the mailing supplier affixes to the direct mail pieces.

3. *Procure mailing permit.* Either the company or the supplier can obtain a mailing permit for the mailing from the post office.

4. *Conduct feedback sessions.* Once the responses from a mailing have been collected and summarized, the functional coordinator can meet with supplier management to go over the results of the mailing. This can result in the modification of the mail piece or a switch to a different mailing list. This feedback session is frequently done shortly after an initial test mailing has been completed; by collecting data on a subset of the full mailing, the coordinator can see if the mailing has a high probability of failure and can take steps to correct the mailing before undergoing the expense of mailing out enough mail pieces for the entire mailing list.

This section covered the transition steps for the public relations, distribution, sales, telemarketing, and direct mail functions.

12.4 CREATING CONTROL POINTS

This section discusses a number of control points that can be used to monitor the activities of each supplier that a company uses in the sales and marketing function.

The controls over direct mail center on its costs and resulting revenues. The coordinator should make a monthly comparison of the budgeted direct mail cost to actual year-to-date costs incurred and investigate the size of any incoming costs to ensure that the budget will not be exceeded. The coordinator should also make a monthly review of the response rate from the direct mail campaign. If the response rate is too low, possibly not even covering the cost of the mailing, the coordinator may have to terminate the mailing. Thus, controls over direct mail include a comparison of budgeted to actual costs and a review of mailing response rates.

An excellent control over a telemarketing supplier is the supplier's own status reports. These reports can be customized to fit the company's needs, including such topics as the days and hours when telemarketing was conducted, the dollars of sales, contacts per hour, sales per hour, no-answers, callbacks, busy signals, and depletion percentage of the call list being used by the telemarketer to make calls. The functional coordinator or the specialist assigned to the telemarketer should review these reports regularly to look for any unusual variances, and follow up with the supplier for corrective action. A major point to consider is that the supplier will experience declining performance over time after it contacts everyone on the primary call list and begins work on lesser-quality secondary call lists; the coordinator should consider this drop in performance before terminating a telemarketing firm for a perceived lack of results. Also, since the supplier is issuing reports on its own performance—which is a conflict of interest—the company should regularly appoint an audit team to verify that the information in the reports can be substantiated. Supplier reports are an excellent control over telemarketing companies.

The budget is the primary financial control over an advertising supplier, though creative controls are necessary as well. The advertising area requires particularly tight control, for even the addition of one extra advertisement in a magazine or (especially) on television can result in costs that are far higher than expected. One way to control these costs is to conduct a monthly comparison of the budget and the actual costs for the month. However, since only one extra advertisement can destroy a budget for an entire year (given the price of advertising in some types of media), it is better to have constantly available an updated amount of money not yet spent that is authorized by the budget. The functional coordinator can then refer to this remaining budget amount when authorizing additional advertising. Besides financial control, the functional coordinator is also responsible for creative control over advertising concepts. It is customary for the coordinator to review and approve the storyboards (drawings of print advertising campaigns) or scripts (for radio campaigns) to be used by the advertising supplier. This approval can either be for the overall concept of the advertising or for individual advertisements to be run. The level of approval varies by the amount of management control the coordinator wants to exercise, as well as by the length of the relationship (and corresponding level of trust) that the company has with the supplier. Thus, control over an advertiser centers on budgetary and creative control points.

The controls needed for a public relations supplier are similar to those used for an advertising supplier, since the functions are similar. There is usually a predetermined budget for public relations, so the functional coordinator should regularly compare the budget to actual year-to-date costs to see if the company is holding within its budget. As was the case with advertising, the coordinator or an assistant should review all public relations materials before they are issued. This review can be avoided if the documents are time sensitive and must be issued at once, but otherwise at least a cursory review is common at most companies. An additional control over a public relations supplier is to compare the hourly rates appearing on its billings to the billings shown in the contract, in order to verify that the supplier is billing the correct rates. In short, advertising controls include comparisons to the budget and contract, as well as reviews of all outgoing publicity materials.

Controls over a distributor are much less important, since the company is not buying from the distributor, and therefore has no money at risk. However, there are cases where distributors either hold inventory on consignment (i.e., the company continues to own the inventory, no matter where it is located) or the distributor has an unlimited right to return the inventory for credit (as is the case in the publishing industry). In these two instances, the functional coordinator should work with the company's internal audit team to regularly compare the amounts of consigned inventory to the company's records of what the distributors are supposed to have, and resolve any differences. The most common control, and the one that applies to *all* distributors, is to compare each distributor's sales levels to the sales budget. If actual sales are consistently dropping below the planned amounts, the coordinator may have to look for a new distributor. The primary distributor controls are audits of consigned inventory and comparisons of sales to planned amounts.

There are two good controls over outside salespeople. One is the level of sales generated by each salesperson. If the sales volume is less than expected, the salesperson should be terminated. However, since sales may fluctuate considerably due to any number of factors—seasonality, a drop in the economy, or the timing of orders—it is best to track sales on a trend line or at least to track average sales over several months to see if there is truly a continuing drop in sales, or if it is only a one-time variance. The second control is to review bad debt on sales made by a salesperson. This can vary significantly by salesperson, for some salespeople will go after sales to companies with high credit risks, which can result in much higher levels of bad debt. A less ethical salesperson may even mislead customers into either ordering a product they do not want or forcing them to take delivery far sooner than they need. In either case, the customer may repudiate the debt or wait a very long time to pay. The quality of a salesperson's sales is readily apparent by reviewing the accounts receivable aging. In short, the best controls over an outside salesperson are to review an average or trend line of that person's sales and to continually review the credit problems with previous sales generated by that person.

A control that is useful for several of the outsourced areas within the sales and marketing function is a customer complaint database. This is useful for gauging the customer response to a media release by a public relations supplier, a direct mail piece, or an advertisement by an advertising supplier. It can also spotlight problems with distributors or outside salespeople who are not treating customers properly. A card enclosed with the company's product is one way to make customers aware of the complaints database, to which they can mail or call in a problem. The complaint address or phone number can also be listed on the company's product catalog or sales brochures, on its trucks, or even on its business cards. By making it as easy and convenient as possible for customers to complain about the company's sales and marketing suppliers, the functional coordinator gets a second opinion on their performance.

In short, the primary controls over the sales and marketing functions are comparisons to budgeted amounts (with other variations to determine the reasonableness of supplier billings) and direct approval of the creative activities of the direct mail, telemarketing, public relations, and advertising suppliers. These controls allow a company to have an in-depth knowledge of the activities of its sales and marketing suppliers.

12.5   MEASURING THE OUTSOURCED FUNCTION

This section covers the array of performance measurements that can be used to assist in managing the many sales and marketing suppliers. Do not be overwhelmed by the number of measurements—these do not all have to be used, but the reader should take a selection of the most relevant measurements from this list in order to compile a set of measurements that works for a company's specific needs. Each measurement includes a discussion of its strengths and weaknesses, as well as how it can be calculated. The measurements are as follows:

DIRECT MAIL

- *Cost per piece.* A company can spend far too much on a direct mail piece by using excessively heavy or odd-sized kinds of paper or by using too many colors or photos. The best way to avoid this problem is to go over various layout and specification options with the supplier in advance, based on the most likely quantity to be used. The decision of what kind of mail piece is economical should be based on this "most likely" quantity. Take the total development and production cost from the supplier's billing statements and divide this amount by the total number of direct mail pieces produced. The problem with this measurement is that it can be badly skewed by purchasing too many mail pieces. The supplier can supply many extra copies nearly for free, since most of its costs are in the setup stage, so an unscrupulous functional coordinator could make the cost per piece look very good simply by ordering too many pieces. For example, a company may only need 1,000 copies of an item, which costs $500 to produce, or $.50 each. By ordering 5,000 copies for $750, the coordinator can drive the measurement down to 15 cents, even though the majority of the pieces will never be used.

- *Total cost per month.* A direct mail campaign involves more costs than the production of the mail piece. There is also the initial design cost, as well as the cost of the mailing permit, the mailing list, and the manual labor to stamp the mail pieces with labels. These costs are substantial, and may exceed the cost of the mail piece. The best way to track all of these costs is to summarize them at the end of the mailing to determine the total cost after the fact, but most companies prefer a monthly analysis. This allows them to spot cost overruns in mailings that carry through many months, and modify the mailings if the costs seem excessive. To calculate this measurement, extract the information from the supplier's monthly billing and track it on a trend line. If costs are coming in from more sources than the supplier, it is best to charge all mailing-related costs to a single general ledger line item and summarize costs from that account.

- *Revenue per mailing dollar.* A mailing does not work if it does not bring in any money. A mail piece may even garner awards for a good layout, but it is still a failure if it does not increase a company's revenues. Thus, the revenue per mailing dollar is the most important measurement in the direct mail area. To calculate it, store the revenues that come in through direct mail pieces in a separate general ledger account, and divide this amount by the total monthly direct mail cost. This measurement is easily skewed if there is a time lag between the time when costs are incurred to produce a mailing and the time when revenues arrive. This is a particular problem if the mailing is only intended to produce leads that may be converted into sales many months in the future. In these cases, it is best to summarize the costs and revenues for a number of months to determine the success of the mailing.

- *Gross profit per mailing dollar.* It does little good to generate large volumes of revenue from the use of a direct mailing if customers only purchase low-margin goods that do not cover the cost of the mailing. To see if this is a problem, charge the cost of goods sold on each sale through a direct mail piece to a separate cost-of-goods-sold account. Subtract this amount from the revenues that come in through direct mail pieces (which must also be stored in a separate general ledger account), then divide the resulting gross profit by the total monthly direct mail cost. Most companies do not track information in this level of detail because they do not store margin information in their databases for each product sold. A way of avoiding this problem (and the need for the measurement) is to predetermine the margin on each product to be sold through direct mail, and only sell those items that have high margins through this sales channel.

- *Profit per mailing dollar.* The most advanced companies are less concerned with the revenues or gross margins earned from the direct mail sales channel— they just want to know how much money they made in profits. To determine this amount, either multiply a standard profit percentage by the revenue per mailing dollar (see the prior measurement) or manually determine the profit for each sales item sold through direct mail. Then divide the resulting profit by the total monthly direct mail cost. If the second (and more accurate) approach is used, this is a time-consuming measurement, which is why very few companies use it. A company that is willing to go this far to find out its profit may want to go a step further and obtain an activity-based costing software package that, when properly installed, will give a more accurate profit number for the direct mail program than any other costing method.

- *Leads per mailing dollar.* Some direct mail campaigns are not designed to directly bring in sales. Instead, they bring in leads on potential customers who may then warrant an additional sales pitch. This approach is used for sales of high-dollar items, such as time-share condominiums. The measure of success for this type of mailing is a high percentage of leads per mailing dollar. To calculate it, track the number of leads manually or store them in a general ledger statistics account. Divide the monthly sum by the total monthly direct mail cost.

DISTRIBUTOR

- *Revenue volume.* The only measure that a distributor is judged on is the amount of sales volume it can generate. Any other measurements—such as gross margins, profitability, or bad debts—are the problem of the distributor and are of no concern to the company. If the revenue volume is lower than expectations or following a downward trend, the company should consider replacing the distributor. To calculate this measurement, code all sales for each distributor with a different sales code or general ledger account code, so that it can be sorted and printed by each distributor for each reporting period. Then track this information on a trend line to spot any revenue trends.

MARKETING

- *Total cost per month.* The total cost of a marketing supplier is not always so easy to determine, for it may arrange for expenses to be incurred by third parties, who then forward their billings directly to the company for payment. However, since many marketing suppliers prefer to charge a premium on these extra services, they pay the subcontractor's bills and then forward a single (and larger) invoice to the company. In the first case, all incoming bills must be stored in a single general ledger account, which can easily be summarized. In the second case, take the total cost from the supplier's monthly billing. In both cases, it is useful to track the total monthly cost on a trend line to spot any long-term variances.

- *Percentage of advertising expenditures.* Many marketing suppliers make their money by selling a marketing concept to a company and then managing the conversion of that concept into an advertising campaign; their compensation comes from charging the company a percentage of the total billings from the advertisers who were used in the advertising campaign. To determine this percentage, take the percentage of advertising expenditures paid to the marketing supplier from the contract with the supplier.

OUTSIDE SALES

- *Commission percentage.* An outside salesperson takes a much larger commission percentage than an in-house salesperson, since the outside person gets no base pay or compensation for travel and entertainment expenses. To offset these other sources of income, the commission percentage must be high. To ensure that outside salespeople are receiving the correct commission, the coordinator should review the commission percentage paid every month. To do so, take the percentage rate from the contract with the supplier.

- *Bad debt percentage.* A sign of a bad outside salesperson is when there is an excessive amount of bad debt resulting from sales generated by that salesperson. This can be a result of not obtaining purchase orders from customers, ordering the wrong products for them, or authorizing shipment when the customer does not even want the product. To determine this percentage, extract the amount of bad debt per month as noted in the general ledger bad-debt account that was from sales made by the outside sales supplier. Then divide this amount by the total sales generated by the outside sales supplier.

TELEMARKETING

- *Cost per call.* A good way to compare telemarketing suppliers is to review the costs that each one charges to make a call on behalf of the company. Though there can also be minimum fees per month, the cost per call is the primary means that most companies use to pay telemarketing suppliers. To determine the cost per call, take the total cost billed to the company in one month and divide this amount by the number of calls sent by the supplier, as noted on the supplier's monthly call report.

- *Revenue per call.* The primary measure of the effectiveness of a telemarketing supplier is the revenue it brings in on behalf of a company. This measure is not useful if the purpose of the telemarketing call is not to achieve an immediate sale, but it still applies to many types of telemarketing calls. To calculate it, summarize the revenues entered into the system by the supplier from outbound calls, and divide this amount by the number of calls sent by the supplier, as noted on the supplier's monthly call report.

- *Retention rate.* Some companies have their telemarketing suppliers handle incoming calls from customers who want to cancel products or services. It is the job of the telemarketing employees to persuade the customers not to cancel. A supplier with a high retention rate is quite valuable, since it keeps a company from losing revenue. To calculate this measurement, locate the number of calls made into the call center to cancel a sale, and divide this amount into the number of callers who were persuaded not to cancel.

- *Total cost per month.* Since there may be several types of costs that a telemarketing supplier charges a company, it is not always enough to only track the cost per call or baseline fee per month. Some suppliers even charge a percentage of all money collected. Thus, it can be better to summarize all of these costs each month to get a bigger picture of this expense. To do so, extract the total cost from the supplier's monthly billing and track it on a trend line. The trend line is useful for seeing if there are costing variances that are building over time, which may require correction.

This section presented a number of measurements for use in tracking the performance of suppliers in the direct mail, marketing, outside sales, and telemarketing areas. The primary focus of these measurements is the revenue and cost of each function, either in total or on a per-transaction basis. Though it is not necessary to use all of these measurements, a selection of them will give a company a good overview of the performance of its suppliers.

12.6 MANAGING THE OUTSOURCED FUNCTION

When outsourcing the sales and marketing function, one of the prime considerations is how to manage them. This is a more difficult management task than some functions, for there are a number of distinct and highly differentiated tasks within the functions that are normally handled by different suppliers, all of which require management oversight. This section discusses the difficulty of managing an outsourced sales and marketing function, as well as the type of support the functional coordinator needs and the job description of a typical coordinator.

The functional coordinator for sales and marketing can have one of the more difficult tasks of any of the functional coordinator positions. This is because there can be a number of suppliers to manage, and the tasks of those suppliers are so different that it takes a coordinator with an unusual range of experience to handle them all. With suppliers taking care of such areas as direct mail, public relations, sales, distribution, telemarketing, and advertising, it is clear that the coordinator needs a number of functional specialists for assistance in managing them. The number of assistants will vary based on the size of the sales and marketing function, with a very small company not having the financial resources to support any at all. The assistants may work directly with the suppliers, and then report on the results of their work to the coordinator, who does not have direct contact with the suppliers. The primary exception to this reporting relationship is a company's distributors, where the primary contact is the president of the distributor—because of the high level of contact, distributors typically deal directly with the coordinator. The functional coordinator reports directly to the vice president of sales and marketing, and may very well fill this position in many companies. These reporting relationships are noted in Figure 12.1. In short, the sales and marketing coordinator should be supported by a group of functional specialists, and report directly to top management.

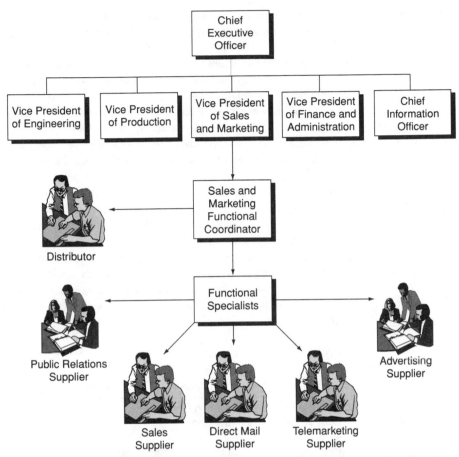

Figure 12.1   Organization Chart for Outsourcing the Sales and Marketing Function

What background should the functional coordinator have? The person's background should be solidly anchored in the sales and marketing area, since there is a large amount of specialization in this area and someone coming from outside the function would require a considerable amount of time to learn. These knowledge areas include product specifications, the commission structure, the timing and content of advertising campaigns, how to write a good telemarketing script, and the proper language to use in a public relations release. Also, because the coordinator must manage a critical function and deal with the senior management of many suppliers, this should be a high-level manager, not someone who is new to the management ranks. Experience is critical.

What skills should the functional coordinator have? The primary one is people-management, since there are functional specialists to manage as well as suppliers.

Also, if there are many independent outside salespeople instead of one sales supplier, this can involve dealing with a large number of people. Since the functional specialists may deal directly with suppliers on behalf of the coordinator, it is also important that the coordinator have sufficient training skills to show these employees how to deal with suppliers. Also, the sales and marketing functions frequently work together to tie marketing campaigns to sales drives. If so, the coordinator must have considerable planning ability to ensure that media messages, promotional materials, sales brochures, and salesperson training are linked to ensure a properly coordinated campaign. The sales and marketing budget can be enormous, depending on the size of the company and the industry. If so, the coordinator must have sufficient budgeting skills to keep from overspending the budget and incurring very large additional expenses. This can be a particular problem in the advertising area, where costs can quickly spiral out of control. Finally, negotiation skills are paramount. There will be contracts to negotiate with as many as five suppliers (or more, if the company opts to have suppliers in such areas as advertising cover only specific geographical markets, with more suppliers added for other regions), so some sort of contract-related dealing is bound to occur every month. In short, the coordinator must have in-depth personnel-management skills, plus experience with planning, budgeting, training, and negotiation. These skills are noted in the job description shown in Figure 12.2.

Figure 12.2   The Sales and Marketing Coordinator's Job Description

Employee Title: Sales and Marketing Outsourcing Coordinator
Reports to: Vice President of Sales and Marketing
Responsibilities:
- Sign off on all agreements with the sales and marketing suppliers.
- Authorize the release of funds for payment to suppliers.
- Plan with suppliers for major sales and marketing campaigns.
- Review the results of the telemarketing program.
- Approve proposed scripts for use by the telemarketing supplier's staff.
- Meet regularly with distributors to discuss problems and upcoming product changes.
- Review the results of the direct mail campaign and implement needed changes.
- Review the sales results of outside salespeople and hire or fire as necessary.
- Review and approve outbound public relations materials.
- Review and approve advertising materials prior to distribution.
- Review the results of the customer complaints database and fix any problems.
- Compare actual costs charged to costs listed in contracts to determine the causes of variances; follow up on these variances with the supplier.
- Manage the transfer of functions from the company to the suppliers.
- Train the functional specialists in how to deal with their assigned suppliers.
- Advise the Internal audit team regarding supplier control points to investigate.

This section covered how to manage an outsourced sales and marketing function. To be done properly, this requires a functional coordinator who may be assisted by functional specialists with in-depth knowledge of the type of supplier that each one is monitoring. The coordinator should have a sales and marketing background with good product and industry knowledge, and should be of sufficient seniority to deal with the top management of suppliers. If this in-house team is in place, a company can exercise good control over its sales and marketing suppliers.

12.7   POTENTIAL CUSTOMER SERVICE ISSUES

The sales and marketing function has direct contact with customers, so there is a high risk of having customer service problems in this area. This section covers those problems.

A company talks to its customers through its pubic relations releases, direct mail pieces, and advertising. A mistake in the format or script of any of these communication media can cause a variety of responses from customers, varying from laughter to outrage, depending on the message (inadvertent or otherwise) that was conveyed. The best way to avoid this problem is to have the functional coordinator approve all public relations releases, direct mail pieces, and advertising scripts and storyboards prior to their release to the public. A company should only risk the unapproved release of materials by a supplier if the company has a long relationship with that supplier and trusts its judgment.

A company must know if its suppliers are causing problems with its customers. Since the suppliers are unlikely to point out problems, it is up to the company to go straight to its customers to find out. The easiest way to do this is to set up a complaint phone line, the results of which go straight to top management. The phone number for the hot line should be made as easy as possible for customers to find, so inserting it on packaging materials or (even better) in instruction books will make it easily available to customers. The phone line should be manned for the longest number of hours per day that is possible, so that customers have a very easy time getting through to the company. This can be accomplished by having a customer service supplier answer the phones through a call center, either all of the time or only when the company is closed. This information should then be logged into a customer complaints database that summarizes problems into categories while still retaining all of the detailed information for follow-up purposes. This file should be made available to as many people as possible through the company's computer system so that everyone can see where the problems are occurring. A customer complaints database is a crucial means for tracking down and fixing customer service issues that arise when the sales and marketing functions are outsourced.

This section noted that customer service problems can arise through misrepresentation of marketing and sales messages to customers. This problem can be fixed by reviewing sales and marketing materials before release, while other problems can be spotted by actively promoting the use of a customer complaint phone line.

12.8   GETTING OUT OF
THE OUTSOURCING ARRANGEMENT

There are varying levels of difficulty involved in getting out of a sales and marketing outsourcing agreement, depending on the type of supplier. This section discusses those problems.

If an outside sales supplier is dismissed, the company is obligated to pay the commission due on all outstanding orders that were sold by the sales supplier. There are many variations on how this commission is paid. For example, the company may pay all remaining commissions at the time of termination, even though it would not otherwise be obligated to do so until the sales were finalized. Another option is to offer partial payment to the sales supplier for commissions that would not otherwise be due for some time; this would be a final payment. Another option is to hold the final commission payment to see if the company should reduce the final amount based on any bad debts that arise within a specific time period following the termination. Whichever of these methods is used should be specified in the initial agreement so that there is no argument about how commissions are to be paid at the time of termination.

If a company wants to terminate its advertising supplier, it must consider how to wind down the advertising campaign being run by the supplier. The most common service provided by a supplier is for it to not only create the advertising campaign, but to also manage its dissemination through a variety of media, charging a percentage of the total cost of that campaign as its compensation. When the supplier goes, so too does the advertising. This means that there will be a lag while the company locates a new supplier who can create a new campaign. The best way to avoid this lag is to arrange with the outgoing supplier to continue its advertising while the new supplier works on a new campaign. Since the old supplier may be tempted to expend large amounts at the last minute on lots of advertising in order to increase its commission, it is best for the company to authorize a specific amount of advertising during the termination period that the supplier is not allowed to exceed. Terminating an advertising supplier may include payments for additional advertising during the interim period when a new supplier is being selected.

When terminating a direct mail supplier, the primary consideration is getting the supplier to release all camera-ready masters of the direct mail documents. It is important to keep the originals so that the cleanest possible copies can be made for future use. The easiest way to do this is to require the return of the camera-ready documents in the original contract with the supplier. If the company has no interest in using this information again, then there is no reason to try to obtain its return, and the supplier can simply be terminated with written notice. The outsourcing contract should require the return of all direct mail master copies at the time of termination.

Depending on the circumstances, terminating a telemarketing supplier can be an expensive proposition. If at the beginning of the relationship the supplier was required to build a call center in order to service the company's telemarketing needs, it will probably have demanded a contract clause that requires a minimum number of months of minimum payments in order to recoup its expenses. If the company terminates early, it will likely face a termination fee. On the other hand, terminating a supplier who has not made this capital investment normally requires nothing more than written notification. A company will typically require the return of all mailing lists being used by the supplier for its telemarketing, since this is considered the property of the company. (This requirement should be noted in the contract.) Also, strange though it may seem, customers who are contacted by telemarketers sometimes notice on their caller identification boxes the phone number of the supplier that called, and will call back to see what the call was about. This can result in additional sales. If the company thinks that this is important, it can request that the phone number from which the telemarketing calls were made be transferred over to the company, which can then answer all return calls or give them to another supplier who can perform the same function. Finally, a company may want to continue its telemarketing efforts elsewhere, possibly with no letup on this activity. If so, it should either create an in-house call center or find another supplier at the same time that it is terminating its current supplier—either of which requires some advance planning. Ending a telemarketing arrangement may require the payment of a termination fee by the company and the return of mailing lists by the supplier, as well as the transfer of the phone number used to make calls and the creation of new calling capacity.

When terminating a distributor, three issues arise. First, it is customary to give some written notice, usually including a notice period of at least 90 days. This gives the distributor time to look for an alternate product line to represent. Second, the distributor is under no obligation to give its customer list to the company, so the company must consider the impact on its sales of giving its business to a new distributor who will have to build up the business from scratch. This is also a consideration if the company wants to bring the sales back in-house, for it must also generate all sales leads without any assistance from the distributor. It is highly unlikely that the distributor will hand over its customer list to the company even for monetary consideration, because the distributor will want to sell other competing products to the same customers, and will not want to compete with the company to make those sales. Finally, depending on the type of product and industry, the distributor may have invested a large amount in storing spare parts to service the company's products, and will want to return these parts. This can be a significant amount of inventory, and some of it may be obsolete. This is a major expense to a company if it must pay a supplier for all of its parts. However, in all cases except consignment sales and guaranteed returns, a company has legitimately sold the parts and does not have to take them back. If the company has guaranteed full payment for returned goods, it can at least try to modify the original contract so that lesser amounts are paid for older goods, with no payment at all for parts that are older than a specific date. Even if the company is under no obligation to buy back parts, it may want some of them for resale elsewhere. If so, it should charge a reasonable restocking fee, such as 20% of the wholesale price, to take back the inventory. The exact terms should be noted in the distribution agreement, so that there will be no arguments about return policies at the point of termination. In short, distributor termination problems include sufficient written notice, the lack of a customer base, and the cost of inventory returns from the distributor.

To summarize, sales and marketing outsourcing termination problems include calculating the timing and amount of commission payments for sales suppliers, obtaining mail piece master copies from direct mail suppliers, and making termination payments to telemarketing suppliers, as well as obtaining new call center capacity and picking up the sales shortfall from a distributor who may also want to return its inventories. The most significant of these problems is in the distribution area, where a company can suffer a severe shortfall in sales if it terminates a distributor who was generating a significant sales volume.

12.9 SUMMARY

This chapter covered the outsourcing of the sales and marketing function. This can involve a large number of suppliers, since there are many specialties within this function: advertising, public relations, direct mail, telemarketing, outside sales, and distribution. Each specialty requires different handling in terms of transitions to the supplier, contract terms, performance measurements, controls, management techniques, and customer service problems, all of which were discussed in this chapter. Due to the large amount of specialization, the functional coordinator in a larger company is frequently assisted by a staff of specialists. The greatest risk in this area is not excessive pricing, as is the case with many other functions, but a combination of not achieving adequate sales through the efforts of the suppliers and not achieving good customer relations. Both of these problems are significant enough to severely damage a company's profitability, so the function must be managed by a senior-level manager with great operational experience in this functional area. If the correct functional manager is hired and supported with a quality staff that closely monitors supplier activity, this area can be a good choice for outsourcing.

CHAPTER THIRTEEN

Outsourcing the Administration Function

There are a number of service areas within the administration function, and all of them can be outsourced to suppliers. These functions include temporary clerical help, record storage, copying, desktop publishing, and security. Most companies outsource at least a few of these functions, and more appear to be doing so, based on the size and number of suppliers now offering services in these areas. Examples of the largest temporary clerical help suppliers are Robert Half, Norrell Staffing Services, and Olsten Staffing Services. The record storage industry is now a billion-dollar industry with more than 2,500 suppliers, represented by Professional Records & Information Services Management, a Raleigh, N.C., trade group. Some of the largest copy services are Kinko's and Sir Speedy, with the giant Xerox Business Services company also offering a high-end electronic document management system. Desktop publishing is mostly offered by local companies. Security is offered by many local firms, as well as such large suppliers as Burns International Security Services, Pinkerton Security, and Wells Fargo Guard Services. In short, there is a thriving field of suppliers available if a company wants to outsource its administration services area.

What can a supplier do to handle a company's administration needs? The following bulleted points note the available services:

- *Clerical.* These suppliers provide temporary labor on short notice and with a specific skill set that a company may not be able to find internally.

- *Record storage.* These suppliers store records in low-cost, off-site locations; retrieve selected records; and destroy and dispose of records as requested by the company.

- *Copying.* These suppliers can copy documents in a variety of sizes and colors, and can do so in any quantity. Many will pick up and drop off documents, as well as provide binding services for booklets. Some suppliers will go further and take over a company's in-house copying facilities with its own equipment and staff. A more advanced service is provided by Xerox Business Services, which can do all of the above on a global scale. For example, it provides a "distribute-then-print" service that digitizes documents, sends them electronically to its own printing centers near a company's various locations, and then prints them out and distributes them from those locations—this speeds the distribution of documents to all of a company's facilities. Xerox can also digitally store and index a company's documents, which is useful for engineering and technical companies that constantly review, revise, and distribute documents. It provides these services to Ericsson, where it stores thousands of drawings for transmission to various company locations in digital format, as well as Empire Blue Cross and Blue Shield, where it manages the company's electronic print and production services.

- *Desktop publishing.* These suppliers are primarily local shops that can provide enhanced graphics work on documents, such as those used for presentations or company-specific booklets or sales tools. They can frequently provide a higher level of expertise than a company has available internally.

- *Security.* These suppliers guard company facilities around-the-clock or only during specific periods when the work force is absent, providing patrol and check-in services. Guards can be armed or unarmed, depending on a company's needs and the prices it is willing to pay. Large security firms can provide security services in most locations throughout the world, which is useful for multinational companies who want consistent security service from a reliable supplier.

This chapter covers the major issues surrounding the outsourcing of administrative services. The issues include the advantages and disadvantages of doing so, contractual issues to be aware of, and transition problems to be surmounted. The chapter also covers the best control points to use when managing suppliers, as well as how to measure and manage them. It concludes with a review of customer service problems and how to resolve them, and examines problems associated with terminating a supplier.

13.1 ADVANTAGES AND DISADVANTAGES

This section covers the advantages and disadvantages of outsourcing the various administration functions. The advantages and disadvantages are clustered together for each of the outsourced services.

One advantage of using a clerical services provider is that it reduces a company's fixed costs. If the service were kept in-house, a company would incur the continuing expense of maintaining a pool of clerical help that may not be fully utilized at all times. By only incurring costs when clerical staff are requested for specific tasks, and then brought in from a supplier, a company can convert this fixed cost to a variable cost. A variation on this issue is to only maintain a small pool of in-house clerical help that is staffed to meet the company's minimum temporary clerical needs at all times, with the company calling the clerical services supplier only when that minimum level is exceeded. This option keeps a company's fixed clerical costs at a minimum while reducing the higher variable cost of a clerical supplier's employees. Using a clerical supplier can reduce or eliminate a company's fixed clerical costs.

Another advantage of using a clerical supplier is that a company can avoid the continuing hassle of recruiting and interviewing temporary workers, as well as of handling the payroll and benefits paperwork associated with the additional staff. This can be a considerable administrative headache if a company uses a large number of temporary personnel. In addition, a company must incur the time and expense of generating and distributing year-end W-2 tax forms to all of the clerical personnel that were employed during the year. All of the administrative problems are handled by the supplier when the clerical services function is outsourced.

If a company needs rapid and short-term access to someone with specialized skills, one of its best avenues is to contact a clerical supplier, who has contacts with many potential temporary workers who may be available immediately to work. This is more efficient than advertising for the temporary position, which may produce a low response rate and may not attract the right kind of person, while also costing the company for the advertisement. Quick access to a diverse skill set is a good reason to outsource the clerical function.

A final advantage of using a clerical supplier is that the company does not have to terminate clerical staff who are not performing to expectations. This is a task that many managers dread. Instead, the company can contact the supplier and request that a clerical person not be sent back to the company the next day, which shifts the termination task to the supplier. This is also good for the clerical person, who is not fired, but just made available for temporary work elsewhere with the same supplier; this is much less of a traumatic experience for the clerical person than a formal firing. An easier termination process is an excellent reason for using a clerical services supplier.

The primary disadvantage of using a provider of temporary clerical help is that this service is expensive. A supplier typically adds a premium of 30% to 50% onto the rate that is paid to the clerical person, which far exceeds the tax and benefits costs of most companies if they were to hire employees directly. A company has some leverage over a supplier if it is a heavy user of the supplier's clerical personnel, since it has enough volume to negotiate lower rates. An incidental user of clerical help has no such basis for negotiation, and must pay the higher rates. Price is the primary disadvantage of using a temporary clerical services supplier.

There are several excellent reasons for using a record storage supplier. One is that a company can eliminate a large amount of storage space. This is a particularly valid reason if a company is using prime office space for storage. Moving records to a cheap supplier warehouse is much less expensive for the company. Also, a record storage supplier may do a much better job of organizing its storage facilities than a company, which tends to pile records in a haphazard manner. A record storage supplier may base its reputation in the rapid retrieval of documents, so it must do a good job of record organization. Thus, record storage advantages include reduced storage requirements and better organization.

Offsetting the advantages of using a record storage supplier are the cost of the service and the retrieval time. Though a supplier may do a better job of organizing its records than a company, it still must transport them back to the company once a document has been requested, and that transportation time is one that a company does not have to worry about if it stores its own documents on-site. This delay can be several days, depending on the distance of the supplier's warehouse from the company. Another problem is price. The basic storage fee is typically much cheaper than a company's cost to store its records internally, but there are ancillary fees for such services as retrieval, transportation, and document destruction, which all add to the base cost. Only by adding together all of these costs can it be determined that a supplier is providing this service cheaper than the company. A company's outsourcing costs are much lower if there are few retrievals from storage. In short, the disadvantages of using a record storage supplier are the total price of the service and the retrieval time.

One of the many advantages of outsourcing the copying function is that the supplier absorbs the cost of the equipment. This can be a considerable expense, especially for larger companies with many copiers, or for those with a need for high-speed or color copiers, which are particularly expensive. A company can also divest itself of some existing copiers when it outsources, which will bring in some extra cash. In addition, suppliers constantly upgrade their equipment, so a company constantly benefits from having new copier equipment, instead of working with older equipment of its own. Suppliers also maintain their own equipment, which saves a company the expense, disruption, and administrative expense of doing so. Outsourcing the copying function reduces a company's fixed costs and eliminates its copier maintenance expense.

A copy supplier is especially useful in overflow situations as well as for printing to unusual specifications. Overflow situations are the times when a company has a sudden need for a large volume of printed materials, and cannot produce them on time with its existing copier equipment. This also applies to special paper sizes or colors that a company's copier equipment cannot handle. Special printing requirements and quantities are ideal reasons to outsource to a copy supplier.

If a company takes advantage of a print-on-demand document-management system that is linked to a digital document library (such as the one marketed by Xerox Business Systems), the advantages are particularly apparent. Using a supplier for this service gives a company expert advice on setting up the system, as well as ongoing maintenance of the service by a knowledgeable staff. It is also much easier to find documents through the digital document database, which represents a large time savings in searching for paper-based documents. Storing documents in a computer database also lessens the need for on-site storage of paper documents, which reduces a company's need for storage space. In addition, since the documents are centrally stored in a computer, more than one person can access the same document at once, resulting in better document access for all employees. Due to the central storage, it is no longer possible to misplace a paper file—you can just recreate it by accessing the computer. It is also less likely to lose digital documents, since they can be stored on backup files, preferably in multiple locations for greater security. The system can also distribute documents to many company locations at once by transmitting digital images through the phone lines, which eliminates the need to mail documents to those locations. In short, a digital document library that is linked to multisite printing locations is the ultimate in the craft of the copy supplier—excellent document and print availability, anywhere in a company, with no lost documents.

A minor advantage of outsourcing is that the supplier, owning many copiers, can purchase maintenance parts and supplies at lower prices, since it buys them in larger quantities than most single companies would. This allows the supplier to shave its prices to the company slightly, though these prices are generally still higher than the internal cost at which a company could produce its own copies.

There are two problems with outsourcing the copying function. One is that the price is higher than what a company would incur if it kept the function in-house. The higher price is not only caused by the inclusion of the supplier's profit in its billings, but also by its capital costs—it is paying for very expensive copier equipment that the company no longer has to pay for. The other problem is turnaround time. If a company has a profusion of copiers throughout its facilities, employees can achieve the fastest possible turnaround time. By moving the function to a supplier that is either off-site or consolidated into a small number of on-site service centers, the turnaround time generally increases. This second problem can be partially resolved by maintaining a small number of copiers for direct use by employees for the most rush jobs. Another approach is to have a centralized copy-job logging database that tracks the supplier's turnaround time. If the time is longer than expected, the company can persuade the supplier to increase its copying speed by various means, or it can find a new supplier. The biggest problems with outsourced copying are cost and turnaround time.

Outsourcing the security function presents several advantages. One is that a company no longer has to deal with the hiring, firing, and other personnel issues of a security force—the supplier takes care of all these administrative details. This is a particular advantage in the security area, where turnover tends to be high, so the related amount of paperwork is also high. An additional paperwork issue that can be transferred to the supplier is the tracking of firearms permits for the security staff. In addition, the reliability of the security staff can sometimes be a problem, since they are sometimes guarding valuable assets, and there is no one to see them if they were to steal those assets. This problem is avoided by using a bonded supplier, since the company can go to the supplier's insurance company for reimbursement. Also, many suppliers offer security training to their staffs, which gives a company the assurance of consistent and reliable service wherever the security supplier does business. Using a security supplier eliminates personnel-related paperwork while improving the reliability and training of the security staff.

The primary disadvantage of outsourcing the security function is its higher price. The supplier charges a significant premium over the amount paid to its security employees, which includes its bonding, training, and administration fees. A company must also incur these costs if it keeps the function in-house, but not the profit and sales overhead costs that the supplier must charge. A supplier sometimes gets around the high-price problem by paying very low rates to its security employees, which results in a company being given a very junior security force. The only case in which a company can reduce its security costs by outsourcing is if its internal security staff is very well paid. In short, the advantages of outsourcing security are somewhat counterbalanced by its high price and (sometimes) by the inexperience of the supplier's personnel.

The desktop publishing function is frequently outsourced by smaller companies who do not have enough need for document work to justify hiring a full-time employee for the task. The best alternative is to outsource the function to a supplier who has a high enough level of skill to rapidly respond to the company's publishing requests. There are two problems with using a desktop publishing supplier, however. One is the price, which tends to be much higher than the hourly cost of an in-house employee who does the same work. The other problem is that, because the supplier is usually located off-site, it takes longer to review and revise documents than if the person doing the work were located in the same building as the reviewer. This problem is easy to avoid by using a fax machine, which drastically shrinks the document-transmission time. In short, outsourcing desktop publishing is a good idea if a company does not have enough need for it to hire a full-time employee, though the price is high and the turnaround time is slightly longer.

This section covered the advantages and disadvantages of outsourcing the clerical, record storage, copying, desktop publishing, and security services of the administrative services function. The most important advantages are shifting the management of staff to a supplier, reducing fixed and capital costs, and using suppliers for tasks that cannot otherwise be easily handled internally. The most prevalent disadvantage is that a company can usually take care of these functions internally at a lower cost than what is charged by a supplier.

13.2   CONTRACT-SPECIFIC ISSUES

This section covers the contractual issues for service providers in the administration area. The primary contract issues are for supplier pricing, followed by service turn-around time and termination issues.

Pricing is the primary contractual issue for administration suppliers. The following bulleted points include a brief description of pricing issues for each of the administration service areas:

- *Copy center.* A provider of copying services can have many fees, such as for binding, delivery, and rush orders, but the two primary rates are the fee per page to copy black-and-white documents and the fee per page to copy color documents. There are additional charges for copying large-size documents. The primary issue is for the contract to include the copying fees for the copying of blank-and-white and color documents, which covers the vast majority of all supplier fees. The other fees do not have to be included in the contract, unless a company has a special situation where the other fees take up a larger proportion of the total fees from a copy center than is normal.

- *Records storage.* A record storage facility has one primary charge, which is the monthly storage cost per cubic foot (or some similar measure), as well as other fees for document pickup, retrieval, and destruction. All of these fees can be noted in the contract, but the bulk of the supplier's billings will come from the storage fee, so this is the one that must be included in the contract. The others can be included at the option of management.

- *Desktop publishing.* The contract should note the cost per page, which may vary for a written page and a graphics-oriented page.

- *Clerical.* A provider of temporary clerical help will charge a variety of hourly rates based on the type of temporary help needed. A receptionist may only cost $10 an hour, while a temporary engineer may cost 60. Due to the wide range of prices, it is not possible to include all of them in the contract. Instead, the contract can include the supplier's percentage markup over the price actually paid to each temporary worker.

- *Security.* A supplier of security services is essentially the same as a provider of temporary clerical help, and charges in the same manner: the price of a security guard's hourly pay plus a markup percentage. As was the case for temporary clerical personnel, there can be a wide variety of hourly rates, since the levels of experience for staff can vary considerably. Therefore, as was the case for the clerical supplier, the contract should avoid itemizing all possible hourly rates and instead focus on the supplier's percentage markup over the price actually paid to each temporary worker.

Service turnaround time applies to most of the administration functions, especially desktop publishing, copy suppliers, and record storage facilities. In all cases, the supplier must be held to a reasonable service turnaround time. For example, a copy center must be able to complete and return copy jobs within three days for all jobs during a month. If not, the company can terminate the outsourcing agreement at any time. A less common approach is to pay bonuses or impose fines if a supplier departs from the targeted average turnaround time. The turnaround time can be skewed by an unexpected surge in requested jobs in any of these service areas, so it is best to build some slack into the performance standards or at least an option to mutually adjust the performance standards after the contract has been in effect for 90 days, based on the results during the first 90 days. An administration supplier should be held accountable in the contract for service turnaround time.

The contract with a copy supplier requires some extra clauses if the copy center is to be located within the company. There should be a requirement for the copy center's minimum operating hours, in case the company has a need for copying outside of normal business hours. Also, the contract should specify the prices at which the supplier will purchase the company's copiers, if this is planned. Also, in the event of termination, the contract should include a pricing schedule that shows the prices at which the company can buy the in-house copiers from the supplier, with prices declining in future years due to depreciation. The contract may also state that the company is allowed to offer jobs to the supplier's in-house staff in case the company elects to take the function back in-house. Any or all of these clauses may be necessary depending on the type of outsourcing arrangement a company is trying to create with a copy supplier.

In case of termination, it is best to specify record storage obligations and pricing in the contract. Otherwise, the supplier can charge excessive fees to move the stored records to a new supplier's facility, and can refuse to allow the records to be moved unless this fee is paid in advance. By noting in the contract that the supplier shall render all reasonable assistance to the company during the records transfer, and also by specifying the hourly rates to be charged for help by the supplier's staff, a company can avoid several problems that might otherwise arise when terminating a record storage supplier.

When a desktop publishing supplier is terminated, it is possible that the supplier will have a number of confidential documents in its computer storage that the supplier worked on for the company. The company should require the supplier to delete these files upon termination, to eliminate any risk of the information leaking to competing companies. The contract can cover this problem in two ways—either by requiring the supplier to sign a confidentiality agreement in advance or by requiring the supplier to destroy all files at the time of termination. Since both contract clauses have the same result, either one is acceptable.

This section focused on the key contractual issues to consider when negotiating terms with administration suppliers. The primary factors are pricing and service turnaround time, though some attention must also be paid to termination issues for selected services.

13.3 TRANSITION ISSUES

This section covers the transition issues for several administration areas. It is quite short, since the transition process is very simple for all service areas. There are no transition steps noted here for the selection of a supplier or for contract negotiations—duplicating the description of these steps for each of the administration service areas is too repetitive. Also, there is no Gantt chart for the transition steps, since there are so few transition steps for each service area. The transition issues for each administrative area are as follows:

- *Clerical.* There should be a primary contact person through whom all requests for clerical help will flow. Otherwise the supplier may be flooded with unauthorized requests for help. The primary contact person should also maintain a request log, which is useful for measuring the supplier's turnaround time for clerical requests, as well as for verifying the detail on supplier billings.

- *Copy center.* There are different levels of difficulty in transitioning a company's copying service, depending on the complexity of the system to which the company is moving. Each one is noted separately:

  - *External copy center.* When switching to a copy supplier that is located off the company premises, the only mandatory transition step is to have all copying requests go through a single coordinator, who logs the requests into a transaction log. This log is later used to measure the timeliness of the supplier's service. It may also be necessary for the company to sell off some of its copiers that are no longer used as a result of outsourcing to the supplier.

  - *Internal copy center.* If the supplier is to be stationed in-house, the first step is for the supplier to review the company's current copying locations, capacity, and state of repair, and recommend changes to the equipment as needed. The supplier may then hire the company's internal copier staff to attend its own internal copier stations. Finally, company personnel should be notified just prior to the change and told about any new procedures, such as funneling all copy requests through a single log-in point so that the supplier's timeliness in completing copy jobs can be tracked.

  - *Internal electronic printing and publishing center.* The most advanced suppliers can create and maintain a database of documents that are stored in a digital format, and electronically disseminate them anywhere in a company for local printing. This transition includes all of the steps noted for an internal copy center, but also requires that the supplier run wiring to all printer locations in the company from the central computer facility that stores the documents. This can be a major process if the company wants to include multiple locations in a single electronic printing database, and must lease dedicated phone lines to link them. Also, documents must be scanned into a digital database, which requires a large amount of work, depending on the number of documents to be converted. The supplier must also set up procedures for updating these documents and maintaining an index that tracks document change dates. The supplier must also train company employees in how to use the electronic document systems, a process that should include how to change and print existing documents.

- *Desktop publishing.* A supplier of desktop publishing services may be asked to create or modify a company's confidential documents. If so, the supplier should sign a confidentiality agreement before being allowed to see these documents. Also, company personnel should be notified that all desktop publishing requests must be routed through the functional coordinator, who can log in the date and time of each request so that the company can measure the supplier's turnaround time.

- *Record storage.* The transition to a record storage supplier starts with tagging all documents to be sent into storage, so that they can be easily retrieved. The supplier may have a tagging system that it prefers to use, so the functional coordinator should consult with the supplier to see what location codes will work best. The documents are then moved to the supplier location. (This move is normally handled by the supplier, so the company does not need to separately hire a team of movers to shift the documents to the supplier.) The functional coordinator should then visit the storage facility to ensure that the documents have been properly stored in an area where they will not be easily damaged, and where all items can be easily accessed for retrieval.

- *Security.* A company should work with its new security supplier to conduct a review of each facility's security risks, and agree upon the security measures the supplier will implement that will mitigate those risks. The company must then transfer keys and access codes to the supplier, agree upon a schedule for the security staff, and notify company employees of the change. This last step is critical, especially if the company has not used a security supplier in the past, so that employees will know who the new people are and why they are there. The employee notification should include a reason why the security is being added, otherwise rumors may arise that they are present to prevent theft by the employees, which is not good for morale.

This section covered the key transition steps to be aware of when moving an administration function to a supplier. Most transitions are quite simple. The most complicated one is when a supplier creates an in-house electronic printing and publishing center. With the exception of the last item, most transitions can be completed quite rapidly.

13.4   CREATING CONTROL POINTS

This section describes the best ways to control the activities of suppliers in the administration area. The primary controls are through request tracking and comparisons to budgets and contracts.

One of the best controls in the administrative services area is the request log. This is a paper-based log in which employees note their requests for service, and which a clerk completes when the requested service has been completed. When summarized, this gives the functional coordinator an excellent view of each supplier's turnaround time. An example of a turnaround log for the record storage service area, requesting the return of several documents from storage, is shown in Figure 13.1. This request log is equally useful for the clerical, copying, and desktop publishing areas, with slight modifications to the format to allow for differences in what is being requested. The information can be used to force the supplier to increase its capacity (such as with copiers) so that turnaround time improves, and it can be the basis for bonus or penalty payments based on average turnaround times, which may be stipulated by the contract with the supplier. The supplier can also use the log to get a historical perspective on when there are sudden increases in the demand for services, which they can use to expand or contract capacity as needed. The request log is an excellent control for most administrative services that can be used by both the company and the supplier.

Figure 13.1   A Sample Request Log for Record Retrieval

Request Date	Complete Date	Requested By	Document Location Code	Document Year	Document Description
1/17/19XX	1/22/19XX	J. Smithers	A-08-C	19XX	A/R file for "P"
1/19/19XX	1/25/19XX	E. Brophy	A-09-F	19XX	A/P file for "L-M"
1/23/19XX	1/27/19XX	Q. Friend	B-01-B	19XX	Job file #45718
1/25/19XX	1/29/19XX	R. Sampson	B-01-D	19XX	Year-end tax records
1/30/19XX	2/15/19XX	P. Montague	C-00-A	19XX	Fixed asset file
2/03/19XX	2/11/19XX	L. Davis	A-07-G	19XX	Job file #40032
2/07/19XX	Open	O. Brother	B-03-B	19XX	Time cards for March

Another important control is to regularly compare the unit prices noted on each supplier's billing to the prices noted in the contract with the supplier. This control applies to all administrative areas: clerical, copying, desktop publishing, record storage, and security. This can be a problem if the supplier does not itemize its billings, so the functional coordinator may have to persuade each supplier to submit a sufficiently detailed invoice. Any significant variances between the billed prices and contract prices should be brought to the attention of the supplier for correction. Billings from administration suppliers should be periodically compared to contract rates.

The functional coordinator should also arrange with the company controller to create a separate line item in the chart of accounts for each supplier. This is very useful as a control, for the coordinator can then insert a monthly and annual budget amount into the accounting system and receive a monthly report back from the accounting staff that lists the amount of expenditures to date for each supplier, as compared to a budgeted amount. This information can even be released daily if a supplier is approaching the limits of its budget, so that the coordinator will not authorize any work that exceeds the budget.

Another control is a complaint database. This is used mostly by company employees, since customers would not normally have any direct interaction with a company's administrative service functions, with the exception of the security function. One person is usually assigned to collect complaints, which may arrive by phone, electronic mail, or the postal service, and enter them into a database that is accessible by the functional coordinator as well as by top management. The coordinator should review this database frequently and bring complaints to the attention of suppliers as soon as possible, so that employees see that their complaints are resulting in some action. Without some evidence of improvement, the number of complaints will likely drop, since employees will see no corresponding action resulting from their complaints. A complaint database is an effective control over the administrative services function.

This section covered the most commonly used controls for the administrative services function, which include request tracking, comparisons to budgets and contracts, and a complaint database.

13.5   MEASURING THE OUTSOURCED FUNCTION

This section describes the measurements used to track the performance of the administration suppliers. The measures are primarily concerned with the cost and turnaround time of each supplier. There are no error rates or revenues in this function, so no measurements pertain to those items. There is a brief discussion of each measurement, along with a description of how it can be calculated. The measurements are as follows:

CLERICAL

*   *Average cost per hour.* A supplier of clerical staff is chiefly judged by the rate at which it bills out its personnel to a company. If its rates are excessive, it is unlikely that it will continue to do business with very many companies. In this highly competitive industry, suppliers who charge too much per hour will not last. To calculate this measurement, extract the cost per hour from the supplier's billing statement. If this is not clearly shown, divide the total number of hours worked into the total price charged to determine the average cost. One problem with this measure is that it is easily skewed if the company uses the services of even a small number of highly skilled temporary workers who are charged out at high hourly rates. This can give the functional coordinator the impression that a supplier is charging inordinately high rates, which only a close review of the underlying detailed records will resolve.

*   *Percentage hired from temporary.* It is difficult to make a qualitative judgment about a clerical supplier's ability to send the company top-notch temporary help. One way to get this information is to determine the percentage of temporary personnel who are hired from the supplier. To do so, manually track the number of temporary employees who are hired from each supplier. Then divide this number by the total number of temporary employees the company has used from the same supplier. The measurement must be used with care, for it can be skewed by the financial condition and revenue growth pattern of the company—if the company is flush with cash or especially if it is in need of new staff due to an increase in business, it may hire temporary workers with less regard for their quality.

COPY CENTER

*   *Cost per piece.* A copy center charges for each page copied. To calculate this measurement, extract from the supplier billings the total cost and divide it by the total number of pages copied. The measure can be skewed because there are very different rates for black-and-white copies and color copies; if both fees are combined into one measurement, the cost per piece will be very high. The best way to avoid this problem is to use two measurements, one for black-and-white copies and the other for color.

- *Turnaround time.* It is important to find out how responsive the supplier is to requests for copying. This applies to both internal and external copy centers. To do so, track the date and time when a copying job is requested from the supplier, and log in the date and time when it is delivered. Summarize this information for each month and divide it by the total number of separate copying requests during that period.

DESKTOP PUBLISHING

- *Cost per page.* A desktop publishing supplier normally charges on a per-page basis, though the fee can vary depending on the amount of graphics on each page. To track this measurement, extract from the supplier billings the total cost and divide it by the total number of pages created. A desktop publisher may also charge by the hour, but this is still the measurement to use, since it shows the productivity of the supplier in completing pages.

- *Turnaround time.* Desktop publishing work may be extremely time sensitive, especially when it is needed for sales presentations or client deliverables. It is therefore crucial to know the track record of a supplier in completing work on time. To calculate this measurement, track the date and time when a document is requested from the supplier, and log in the date and time when it is delivered. Summarize this information for each month and divide it by the total number of separate requests during that period.

RECORD STORAGE

- *Cost per cubic foot.* There are several fees that a record storage supplier can charge a company, such as charges for record pickup, return, or destruction, but the primary one, and the cost that makes up the bulk of most supplier billings, is the storage cost. To calculate it, either take this number from the supplier contract or determine the total cubic feet of storage used at the supplier's location each month and divide this amount into the monthly billing from the supplier.

- *Retrieval speed.* It may be critical to obtain information from storage on short notice. If so, a company should track the record storage supplier's ability to locate the correct records and bring them to the requesting person. To calculate this measurement, track the date and time when records were requested from the supplier and log in the date and time when they are delivered. Summarize this information for each month and divide it by the total number of deliveries during that period. The measure can be flawed if the supplier delivers the wrong information but it is logged in anyway as having been received. This problem can be avoided by having the receiving person verify that the documents match those requested prior to logging them in as received.

SECURITY

- *Average cost per hour.* There are a variety of charges that a security supplier can include in its billings, such as extra fees for security services during holidays or a premium for using armed guards, but the primary cost is the rate per hour. To calculate this measurement, extract the cost per hour from the supplier's billing statement. If this is not evident, divide the total number of hours worked into the total price charged to determine the average cost.

The above measurements are useful for tracking the performance of the suppliers of clerical, copy center, desktop publishing, record storage, and security services. They are focused on the cost of each function, along with the responsiveness of service in some areas. Using a selection of these measurements allows a company to track the key variables for its administration suppliers.

13.6 MANAGING THE OUTSOURCED FUNCTION

This section covers the management of the administration function after it has been outsourced. The topics covered are the structure of management needed and the skills and job descriptions of the management personnel assigned this role.

The multitude of tasks clustered within the administration function are usually assigned to the accounting department for day-to-day management, primarily because this function has a history of handling not only accounting, but also a catch-all of other tasks. Perhaps more importantly, no other company functions have (or want) a history of managing this area. The administration services are typically assigned to the controller, who divides them among assistant controllers for daily management. This reporting relationship is shown in Figure 13.2. An assistant controller's ability to manage these disparate tasks can even be a significant factor in promotion decisions. The only service that is commonly managed elsewhere is security, which may be given to the plant manager. However, it is assumed for this discussion that all administration functions stay within the accounting area.

The person who manages administration services is generally a low-level manager, since these are not mission-critical functions and do not involve large quantities of money. If contract negotiation is an issue, the manager can be assisted by a lawyer. The manager should have sufficient authority to sign off on supplier contracts and approve expenditures, though excessively high dollar amounts may require a secondary approval by the controller. Asset sales or purchases, as well as approval of contracts lasting multiple years, should be shifted up to the controller for approval. In short, the manager assigned to administration should be a lower-level manager who can be assisted in the more difficult management tasks and should not be allowed to commit the company to contracts of excessive size or duration without higher-level approval.

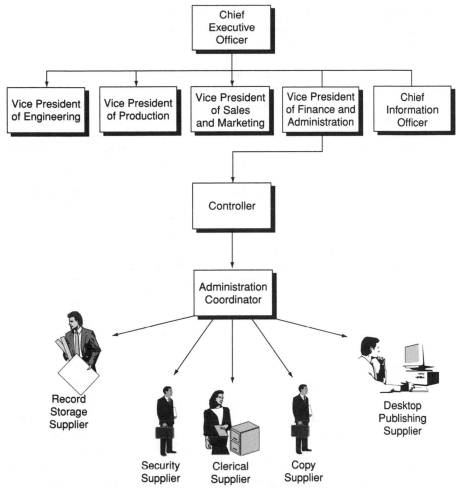

Figure 13.2   Organization Chart for Outsourcing the Administration Function

The skills required to manage the administration function do not require an especially large amount of service in the functional area, nor any specific training. The manager normally employs one or more personnel at the administrative assistant level, who logs in requests for service by employees and tracks supplier fulfillment of these requests. This requires low-level monitoring skill by the manager. Besides a small amount of management skill, it is helpful that the coordinator have some background in document management, since this gives him or her some familiarity with the issues surrounding the record storage, desktop publishing, clerical, and copying service areas. This all points toward a background in accounting, where document management is an underlying skill. The job description

Figure 13.3   The Administration Coordinator's Job Description

Employee Title: Administrative Services Outsourcing Coordinator
Reports to: Controller
Responsibilities:
- Sign off on all agreements with all administration suppliers.
- Authorize the release of funds for payment to suppliers.
- Compare actual costs charged to costs listed in contracts to determine the causes of variances; follow up on these variances with each supplier.
- Manage the transfer of functions from the company to the suppliers.
- Train company employees in how to log in job requests for copying, records retrieval, desktop publishing, and clerical assistance.
- Manage the clerical staff that logs in job requests.
- Monitor supplier performance by tracking the turnaround time needed to respond to employee requests.
- Periodically review security requirements with the supplier.
- Periodically review the adequacy of record storage facilities.
- Periodically review employee complaints regarding supplier service.
- Periodically review the security supplier's incident reports.

of a typical administration coordinator is noted in Figure 13.3. In short, no in-depth background or training in administration is needed to be a functional coordinator in this area.

The above discussion makes it quite clear that a low-end manager is the most common type of functional coordinator. However, this may not be the case in two situations. One is if the company is a large one where administrative costs are enormous. For example, the record storage cost of a Fortune 500 company can reach far into the millions of dollars, as can the cost of all of the other administrative services. In these companies, the potential costs are so much greater than in a small or midsized company that a specialist who has significant experience and training in the field may be assigned to each supplier. The second situation is when a company uses a supplier, such as Xerox, who implements a complex electronic document storage and retrieval system. This calls for a functional coordinator with a working knowledge of computer systems, who can operate the system and track its performance. This may also require some people skills, since the coordinator may have to work with the company's computer services staff to evaluate the installation and performance of supplier systems. Thus, the coordinator's skill level may be significantly higher if the administrative services area has a large budget or involves complex document-management systems.

This section covered the organizational structure used to manage an outsourced administrative services function, as well as the job description and skills of the functional coordinator who would manage the suppliers on behalf of the company. With the exception of large companies or those with complex document-management systems, this function tends to be assigned to a lower-level manager.

13.7   POTENTIAL CUSTOMER SERVICE ISSUES

There are a surprising number of customer service issues in the administration function. Though the services in this area do not normally interact directly with customers (with the exception of security), they can have a secondhand impact when they do not perform services quickly enough for other functional areas that do interact directly with customers. These problems, and ways in which they can be resolved, are noted in this section.

The only area that has some direct interaction with customers is the security function. Security personnel are not visible in most companies during regular business hours, so there is no interaction. However, for companies dealing with dangerous materials or top-secret information, all visiting customers must be cleared through the security staff. When this happens, customers can receive a wrong impression of the company if the security staff is too confrontational. A company can indirectly monitor this problem through a customer database, but this is an area where customers will not go out of their way to report bad treatment unless it is an exceptional situation. An easier alternative is to use the security cameras that monitor incoming visitors—rather than train them on customers, management can use them occasionally to view the manner in which the security staff deals with customers, and make any necessary corrective action. The best way to keep any customer problems from ever occurring is to put new security staff through customer-relations training and to give refresher training to long-term security personnel. In short, there is a potential for the security staff to improperly treat visiting customers, which can be avoided by training and video monitoring.

All other administration services can harm customer relations by not completing deliverables on time. For example, a record storage company may not locate and return a requested file that is needed for a customer presentation; a temporary clerical worker cannot complete a task that is required for a presentation to a customer; a copy service does not deliver copies of a final report for a customer until after the final meeting with the customer; a desktop publishing supplier cannot complete a set of graphics that is needed for the same presentation to a customer. In all of these cases, the customer does not know why the service it is receiving is inadequate, and it may blame some other functional area in the company for the problem, but the administration function is at fault. This problem, no matter which administration service is being provided, is solved with the same technique: job tracking. This is a simple log that is kept by the functional coordinator, in which the date on which a service request was made and the desired completion date are noted, along with the date when the service was actually completed. The functional coordinator should summarize this information for each supplier and review it regularly. The supplier must be notified if there are continuing problems with the timely delivery of service. Since this is an important problem that can impact customer relations, it is most acceptable to terminate a supplier for a continuing inability to provide services on time. In short, on-time service delivery can have a secondary impact on customer service, which can be tracked and resolved through the orderly logging and review of service requests.

This section covered the customer service issues involving the administration function, which include direct customer service problems through the security function and indirect problems through the other administration services.

13.8   GETTING OUT OF THE OUTSOURCING ARRANGEMENT

This section covers the problems to be aware of when terminating an outsourcing contract for an administration supplier.

It is a simple matter to terminate the services of an external copy center: Just stop sending documents to it for copying. It is another matter to terminate the services of a supplier who is providing on-site copying services. One problem is that the supplier may own the copying equipment. If so, the company should have a clause in its outsourcing contract allowing it to purchase the equipment, or it must move quickly to have new equipment brought in to replace the outgoing equipment that will leave with the supplier. Another problem is the lack of equipment servicing. If the supplier's in-house staff was maintaining the copying equipment and that staff is now leaving, the company must find a new equipment servicing supplier. This can be the outgoing supplier if the company is buying the supplier's copy equipment, or it may be a new supplier if the company elects to purchase a different brand of equipment. Finally, the company will have no staff to operate the equipment. It may have the option of hiring the staff of the outgoing supplier, or it may hire new staff. No matter what option a company takes, advance planning is necessary to avoid a drop in service when an internal copy center supplier is terminated.

The primary difficulty when terminating a record storage supplier is moving the records to a new storage facility. The supplier who has been terminated must be called upon in the contract to render all reasonable assistance to the company and its new supplier in helping to move the records to the new storage facility. This point should be noted in the contract with the supplier. The outgoing supplier may also charge a steep fee for helping to move the records; since this is the last billing it can charge the company, there is a temptation to charge a very high rate for this service. The problem can be avoided by specifying in the contract the rate per hour to move records out in the event of termination. In short, a company can use the contract with its record storage supplier both to avoid problems with moving records to a new supplier and to avoid any overbillings for this service.

A desktop publishing supplier is easier to terminate, since the company does not keep any assets at the supplier. However, the publisher may have a number of documents in computer storage that it has previously created or modified for the company. Some of these documents may contain confidential information, so the contract with the supplier should include a clause requiring the supplier to delete all of these files upon notice of termination. This does not mean that the company can prove the supplier's compliance with this order, but it does give the company a legal position in case it later becomes apparent that the supplier has used these files for services provided to other companies. Thus, the wording of the initial contract with a desktop publisher should require a supplier to destroy all documents it has stored for the company.

There are several tasks to complete when a company terminates its security supplier. First, depending on the supplier's attitude towards being terminated, the company may have to change all of its locks and access codes. This is a major issue if the company intends to leave the company facility unprotected rather than bring in another security service as a replacement. If there will be replacement personnel, these people can guard against unauthorized access, though it is still best to change the locks and access codes if the facility has many access points that cannot all be guarded. Another related task is to ensure that the outgoing supplier turns in all of its keys. Though keys can be easily replicated, it is best to retrieve the originals if a company does not intend to change its locks. One way to prevent the duplication of keys is to only use keys that are stamped "Do Not Duplicate," which keeps a reputable locksmith from making copies. Finally, if a facility is in a high-crime area or contains materials or information of high value, the functional coordinator must be sure to have a replacement team of security personnel on hand to guard the facility as soon as the old supplier's employees have departed. This requires advance planning to locate a qualified supplier. When terminating a security supplier, be sure to find a replacement supplier at once, and either retrieve all keys or (better yet) replace all locks and change all access codes.

This section covered the problems with terminating an administration supplier, including copier equipment and staffing problems, moving records from a record storage center, destroying documents at a desktop publisher, and changing facility access codes and locks.

13.9 SUMMARY

This chapter covered the highlights of administration outsourcing. "Administration" is a catch-all term for a number of key functions that are not closely linked, and which may not be managed by the same person. The service areas covered were security, temporary clerical help, desktop publishing, record storage, and copying. The advantages of outsourcing administration include reductions in fixed cost and storage space, as well as less need to manage these services. The primary contractual issues are pricing and service turnaround time. The best controls include a request tracking log to monitor turnaround time along with a complaints database and a comparison of billed costs to the budget and to the supplier's contract. The most important measurements are for the unit cost of the service provided and for the average turnaround time. Management of these suppliers is normally given to one or more low-level managers, frequently in the accounting area. Also, with the exception of security, all of the administration areas only have a secondary impact on customer service, which can be improved by monitoring service turnaround time. Finally, most supplier termination problems can be handled in advance by changes to the outsourcing contract, though a company may have to purchase copier equipment if it had previously sold these machines to a supplier. In short, outsourcing the administration functions makes sense in many cases because it shifts an administrative headache to a supplier while reducing a company's fixed costs.

CHAPTER FOURTEEN

Summary
of the Functional Areas

This chapter summarizes the previous chapters, which discussed all of a company's functional areas that can be outsourced. The layout of this chapter is similar to the chapters that it summarizes, with separate headings for such topics as controls, contractual issues, and customer service concerns. The only difference is the advantages and disadvantages heading, which is split into a separate section for each one. There is a table under each of these headings that lists the functional areas across the top, in the order in which they were presented in this book. Down the left side of each chart are the various outsourcing topics that were covered in each chapter, listed in alphabetical order. If a topic applies to a specific functional area, there is an asterisk in the table under that function heading that is level with the topic. There is also a brief discussion of the contents of each table. The purpose of these tables is to give a visual presentation of all of the data located in the previous chapters, so that the reader can gain a quick understanding of the issues for each functional area. However, in order to present a brief and readable set of tables, many of the lesser points noted in the chapters are not listed in them. Thus, it is important for the reader to thoroughly read each chapter covering a functional area, rather than relying on just the tables in this chapter, in order to gain the most thorough understanding of all issues surrounding the outsourcing of a functional area.

14.1 COMPARISON OF ADVANTAGES

This section compares the advantages of outsourcing the various company functions. The comparison of advantages for all functions is noted in Figure 14.1. There is great similarity in advantages for all areas, particularly the avoidance of fixed and capital costs. Some functions are outsourced because they are not strategic functions. It is also common to use suppliers to handle overflow situations within functions. A

Figure 14.1   Comparison of Outsourcing-Related Advantages for All Functions

Description	Acctg	Cmptr Service	Cust Service	Engi- neering	H/R	Main- tenance	Manufac- turing	Mtl Mgmt	Sales & Mktg	Admin
Avoids fixed costs	*	*	*		*		*	*	*	*
Avoids risk of loss					*					
Creates extra space	*	*	*	*		*	*	*	*	*
For overflow tasks			*	*						*
Hard to manage		*	*	*			*	*	*	
Has better staff	*	*	*	*		*	*	*	*	*
Knowledge of best practices	*	*	*			*		*	*	*
Less admini- stration	*	*	*	*	*	*	*	*	*	*
Lower cost		*		*	*					*
No capital needed		*	*			*	*	*	*	*
Not a strategic function		*			*	*				*
Not enough work to justify internal staff			*		*	*		*		*

common byproduct of outsourcing is the creation of extra space internally that had previously been used for the outsourced function. A very important point is that functions are outsourced because the supplier can do it better—it has better management, staff, or knowledge of best practices. The most unusual item is outsourcing in order to achieve *lower* costs; since *high* costs are listed as a disadvantage in the next section, it is evident that suppliers can only offer lower costs in limited situations, such as when they can negotiate lower prices on larger purchase volumes than a company can obtain. Thus, the most common outsourcing advantages are that the supplier can do the work better while absorbing all associated fixed and capital costs, which allows companies more time to work on their most strategically important functions.

14.2   COMPARISON OF DISADVANTAGES

This section compares the disadvantages of outsourcing the various company functions. The comparison of disadvantages for all functions is noted in Figure 14.2. The

Figure 14.2   Comparison of Outsourcing-Related Disadvantages for All Functions

Description	Acctg	Cmptr Service	Cust Service	Engi- neering	H/R	Main- tenance	Manufac- turing	Mtl Mgmt	Sales & Mktg	Admin
Cannot shift licences	*	*		*						
Distance to supplier				*		*	*			
High variable cost	*	*	*	*	*	*	*	*	*	*
Lose confidential information	*		*	*			*			
Lose own staff	*	*		*		*	*	*	*	
Low quality possible			*	*		*	*			
Need to train	*	*				*	*		*	
No company knowledge	*		*	*			*		*	
No loyalty to company									*	
Slow turnaround time	*	*		*		*	*	*		*
Too strategic		*		*			*			

most common disadvantage is the high variable cost of a supplier. Despite supplier claims to the contrary, there are only a limited number of situations where a supplier can perform the same tasks as a company for less cost. There is also a risk of losing confidential information, since suppliers will have access to company secrets in several functional areas. Another area of concern is slow turnaround time. A company can always complete a service faster than a supplier, because it is not distracted by the demands for service by its other customers, as is the case with a supplier. Thus, the most common disadvantages of outsourcing most functional areas are the cost and response time, with confidentiality being an issue for a smaller group of functions.

14.3   COMPARISON OF CONTRACTUAL ISSUES

This section compares the contractual issues that arise when outsourcing the various company functions. The comparison of contractual issues for all functions is noted in Figure 14.3. The following figure shows that, though there are many contractual issues that only apply to a small number of functional areas, a few are applicable to all or most functions. For example, all suppliers should be required to supply detailed billings so that the company can carefully compare the supplier's prices to the original contract rates, which should also be clearly specified in the contract. There should also be some mention of target turnaround times in the contract for most functions, as well

Figure 14.3　Comparison of Outsourcing-Related Contractual Issues for All Functions

Description	Acctg	Cmptr Service	Cust Service	Engi- neering	H/R	Main- tenance	Manufac- turing	Mtl Mgmt	Sales & Mktg	Admin
Baseline pricing	*	*				*				
Computer linkages	*	*	*				*	*		*
Confidentiality	*	*		*		*	*			
Copyright ownership					*		*			
Detailed billings	*	*	*	*	*	*	*	*	*	*
Equipment buyback	*	*		*		*	*	*		*
Free add-on services					*					
Insurance					*			*		
Joint marketing				*						
Methodology	*	*								
Patent ownership				*						
Penalties and bonuses	*	*		*			*	*		
Predefined reasons to terminate	*	*		*			*	*	*	
Right to return inventory						*	*	*		
Staffing approval	*	*		*						
Termination payments	*	*	*				*			*
Territories									*	
Turnaround time	*	*	*	*		*	*	*		*
Unit pricing	*	*	*	*	*	*	*	*	*	*
Upgrade payments	*	*		*						

as penalties and bonuses that are linked to achieving those targets. Also, the contract should note the conditions that will bring about the termination of the contract, as well as terms for having the company buy back equipment from the supplier in the event of termination. In summary, the primary contractual issues that apply to nearly all functions are pricing, billing formats, turnaround time, and conditions for termination.

14.4　COMPARISON OF TRANSITION ISSUES

This section compares the transition issues that arise when outsourcing the various company functions. The comparison of transition issues for all functions is noted in

Figure 14.4 Comparison of Outsourcing-Related Transition Issues for All Functions

Description	Acctg	Cmptr Service	Cust Service	Engi- neering	H/R	Main- tenance	Manufac- turing	Mtl Mgmt	Sales & Mktg	Admin
Confidentiality agreement	*	*		*		*	*			
Create computer linkages	*	*	*	*			*	*	*	
Hire coordinator	*	*	*	*	*	*	*	*	*	*
Inspect supplier facilities	*	*	*	*		*	*	*	*	
Sell equipment	*	*		*		*	*	*		*
Sell excess space	*	*	*	*	*	*	*	*	*	*
Train supplier	*	*	*	*		*	*		*	
Transfer key information	*	*		*	*	*	*			
Transfer staff	*	*	*	*		*	*	*		*

Figure 14.4. There are many similarities in transition steps for all of the functions. For example, all of them begin with the hiring of a functional coordinator and end with the disposition of excess space that was created by moving each function to a supplier. Many functions also require the transfer of staff, information, and equipment to suppliers. A majority of functions also require the inspection of supplier facilities and the signing of confidentiality agreements. Thus, the bulk of all transition issues apply to all functional areas.

14.5 COMPARISON OF CONTROL POINTS

This section compares the control points that arise when outsourcing the various company functions. The comparison of control points for all functions is noted in Figure 14.5. A few control points can be applied to most of the functional areas, such as comparisons of supplier billing statements to the budget or the supplier's contract. Other common controls are the use of a complaint database, keeping minutes from meetings with suppliers, reviewing expense trend lines, and storing supplier-specific expenses in separate general ledger accounts. However, there are many controls that can only be used for a small number of functional areas, such as change order tracking or milestone tracking, which are only useful for the computer services and engineering functions. To get a true picture of the full range of controls that are available for each functional area, it is best to consult the chapter pertaining to each function.

Figure 14.5   Comparison of Outsourcing-Related Control Points for All Functions

Description	Acctg	Cmptr Service	Cust Service	Engi-neering	H/R	Main-tenance	Manufac-turing	Mtl Mgmt	Sales & Mktg	Admin
Audit supplier		*	*			*	*	*		
Change order tracking		*		*						
Compare billings to budget	*	*	*	*	*	*	*	*	*	*
Compare billings to contract	*	*	*	*	*	*	*	*	*	*
Completed project review		*		*						
Keep meeting minutes	*	*	*	*	*	*	*	*	*	*
Review expense trends	*	*	*	*	*	*	*	*	*	*
Review insurance				*			*			
Separate general ledger account	*	*	*	*	*	*	*	*	*	*
Track milestones		*	*							
Use benchmarking		*								
Use complaint database	*	*	*	*	*	*	*	*	*	*
Use evaluation forms					*					

14.6   COMPARISON OF PERFORMANCE MEASUREMENTS

This section compares the performance measurements that arise when outsourcing the various company functions. The comparison of measurements for all functions is noted in Figure 14.6. There are a vast array of performance measurements that can be used to determine how well a supplier is completing its assigned tasks. Many are specific to a single functional area, such as evaluation scoring for training classes. However, there are many measurements that are common to most functional areas, some of which are mandatory for proper performance measurement. The single most important measurement is the unit price charged for a service. This applies to all functional areas, and is an excellent way to compare a supplier's prices to those of its competition. Another significant measure is turnaround time, which is crucial for determining how rapidly a supplier can complete its assigned tasks. Some kind of tracking system for determining the proportion of complaints from customers is also a prime indicator of a supplier's performance. In short, special measurements need to be used for tracking function-specific issues, but there are also measurements—such as unit pricing and turnaround time—that are needed to determine the overall performance of nearly all functional areas.

Figure 14.6   Comparison of Outsourcing-Related Measurements for All Functions

Description	Acctg	Cmptr Service	Cust Service	Engi-neering	H/R	Main-tenance	Manufac-turing	Mtl Mgmt	Sales & Mktg	Admin
Complaints	*	*	*	*	*	*	*	*	*	*
Completion dates	*	*		*		*	*	*		
Downtime		*	*						*	
Evaluation scoring					*					
Failure rates				*		*	*			
Percentage complete		*		*						
Percentage margins							*			
Retention									*	
Staff experience	*	*		*	◡	*				
Total cost	*	*	*	*	*	*	*	*	*	*
Turnaround time	*		*	*	*	*	*	*		*
Turnover					*					
Unit prices	*	*	*	*	*	*	*	*	*	*
Variance from baseline		*		*						
Working capital		*					*	*		

14.7   COMPARISON OF MANAGEMENT ISSUES

This section compares the management issues that arise when outsourcing the various company functions. The comparison of management issues for all functions is noted in Figure 14.7. Except for the presence of a functional coordinator, there are no management issues that are common to all functional areas. However, several issues are of importance for a large number of functions. These include having an in-house support staff to assist in managing suppliers and requiring that the functional coordinator have significant experience and training in the functional area to be managed. Otherwise, there is a large dispersion in management issues, ranging from having many suppliers to just one, and from needing only a low-level functional coordinator to having one at the highest levels of company management. Thus, there are few common management issues that apply to all functional areas—special management problems arise for each one.

14.8   COMPARISON OF CUSTOMER SERVICE ISSUES

This section compares the customer service issues that arise when outsourcing the various company functions. The comparison of customer service issues for all functions is noted in Figure 14.8. The two most important customer service issues that relate to the

Figure 14.7 Comparison of Outsourcing-Related Management Issues for All Functions

Description	Acctg	Cmptr Service	Cust Service	Engi-neering	H/R	Main-tenance	Manufac-turing	Mtl Mgmt	Sales & Mktg	Admin
Additional in-house support staff	*	*		*	*	*	*	*	*	
Background in the functional area	*	*		*	*	*	*	*	*	
Coordinator, high-level	*	*		*			*	*	*	
Coordinator, low-level					*					*
Coordinator, mid-level				*		*				
Different bosses						*				
Large budget	*	*		*			*	*		
Multiple suppliers	*	*		*	*		*		*	*
Process flow knowledge	*	*			*					*
Single supplier			*	*			*			
Small budget										*

Figure 14.8 Comparison of Outsourcing-Related Customer Service Issues for All Functions

Description	Acctg	Cmptr Service	Cust Service	Engi-neering	H/R	Main-tenance	Manufac-turing	Mtl Mgmt	Sales & Mktg	Admin
Damaged deliveries							*	*		
Incorrect payments	*									
Incorrect receipt handling	*									
Late service delivery	*	*		*	*	*	*	*		*
Lose insurance					*					
No customer access		*							*	
Poor assembly							*	*		
Poor message									*	
Poor product or service quality	*	*	*	*	*	*	*	*	*	*
Poor training	*	*	*	*	*	*	*	*	*	*

supplier of a functional area are the late delivery and poor quality of service or products. Other, lesser concerns are incorrect billings, lost insurance, and lack of access to the company by customers, but the most important issues by far are late service and poor quality. The discussion of how to mitigate these problems is noted in the chapter that deals with each functional area.

14.9   COMPARISON OF TERMINATION ISSUES

This section compares the termination issues that arise when outsourcing the various company functions. The comparison of termination issues for all functions is noted in Figure 14.9. The most significant termination issue is that a company must arrange for alternate methods of supplying a service if it terminates the work of a supplier. This may involve bringing the work back in-house or shifting it to another supplier. In either case, some lead time is required to do so, especially if new facilities and equipment are needed. The next most common termination problem is that a company may have to shut down any computer linkages to the supplier, depending on the service it is providing, and recreate them for whichever supplier is replacing the old one. Thus, the most common termination issue is that it takes time to move away from a supplier, due to the need to create other facilities elsewhere, either in-house or by finding a new supplier.

Figure 14.9   Comparison of Outsourcing-Related Termination Issues for All Functions

Description	Acctg	Cmptr Service	Cust Service	Engi-neering	H/R	Main-tenance	Manufac-turing	Mtl Mgmt	Sales & Mktg	Admin
Access to former staff	*	*		*						
Finish existing projects		*		*					*	
Need alternate facilities	*	*	*	*		*	*	*	*	*
Reroute computer linkages	*	*	*	*			*	*	*	
Shift phone number			*						*	
Take back equipment	*	*		*		*	*	*		*
Take back inventory						*	*	*		
Termination fees	*	*	*			*	*	*	*	*
Wait until end of contract period					*					

14.10   SUMMARY

A cursory review of the figures listed in this chapter shows that there are great similarities between the issues that impact each of the functional areas. For example, a reduction in administrative time is an advantage that is common to all functional areas, while high variable pricing is a disadvantage that also applies to all functional areas. In addition, unit pricing must be included in all contracts, while the transition for all functional areas begins with the appointment of a functional coordinator. Many of the same issues must be considered when handling the details of outsourcing a functional area.

Having pointed out the similarities between outsourcing the functions, it is equally important to note that there are many issues that only apply to a small number of functions. In order to save space, some issues were not included in these figures, and may only be found in the chapters that deal with a specific function. Thus, it is important not to read just this chapter, which is meant to be nothing more than an overview and comparison of outsourcing issues, and ignore the previous chapters, which give much more information regarding outsourcing issues.

CHAPTER FIFTEEN

The Future of Outsourcing

This chapter discusses various ways in which outsourcing may evolve in the future. There will be changes in the size and interrelationships of suppliers that will be driven by the need of large corporations to deal with suppliers with a global presence and a wide range of skills. Also, the profitability of suppliers will change as more suppliers enter the field, making pricing pressures more intense. In addition, companies will become more knowledgeable in dealing with suppliers, and will take steps both internally and externally to improve their level of skill in this area. As suppliers begin to look for more business, it is likely that they will expand their sales efforts both geographically and strategically, targeting down to smaller-sized companies. These issues and others are discussed in this chapter.

15.1 OVERALL MARKET PENETRATION

Several factors will influence the market penetration of outsourcing. One factor is the level of comfort that companies have with handing some of their functions to outside organizations. This comfort level is not a problem for low-cost functions or those with low strategic value, such as janitorial services. If a company engages a supplier to provide such "introductory level" services and has a good experience, then there is a greater chance that the company will eventually try to outsource more sophisticated functions. It takes a long time for a company to work its way from outsourcing low-level functions to doing the same for such expensive or strategically important functions as computer services and engineering. If there is a bad outsourcing experience along the way, it is likely that the company will stop any further outsourcing and may even bring some previously outsourced functions back in-house. Thus, the depth of market penetration depends to a large extent on the experience companies have with outsourcing other functions.

Another key determinant of market penetration is the level of sales work suppliers must undertake to convince a company that outsourcing is a viable option. This sales effort can require many contacts with the company and may continue for many months or years before a decision is reached. Since a supplier wants the largest possible return for its sales investment, only the largest companies will be the target of concentrated sales efforts by suppliers. Small companies may receive only the most rudimentary sales efforts, if any. Thus, it is likely that the market penetration among smaller companies will not be significant, especially for those functions—such as manufacturing or computer services—that require a concentrated and prolonged sales effort.

The final determinant of market penetration is the proclivity of management to keep all functions under its direct control. Some managers have an underlying need to directly control every aspect of a company's functions, and will not consider any outsourcing for that reason—they would be continuously uncomfortable with the thought of having an outside organization take over some part of the company. In these cases, the chance of having any penetration by a supplier is slim. The only possibility for a determined supplier would be to go around management by appealing to the board of directors. This approach does not have a high percentage of success, but there is a trend towards having more independent boards, so the option may work in a few cases, however unlikely it may seem. However, even if outsourcing is approved by the board of directors, the same management team that already shot down previous supplier advances will be in charge of implementing the board's directive, so the supplier can count on a very difficult time dealing with the management group that it just circumvented. In short, some management teams simply will not adopt outsourcing unless forced to by the company's board of directors.

In summary, the level of market penetration by suppliers will be subject to the previous experiences of individual companies with outsourcing, the sales efforts expended by suppliers (which will likely be concentrated on only the largest companies), and the proclivity of company managers to accept outsourcing as a viable alternative to having the company handle all functions in-house.

15.2   MARKET PENETRATION AMONG FINANCIALLY TROUBLED COMPANIES

Outsourcing originally caught on the quickest among those companies experiencing financial difficulties. This was because suppliers were trying to establish a market presence and did so by pushing the lower cost of their services to those companies who were desperately in search of anything that could reduce their costs. Another technique was for the supplier to purchase some company assets, thereby giving the company a one-time cash infusion. As outsourcing has become more established, the suppliers who have achieved a high level of market penetration have not pursued business with financially troubled companies. However, a new group of suppliers have entered the market in all functional areas, and are willing to take on this sort of business in order to gain a foothold in the outsourcing market. Thus, it appears likely that not only will the existing market penetration of suppliers among financially troubled companies continue, but that the level of penetration will increase, these being the easiest targets for suppliers who are new competitors in the outsourcing arena.

15.3   MARKET PENETRATION BY FUNCTION

Suppliers will have much greater market penetration for those functions that are perceived to be of low cost or low strategic value. For example, many companies outsource their janitorial, security, and maintenance functions. These functions require minimal management, have a relatively low cost, and cannot harm the company even if the supplier does a poor job of providing the service. In addition, the sales effort required to get a company to take on a supplier's services is minimal—sometimes a brochure in the mail and a follow-up phone call are all that is required to secure a sale. Accordingly, these functions will enjoy high market penetration for companies of all sizes.

Market penetration will be progressively less for those functions that require higher costs or which will damage the company if a supplier does a poor job of supplying the service. Telephone support services fall into this category, since low-quality support can damage a company's relations with its customers. Manufacturing services can create similar problems if a company's products are not assembled correctly. Likewise, computer services are both expensive and can bring company functions to a halt if they are not handled properly. Also, because of these perceived difficulties, the sales effort required to sell companies these services will be much higher and more long term, which will confine the most intensive sales work to the largest companies. For these functions, market penetration will be considerably lower due to the added sales effort required to sell them, the higher cost of the service, or the possibility of damaging a company's operations if poor-quality service is provided.

15.4   MARKET PENETRATION BY GEOGRAPHICAL AREA

Outsourcing will gain the greatest market penetration in urban areas and later move into suburban and rural company locations; however, these regions will never see the level of market penetration achieved in urban areas. Those locations with large concentrations of potential customers are where suppliers will target their marketing efforts, since it is more efficient for their sales teams to cover the smallest regions possible. As competition becomes more intense in these urban areas and the number of available customers declines, suppliers will be forced to move further afield in search of new customers. It is more likely that they will jump to other urban areas than that they will stay in one area and branch out into the countryside, so it may be a very long time before outsourcing is seen with any regularity in the less populated areas. The jump to other urban areas is also likely to include those areas in other countries. Due to the difficulty of access, outsourcing will always have more presence in high-population areas.

The level of geographical market penetration will vary greatly by the type of function being outsourced. Some functions require that the supplier be able to regularly visit the company's location to provide services. Examples of these functions are the janitorial, maintenance, administration, and materials-management functions. For these functional areas, suppliers will have to travel a long way to service the more geographically isolated companies, and so those companies may never see any bids for outsourcing. However, other functions do not require the continual presence of suppliers at the company location. Examples of these functions are telephone-based customer service and telemarketing, manufacturing, payroll, and sales. For these functions, suppliers can provide service to the company without having to visit the company location with any regularity (except for initial sales calls and later visits to maintain the relationship), since the service they provide can be handled elsewhere. For these functions, then, it is less relevant where the company is located, though sales teams pursuing these companies are still likely to go after companies in higher-population areas first, since they can call on more companies in one day by doing so. In short, the market penetration of suppliers will vary drastically by function, with those functions requiring on-site supplier presence having minimal market penetration in rural areas, whereas the penetration will be higher for those functions that do not require continual on-site supplier presence.

15.5 CHANGES IN COMPETITION

As outsourcing matures, there will be a number of changes in the competitive situation in all functional areas and industries. One change will be an increase in the number of niche suppliers. These are suppliers who have a very small area of specialization, and who work as subcontractors for lead suppliers who, in turn, sell their services to companies. The technical skills of these suppliers are usually quite good, while their sales and management skills are lacking; this is why they work through a lead supplier who possesses these missing skills, and can use them to sell a subcontractor's services to a supplier and manage the subcontractor's activities once the company has agreed to accept its services. Over time, it is likely that subcontractors will associate themselves more firmly with those lead suppliers who can bring them the most business, and will eventually form formal links with those lead suppliers. It is also likely that lead suppliers will purchase equity stakes in those subcontractors that possess truly unique skills, thereby denying the services of those subcontractors to other lead suppliers—locking in the services of the best subcontractors will become a barrier to entry for potential new suppliers. Thus, the appearance of a large number of supplier subcontractors is likely, with this trend evolving into the formation of associations of subcontractors with lead suppliers who market and manage their services, and who may purchase some subcontractors to lock in necessary skills.

The other competitive trend will be the continuing appearance of new suppliers, especially in those high-skill areas that allow high profits by suppliers, such as engineering and computer services. New suppliers will be most inclined to enter these areas in search of the highest profits and less likely to enter those functional areas that are more competitive, and which therefore yield lower levels of profit. The success rate among these new suppliers in the high value–added functions will be poor; the reason is that a company that is reviewing potential suppliers to take over a strategically important function will be much more inclined to give its business to a supplier that has a great deal of previous experience in this area. The company cannot afford to give its business to a new entrant in the field, since the function is too important to entrust to a new supplier, however low a price the supplier may bid. Thus, the likeliest pattern to be seen among these new entrants will be a significant investment in sales efforts targeted at the largest companies (with the intention of giving the new supplier an immediate set of well-known references for its later sales efforts), accompanied by exceptionally low pricing and contract terms that are advantageous to the targeted companies. Most of these efforts will fail, since the new suppliers have no track record, and the suppliers will withdraw from the marketplace after having sustained significant losses from the few disadvantageous contracts that were signed.

Perhaps the only reasonable way to enter a functional area where previous experience is considered a strong selling point is to buy a supplier who has been competing in the target area for some time and pump additional resources into that supplier in an effort to increase its market share. If new suppliers want to enter a market quickly, this may lead, as a side benefit, to a rapid increase in the market value of established suppliers, since they may be the targets of takeover bids by the new suppliers. In short, spending capital on the purchase of an existing supplier may be a better investment than attempting to enter a market without any previous experience in that area.

Competition among suppliers will change in several ways. There will be more subcontractors that work through lead suppliers that are skilled in managing these smaller suppliers. Many new suppliers will attempt to compete in those markets where high profit levels are expected, but will generally fail due to their lack of a track record, which is a major selling point. Finally, new suppliers will purchase established suppliers in order to gain an immediate market share; this trend will drive up the market value of established suppliers.

15.6   CHANGES IN PRICING

Outsourcing can yield abnormally high profit margins, especially in those functional areas that require high levels of skill to properly service. These high margins will attract additional competitors, who will offer lower prices to companies in order to obtain their business. More established suppliers will drop their prices in order to prevent the new competition from gaining a toehold in the market. As a result, there will be price erosion and a drop in profitability across all functional areas for suppliers. However, this reduction in margins will be minimized in those areas where the supplier can provide a service that requires great technical skill, since the supplier can use this skill to differentiate itself from its competition. Thus, those suppliers trying to maintain their traditionally high levels of profitability will be most successful in the high-skill service areas, such as engineering and computer services, and least successful in the low-skill areas, such as janitorial services.

Another way for a supplier to maintain margins is to concentrate on providing extra services to companies for which a premium can be charged. For example, an equipment-maintenance supplier may earn low margins from providing scheduled maintenance to a company's truck fleet, which is a very competitive business; however, it can earn higher profits by also providing complete engine and transmission overhauls, which requires far more skill to properly complete. As another example, a computer services company may earn average margins by providing network maintenance to a company, but may earn more by offering to install an internal fiber optic network, which requires a higher skill level and is therefore a more valuable and profitable service. These extra services may even take the form of offering services in a completely unrelated area, so that a company will have the added convenience of only dealing with one supplier when having several functional areas serviced. This has already happened in the computer services area, where data center providers have purchased desktop support as well as network service suppliers. It is unlikely that a supplier will begin to provide services in an entirely different functional area, since this would require either purchasing another supplier or developing an entirely new area of expertise, and since the perceived benefit by the company is only that of dealing with one less supplier, it is unlikely that this would result in significantly higher profits being earned by the supplier.

In short, more competitors will enter all functional areas in pursuit of higher-than-average earnings. This will force existing suppliers to either drop their prices in order to compete, migrate their service areas to those functions that require high skill levels (and therefore demand higher profits), or begin to offer high-margin add-on services to supplement the margins from their core businesses.

15.7 CHANGES IN CONTRACT TERMS

As competitive conditions and the experience of companies with outsourcing changes, there will be some modification of outsourcing contracts. One item will be the push by companies for more shared risk and reward terms. These terms involve changing supplier payments based on how the performance of the company is altered by the supplier—if there is more profit, the supplier's compensation is greater, and vice versa. These sorts of deals are not likely to achieve great acceptance in the marketplace, because established suppliers will realize that these terms will introduce a high level of variability into their earnings, and could even threaten their existence if a number of such deals were to produce less-than-stellar earnings. However, new suppliers who are trying to gain an edge in the marketplace will be more willing to take on these deals just to take on some customers, and so the acceptance of shared risk and reward terms will be greatest among new suppliers.

As new suppliers appear and try to take business away from established suppliers, it is likely that the established suppliers will try to lock companies into longer-term outsourcing deals with them. This will keep the potential number of companies available to the new suppliers at a minimum, and may lock them out of the more lucrative deals for so long that they will quit the market rather than wait until contracts terminate and companies look to rebid their outsourcing situations. Longer contract terms will be pushed by suppliers to keep out new competitors.

New suppliers will allow the softening of a number of contract terms in order to get more business. For example, a new supplier might accept only minimal increases in the contract price based on inflationary adjustments. It also might allow a company to easily terminate the agreement or at least do so with a much smaller termination fee than is customary. Another option might be allowing very large penalty payments if the level of service is substandard. Finally, a supplier might allow a company to include all or most services to be provided under a single contract price, rather than trying to move some services into higher-priced categories of service. Though this sort of arrangement is highly beneficial to the company, it puts the supplier under the thumb of the company. The supplier has gained a foothold in the marketplace by signing this contract, but is in a highly disadvantageous position, and will try to get out of or renegotiate the contract once it has gathered enough other service agreements with other companies to give it a viable position in the market. Generally, it is best for a company to avoid this kind of contract, and to avoid the supplier that is willing to agree to such terms.

In summary, new suppliers will make a number of concessions in contract terms in order to win new business, while more established companies may also do so in order to avoid losing business to new competitors. Existing suppliers will also try to push companies into long-term agreements, which effectively keeps new suppliers out of the market by shrinking the number of potential customers for new suppliers.

15.8   SUPPLIER ALLIANCES

One of the most likely trends in the outsourcing field will be the creation of alliances between suppliers. This trend will be driven by larger companies who demand a large variety of services from a single supplier. Since most suppliers have a limited set of skills, they will have to work together to offer bids to companies that contain the full spectrum of services demanded. This trend is most likely for those smaller suppliers who cannot otherwise compete against the largest suppliers who have larger numbers of skilled employees to use to service a company. However, the demands of the largest companies will require even the largest suppliers to find partners for some of the more specialized services being requested, or because the company may require that services be delivered in a geographical area in which the supplier has no presence—hiring a subcontractor in that area may be the only viable option for winning the bid to work for the company. It is even possible that companies may require that specific subcontractors be used, since the company may be comfortable with the services already provided by those subcontractors, or may be impressed enough by their reputation to make it clear that no bid will be accepted unless such subcontractors are included. There will be an increasing trend towards alliances among suppliers to provide a greater range of services to companies.

As these alliances evolve, it will be necessary for one supplier to take the lead in managing the other suppliers, since the company will not want the hassle of going to a large number of suppliers to request services or to have problems fixed. This means that suppliers skilled in managing subcontractors will arise, with good project management skills. These lead suppliers are likely to earn a somewhat larger profit than their subcontractors, since they will take on additional management chores. Also, it is possible that the lead suppliers will cherry pick the subcontractors and buy those suppliers that provide core skills that are necessary for most bids submitted by the lead suppliers. This is likely to happen in particular for those subcontractors who have especially valuable skills that cannot be procured elsewhere. By purchasing these subcontractors, lead suppliers can lock in those critical skill sets needed to win bids. The formation of alliances will create a new class of lead suppliers who may acquire those of their subcontractors who possess the skills most critical for winning bids.

Supplier alliances will become more common as companies demand a larger number of services over a greater geographical range. Lead suppliers that are noted for their management skills will arise among these alliances, and will be likely to purchase those subcontractors who possess the most critical skills.

15.9   SUPPLIER–VENTURE CAPITAL ALLIANCES

A less likely scenario is that venture capital firms will form partnerships with suppliers to provide services to newly formed companies in which the venture capital firms have purchased equity stakes. It is in the interests of a venture capital firm to do this, for it can reduce the risk that its investment in a start-up company will be lost because the start-up cannot manage those functions that can more easily be left to suppliers to handle. Venture capital firms could have preexisting arrangements with a variety of suppliers, allowing them to take over various functions as soon as the firm purchases a stake in a start-up. This guarantees some business for a supplier, which means that the supplier may have to offer especially low pricing in exchange for this guaranteed business. However, such an arrangement may be less palatable to a supplier because the typical start-up company is very small and will not provide much of a revenue boost for the supplier. However, there is the chance that a start-up will greatly increase in size (which is why the venture capital firm chose to invest in it in the first place), which means that there is a chance that the supplier's revenue volume will drastically increase as the start-up's revenue increases. Thus, it is reasonable for venture capital firms to seek alliances with suppliers who will provide services to start-up companies, but the size of the start-up companies means that suppliers will not receive large volumes of business from such deals, and will therefore be lukewarm about entering into this type of agreement with a venture capital firm.

An alternative scenario is that a company with a track record of purchasing large numbers of other companies will form alliances with suppliers. As the company purchases other companies, suppliers will take over specific functions as part of the takeovers. This is a very advantageous position for a supplier to be in, since an established company that is acquired may be far larger than a start-up, which means that the supplier will earn far more revenues. The acquiring company will be doing so much business with its suppliers that it will justifiably be able to extract excellent pricing terms from them. In short, it is very advantageous for both suppliers and acquiring companies to form alliances to provide services to acquired companies, and is something that suppliers should aggressively pursue.

Venture capital and acquisition-minded companies should enter into arrangements with suppliers to provide services for a variety of functions to those companies in which equity stakes have been purchased, or which have been bought. This increases the reliability of services for the venture capital and acquiring companies, while greatly increasing the sales volume of the suppliers.

15.10   SUPPLIER-COMPANY ALLIANCES

There may be several instances in which supplier-company alliances will arise. One possibility (that has already occurred several times) is that the supplier will develop a highly advanced application while servicing a company. The company and the supplier then agree to jointly market the application. This is most common with software development and is not a factor with nearly all other functional areas. The most common case so far is for the supplier to own the software application but to pay the company some portion of its profits from the sale of the application to other companies. The company retains an ownership interest in the software because it provided the original funding for software development. These alliances are especially useful for suppliers, since the company may be very interested in continuing to develop new applications with the supplier if the first application proved to be profitable through sales to other companies. Thus, supplier-company alliances may arise to market software that was created by the supplier to service the company.

Another supplier-company alliance may arise if one party purchases the other. This may occur if the company feels that the supplier provides a service so valuable that it must lock in as much of the supplier's available capacity as possible. A good example of this is the (now defunct) acquisition of Electronic Data Systems by General Motors. The reverse situation may arise if a supplier feels that it must purchase a company either to share in its above-average profit levels or to keep the company from going bankrupt; a more common variation on this option would be to invest just enough equity or debt in the company to give the supplier a seat on the board of directors, through which it could influence company policy. The danger for a supplier in purchasing a company is that it may lose any business it has with other companies in the same industry, since it now has a controlling interest in a competitor. Supplier-company alliances may arise that are caused by the ownership of one entity by the other.

In short, supplier-company alliances may arise to jointly market products. This type of arrangement has so far been restricted to the computer services suppliers, but may expand into other areas where leading-edge services can be created through the joint efforts of suppliers and companies. Also, alliances may arise through the purchase of suppliers by companies (or vice versa) for a variety of reasons.

15.11   IN-HOUSE OUTSOURCING DEPARTMENTS

As companies use suppliers to handle a greater proportion of company functions, it is likely that they will create in-house outsourcing departments, as some have already done, that will act as a resource for management in finding suppliers, issuing requests for proposals, evaluating bids, negotiating contracts, handling transitions to the winning suppliers, and providing support to management in handling current supplier relationships. These outsourcing departments could be composed of lawyers who specialize in contract negotiations with suppliers, internal auditors with knowledge of the control systems needed to manage a supplier, accountants who know how to set up accounting transactions with suppliers, human resources personnel who specialize in moving employees to supplier organizations, and analysts who comb industry literature for information about how other outsourcing deals have developed, and what lessons can be learned from these situations. The goal of this department would be to ensure that all company outsourcing deals are completed in accordance with a standardized format that is used throughout the company; this format will keep the company from missing any important implementation steps, help it to select the correct supplier, create a contract with no major flaws, and manage the supplier relationship in a way that benefits both parties. It is unlikely that this type of department will arise in smaller organizations, since the overhead cost of maintaining it would be too great; nor would it be seen even in a larger corporation if the organization was not committed to the outsourcing of many functions. The department would only come into existence if the company were both large enough to support its expense and interested in outsourcing a large number of functions. For smaller companies that cannot afford this type of in-house service, it is possible that they will band together to form industry-specific outsourcing advisory groups that will provide the same type of advice to those companies that give them support through some kind of membership fee structure. Any company that is unwilling to pay a fee would not have access to the specialized assistance of an advisory group. It is likely that companies will form either in-house or industry-specific advisory groups that specialize in how to outsource various functions and how to manage suppliers once the initial outsourcing steps have been completed.

In-house outsourcing departments will arise that are skilled in assisting the management of all company functions through the various steps of the outsourcing process. For smaller firms who cannot afford this luxury, there will be industry-sponsored groups that provide the same service.

15.12   CONTROL OVER SUPPLIERS BY COMPANIES

Companies will become more sophisticated in the ways they control the performance of their suppliers. This will happen in two ways. One will be the increased use of standard internal audit programs to review the performance of suppliers. There will be an increase in the body of literature that addresses audit programs for outsourcing, and this literature will eventually cover all functional areas. Corporate internal audit staffs can either purchase these audit programs or develop their own programs in-house. Using internal audits to review suppliers will increase as corporate controllers begin to understand the operational and financial risks of outsourcing, and seek to understand their current levels of risk. The second area of control will be the use of outside benchmarking organizations. These organizations will periodically measure the performance of a company's suppliers and compare those measurements to a baseline set of metrics they have collected from other companies that indicate world-class performance. This information will then be sent to the functional coordinator of whatever functional area was reviewed, who will then use it to evaluate the supplier in question. This sort of periodic review would be intended to keep current suppliers from adopting sloppy business practices, as well as to decide when to switch to a better supplier. These independent review organizations might even take on the role of reporting on the performance metrics of a supplier as a form of certification—the supplier could then use this information as a marketing tool (if the resulting metrics were good enough). However, since only the best supplier would welcome this sort of attention, it is questionable whether there is enough demand to warrant the use of these organizations in providing certified metrics to suppliers. In short, companies will become more sophisticated in their use of both internal and external resources to control their suppliers, the most notable change being the appearance of independent performance-measurement organizations.

15.13   INCREASE IN GOVERNMENT INTERVENTION

There is some chance that government intervention in the outsourcing industry will increase, though the probability is not high. One form of intervention would be the prohibition of mergers among suppliers if some suppliers are beginning to take over a large proportion of their respective industries. This is not likely yet, because there are no very large suppliers in any functional areas (with the exception of computer services, and even in that area, the largest suppliers do not have an excessive proportion of the market). If the government were to prohibit certain mergers, it would likely be at the instigation of competitors of the two suppliers seeking to merge, since the merger would not help the competitive situation of other suppliers. Thus, one form of possible government regulation would be to prohibit the merger of suppliers that might potentially create monopoly situations.

A second area of possible government intervention would be in the regulation of suppliers. This regulation might take the form of rules for how outsourcing work is to be performed, the presence of a regulatory body with oversight powers, or even the issuance of licenses that would be required before a supplier could solicit business. There is not a high likelihood that this type of regulation will occur, for several reasons. First, outsourcing covers so many functional areas that government regulation of all possible areas of outsourcing would be a huge task; the sheer magnitude of the potential regulation work might turn the government away from considering creating a set of regulations or an oversight body to enforce those regulations. The second reason is that outsourcing is self-governing—if a supplier does not behave properly, it will lose customers and go out of business. No government regulation is needed to enforce quality business practices if the market itself is quite capable of enforcing them. However, the government might be tempted to enforce some regulation if there were one or more high-profile cases where sloppy work by suppliers were to force a prominent company into a serious financial position. The resulting public outcry might force the government to take on some oversight role. In short, the government could create laws to govern suppliers and create a government entity to enforce those laws; this is not likely for several reasons, but if the actions of a few suppliers were to inflict heavy damage on well-known companies, the likelihood of some government action would increase.

In summary, government intervention in the outsourcing arena is not likely. If it were to occur, however, it would be in the prohibition of any supplier mergers that might reduce competition, and in the imposition of regulations resulting from high-profile problems at suppliers that damaged their customers.

15.14   IMPACT OF OUTSOURCING ON THE NATIONAL ECONOMY

What will be the impact of outsourcing on the national economy? Outsourcing improves the efficiency and competitiveness of a company by upgrading its functions and (in some cases) reducing its costs. If all companies were to adopt outsourcing across many functional areas, there would be a considerable improvement in national productivity, resulting in higher corporate earnings. However, this improvement is unlikely to take place rapidly, if at all. The reason for the slow improvement is that a company requires a long time to accept outsourcing. It usually outsources a small function, waits a while to see how it works, and gradually brings in more suppliers as it gains confidence in the use of outsourcing. Also, suppliers are more concerned with marketing their services to the largest companies, since they can gain the greatest revenue volume for the smallest sales effort; this means that the hundreds of thousands of smaller companies that make up the bulk of the economy are receiving only the most indifferent sales pitches from suppliers. Thus, since outsourcing acceptance is a slow process and the efforts of suppliers are primarily directed at the largest companies, it is unlikely that the efficiencies and improved competitiveness provided by the outsourcing solution will have a significant impact on the performance of the national economy.

An area where outsourcing might have a significant impact on a national economy is if it were to be introduced into a developing country. In this instance, introducing the world-class efficiencies of a top-notch supplier into a few of the developing country's largest corporations could have a measurable impact on the economy. This is because many smaller countries are dominated by a few large businesses, with the remaining companies making up a smaller proportion of the economy than would be the case in a mature, well-developed business environment. Thus, helping a small number of the largest companies in a developing country could bring about a noticeable improvement in the economy as a whole.

Outsourcing would have a minimal impact on the efficiency of a large, well-developed economy, because it is requires a large amount of time to sell this service, and because suppliers usually concentrate their efforts on a small number of large companies. However, outsourcing may bring about a significant improvement for a small, developing country if only a few of the largest corporations try it, since they make up a much larger percentage of the business activity in their country.

15.15   SUMMARY

In this chapter, a number of changes in market penetration for suppliers were predicted—in general, among geographical areas, among financially troubled companies, and by function. In addition, a number of changes were predicted in the areas of supplier competition, pricing, and contract terms. Also, the forming of a number of alliances were predicted, not only among suppliers but also between suppliers and venture capital firms, acquisition-minded companies, and financially troubled companies. A number of changes were also predicted within companies, such as the appearance of in-house outsourcing departments and new controls over suppliers. It is also possible that new government controls will be implemented to govern outsourcing. Finally, the impact of outsourcing on the performance of the national economy was discussed. In short, outsourcing is a maturing concept that will involve the consolidation of existing suppliers, the entrance of new competitors into the marketplace, stiffer price competition, and the movement of suppliers into higher value–added services as they continue to search for new products that yield above-average profits. Companies will mature in their approach to suppliers, resulting in better out-sourcing of functions and better management of those functions once they have been given to a supplier. This higher degree of comfort with the outsourcing concept will lead to greater market acceptance, which will have a modest impact on the perfor-mance of the national economy as functions are run more efficiently.

APPENDIX A

Suggested Readings

Ambrosio, J. "Outsourcing at Southland: Best of Times, Worst of Times." *Computerworld,* March 25, 1991, 1, 119.

Anthes, G. "Perot Wins 10-year Outsourcing Deal." *Computerworld,* April 8, 1991, 96.

Avish, Shimon. "T&E Expense: To Outsource or Not?" *Management Accounting,* September 1997, 44–48.

Barr, Stephen. "Payroll Quandaries." *CFO,* May 1997, 83–88.

Bostwick, William J., and J. Ralph Byington. "Outsourcing of Internal Audit: Concerns and Opportunities." *The Journal of Corporate Accounting & Finance,* Summer 1997, 85–93.

Burt, David N. "Managing Suppliers Up to Speed." *Harvard Business Review,* July–August 1989, 129.

Czegel, Barbara. *Running an Effective Help Desk: Planning, Implementing, Marketing, Automating, Improving, Outsourcing.* QED Publications, 1995.

Davidow, William H., and Michael Malone. *The Virtual Corporation.* New York: HarperCollins, 1992.

The Economist Intelligence Unit. *New Directions in Finance: Strategic Outsourcing.* New York: The Economist Intelligence Unit and Arthur Andersen, 1995.

Finegan, Jay. "New Biz Puts 7,300 on Payroll." *Inc.,* May 1997, 17.

Gruner, Stephanie. "The Secrets of Cross-Promotion." *Inc.,* June 1997, 99–100.

Halvey, John K., and Barbara Murphy Melby. *Information Technology Outsourcing Transactions: Process, Strategies, and Contracts.* New York: John Wiley & Sons, 1996.

Horwitt, E. "Signet Signals Outsourcing Vendors." *Computerworld,* December 10, 1990, 2.

Kass, E., and B. Caldwell. "Outsource Ins, Outs." *Information Week,* March 5, 1990, 14.

Kiely, Thomas. "Business Processes: Consider Outsourcing." *Harvard Business Review,* May–June 1997, 11–12.

Klepper, Robert. *Information Systems Outsourcing.* Englewood Cliffs, NJ: Prentice-Hall, 1997.

Krass, P. "The Dollars and Sense of Outsourcing." *Information Week,* February 26, 1990, 26–31.

Lacity, Mary Cecilia, and Rudy Hirschheim. *Beyond the Information Systems Outsourcing Bandwagon: The Insourcing Response.* New York: John Wiley & Sons, 1995.

Lacity, Mary Cecilia, and Rudy Hirschheim. *Information Systems Outsourcing: Myths, Metaphors and Realities.* New York: John Wiley & Sons, 1995.

Leinfuss, E. "IS Staffs Can Win When Outsources are Employers." *Computerworld,* September 23, 1991, 80.

Marcella, Albert. *Outsourcing, Downsizing, and Reengineering.* Altamonte Springs, FL: Institute of Internal Auditors, 1995.

Maynard, Roberta. "Striking the Right Match." *Nation's Business,* May 1996, 18–28.

Minoli, Daniel. *Analyzing Outsourcing: Reengineering Information and Communication Systems.* New York: McGraw Hill, 1994.

Mylott III, Thomas R. *Computer Outsourcing: Managing the Transfer of Information Systems.* Englewood Cliffs, NJ: Prentice Hall, 1995.

Narus, James A., and James C. Anderson. "Rethinking Distribution: Adaptive Channels." *Harvard Business Review,* July–August 1996, 112–120.

Oltman, J. "21st Century Outsourcing." *Computerworld,* April 16, 1990, 77–79.

Rohan, Thomas M. "Supplier-Customer Links Multiply." *Industry Week,* April 17, 1989, 20.

Rothfeder, J., and P. Coy. "Outsourcing: More Companies are Letting George Do It." *Business Week,* October 8, 1990, 148.

Sanders, Lisa. "Consultants Need Not Apply." *Business Week,* June 9, 1997, 6.

Sheridan, John H. "Suppliers: Partners in Prosperity." *Industry Week,* March 19, 1990, 14.

Stefanides, E. J. "Turning Suppliers into Partners." *Design News,* July 3, 1989, 82.

Useem, Jerry. "Company Goes Crazy Over Partnerships, Gets Committed." *Inc.,* June 1997, 24.

Wilder, C., and N. Margolis. "Outsourcing's Hidden Cost Bite." *Computerworld,* September 24, 1990, 1, 12.

Williams, Kathy. "Has Your Company Outsourced Yet?" *Management Accounting,* March 1997, 14.

Summary of Performance Measurements

This appendix lists the measurements that can be used to determine the performance of a supplier. The measurements are grouped by functional area, and include a brief description of each measurement. However, some measurements are more effective than others—for a more complete discussion of each measurement, including where it is most (and least) useful, it is necessary to consult the more complete measurement descriptions noted in the chapter devoted to each functional area. The additional text in the chapters is especially useful for a discussion of how each measurement's results can be skewed, giving company management a false or misleading sense of how a supplier is performing.

ACCOUNTING

Measurement	Description
Cash management: Earnings rate on investments	Take the total investment income from the bank statement and divide it by the total average balance invested.
Cash management: Transaction fees	Take from the bank's monthly reporting statement.
Collections: Percentage collected of dollar volume assigned	Divide the total cash received from the collections agency by the total amount of accounts receivable turned over to it for collection.
Financial statements: Accuracy of accruals	Have the internal audit team periodically review the calculations used for each accrual.
Financial statements: Number or percentage of material irregularities	Have the internal audit team review the statements for material irregularities, determine the amount by which the financial statements are incorrect, and derive a percentage of inaccuracy based on how far off the profits are from what they should have been.
Financial statements: Time to release statements	Record the number of days lag between the end of the reporting period and the receipt date.
Internal auditing: Percentage of audits completed	Divide the total number of completed audits by the total number of audits listed in the annual audit plan.
Internal auditing: Cost per audit	Take from the supplier's billing statement.

Measurement	Description
Investments: Accuracy of trades	Have the internal audit team compare the company's records of what it authorized for trades to the supplier's periodic statements showing the actual trades made.
Investments: Brokerage fees as a percentage of the amount invested	Take from the supplier's billing statement.
Payroll: Timeliness in paying payroll taxes	The government will notify the company of any late payments.
Payroll: Transaction fees per person	Summarize all costs per payroll for each person for whom a paycheck was created. Then summarize these fees and divide them by the total number of employees paid during the period. If the company has several payrolls of different lengths, then the costs should be annualized to properly account for the costs of all payrolls.
Payroll: Proportion of fees for extra services	Summarize the total additional fees per reporting period, divided by the total fees during that period.
Payroll: Proportion of payrolls delivered to correct locations	Summarize all instances when payroll was incorrectly delivered and divide this by the total number of payroll deliveries in the reporting period.
Pension: Investment returns	Have the supplier provide a quarterly statement of investment return for each fund in the pension plan.
Pension: On-time release of funds	Look for a pattern of employee complaints.
Pension: On-time release of statements	Compare the date when statements are received to the date when they are due.
Taxes: Absence of penalties	Total all penalty and related charges paid to tax authorities in a given time period.
Taxes: Timeliness of filing	The government will notify the company of any late filings. The number of these late filings can be divided by the total number of tax filings to determine the proportion of late filings.
Transactions: Average employee expense report turnaround time	Periodically review the time required to pay employees after they have submitted expense reports.
Transactions: Cost per transaction	Take from supplier billing statements.
Transactions: Error rate on processing	Schedule periodic audits of all processed transactions to determine the percentage of errors in such areas as billing addresses, accounts payable matching, and tax rates on billings.
Transactions: Timeliness of processing	Either rely on a supplier to track this measure or send in an audit team.
Transactions: Percentage of invoices paid on due date	Compare the date of arrival of paperwork at the supplier to the date when the transaction was completed.

Measurement	Description
Transactions: Percentage of payment discounts taken	Have the supplier generate a monthly report listing all payments and those for which discounts were taken. An audit team can then sample the payments listed on this report to verify that all discounts were taken, as well as to verify that all payments made during the month are listed on the report.

COMPUTER SERVICES

Measurement	Description
Time from update release to installation	Obtain release date from software supplier and compare to actual installation date.
Help desk average response time	Either have the supplier collect this information or use the internal audit staff to derive the measurement based on a sample of calls.
Mission-critical problem: Average response time	Rely on the supplier to track the time from receipt of problem notification to the commencement of repair work.
Mission-critical problem: Average time to fix	Rely on the supplier to track the time from the commencement of repair work to resolving the problem.
Percentage of mission-critical downtime	Obtain downtime from computer log that tracks the times when the system is not available to users; summarize all instances of downtime during the month and divide this total by the total amount of time in the month.
Average length of downtime	Obtain the computer log that notes the times of operation and calculate from it the total time during the month when the system is down. Then divide this number by the total number of instances when the system was down during the month.
Mean time between failures	Measure the time intervals between downtime periods and divide by the total number of failures in the month.
Downtime percentage during regular working hours	Determine the duration of "regular business hours." Then refer to the computer log and measure all instances of downtime. Then divide the total downtime by the total time taken by regular business hours during the month.
Network downtime	Review the activity log on the network file server to derive the percentage of downtime to total time during the month.
Cost as a percentage of revenue	Summarize all computer service costs for the month and divide them by monthly revenues.

Measurement	Description
Cost per line of programming	Add up the number of program lines created since the last billing and divide this number into the total cost of application development as shown on the supplier's last billing.
Cost per network connection	Add up the number of network connections added during the last billing period and divide this amount into the total network connection cost on the last supplier billing.
Cost per help desk response	Should be listed on the supplier's billing statement.
Days variance from programming milestones	Extract milestone dates from supplier-company agreements and compare them to the actual dates when milestones were achieved.
Number of program bugs found subsequent to program release	Either conduct a separate test to find bugs or collect this information from users.
Average years experience of supplier personnel	Request this information from supplier; it can be for total years experience, years of experience in the industry, or years of experience with the service being provided to the company.
Average number of complaints by employees	Keep a file of all complaints received and summarize it once a month.

CUSTOMER SERVICE

Measurement	Description
Cost per call received	Take the total cost billed to the company in one month and divide this amount by the number of calls received by the supplier, as noted on the supplier's monthly call report.
Revenue per call	Summarize the revenues entered into the system by the supplier from inbound calls, and divide this amount by the number of calls received by the supplier, as noted on the supplier's monthly call report.
Retention rate	Locate the number of calls made into the call center to cancel a sale, and divide this amount into the number of callers who were persuaded not to cancel.
Total cost per month	Use the total cost shown on the supplier's monthly summary billing. Track this on a trend line.
Percentage of system downtime	Take this information from the supplier's report, or poll customers to determine an approximate downtime percentage.

Measurement	Description
Percentage of changes on callback	Review the report of an independent callback supplier to determine the percentage of changes made to orders placed during calls to the original supplier.
Percentage of overflow calls	Take the total number of overflow calls received by the supplier and divide by the total number of calls fielded by the in-house customer service staff.

ENGINEERING

Measurement	Description
Cost per drawing	Add up the total number of drawings completed and signed off on, and divide by the total cost incurred by the drafting function during that period.
Cost by milestone	Summarize the total cost incurred during the time interval between adjacent milestones of a project.
Cost as a percentage of revenue	Compare the total engineering cost, including the cost of the engineering coordinator and staff, to the company's total revenues.
Days variance from milestone budgets	Work out a project timeline and milestone, and then track the days variance from those milestones, both for each milestone and cumulatively.
Percentage of drawings that have passed review	Derive the total number of drawings required for an entire project, and then divide this number into the total number of drawings that have been completed and signed off on by the project manager as being complete.
Percentage of customer complaints / warranty claims	Accumulate either the total number of customer complaints or warranty claims received for a product, and divide this number by the total number of units sold.
Percentage of customer complaints / warranty claims after fixes	Accumulate either the total number of customer complaints or warranty claims received for a product subsequent to design changes made by the supplier, and divide this number by the total number of units sold.
Average years experience of supplier personnel	Can track either the total number of years since leaving college, the total number of years of engineering experience, or the total number of years with a specific job title or function.
Number of errors found during peer review	Accumulate the number of errors written down during peer reviews of drawings and given back to the drafter for correction, and divide by the total number of drawings reviewed for each drafter.

HUMAN RESOURCES

Measurement	Description
Medical insurance cost per person	Multiply the single and family insurance rates by the number of employees who are likely to take each type of insurance, subtract the amounts that employees will pay to derive the amount to be paid by the company, summarize this information, and divide it by the total number of employees.
Proportion of rejected medical claims	Notify employees that they should appeal all claim rejections to the functional coordinator, who then compiles this information and divides it by the total number of claims submitted.
Life insurance cost per dollar of insurance	Multiply the amount of life insurance offered for each employee by the number of employees covered, and then divide this amount by the annual cost of the insurance.
Workers' compensation cost per person	Throw out all clerical personnel who have minimal workers' compensation charges to derive the number of employees with significant insurance risk. Then divide this number into the total annual workers' compensation cost, as adjusted by the year-end audit.
Recruiting cost per person	Measure based on the percentage of first-year pay charged by the recruiter, or, if paying by the hour, then measure based on the total recruiting cost per person hired.
Outplacement cost per person	Extract the per-person fee from the supplier's periodic billing statement and track this information over time to spot any costing trends.
Relocation administration cost per person	Extract the fixed fee per person relocated from the supplier's periodic billing statement and track this information over time to spot any costing trends.
Relocation moving cost per mile	Determine the cost per moving van. Then divide the cost per van by the number of miles the goods must be moved to the new location.
Training cost per person/hour	Extract the training cost from the general ledger expense account, and divide it by the hourly length of classes offered.
Training evaluation scoring	Issue an evaluation form to employees who take classes. Then summarize the scores and divide them by the number of people who submitted completed evaluation forms.
Average number of complaints per move	Divide the total number of complaints received by the total number of moves. Track this information separately for each moving company used.

Measurement	Description
Employee turnover percentage	Add up the number of people who left the company during the year and divide it by the total number of people employed by the company at the beginning of the year.

MAINTENANCE AND JANITORIAL

Measurement	Description
Janitorial: Cost per square foot	Determine the company's total square footage subject to janitorial services, and divide this amount by the monthly supplier billing.
Janitorial: Cost per person	Determine the company's total janitorial costs assigned to the production and administration areas, and divide by the total number of employees in each area.
Janitorial: Cost per office	Determine the company's total square footage of office space and divide by the supplier billing for the cleaning of this space.
Janitorial: Average number of complaints per employee	Tally the complaints received about janitorial services during a month and divide this number by the total number of employees.
Janitorial: Proportion of missed cleaning points	Audit the areas to be cleaned to determine the average number of cleaning points that were missed, and divide this amount by the total number of cleaning points.
Maintenance: Mean time between failures	Track the times when equipment failures occur for each piece of equipment, and create a monthly average for each equipment type.
Maintenance: Proportion of preventive maintenance conducted on schedule	Audit a fixed number of preventive maintenance steps and determine the number that have been completed. Then divide this by the total number of activities audited to arrive at the proportion of preventive maintenance activities that were actually completed.
Maintenance: Average time required to initiate repairs	Measure the time period between the first report of equipment failure and the arrival at the equipment of the supplier's maintenance staff.
Maintenance: Average time required to complete repairs	Record the time when repairs were initiated and completed. Average this repair time duration each month to arrive at the average time required to complete repairs.
Maintenance: Average time to failure after servicing	Record the time when a failure occurs and compare this to the date of the last maintenance work on

Measurement	Description
	that equipment. When averaged over a sufficiently large number of pieces of equipment, this yields an accurate average time to failure after servicing.
Maintenance: Average number of complaints per employee	Add up the number of complaints in a reporting period and divide it by the total number of company employees.
Maintenance: Average maintenance cost per piece of equipment	Divide the total monthly maintenance cost by the total number of pieces of equipment being maintained.

MANUFACTURING

Measurement	Description
Percentage of times shipped within promise date	Add up the number of complete orders received from the supplier on the correct date, as noted in the receiving log, and divide it by the total number of shipments that should have been received.
Percentage of variance from contract prices	Take the unit price from the supplier's invoice and divide it by the unit price listed on the contract.
Percentage of customer returns	Divide the total number of units received by the total number shipped.
Percentage of products shipped DOA	The number of DOA units is easy to track, for it is forcefully brought to the company's attention by irate customers. This number should be divided by the total number of units shipped to determine the percentage of products shipped DOA.
Percentage of accurate picking for assembled products	Break down a sample of ready-to-ship products and compare the actual number of parts to the bill of materials. If any parts are missing, count the product as incorrect. Divide the total number of incorrect products by the total number sampled to arrive at the percentage of accurate picking for assembled products.
Production backlog	Obtain from the supplier the total dollar amount of its backlog, as well as the amount of production it is capable of handling in one month. Then reduce the amount of the total backlog by the amount that the company obtained from the supplier in order to arrive at the total dollar amount of orders from other customers of the supplier. Then divide the amount of the supplier's production per month into the reduced backlog figure. This yields the total backlog assigned to other customers.

Measurement	Description
Scrap as percentage of material cost	Take the scrap figure recorded in the general ledger and divide it by the total material expense cost for the same time period.
Component defect rate	Find the supplier's records of defective components. The easiest place to find this information is some kind of log for returned parts, which is occasionally included in the receiving log. Once this information is found, compare the receipt dates when all defective orders were received to the same dates in the receiving log. Then divide the total number of defective orders received during a month to the total number of orders received during the same month to derive the component defect rate.
Material cost	Review the invoices for parts that make up the finished product and derive the product cost from them.
Labor volume variance	Collect from labor routings the total budgeted labor hours per unit. Then multiply this amount by the total number of units produced to arrive at the total number of budgeted hours for the actual production volume. Then compare this number of hours to the total number of hours actually used to complete the job—this yields the labor variance, expressed in hours. To translate this into dollars, multiply the labor variance by the budgeted cost per hour.
Labor cost variance	Subtract the budgeted labor cost per hour from the actual cost per hour to determine the per-unit variance, and then multiply this amount by the total number of units produced.
Bill of material accuracy	Have a team of engineers review the bill of materials. Mark any missing or excessive component quantities as errors, and then divide this number by the total number of components in the bill to determine the total percentage of incorrect items in the bill. The inverse of this percentage is the bill of material accuracy percentage.
Inventory accuracy	Print out a listing of the inventory and compare a random sample from the printout to the actual inventory. If an item quantity or location code is incorrect, this is an error. Also take a sample of items from the actual inventory and trace them back to the inventory report. If the same information is missing or incorrect, this is also an error. Then divide the total number of correct sample items by the total number of items sampled to arrive at the inventory accuracy percentage.

Measurement	Description
Capital investment	Compare the supplier's fixed asset records to the equipment located on the production line that is manufacturing products for the company.

MATERIALS MANAGEMENT

Measurement	Description
Freight audit: Cost per dollar collected	Obtain from the freight auditor's billing statement or contract with the company.
Freight audit: Recovery rate per dollar of bills reviewed	Determine the total dollar amount of freight billings given to a supplier and divide this into the total dollar amount that the freight auditor has recovered from trucking suppliers.
Freight brokering: Cost per mile	Take the total expense shown on the freight broker's billing statement and divide it by the cubic volume of the shipment to determine the cost per cubic foot. Then divide this amount by the total miles traveled to determine the cost per mile per cubic foot.
Freight brokering: Insurance cost per dollar shipped	Determine the total cost of a shipment, break out the insurance cost from the freight billing, and divide this insurance cost by the total cost of the shipment.
Trucking: Cost to load/unload truck	Take from billing statement.
Trucking: Full-load cost per mile	Divide supplier billings by the number of miles traveled, which are easily obtained from a variety of distance rating guides.
Trucking: Partial-load cost per mile	Take the freight cost from the supplier billing and divide it by the cubic volume shipped to determine the cost per cubic foot shipped. Then divide this figure by the number of miles traveled, which yields the cost per mile per cubic foot shipped.
Trucking: Trailer rental rate per month	Extract the price per trailer from the supplier's billing statement.
Warehouse: Cost per square foot	Take it directly from the supplier's billing statements. If the statement does not contain this level of detail, an audit team can calculate the actual warehouse space used and divide this amount into the monthly fee to determine the cost per square foot.
General: Working capital employed	Take the inventory figure from the balance sheet at the end of the month and track it on a trend line to monitor changes.
General: Fixed assets employed	Assign a department code to each fixed asset in the fixed asset ledger and sort the ledger by that department code to extract all assets belonging to the materials-management function. Then track this number on a trend line to monitor changes.

SALES AND MARKETING

Measurement	Description
Direct mail: Cost per piece	Take the total development and production cost from the supplier's billing statements and divide this amount by the total number of direct mail pieces produced.
Direct mail: Total cost per month	Extract this information from the supplier's monthly billing and track it on a trend line.
Direct mail: Revenue per mailing dollar	Store the revenues that come in through direct mail pieces in a separate general ledger account, and divide this amount by the total monthly direct mail cost.
Direct mail: Gross profit per mailing dollar	Charge the cost of goods sold on each sale through a direct mail piece to a separate cost-of-goods-sold account. Subtract this amount from the revenues that come in through direct mail pieces (which must also be stored in a separate general ledger account). Divide the resulting gross profit by the total monthly direct mail cost.
Direct mail: Profit per mailing dollar	Either multiply a standard profit percentage by the revenue per mailing dollar (see prior measurement) or manually determine the profit for each sales item sold through direct mail. Divide the resulting profit by the total monthly direct mail cost.
Direct mail: Leads per mailing dollar	Track the number of leads manually or store them in a general ledger statistics account. Divide the monthly sum by the total monthly direct mail cost.
Marketing: Total cost per month	Take the total cost from the supplier's monthly billing and track it on a trend line.
Marketing: Percentage of advertising expenditures	Take the percentage of advertising expenditures paid to the marketing supplier from the contract with the supplier.
Outside sales: Commission percentage	Take the percentage rate from the contract with the supplier.
Outside sales: Bad debt percentage	Extract the amount of bad debt per month as noted in the general ledger bad-debt account that was from sales made by the outside sales supplier. Then divide this amount by the total sales generated by the outside sales supplier.
Telemarketing: Cost per call	Take the total cost billed to the company in one month and divide this amount by the number of calls sent by the supplier, as noted on the supplier's monthly call report.
Telemarketing: Revenue per call	Summarize the revenues entered into the system by the supplier from outbound calls, and divide this amount by the number of calls sent by the supplier, as noted on the supplier's monthly call report.

Measurement	Description
Telemarketing: Retention rate	Locate the number of calls made into the call center to cancel a sale, and divide this amount into the number of callers who were persuaded not to cancel.
Telemarketing: Total cost per month	Extract the total cost from the supplier's monthly billing and track it on a trend line.

ADMINISTRATION

Measurement	Description
Clerical: Average cost per hour	Extract the cost per hour from the supplier's billing statement. If this is not clearly shown, divide the total number of hours worked into the total price charged to determine the average cost.
Clerical: Percentage hired from temporary	Manually track the number of temporary employees who are hired from each supplier. Then divide this number by the total number of temporary employees the company has used from the same supplier.
Copy center: Cost per piece	Extract from the supplier billings the total cost and divide it by the total number of pages copied.
Copy center: Turnaround time	Track the date and time when a copying job is requested from the supplier, and log in the date and time when it is delivered. Summarize this information for each month and divide it by the total number of separate copying requests during that period.
Desktop publishing: cost per page	Extract from the supplier billings the total cost and divide it by the total number of pages created.
Desktop publishing: Turnaround time	Track the date and time when a document is requested from the supplier, and log in the date and time when it is delivered. Summarize this information for each month and divide it by the total number of separate requests during that period.
Record storage: Cost per cubic foot	Either take this number from the supplier contract or determine the total cubic feet of storage at the supplier each month and divide this amount into the monthly billing from the supplier.
Record storage: Retrieval speed	Track the date and time when records were requested from the supplier, and log in the date and time when they are delivered. Summarize this information for each month and divide it by the total number of deliveries during that period.
Security: Average cost per hour	Extract the cost per hour from the supplier's billing statement. If this is not evident, divide the total number of hours worked into the total price charged to determine the average cost.

Index